D1016912

The Mind's
New Science

Other Books by Howard Gardner

The Quest for Mind (1973; second edition, 1981)

The Arts and Human Development (1973)

The Shattered Mind (1975)

Developmental Psychology (1978; second edition, 1982)

Artful Scribbles: The Significance of Children's Drawings (1980)

Art, Mind, and Brain: A Cognitive Approach to Creativity (1982)

Frames of Mind: The Theory of Multiple Intelligences (1983)

THE MIND'S

NEW

SCIENCE

A History of the
Cognitive Revolution

HOWARD GARDNER

Basic Books, Inc., Publishers / New York

Quotes on pp. 66 and 88 from H. Putnam, *Mind, Language, and Reality: Philosophical Papers,* *vol. 2,* 1975. Reprinted with permission, Cambridge University Press.

Quotes on pp. 20, 24, 132, and 295 from N. Wiener, *Cybernetics, or Control and Communication in the Animal and the Machine,* 2nd ed., 1961/1948. Reprinted with permission, MIT Press.

Quote on p. 244 from Jonathan Miller, *States of Mind,* 1983. Reprinted with permission, Pantheon Books, a Division of Random House, Inc.

Quotes on pp. 72, 73, 74, 75, and 85 from Richard Rorty, *Philosophy and the Mirror of Nature.* Copyright © 1979 by Princeton University Press. Excerpts reprinted with permission of Princeton University Press.

Quote on p. 70 from Jerome Bruner, *In Search of Mind* (in press). Reprinted with permission of the author.

Library of Congress Cataloging in Publication Data

Gardner, Howard.
 The mind's new science.

 Bibliography: p. 393.
 Includes index.
  1. Cognition—History. 2. Cognition—Research—
Methodology—History. 3. Artificial intelligence—
History. I. Title.
BF311.G339 1985   153   85-47555
ISBN 0-465-04634-7

For my parents,

Hilde Weilheimer Gardner and Ralph Gardner

CONTENTS

PART II

THE COGNITIVE SCIENCES: A HISTORICAL PERSPECTIVE

Contents

PART III

TOWARD AN INTEGRATED COGNITIVE SCIENCE: PRESENT EFFORTS, FUTURE PROSPECTS

PREFACE

In the mid-1970s, I began to hear the term *cognitive science*. As a psychologist interested in cognitive matters, I naturally became curious about the methods and scope of this new science. When I was unable to find anything systematic written on the subject, and inquiries to colleagues left me confused, I decided to probe further. Some immersion in the writings of self-proclaimed cognitive scientists convinced me that cognitive science was deeply rooted in philosophy and therefore, in a sense, had a long history. At the same time, the field was so new that its leading figures were all alive, and some of them were still quite young.

I decided that it would be useful and rewarding to undertake a study in which I would rely heavily on the testimony of those scholars who had founded the field as well as those who were at present its most active workers. But in lieu of an oral history or a journalistic account of current laboratory work (both of which subsequently were undertaken by other authors), I decided to make a comprehensive investigation of cognitive science in which I could include the long view—the philosophical origins, the histories of each of the respective fields, the current work that appears most central, and my own assessment of the prospects for this ambitious field.

It had not escaped my attention that the Alfred P. Sloan Foundation was a major supporter of work in the cognitive sciences. I therefore approached its program officer Kenneth Klivington about the possibility of writing a history of cognitive science. To my delight, the Foundation proved receptive, and I began my formal study at the beginning of 1981. I want to express my gratitude to the entire administration of the Sloan Foundation, and to its two responsible program officers, Kenneth Klivington and Eric Wanner, who were totally supportive of my efforts to carry through this somewhat risky undertaking.

In the course of my study, I interviewed formally, or conducted informal discussions with, dozens of cognitive scientists in this country and abroad. As far as I can recall, no scientist whom I approached denied me an interview, and most—even those who expressed skepticism about cognitive science—were gracious and informative. I regret that I had to stop interviewing and begin writing after a time, and I regret even more that I ultimately was not able to discuss in print the work of many of those from whom I learned much. Unfortunately, if I had included even half of the work worthy of review, this book would be several times longer than it is.

I want to mention first and thank the many individuals who willingly discussed their work and the field of cognitive science with me. (I also must apologize to those whom I have inadvertently omitted from this list.) I am indebted to Jonathan Adler, Allan Allport, John Anderson, Dana Ballard, Jon Barwise, Elizabeth Bates, Brent Berlin, Ned Block, Daniel Bobrow, Margaret Boden, Stanley Brandes, Joan Bresnan, John Seely Brown, Roger Brown, Jerome Bruner, Peter Bryant, Alfonso Caramazza, Noam Chomsky, Gillian Cohen, Michael Cole, Roy D'Andrade, Daniel Dennett, Hubert Dreyfus, Jerome Feldman, Charles Fillmore, Jerry Fodor, Michael Gazzaniga, Clifford Geertz, my late and beloved mentor Norman Geschwind, Samuel Glucksberg, Nelson Goodman, Charles Gross, Patrick Hayes, Geoffrey Hinton, Stephen Isard, Philip Johnson-Laird, Ronald Kaplan, Paul Kay, Samuel Jay Keyser, Stephen Kosslyn, George Lakoff, Jean Lave, Jerome Lettvin, Robert LeVine, Claude Lévi-Strauss, Christopher Longuet-Higgins, John McCarthy, Jay McClelland, Jean Mandler, Alexander Marshack, John Marshall, Jacques Mehler, Susanna Millar, George Miller, Marvin Minsky, Julius Moravcsik, John Morton, Ulric Neisser, Freda Newcombe, Allen Newell, Donald Norman, Daniel Osherson, Domenico Parisi, Stanley Peters, Michael Posner, Karl Pribram, Hilary Putnam, Raj Reddy, Richard Rorty, Eleanor Rosch, David Rumelhart, Roger Schank, Israel Scheffler, John Searle, Robert Siegler, Herbert Simon, Aaron Sloman, Brian Cantwell Smith, Stuart Sutherland, Leonard Talmy, Sheldon Wagner, Terry Winograd, and Edgar Zurif.

Several friends and colleagues were good enough to read and comment critically on one or more of the drafts of this book. I am considerably in their debt. I wish to thank Margaret Boden, Hiram Brownell, Daniel Dennett, Martha Farah, Josef Grodzinsky, Jerome Kagan, Benny Shanon, Eric Wanner, my wife, Ellen Winner, and several anonymous reviewers for their useful comments, criticisms, and words of encouragement. I know that I benefited greatly from their feedback; I fear that remaining errors and infelicities are my own responsibility.

Over the several years in which this book was in preparation, I was fortunate enough to have the help of Linda Levine, Susan McConnell, Christine Meyer, and Claudia Strauss, who served as research assistants.

Preface

Mara Krechevsky, my current research assistant, has been invaluable in helping me to bring the manuscript to publication. In addition, she has made many substantive contributions to the manuscript. I thank Connie Wolf at Harvard and Carmella Loffredo at the Sloan Foundation for their help. The manuscript in its various guises was ably typed and word-processed by Dolly Appel, Damaris Chapin, Isabel Eccles, Nan Kortz, and Laura Stephens-Swannie. I am sure they would agree with the sentiment expressed by Samuel Johnson with respect to *Paradise Lost:* "No man could wish it longer."

As with my last three books, I have been fortunate to have the support of many individuals at Basic Books. On the editorial side I am tremendously grateful to Judith Greissman, Jane Isay, and Martin Kessler for their thoughtful reactions to earlier versions of this manuscript. Linda Carbone performed ably as the project editor; and Phoebe Hoss, as development editor, helped me to deal with many expositional problems and also displayed an uncanny sense of where I (and, at times, where cognitive science) had fallen short. In another life, she is at risk of becoming a cognitivist herself.

My greatest pleasure is to have the opportunity to dedicate this book to my parents.

HOWARD GARDNER
Cambridge, Massachusetts
April 1985

PART I

THE COGNITIVE
REVOLUTION

1

Introduction: What the *Meno* Wrought

> One thing I would fight for to the end, both in word and deed if I were able—that if we believed that we must try to find out what is not known, we should be better and braver and less idle than if we believed that what we do not know it is impossible to find out and that we need not even try.
>
> —Socrates, The *Meno*

> The safest general characterization of the European philosophical tradition is that it consists in a series of footnotes to Plato.
>
> —Alfred North Whitehead

The Greek Agenda

In the *Meno,* a Platonic dialogue, Socrates persistently questions a young slave about his knowledge of geometry. At first the slave appears quite knowledgeable, readily asserting that a square composed of sides two feet in length contains four square feet. But when, in response to a problem posed by Socrates, the slave indicates that a figure of eight square feet contains sides four feet long, Socrates demonstrates that the boy is thoroughly confused and does not realize that the length of the side must be the square root of eight.

The centerpiece of the dialogue features many questions and responses in the approved Socratic manner. Through this interchange, the philosopher ultimately succeeds in drawing out from the boy the knowledge that a square with a four-foot side would actually be sixteen square feet—that is, twice as great an area than he had supposed; and the knowledge that one can, by geometric maneuvers, inscribe a square that is actually eight square feet within this larger square. In so doing, Socrates has demonstrated to his satisfaction, and to the satisfaction of the slave's master, Menon, that the youth possesses within him all of the knowledge necessary to compute the various geometrical relationships in question.

At issue in this Platonic dialogue was far more than an exploration of the extent of knowledge possessed by a single slave boy. Here, for perhaps the first time in human intellectual history, was an extended rumination on the nature of knowledge: where does it come from, what does it consist of, how is it represented in the human mind? And, for good measure, there was also proposed a specific—if ultimately highly controversial—theory of human knowledge.

According to Plato (and, presumably, Socrates as well), the domain of knowledge par excellence inhered in mathematics and the exact sciences it had spawned. Indeed, the purest forms of knowledge were idealized forms or archetypes which can merely be glimpsed in mundane reality. An understanding of geometrical matters—indeed, of all matters of genuine knowledge—was already implanted in the human soul at birth. The task in instruction, as demonstrated in the dialogue of the *Meno*, was simply to bring this innate knowledge to conscious awareness.

The Greeks' interest in the nature of knowledge, no less than their particular contentious theories and evocative images, continued to reverberate through the Western intellectual tradition. Aristotle's version was the principal cornerstone of the Middle Ages, when discussions about knowledge were principally the purview of theologians. Then, during the Renaissance and Enlightenment periods, philosophers continued the discussions and began to draw regularly on findings obtained in the newly emerging empirical sciences. Such thinkers as Descartes, Locke, and Kant dealt comfortably with theoretical and empirical issues concerning knowledge, and the Neapolitan scholar Giambattista Vico even christened a New Science *(Scienza Nova)* to deal with these and related matters. By the end of the nineteenth century, there had been a proliferation of new sciences and philosophical specialties, several of which purported to deal with the nature of the human mind.

Today, armed with tools and concepts unimaginable even a century ago, a new cadre of thinkers called cognitive scientists has been investigating many of the same issues that first possessed the Greeks some twenty-five hundred years ago. Like their earlier counterparts, cognitive scientists today ask what it means to know something and to have accurate beliefs, or to be ignorant or mistaken. They seek to understand what is known—the objects and subjects in the external world—and the person who knows —his* perceptual apparatus, mechanisms of learning, memory, and rationality. They ponder the sources of knowledge: where does it come from, how is it stored and tapped, how might it be lost? They are curious about the differences among individuals: who learns early or with difficulty; what can be known by the child, the inhabitant of a preliterate society, an individual who has suffered brain damage, or a mature scientist?

Further, cognitive scientists, again as did the Greeks, conjecture about the various vehicles of knowledge: what is a form, an image, a concept, a word; and how do these "modes of representation" relate to one another? They wonder about the priorities of specific sense organs as against a central "general understanding" or "common sense." They reflect on language, noting the power and traps entailed in the use of words and their possible predominant influence over thoughts and beliefs. And they speculate at length on the nature of the very activity of knowing: why do we want to know, what are the constraints on knowing, and what are the limits of scientific knowledge about human knowing?

This "new science," thus, reaches back to the Greeks in the commitment of its members to unraveling the nature of human knowledge. At the same time, however, it is radically new. Proceeding well beyond armchair speculation, cognitive scientists are fully wedded to the use of empirical methods for testing their theories and their hypotheses, of making them susceptible to disconfirmation. Their guiding questions are not just a rehash of the Greek agenda: new disciplines, like artificial intelligence, have arisen; and new questions, like the potential of man-made devices to think, stimulate research. Moreover, cognitive scientists embrace the most recent scientific and technological breakthroughs in a variety of disciplines. Most central to their undertaking is the computer—that creation of the mid-twentieth century that holds promise for changing our conceptions of the world in which we live and our picture of the human mind.

Definition and Scope of Cognitive Science

In the course of proposing and founding a new field of knowledge, many individuals will formulate their own definitions. Indeed, since the term *cognitive science* first began to be bandied about in the early 1970s, dozens of scientists have attempted to define the nature and scope of the

*For ease of exposition, the pronoun *he* is used in its generic sense throughout this book.

field (see, for example, Bruner 1983; Collins 1977; Mandler 1981; Miller 1979; Norman 1980; Rumelhart 1982). It therefore becomes important for me at the outset to state what I take cognitive science to be.

I define cognitive science as a contemporary, empirically based effort to answer long-standing epistemological questions—particularly those concerned with the nature of knowledge, its components, its sources, its development, and its deployment. Though the term *cognitive science* is sometimes extended to include all forms of knowledge—animate as well as inanimate, human as well as nonhuman—I apply the term chiefly to efforts to explain human knowledge. I am interested in whether questions that intrigued our philosophical ancestors can be decisively answered, instructively reformulated, or permanently scuttled. Today cognitive science holds the key to whether they can be.

Of the various features or aspects generally associated with cognitive-scientific efforts, I consider five to be of paramount importance. Not every cognitive scientist embraces every feature, of course; but these features can be considered symptomatic of the cognitive-scientific enterprise. When all or most are present, one can assume that one is dealing with cognitive science; when few, if any, are present, one has fallen outside my definition of cognitive science. These features will be introduced more formally at the end of chapter 3 and will be revisited repeatedly throughout the book, but it is important to make an initial acquaintance with them at this point.

First of all, there is the belief that, in talking about human cognitive activities, it is necessary to speak about mental representations and to posit a level of analysis wholly separate from the biological or neurological, on the one hand, and the sociological or cultural, on the other.

Second, there is the faith that central to any understanding of the human mind is the electronic computer. Not only are computers indispensable for carrying out studies of various sorts, but, more crucially, the computer also serves as the most viable model of how the human mind functions.

While the first two features incorporate the central beliefs of current cognitive science, the latter three concern methodological or strategic characteristics. The third feature of cognitive science is the deliberate decision to de-emphasize certain factors which may be important for cognitive functioning but whose inclusion at this point would unnecessarily complicate the cognitive-scientific enterprise. These factors include the influence of affective factors or emotions, the contribution of historical and cultural factors, and the role of the background context in which particular actions or thoughts occur.

As a fourth feature, cognitive scientists harbor the faith that much is to be gained from interdisciplinary studies. At present most cognitive scientists are drawn from the ranks of specific disciplines—in particular, philosophy, psychology, artificial intelligence, linguistics, anthropology, and neuroscience (I shall refer to these disciplines severally as the "cognitive sciences"). The hope is that some day the boundaries between these disciplines may become attenuated or perhaps disappear altogether, yielding a single, unified cognitive science.

A fifth and somewhat more controversial feature is the claim that a key ingredient in contemporary cognitive science is the agenda of issues, and the set of concerns, which have long exercised epistemologists in the Western philosophical tradition. To my mind, it is virtually unthinkable that cognitive science would exist, let alone assume its current form, had there not been a philosophical tradition dating back to the time of the Greeks.

Purpose and Plan of This Book

I have chosen to write a book on cognitive science because I consider this area to be the most exciting new line of inquiry undertaken by scientists in the past few decades. Whether it will ultimately achieve all of its objectives, no one can say at this point; but this seems an opportune time to present a history and a current assessment. For contemporaries present during the opening decades of cognitive science, I hope to convey something of the enthusiasm I have noted, the difficulties that are being confronted, and the nature of the research enterprises in which investigators are presently engaged.

My history has two components. The first consists of the various interdisciplinary conversations and projects that took place in this century —both those preceding and those surrounding the unofficial launching of cognitive science in the mid-1950s. I relate the founding of cognitive science in the next two chapters of the book. The second component— spanning chapters 4 through 9—consists of brief targeted histories of each of the six aforementioned fields of cognitive science. (Other disciplines, such as sociology or economics, might have been added; the "borderline" disciplines of anthropology and neuroscience might have been eliminated; but I believe that the major points about cognitive science are made effectively by these six fields.) In my view, a brief targeted history of each of the several cognitive sciences serves as an optimal introduction to the principal issues of today, to the ways in which they are currently approached and explored, and to the lines of work likely to be undertaken in the future.

I have built each historical chapter around one or two major themes, which have been selected to convey a feeling for the kinds of issues that have recurred and the kinds of approaches that are especially central within a particular field. For example, in philosophy I trace the perennial dispute between those of a rationalist persuasion (who view the mind as actively organizing experiences on the basis of pre-existing schemes); and those of an empiricist bent (who treat mental processes as a reflection of information obtained from the environment). In anthropology I survey various attempts over the years to compare the thought of primitive peoples with that exhibited by typical individuals in modern Western society. Approaching these same fields from a methodological point of view, I raise the questions whether philosophy will eventually come to be supplanted by an empirically based cognitive science, and whether anthropology can (or even should) ever transcend the individual case study.

Of course, such organizing themes can only scratch the surface of the complex territory that underlies any scientific discipline. Still I hope that through such themes I can convey how a linguist views an issue, what a psychologist deems a problem (and a solution), which conceptions of process obtain in neuroscience and artificial intelligence. Only through such an immersion in the daily (and yearly) concerns of a cognitive scientist drawn from a particular discipline can one appreciate the possibilities —and the difficulties—that arise when workers from different fields collaborate in cognitive-scientific research. In the end I will in each case take stock and indicate where things stand with reference to the principal lines of contention in a particular cognitive science—a discussion that will, in turn, suggest some of the principal factors that have stimulated cognitive scientists to join forces.

While each of the histories stands on its own, their juxtaposition points up fascinating and difficult-to-anticipate parallels. Scientific fields hardly develop in a vacuum: such disparate factors as the dissemination of Darwin's pivotal writings, the outbreak of wars, the rise of great universities have had reverberations—and sometimes cataclysmic ones—across apparently remote fields, which may well have had little direct contact with one another. For the most part, I shall simply allow these parallels to emerge, but at the beginning of part III I shall specify certain historical forces that seem to have exerted influence across a range of cognitive sciences.

Having taken the measure of the individual cognitive sciences, I turn in the third part of the book to review ongoing work that is quintessentially cognitive-scientific. Thus, in chapters 10 to 13, the focus shifts from work within a traditional discipline to those lines of research that stand most squarely at the intersection of a number of disciplines and therefore can be considered prototypical of a single, unified cognitive science. I have sought to identify work that is of the highest quality: if cognitive science is to be assessed as an intellectual enterprise, it ought to be judged by the most outstanding instances.

There is a common structure to these four essays on current cognitive-scientific work. Consistent with my claim that cognitive science seeks to elucidate basic philosophical questions, each chapter begins with a perennial epistemological issue. For example, in chapter 10, I describe work on how we perceive the world; in chapter 13, I review competing claims on the extent of human rationality. Across chapters 10 to 13, there is a progression from those issues that seem most circumscribed to those that are most global. Not surprisingly, the most confident answers exist for the delimited questions, while the global topics remain ringed by unresolved questions.

My personal reflections on cognitive science are reserved for the final chapter. There I revisit the major themes of cognitive science in light of the histories sketched and the interdisciplinary work reviewed. I also discuss two themes that emerge from the inquiry and that will be introduced at greater length in chapter 3: the computational paradox and the cognitive challenge. In my view, the future of cognitive science rests on how the computational paradox is resolved and on how the cognitive challenge is met.

One might say that cognitive science has a very long past but a relatively short history. The reason is that its roots go back to classical times, but it has emerged as a recognized pursuit only in the last few decades. Indeed, it seems fair to maintain that the various components that gave rise to cognitive science were all present in the early part of the century, and the actual birthdate occurred shortly after mid-century. Just why cognitive science arose when it did in the form it did will constitute my story in the remainder of part I.

2

Laying the
Foundation for
Cognitive Science

The Hixon Symposium and the Challenge to Behaviorism

In September of 1948 on the campus of the California Institute of Technology, a group of eminent scientists representing several disciplines met for a conference on "Cerebral Mechanisms in Behavior," sponsored by the Hixon Fund (Jeffress 1951). This conference had been designed to facilitate discussions about a classic issue: the way in which the nervous system controls behavior. And yet the discussions ranged far more widely than the official topic had implied. For example, the opening speaker, mathematician John von Neumann, forged a striking comparison between the electronic computer (then a discovery so new that it smacked of science fiction) and the brain (which had been around for a while). The next speaker, mathematician and neurophysiologist Warren McCulloch, used his provocative title ("Why the Mind Is in the Head") to launch a far-ranging discussion on how the brain processes information—like von Neumann, he wanted to exploit certain parallels between the nervous system and "logical devices" in order to figure out why we perceive the world the way we do.

Less steeped in the latest technological innovations but more versed in the problems of explaining human behavior, the next speaker, psychologist Karl Lashley, gave the most iconoclastic and most memorable address. Speaking on "The Problem of Serial Order in Behavior," he challenged the doctrine (or dogma) that had dominated psychological analysis for the past several decades and laid out a whole new agenda for research. In the terms of my own discussion, Lashley identified some of the major components needed for a cognitive science, even as he castigated those forces that had prevented its emergence before this time.

In order to appreciate the importance of Lashley's remarks, it is necessary to consider the scientific climate in which he (and his numerous colleagues interested in human psychology) had been operating during the past few decades. At the turn of the century, in the wake of the founding of new human sciences, investigators had been addressing the key issues of mental life: thinking, problem solving, the nature of consciousness, the unique aspects of human language and culture. These discussions had linked up with the philosophical agenda of the West, but investigators had sought to go beyond sheer speculation through the use of rigorous experimental methods.

Unfortunately the scientific method favored by most researchers at that time was introspection: self-reflection on the part of a trained observer about the nature and course of his own thought patterns. Though suggestive (indeed, often too suggestive), such introspection did not lead to that accumulation of knowledge that is critical to science. Introspectionism might have collapsed of its own weight, but, in fact, it was toppled in a more aggressive manner by a group of mostly young, mostly American scientists who became known as the "behaviorists."

The behaviorists put forth two related propositions. First of all, those researchers interested in a science of behavior ought to restrict themselves strictly to public methods of observations, which any scientist could apply and quantify. No subjective ruminations or private introspection: if a discipline were to be science, its elements should be as observable as the physicist's cloud chamber or the chemist's flask. Second, those interested in a science of behavior ought to focus exclusively on *behavior:* researchers ought assiduously to eschew such topics as mind, thinking, or imagination and such concepts as plans, desires, or intentions. Nor ought they to countenance hypothetical mental constructs like symbols, ideas, schemas, or other possible forms of mental representation. Such constructs, never adequately clarified by earlier philosophers, had gotten the introspectionists into hot water. According to behaviorists, all psychological activity can be adequately explained without resorting to these mysterious mentalistic entities.

A strong component of the behaviorist canon was the belief in the supremacy and determining power of the environment. Rather than individuals acting as they do because of their own ideas and intentions, or because their cognitive apparatuses embody certain autonomous structuring tendencies, individuals were seen as passive reflectors of various forces and factors in their environment. An elaborate explanatory apparatus detailing principles of conditioning and reinforcement was constructed in order to explain just how such learning and shaping of particular behavior might come about. It was believed that the science of behavior, as fashioned by scholars such as Ivan Pavlov, B. F. Skinner, E. L. Thorndike, and J. B. Watson, could account for anything an individual might do, as well as the circumstances under which one might do it. (What one thinks was considered irrelevant from this perspective—unless thought was simply redefined as covert behavior.) Just as mechanics had explained the laws of the physical world, mechanistic models built on the reflex arc could explain human activity.

Behaviorism spoke to many needs in the scientific community, including some that were quite legitimate: discomfort with the acceptance of introspective evidence on face value, without any means of scientific control or any possibility for refutation; dissatisfaction with vague and global concepts like *will* or *purpose* and the desire to explain human behavior using the same constructs that were applied (with apparently great success) to animal behavior. Indeed, in the wake of the troubles that had arisen from reliance on introspectionism (troubles that are spelled out in chapter 4), behaviorism seemed like a breath of fresh air during the opening decades of the century. Little wonder that it caught on quickly and captured the best minds of a generation of workers.

Yet, in retrospect, the price paid by strict adherence to behaviorism was far too dear. So long as behaviorism held sway—that is, during the 1920s, 1930s, and 1940s—questions about the nature of human language, planning, problem solving, imagination, and the like could only be approached stealthily and with difficulty, if they were tolerated at all. Lashley's paper crystallized a growing awareness on the part of thoughtful scientists that adherence to behaviorist canons was making a scientific study of mind impossible.

Lashley realized that before new insights about the brain, or about computers, could be brought to bear in the psychological sciences, it would be necessary to confront behaviorism directly. Therefore, in his opening remarks, Lashley voiced his conviction that any theory of human activity would have to account for complexly organized behaviors like playing tennis, performing on a musical instrument, and—above all—speaking. He commented, "The problems raised by the organization of language seem to me to be characteristic of almost all other cerebral activity" (quoted in Jeffress 1951, p. 121). In this one sentence, Lashley put at the very center of human psychology a topic that had been relegated to obscurity by his behaviorist colleagues. At the same time, he added, the dominant theoretical explanatory framework in neurophysiology no less than in psychology —that of simple associative chains between a stimulus and a response— could not possibly account for any of this serially ordered behavior. The reason is that these action sequences unfold with such rapidity that there is no way in which the next step in the chain can be based upon the previous one: when one plays an arpeggio, for instance, there is simply no time for feedback, no time for the next tone to depend upon or in any way to reflect the course of the preceding one. Similarly, the kinds of error made by individuals—for example, slips of the tongue—often include anticipation of words that are to occur only much later in a sequence. Again, these phenomena defy explanations in terms of linear "A evokes B" chains.

According to Lashley, these behavioral sequences have to be planned and organized in advance. The organization is best thought of as hierarchical: there are the broadest overall plans, within which increasingly fine-grained sequences of actions are orchestrated. Thus, for instance, in the case of speech, the highest nodes of the hierarchy involve the overall intention prompting the utterance, while the choice of syntax and the actual production of sounds occupy lower nodes of the hierarchy. The nervous system contains an overall plan or structure, within which individual response units can—indeed, have to—be slotted, independent of specific feedback from the environment. Rather than behavior being consequent upon environmental promptings, central brain processes actually precede and dictate the ways in which an organism carries out complex behavior. Or, to put it simply, Lashley concluded that the form precedes and determines specific behavior: rather than being imposed from without, organization emanates from within the organism.

Even as he defied the standard behavioral analysis of the time, Lashley was also challenging two major dogmas of neurobehavioral analysis: the belief that the nervous system is in a state of inactivity most of the time, and the belief that isolated reflexes are activated only when specific forms of stimulation make their appearance. Lashley's nervous system consisted of always active, hierarchically organized units, with control emanating from the center rather than from peripheral stimulation. As he put it, "Attempts to express cerebral function in terms of the concepts of the reflex arc, or of associated chains of neurons, seem to me doomed to failure because they start with the assumption of a static nervous system. Every bit of evidence available indicated a dynamic, constantly active system, or, rather, a composite of many interacting systems" (quoted in Jeffress 1951, p. 135).

In the topics he chose to address, and in the ways in which he addressed them, Lashley was adopting a radical position. Scientists concerned with human behavior had been reluctant to investigate human language, because of its complexity and its relative "invisibility" as a form of behavior; and when they did treat language, they typically sought analogies to simpler forms (like running a maze or pecking in a cage) in simpler organisms (like rats or pigeons). Not only did Lashley focus on language, but he reveled in its complexity and insisted that other motoric activities were equally intricate.

Ordinarily, a scientist who challenges established wisdom is in for a rough time. It is rare, at a scientific meeting, for major scholars (an ambitious and often jealous lot) to pay homage to a colleague. But from comments by those attending the Hixon Symposium, it seemed clear that Lashley's colleagues were deeply impressed by the originality and brilliance of this presentation—coming from a scientist closely associated with the behaviorist tradition. Lashley himself declared, "I have been rather embarrassed by some of the flattering remarks made today" (quoted in Jeffress 1951, p. 144). It is no exaggeration to suggest that entrenched modes of explanation were beginning to topple and that a whole new agenda was confronting the biological and behavioral communities.

A Critical Moment in Scientific History

The scholars in attendance at the Hixon Symposium stood at a critical juncture of scientific history. They were keenly aware of the staggering advances of previous centuries in the physical sciences as well as of recent breakthroughs in the biological and neural sciences. Indeed, by the middle of the twentieth century, two major mysteries of ancient times—the nature of physical matter and the nature of living matter—were well on their way to being unraveled. At the same time, however, a third mystery that had also fascinated the ancients—the enigma of the human mind—had yet to achieve comparable clarification.

Trained (like many scholars of their time) in the humanities as well as in the sciences, the Hixon symposiasts displayed a familiarity with the kinds of epistemological issue that had first exercised the Greeks and had then formed a major part of learned conversation during the Enlightenment. They knew that, in the wake of Darwin's influential account of the origin and evolution of species, many scientists had sought to bring comparable rigor to the study of human behavior and thought. Often spurning direct ties to philosophy (which they regarded as a regressive intellectual force), these scholars at the end of the nineteenth century had launched separate scientific disciplines, like psychology, linguistics, anthropology, sociology, and various neurosciences. That these aspiring scientists of human nature had succeeded in establishing effective institutional bases within the universities could not be disputed; but the extent to which each new discipline had arrived at important truths was still being debated at mid-century. Finally, those attending the Pasadena meeting were well acquainted with the scientific program of the behaviorists. And they shared an intuition—strongly bolstered by Lashley's tightly reasoned paper—that the behaviorist answer to questions of the human mind was no answer at all.

But other factors had also impeded the proper launching of a science of cognition. Fitting comfortably with behaviorism were several philosophical schools—positivism, physicalism, and verificationism—which eschewed entities (like concepts or ideas) that could not be readily observed and reliably measured. There was also the intoxication with psychoanalysis. While many scholars were intrigued by Freud's intuitions, they felt that no scientific discipline could be constructed on the basis of clinical interviews and retrospectively constructed personal histories; moreover, they deeply resented the pretense of a field that did not leave itself susceptible to disconfirmation. Between the "hard line" credo of the Establishment behaviorists and the unbridled conjecturing of the Freudians, it was difficult to focus in a scientifically respectable way on the territory of human thought processes.

Finally, the world political situation had exerted a crippling effect on the scientific enterprise. First, the European scientific establishment had been ripped apart by the rise of totalitarianism, and then the American scientific establishment had been asked to lay aside its theoretical agenda in order to help wage the war.

While the war had been, in many ways, the worst of times, bringing on the death or disability of many talented investigators, it had also stimulated certain scientific and technological activities. Within the United States, the war effort demanded calculating machines that could "crunch" large sets of numbers very quickly. Computers soon became a reality. There were other war needs to be met as well. For instance, the mathematician Norbert Wiener was asked to devise more accurate anti-aircraft machinery. This work required "a good gun, a good projectile, and a fire-control system that enables the gunner to know the target's position, apply corrections to the gun controls, and set the fuse properly, so that it will detonate the projectile at the right instant" (quoted in Heims 1980, p. 183). While working on these problems at the Massachusetts Institute of Technology, Wiener and his associate, a young engineer named Julian Bigelow, concluded that there were important analogies between the feedback aspects of engineering devices and the homeostatic processes by which the human nervous system sustains purposive activity. These ideas of planning, purpose, and feedback, developed with mathematical precision, were directly antithetical to the behaviorist credo. War also produced many victims of gunfire; and medical practitioners who cared for brain-injured patients were being asked to evaluate which tasks could be carried out and which ones had been compromised—temporarily or permanently—by injury to the nervous system. Also, a host of more person-centered issues—ranging from the study of the effects of propaganda to the selection of men fit to lead combat units—enlisted the efforts of behavioral scientists and generated ideas on which the postwar human sciences were to build (Bruner 1944; Murray 1945; Stouffer et al. 1949). So it was in other war-torn lands, from Alan Turing and Kenneth Craik's interest in computers in England, to Alexander Luria's painstaking research with brain-injured patients in Russia during the war.

By the late 1940s, there was beginning to be a feeling abroad—one observable at Pasadena but in no way restricted to that site—that perhaps the time was ripe for a new and finally effective scientific onslaught on the human mind. Interestingly, nearly all of the work that came to fruition in the postwar era was in fact built upon prior theoretical efforts—work often dating back to the beginning of the century. But this work had sometimes been obscured by the behaviorist movement and had sometimes been transformed in unanticipated ways by the events of the war. These ideas, these key inputs to contemporary efforts in cognitive science, were already familiar to the participants at the Hixon Symposium and to other scholars involved in the first concerted efforts to found cognitive science during the 1940s and 1950s. Now it was time to put these ideas to optimal scientific use.

Key Theoretical Inputs to Cognitive Science

Mathematics and Computation

The years around the turn of the century were of exceptional importance in mathematics and logic. For nearly two thousand years, the logic of syllogistic reasoning developed in classical times by Aristotle had held sway; but thanks to the work of the German logician Gottlob Frege, a new form of logic, which involved the manipulation of abstract symbols, began to evolve toward the end of the nineteenth century. Then, in the early twentieth century, as I shall elaborate in chapter 4, the British mathematical logicians Bertrand Russell and Alfred North Whitehead sought, with considerable success, to reduce the basic laws of arithmetic to propositions of elementary logic. The Whitehead-Russell work influenced a whole generation of mathematically oriented thinkers, including both Norbert Wiener and John von Neumann, two of the most important contributors to the founding of cognitive science.

In the 1930s, the logical-mathematical work that ultimately had the greatest import for cognitive science was being carried out by a then relatively unknown British mathematician, Alan Turing. In 1936, he developed the notion of a simple machine (subsequently dubbed a "Turing machine") which could in principle carry out any possible conceivable calculation. The notions underlying this "theoretical" machine were simple. All one needed was an infinitely long tape which could pass through the machine and a scanner to read what was on the tape. The tape itself was divided into identical squares, each of which contained upon it either a blank or some kind of slash. The machine could carry out four moves with the tape: move to the right, move to the left, erase the slash, or print the slash. With just these simple operations, the machine could execute any kind of program or plan that could be expressed in a binary code (for example, a code of blanks and slashes). More generally, so long as one could express clearly the steps needed to carry out a task, it could be programmed and carried out by the Turing machine, which would simply scan the tape (no matter what its length) and carry out the instructions (Davis 1958; McCorduck 1979).

Turing's demonstration—and the theorem he proved—was of profound importance for those researchers interested in computing devices. It suggested that a binary code (composed simply of zeros and ones) would make possible the devising and execution of an indefinite number of programs, and that machines operating on this principle could be constructed. As Turing himself pondered computing devices, he became increasingly enthusiastic about their possibilities. In fact, in 1950 (shortly before his untimely death by suicide in his early forties) he suggested that one could so program a machine that it would be impossible to discriminate *its* answers to an interlocutor from those contrived by a living human being—a notion immortalized as the "Turing machine test." This test is used to refute anyone who doubts that a computer can really think: if an observer cannot distinguish the responses of a programmed machine from those of a human being, the machine is said to have passed the Turing test (Turing 1963).

The implications of these ideas were quickly seized upon by scientists interested in human thought, who realized that if they could describe with precision the behavior or thought processes of an organism, they might be able to design a computing machine that operated in identical fashion. It thus might be possible to test on a computer the plausibility of notions about how a human being actually functions, and perhaps even to construct machines about which one could confidently assert that they think just like human beings.

In building upon Turing's ideas, John von Neumann pursued the notion of devising a program to instruct the Turing machine to reproduce itself. Here was the powerful idea of a *stored program:* that is, the computer could be controlled through a program that itself was stored within the computer's internal memory, so that the machine would not have to be laboriously reprogrammed for each new task (see Goldstine 1972). For the first time, it became conceivable that a computer might prepare and execute its own programs.

The Neuronal Model

A second line of thinking important for those involved in founding cognitive science was put forth during the early 1940s by Warren McCulloch, the second speaker at the Hixon Symposium, and Walter Pitts, a young logician. Again, the core idea was disarmingly simple, though the actual mathematical analysis was anything but trivial. McCulloch and Pitts (1943) showed that the operations of a nerve cell and its connections with other nerve cells (a so-called neural network) could be modeled in terms of logic. Nerves could be thought of as logical statements, and the all-or-none property of nerves firing (or not firing) could be compared to the operation of the propositional calculus (where a statement is either true or false) (Heims 1980, p. 211). This model allowed one to think of a neuron as being activated and then firing another neuron, in the same way that an element or a proposition in a logical sequence can imply some other proposition: thus, whether one is dealing with logic or neurons, entity A plus entity B can imply entity C. Moreover, the analogy between neurons and logic could be thought of in electrical terms—as signals that either pass, or fail to pass, through a circuit. The end result of the McCulloch-Pitts demonstration: "Anything that can be exhaustively and unambiguously described . . . is . . . realizable by a suitable finite neural network" (von Neumann, quoted in Bernstein 1982, p. 68).

The designers of the new computational devices were intrigued by the ideas put forth by McCulloch and Pitts. Thanks to their demonstration, the notion of a Turing machine now looked in two directions—toward a nervous system, composed of innumerable all-or-none neurons; and toward a computer that could realize any process that can be unambiguously described. Turing had demonstrated the possibility in principle of computing machines of great power, while McCulloch and Pitts had demonstrated that at least one redoubtable machine—the human brain—could be thought of as operating via the principles of logic and, thus, as a powerful computer.

Ultimately, McCulloch may have carried his own chain of reasoning too far. He was convinced that fundamental problems of epistemology could be stated and solved only in light of the knowledge of the central nervous system (McCorduck 1979), and he tied his claims about thinking very closely to what was known during his own time about the nervous system. Some commentators even feel that the search by McCulloch and his associates for a direct mapping between logic machines and the nervous system was a regressive element in the development of cognitive science: rather than trying to build machines that mimic the brain at a physiological level, analogies should have been propounded and pursued on a much higher level—for example, between the *thinking* that goes on in human problem solving and the *strategies* embodied in a computer program (McCarthy 1984). On the other hand, it was due in part to McCulloch's own analysis that some of the most important aspects of the nervous system came to be better understood: for he sponsored research on the highly specific properties of individual nerve cells. Moreover, very recently computer scientists have once again been drawing directly on ideas about the nature of and connections among nerve cells (see chapter 10, pp. 318–22). On balance, his polymathic spirit seems to have been a benign catalyst for the growth of cognitive science.

The Cybernetic Synthesis

Even as John von Neumann, working at Princeton, was trying to piece together evidence from mathematics, logic, and the nervous system, mathematician Norbert Wiener was engaged in parallel pursuits at the Massachusetts Institute of Technology (see Heims 1980; Wiener 1964). Even more than von Neumann, Wiener had been a mathematical prodigy and, like his counterpart, had made fundamental discoveries in mathematics while still in his early twenties (Wiener had worked on Brownian motion; von Neumann, on quantum theory). Clearly, in these early choices, both men exhibited a practical bent in their mathematics: further, they aspired to influence the growth of science and technology within their society.

During the 1930s and 1940s, Norbert Wiener, by then ensconced at M.I.T., became involved in a variety of worldly projects. In working on servomechanisms—devices that kept anti-aircraft artillery, guided missiles, and airplanes on course—he had come to think about the nature of feedback and of self-correcting and self-regulating systems, be they mechanical or human. He collaborated closely with Vannevar Bush, who had pioneered in the development of analog computers. Wiener was also struck by the importance of the work of his sometime colleagues McCulloch and Pitts, particularly by the suggestive analogies between a system of logical connections and the human nervous system.

Wiener went beyond all of his contemporaries in his missionary conviction that these various scientific and technological developments cohered. Indeed, in his mind they constituted a new science—one founded on the issues of control and communication, which he deemed to be central in the middle of the twentieth century. He first publicly formulated this point of view in a 1943 paper, "Behavior, Purpose, and Teleology" (Rosenblueth, Wiener, and Bigelow 1943), in which he and his fellow authors put forth the notion that problems of control engineering and communication engineering are inseparable; moreover, they center not on the techniques of electrical engineering, but rather on the much more fundamental notion of the message—"whether this should be transmitted by electrical, mechanical, or nervous means." The authors introduced a then-radical notion: that it is legitimate to speak of machines that exhibit feedback as "striving toward goals," as calculating the difference between their goals and their actual performance, and as then working to reduce those differences. Machines were purposeful. The authors also developed a novel notion of the central nervous system. As Wiener later put it:

> The central nervous system no longer appears as a self-contained organ, receiving inputs from the senses and discharging into the muscles. On the contrary, some of its most characteristic activities are explicable only as circular processes, emerging from the nervous system into the muscles, and re-entering the nervous system through the sense organs, whether they be proprioceptors or organs of the special senses. This seemed to us to mark a new step in the study of that part of neurophysiology which concerns not solely the elementary processes of nerves and synapses but the performance of the nervous system as an integrated whole. (Wiener 1961, p. 8)

The parallels to Lashley's ideas about neural organization—and the challenge to behaviorist reflexology—are striking indeed.

Before long, Wiener had contrived a synthesis of the various interlocking ideas and presented it in the landmark volume *Cybernetics* (first published in 1948, the same year as the Hixon Symposium). He introduced his neologistic science as follows: "We have decided to call the entire field of control and communication theory, whether in the machine or in the animal, by the name Cybernetics" (1961, p. 11). In the following pages, he set down an integrated vision—a linkage of developments in understanding the human nervous system, the electronic computer, and the operation of other machines. And he underscored his belief—echoing von Neumann and McCulloch and Pitts—that the functioning of the living organism and the operation of the new communication machines exhibited crucial parallels. Though Wiener's synthesis was not ultimately the one embraced by cognitive science (it came closer to achieving that exalted status in the Soviet Union), it stands as a pioneering example of the viability of such an interdisciplinary undertaking.

Information Theory

Another key progenitor of cognitive science was Claude Shannon, an electrical engineer at M.I.T. who is usually credited with devising information theory. Already as a graduate student at M.I.T. in the late 1930s, Shannon had arrived at a seminal insight. He saw that the principles of logic (in terms of true and false propositions) can be used to describe the two states (on and off) of electromechanical relay switches. In his master's thesis, Shannon provided an early suggestion that electrical circuits (of the kind in a computer) could embody fundamental operations of thought. I shall describe this work—so crucial for all subsequent work with computers—further in chapter 6.

During the next ten years, working in part with Warren Weaver, Shannon went on to develop the key notion of information theory: that information can be thought of in a way entirely divorced from specific content or subject matter as simply a single decision between two equally plausible alternatives. The basic unit of information is the *bit* (short for "binary digit"): that is, the amount of information required to select one message from two equally probable alternatives. Thus, the choice of a message from among eight equally probable alternatives required three bits of information: the first bit narrowed the choice from one of eight to one of four; the second, from one of four to one of two; the third selects one of the remaining alternatives. Wiener explained the importance of this way of conceptualization: "Information is information, not matter or energy. No materialism which does not admit this can survive at the present day" (Wiener 1961, p. 132).

Thanks to Wiener's insights, it became possible to think of information apart from a particular transmission device: one could focus instead on the efficacy of *any* communication of messages via *any* mechanism, and one could consider cognitive processes apart from any particular embodiment—an opportunity upon which psychologists would soon seize as they sought to describe the mechanisms underlying the processing of any kind of information. Only very recently have cognitive scientists begun to wonder whether they can, in fact, afford to treat all information equivalently and to ignore issues of content.

Neuropsychological Syndromes

A comparable contribution to an incipient cognitive science came from a remote and unexpected scientific corner—the profiles of cognitive incapacities following damage to the human brain. Paradoxically, this area of science relies heavily on the travesties of war. As in the era of the First World War, much was learned during the Second World War about aphasia (language deficit), agnosia (difficulty in recognition), and other forms of mental pathology consequent upon injury to the brain. Laboratories in New York, Oxford, Paris, Berlin, and Moscow were all busily engaged in working with victims of brain damage. When the neuropsychological researchers began to communicate their findings to one another, considerable convergence was noted even across cultural and linguistic boundaries. For instance, aphasia assumed similar forms despite wide differences across languages. There was, it seemed, much more regularity in the organization of cognitive capacities in the nervous system than was allowed for by wholly environmental accounts of mental processes. Furthermore, the patterns of breakdown could not be readily explained in terms of simple stimulus-response disruption. Rather, in many cases, the hierarchy of behavioral responses was altered. For example, in certain forms of aphasia, the general sentence frame was preserved, but subjects could not correctly slot individual words into the frame. In other aphasias, the sentence frame broke down, but individual content words carried meaning. Thus was struck yet another blow against reflex-arc models of thought. At the same time, the particular profiles of abilities and disabilities that emerge in the wake of brain damage provided many pregnant suggestions about how the human mind might be organized in normal individuals.

By the late 1940s, in areas as diverse as communication engineering and neuropsychology, certain themes were emerging principally in the United States, Great Britain, and the Soviet Union. Though I have stressed the American version of this story, comparable accounts could be presented from other national perspectives as well. Scholars in these fields were not only writing but were eagerly meeting with one another to discuss the many exciting new perspectives. Herbert Simon, ultimately one of the founders of cognitive science but then a graduate student at the University of Chicago, recalls a kind of "invisible college" in the 1940s (Simon 1982). He knew McCulloch at Chicago; he knew of Shannon's master's thesis at M.I.T.; he knew that Wiener and von Neumann were working on issues in symbolic logic which had grown out of the philo-sophical writings of Whitehead, Russell, and Frege. Simon himself was studying at Chicago with Rudolf Carnap, who was then putting forth key notions about the syntax of logic. Such leading biologists (and Hixon symposiasts) as Ralph Gerard, Heinrich Klüver, Roger Sperry, and Paul Weiss were working in nearby laboratories on issues of the nervous sys-tem. Many of the same influences were rubbing off during this period on Jerome Bruner, Noam Chomsky, John McCarthy, George Miller, Allen Newell, and other founders of cognitive science.

Catalytic Encounters and Influential Writings

By the 1940s, then, the principal intellectual capital on which cognitive science was to be constructed had already emerged. A few scholars like Norbert Wiener attempted a tentative intellectual synthesis, and more than a few—ranging from students like Herbert Simon to masters like John von Neumann—sensed the imminent emergence of a new field (or fields) of study. There was still the resistance implicit in the behaviorist credo, as well as some doubts that the human mind would be able to study itself as effectively as it had studied matter and genetics; but these factors did not suffice to dampen the enthusiasm of those who sensed the vastness of the prize awaiting the Newton of human cognition.

The intellectual history of this era reveals many meetings among those interested in matters of cognition as well as a significant number of publi-cations that helped to promote a new interdisciplinary science of the mind. It is possible, of course, that cognitive science could have come into being —and perhaps even have assumed its present form—in the absence of these conferences, books, and articles. But particularly when scholars seek to join forces across often remote disciplines, it is crucial for them to have the opportunity to get together regularly, to question one another, and to discover those aspects of scientific method, prejudice, and hunch that are often invisible in the written record.

The Hixon Symposium, then, was but one of many conferences held among cognitively oriented scientists during the 1940s and 1950s. To be sure, it was especially important for our story because of two factors: its linking of the brain and the computer and its relentless challenging of the then-prevalent behaviorism. Nonetheless, in any history of this new field, it is necessary to cite a few other circumstances under which aspiring cognitive scientists met one another.

In the scientific annals of this period, the name of the Josiah P. Macy

Foundation looms large. In the winter of 1944, John von Neumann and Norbert Wiener convened a meeting at Princeton of all those interested in what later came to be called "cybernetics." Present at the Macy-sponsored event were many of the scholars already introduced in this narrative. Wiener later recalled, "At the end of the meeting it had become clear to all that there was a substantial common basis of ideas between the workers in the different fields, that people in each group could already use notions which had been better developed by the others, and that some attempt should be made to achieve a common vocabulary" (1961, p. 15).

Building on these initial contacts, Warren McCulloch arranged with the Macy Foundation in the spring of 1946 for a series of meetings on the problems of feedback. "The idea has been to get together a group of modest size, not exceeding some twenty in number, of workers in various related fields and to hold them together for two successive days in all-day series of informal papers, discussions, and meals together, until they had had the opportunity to thresh out their differences and to make progress in thinking along the same lines" (Wiener 1961, p. 18). Ultimately there were ten such meetings, about one a year, of what was originally the Conference for Circular Causal and Feedback Mechanisms in Biological and Social Systems—soon (and happily) shortened, at Wiener's urging, to the Conference on Cybernetics. In the transcripts of these conferences, one discerns ample evidence of scholars informing one another as well as first intimations of interesting and sometimes unexpected projects. For example, it was in discussions at the Macy meetings that the anthropologist Gregory Bateson first encountered ideas about feedback which he was to mine in his "double-bind" theory of schizophrenia.

Activity was especially intense in the Boston and Princeton areas and in California. During the early 1950s, J. Robert Oppenheimer, director of the Princeton Institute for Advanced Study (of which von Neumann was a permanent member) became interested in the application of some of these new ideas in the field of psychology. He regularly invited a group of psychologists to visit the institute and report on recent developments in their field. Among those who spent a year there were George Miller and Jerome Bruner, gifted young psychologists who would shortly play a fundamental role in the launching of cognitive science.

Again, there was difficult-to-anticipate but promising cross-fertilization of ideas. Oppenheimer was particularly interested in analogies between the problems of perception, as they are viewed by the psychologist, and issues of observation, which had come to loom large in atomic and subatomic physics, once one began to work at the atomic and the subatomic levels. He had been pondering the disturbing implications of the *indeterminacy principle,* according to which it is impossible to ascertain the position and the velocity of a particle without affecting it during the course of measurement. Meanwhile, Bruner had been studying the effects of an observer's attitude and expectations on putatively "objective data." One day Oppenheimer remarked to him, "Perception as you psychologists study it can't, after all, be different from observation in physics, can it?" (quoted in Bruner 1983, pp. 95–96).

In Boston, discussion of these cognitive themes was continuing at M.I.T., and at the associated Lincoln Laboratories, where a group of young engineers and psychologists had assembled to work on applied problems, such as early warning signals in the case of bomb attacks. At nearby Harvard in the prestigious Society of Fellows, the influence of behaviorist thinking was dominant among the senior fellows, but the young junior fellows, including the linguist Noam Chomsky and the mathematician Marvin Minsky, were already proceeding in different (and anti-behaviorist) theoretical directions (Miller 1982). The Ford Foundation, having decided to help stimulate work in the behavioral sciences, established a Center for Advanced Study in the Behavioral Sciences in Palo Alto and also provided funding for a significant proportion (perhaps one third) of all the research psychologists in America. At the Rand Corporation in Southern California, groups of mathematicians and engineers were working on the development of computing machines. Two young scientists, Allen Newell and Herbert Simon, had begun to talk about the possibilities of creating machines that could genuinely think. And, again, there was a British version as well—the Ratio Club, which commenced in 1949. Central to the Ratio Club was the notion of processing information in animals and machines. Members included physiologists, engineers, physicians, and psychologists with interests in the mind or "minding." Turing occasionally attended meetings. The group (which met for several years) had the intriguing rule that any member who reached the rank of full professor must be expelled, because he would then have potential control over other members (McCorduck 1979, p. 78).

In addition to these many face-to-face encounters among those concerned with cognitive matters, there appeared in the late 1940s and early 1950s several books from different quarters which helped to bring the emerging interdisciplinary ideas to wider attention. One such book, perhaps the closest analogy in writing to the Hixon Symposium, was W. Ross Ashby's *Design for a Brain* (1952).

Ashby, a British physician and mathematician, wished to account for human mental activity in a mechanistic manner. He sought to show how, using only logical axiomatic methods, one could design a machine capable of adaptive behavior or learning. In the proper behaviorist fashion of the day, Ashby deliberately avoided talking of anything like consciousness or purposeful behavior. Instead, he directed his attention to the way in which an organism can effect a transition from chaos to stability, thereby enhancing the possibility of survival. Stability can come about because "the machine is a self-organizing system, a system that responds to stimuli, changing its behavior and sometimes its shape in order to achieve stability" (McCorduck 1979, p. 83). Ashby's work intrigued young scholars—like George Miller, Marvin Minsky, Allen Newell, and Herbert Simon—for he was not interested merely in making a machine that worked well. "My aim," Ashby declared, "is simply to copy the living brain. In particular if the living brain fails in certain characteristic ways, then I want my artificial brain to fail too. I have attempted to deduce what is necessary, what properties the nervous system must have if it is to behave at once mechanistically and adaptively" (1952, pp. v, 130). It was the scope of Ashby's aspirations, the doggedly logical way in which he proceeded, and his refusal to "finesse" possible differences between human and mechanical behavior which caught the attention of aspiring cognitive scientists. Indeed, Ashby's maddening adherence to the strictest behaviorist and mechanistic canons served as an additional spur to younger investigators: his challenge continues to hang, at least spiritually, above the desks of many of today's cognitive scientists.

From more remote quarters began to appear books relevant to the discussions in the emerging cognitive sciences. For instance, in the area of linguistics, Roman Jakobson and his colleagues published their first findings about the distinctive features of language—the units or building blocks out of which the phonemes (or basic sounds) of language are constructed (Jakobson and Halle 1956). In neuropsychology, Donald Hebb described the developing nervous system so as to account for many aspects of visual perception and also to illuminate processes of learning and the growth and subsequent decline of intelligence (Hebb 1949). In anthropology, Gregory Bateson introduced his notions about feedback systems in social systems—for example, among members of a family (Bateson et al. 1956). New mathematical innovations, such as Markov processes and stochastic models, quickly came to the attention of young workers in the social sciences. And a few names which had garnered attention on the Continent began to command increasing respect in the Anglo-American community—Frederic Bartlett, Claude Lévi-Strauss, Alexander Luria, Jean Piaget, Lev Vygotsky.

But all this is by way of stagesetting. The basic ideas for cognitive science were immanent in the early papers of McCulloch, Turing, von Neumann, Wiener, and Pitts and were being heatedly debated at the Macy conferences, the Ratio Club, Harvard's Society of Fellows, and various other institutions and venues. Important papers and books were being written and discussed. Still, all of this activity was going on, in a sense, outside established fields of study. It was extracurricular and considered a bit odd by those in the mainstream—behaviorist psychology, structural linguistics, functionalist social anthropology, the neuropsychology of animal learning. It would take more dramatic events to shake these fields to their foundation—events that were not long in coming.

3

Cognitive Science:
The First Decades

A Consensual Birthdate

Seldom have amateur historians achieved such consensus. There has been nearly unanimous agreement among the surviving principals that cognitive science was officially recognized around 1956. The psychologist George A. Miller (1979) has even fixed the date, 11 September 1956.

Why this date? Miller focuses on the Symposium on Information Theory held at the Massachusetts Institute of Technology on 10–12 September 1956 and attended by many leading figures in the communication and the human sciences. The second day stands out in Miller's mind because of two featured papers. The first, presented by Allen Newell and Herbert Simon, described the "Logic Theory Machine," the first complete proof of a theorem ever carried out on a computing machine. The second paper, by the young linguist Noam Chomsky, outlined "Three Models of Language." Chomsky showed that a model of language production derived from Claude Shannon's information-theoretical approach could not possibly be applied successfully to "natural language," and went on to exhibit his own approach to grammar, based on linguistic transformations. As Miller recalls, "Other linguists had said language has all the formal precisions of mathematics, but Chomsky was the first linguist to make good on the claim. I think that was what excited all of us" (1979, p. 8). Not incidentally, that day George Miller also delivered a seminal paper, outlining his claim that the capacity of human short-term memory is limited to approximately seven entries. Miller summed up his reactions:

I went away from the Symposium with a strong conviction, more intuitive than rational, that human experimental psychology, theoretical linguistics, and computer simulation of cognitive processes were all pieces of a larger whole, and that the future would see progressive elaboration and coordination of their shared concerns. . . . I have been working toward a cognitive science for about twenty years beginning before I knew what to call it. (1979, p. 9)

Miller's testimony is corroborated by other witnesses. From the ranks of psychology, Jerome Bruner declares, "New metaphors were coming into being in those mid-1950s and one of the most compelling was that of computing. . . . My "Generation" created and nurtured the Cognitive Revolution—a revolution whose limits we still cannot fathom" (1983, pp. 274, 277). Michael Posner concludes, "This mix of ideas about cognition was ignited by the information processing language that arrived in psychology in the early 1950s" (Posner and Shulman 1979, p. 374). And George Mandler suggests:

For reasons that are obscure at present, the various tensions and inadequacies of the first half of the twentieth century cooperated to produce a new movement in psychology that first adopted the label of information processing and after became known as modern cognitive psychology. And it all happened in the five year period between 1955 and 1960. Cognitive science started during that five year period, a happening that is just beginning to become obvious to its practitioners. (1981, p. 9)

Finally, in their history of the period, computer scientists Allen Newell and Herbert Simon declare:

Within the last dozen years a general change in scientific outlook has occurred, consonant with the point of view represented here. One can date the change roughly from 1956: in psychology, by the appearance of Bruner, Goodnow, and Austin's *Study of Thinking* and George Miller's "The magical number seven"; in linguistics, by Noam Chomsky's "Three models of language"; and in computer science, by our own paper on the Logical Theory Machine. (1972, p. 4)

This impressive congruence stresses a few seminal publications, emanating (not surprisingly perhaps) from the same small group of investigators. In fact, however, the list of relevant publications is almost endless. As far as general cognitive scientific publications are concerned, John von Neumann's posthumous book, *The Computer and the Brain* (1958), should head the list. In this book—actually a set of commissioned lectures which von Neumann became too ill to deliver—the pioneering computer scientist developed many of the themes originally touched upon in his Hixon Symposium contribution. He included a discussion of various kinds of computers and analyzed the idea of a program, the operation of memory in computers, and the possibility of machines that replicate themselves.

Relevant research emanated from each of the fields that I have designated as contributing cognitive sciences.* The witnesses I have just quoted noted the principal texts in the fields of psychology, linguistics, and artificial intelligence, and many more entries could be added. Neuroscientists were beginning to record impulses from single neurons in the nervous system. At M.I.T., Warren McCulloch's research team, led by the neurophysiologists Jerome Lettvin and Humberto Maturana, recorded from the retina of the frog. They were able to show that neurons were responsive to extremely specific forms of information such as "bug-like" small dark spots which moved across their receptive fields, three to five degrees in extent. Also in the late 1950s, a rival team of investigators, David Hubel and Torsten Wiesel at Harvard, began to record from cells in the visual cortex of the cat. They located nerve cells that responded to specific information, including brightness, contrast, binocularity, and the orientation of lines. These lines of research, eventually honored in 1981 by a Nobel Prize, called attention to the extreme specificity encoded in the nervous system.

The mid 1950s were also special in the field of anthropology. At this time, the first publications by Harold Conklin, Ward Goodenough, and Floyd Lounsbury appeared in the newly emerging field of cognitive anthropology, or ethnosemantics. Researchers undertook systematic collection of data concerning the naming, classifying, and concept-forming abilities of people living in remote cultures, and then sought to describe in formal terms the nature of these linguistic and cognitive practices. These studies documented the great variety of cognitive practices found around the world, even as they strongly suggested that the relevant cognitive processes are similar everywhere.

In addition, in the summer of 1956, a group of young scholars, trained in mathematics and logic and interested in the problem-solving potentials of computers, gathered at Dartmouth College to discuss their mutual interests. Present at Dartmouth were most of the scholars working in what came to be termed "artificial intelligence," including the four men generally deemed to be its founding fathers: John McCarthy, Marvin Minsky, Allen Newell, and Herbert Simon. During the summer institute, these scientists, along with other leading investigators, reviewed ideas for programs that would solve problems, recognize patterns, play games, and reason logically, and laid out the principal issues to be discussed in coming years. Though no synthesis emerged from these discussions, the participants seem to have set up a permanent kind of "in group" centered at the

*Full bibliographical references to these lines of research will be provided at appropriate points in the text.

M.I.T., Stanford, and Carnegie-Mellon campuses. To artificial intelligence, this session in the summer of 1956 was as central as the meeting at M.I.T. among communication scientists a few months later.

Scholars removed from empirical science were also pondering the implications of the new machines. Working at Princeton, the American philosopher Hilary Putnam (1960) put forth an innovative set of notions. As he described it, the development of Turing-machine notions and the invention of the computer helped to solve—or to dissolve—the classical mind-body problem. It was apparent that different programs, on the same or on different computers, could carry out structurally identical problem-solving operations. Thus, the logical operations themselves (the "software") could be described quite apart from the particular "hardware" on which they happened to be implemented. Put more technically, the "logical description" of a Turing machine includes no specification of its physical embodiment.

The analogy to the human system and to human thought processes was clear. The human brain (or "bodily states") corresponded to the computational hardware; patterns of thinking or problem solving ("mental states") could be described entirely separately from the particular constitution of the human nervous system. Moreover, human beings, no less than computers, harbored programs; and the same symbolic language could be invoked to describe programs in both entities. Such notions not only clarified the epistemological implications of the various demonstrations in artificial intelligence; they also brought contemporary philosophy and empirical work in the cognitive sciences into much closer contact.

One other significant line of work, falling outside cognitive science as usually defined, is the ethological approach to animal behavior which had evolved in Europe during the 1930s and 1940s thanks to the efforts of Konrad Lorenz (1935) and Niko Tinbergen (1951). At the very time that American comparative psychologists were adhering closely to controlled laboratory settings, European ethologists had concluded that animals should be studied in their natural habitat. Observing carefully under these naturalistic conditions, and gradually performing informal experiments on the spot, the ethologists revealed the extraordinary fit between animals and their natural environment, the characteristic *Umwelt* (or world view) of each species, and the particular stimuli (or releasers) that catalyze dramatic developmental milestones during "critical" or "sensitive" periods. Ethology has remained to some extent a European rather than an American specialty. Still, the willingness to sample wider swaths of behavior in naturally occurring settings had a liberating influence on the types of concept and the modes of exploration that came to be tolerated in cognitive studies.

The 1960s: Picking Up Steam

The seeds planted in the 1950s sprouted swiftly in the next decade. Governmental and private sources provided significant financial support. Setting the intellectual tone were the leading researchers who had launched the key lines of study of the 1950s, as well as a set of gifted students who were drawn to the cognitive fields, much in the way that physics and biology had lured the keenest minds of earlier generations. Two principal figures in this "selling of cognition" were Jerome Bruner and George Miller, who in 1960 founded at Harvard the Center for Cognitive Studies. The Center, as story has it, began when these two psychologists approached the dean of the faculty, McGeorge Bundy, and asked him to help create a research center devoted to the nature of knowledge. Bundy reportedly responded, "And how does that differ from what Harvard University does?" (quoted in Bruner 1983, p. 123). Bundy gave his approval, and Bruner and Miller succeeded in getting funds from the Carnegie Corporation, whose president at that time, the psychologist John Gardner, was sympathetic to new initiatives in the behavioral sciences.

Thereafter, for over ten years, the Harvard Center served as a locale where visiting scholars were invited for a sabbatical, and where graduate and postdoctorate students flocked in order to sample the newest thinking in the cognitive areas. A list of visitors to the Center reads like a Who's Who in Cognitive Science: nearly everyone visited at one time or another, and many spent a semester or a year in residence. And while the actual projects and products of the Center were probably not indispensable for the life of the field, there is hardly a younger person in the field who was not influenced by the Center's presence, by the ideas that were bandied about there, and by the way in which they were implemented in subsequent research. Indeed, psychologists Michael Posner and Gordon Shulman (1979) locate the inception of the cognitive sciences at the Harvard Center.

During the 1960s, books and other publications made available the ideas from the Center and from other research sites. George Miller—together with his colleagues Karl Pribram, a neuroscientist, and Eugene Galanter, a mathematically oriented psychologist—opened the decade with a book that had a tremendous impact on psychology and allied fields—a slim volume entitled *Plans and the Structure of Behavior* (1960). In it the authors sounded the death knell for standard behaviorism with its discredited reflex arc and, instead, called for a cybernetic approach to behavior in terms of actions, feedback loops, and readjustments of action in the light of feedback. To replace the reflex arc, they proposed a unit of activity called a "TOTE unit" (for "Test-Operate-Test-Exit"): an important property of a TOTE unit was that it could itself be embedded within the hierarchical structure of an encompassing TOTE unit. As a vehicle for conceptualizing such TOTE units, the authors selected the computer with its programs. If a computer could have a goal (or a set of goals), a means for carrying out the goal, a means for verifying that the goal has been carried out, and then the option of either progressing to a new goal or terminating behavior, models of human beings deserved no less. The computer made it legitimate in theory to describe human beings in terms of plans (hierarchically organized processes), images (the total available knowledge of the world), goals, and other mentalistic conceptions; and by their ringing endorsement, these three leading scientists now made it legitimate in practice to abandon constricted talk of stimulus and response in favor of more open-ended, interactive, and purposeful models.

The impact of this way of thinking became evident a few years later when textbooks in cognitive psychology began to appear. By far the most influential was *Cognitive Psychology* by the computer-literate experimental psychologist Ulric Neisser (1967). Neisser put forth a highly "constructive" view of human activity. On his account, all cognition, from the first moment of perception onward, involves inventive analytic and synthesizing processes. He paid tribute to computer scientists for countenancing talk of an "executive" and to information scientists for discussing accession, processing, and transformation of data. But at the same time, Neisser resisted uncritical acceptance of the computer-information form of analysis. In his view, objective calculation of how many bits of information can be processed is not relevant to psychology, because human beings are selective in their attention as a pure channel such as a telephone cannot be. Neisser expressed similar skeptical reservations about the claims surrounding computer programs:

> None of [these programs] does even remote justice to the complexity of human mental processes. Unlike men, "artificially intelligent" programs tend to be single minded, undistractable, and unemotional. . . . This book can be construed as an extensive argument against models of this kind, and also against other simplistic theories of the cognitive processes. (1967, p. 9)

After Neisser, it was possible to buy the cognitive science approach in general and still join into vigorous controversies with "true believers."

Enthusiasts of the power of simulation were scarcely silent during this period. In his 1969 Compton lectures, *The Sciences of the Artificial*, Herbert Simon provided a philosophical exposition of his approach: as he phrased it, both the computer and the human mind should be thought of as "symbol systems"—physical entities that process, transform, elaborate, and, in other ways, manipulate symbols of various sorts. And, in 1972, Allen Newell and Herbert Simon published their magnum opus, the monumental *Human Problem Solving,* in which they described the "general problem solver" programs, provided an explanation of their approach to cognitive studies, and included a historical addendum detailing their claims to primacy in this area of study.

Textbooks and books of readings were appearing in other subfields of cognitive science as well. An extremely influential collection was Jerry Fodor and Jerrold Katz's collection, *The Structure of Language* (1964), which anthologized articles representing the Chomskian point of view in philosophy, psychology, and linguistics, and attempted to document why this approach, rather than earlier forays into language, was likely to be the appropriate scientific stance. In artificial intelligence, Edward Feigenbaum and Julian Feldman put out a collection called *Computers and Thought* (1963), which presented many of the best-running programs of the era; while their collection had a definite "Carnegie slant," a rival anthology, *Semantic Information Processing,* edited by Marvin Minsky in 1968, emphasized the M.I.T. position. And, in the area of cognitive anthropology, in addition to influential writings by Kimball Romney and Roy D'Andrade (1964), Stephen Tyler's textbook *Cognitive Anthropology* made its debut in 1969.

But by 1969, the number of slots in short-term memory had been exceeded—without the benefit of chunking, one could no longer enumerate the important monographs, papers, and personalities in the cognitive sciences. (In fact, though my list of citations may seem distressingly long, I have really only scratched the surface of cognitive science, circa 1970.) There was tremendous activity in several fields, and a feeling of definite progress as well. As one enthusiastic participant at a conference declared:

> We may be at the start of a major intellectual adventure: somewhere comparable to the position in which physics stood toward the end of the Renaissance, with lots of discoveries waiting to be made and the beginning of an inkling of an idea of how to go about making them. It turned out, in the case of the early development of modern physics that the advancement of the science involved developing new kinds of intellectual sophistication: new mathematics, a new ontology, and a new view of scientific method. My guess is that the same sort of evolution is required in the present case (and, by the way, in much the same time scale). Probably now, as then, it will be an uphill battle against obsolescent intellectual and institutional habits. (Sloan Foundation 1976, p. 10)

When the amount of activity in a field has risen to this point, with an aura of excitement about impending breakthroughs, human beings often found some sort of an organization or otherwise mark the new enterprise. Such was happening in cognitive science in the early and middle 1970s. The moment was ripe for the coalescing of individuals, interests, and disciplines into an organizational structure.

The Sloan Initiative

At this time, fate intervened in the guise of a large New York–based private foundation interested in science—the Alfred P. Sloan Foundation. The Sloan Foundation funds what it terms "Particular Programs," in which it invests a sizable amount of money in an area over a few years' time, in the hope of stimulating significant progress. In the early 1970s, a Particular Program had been launched in the neurosciences: a collection of disciplines that explore the nervous system—ranging from neuropsychology and neurophysiology to neuroanatomy and neurochemistry. Researchers drawn from disparate fields were stimulated by such funding to explore common concepts and common organizational frameworks. Now Sloan was casting about for an analogous field, preferably in the sciences, in which to invest a comparable sum.

From conversations with officers of the Sloan Foundation, and from the published record, it is possible to reconstruct the principal events that led to the Sloan Foundation's involvement with cognitive science. In early 1975, the foundation was contemplating the support of programs in several fields; but by late 1975, a Particular Program in the cognitive sciences was the major one under active consideration. During the following year, meetings were held where major cognitive scientists shared their views. Possibly sensing the imminent infusion of money into the field, nearly every scientist invited by the Sloan Foundation managed to juggle his or her schedule to attend the meetings. Though there was certainly criticism voiced of the new cognitive science movement, most participants (who were admittedly interested parties) stressed the promise of the field and the need for flexible research and training support.

While recognizing that cognitive science was not as mature as neuroscience at the time of the foundation's commitment to the latter field, officers concluded that "nonetheless, there is every indication, confirmed by the many authorities involved in primary explorations, that many areas of the cognitive sciences are converging, and, moreover, there is a correspondingly important need to develop lines of communication from area to area so that research tools and techniques can be shared in building a body of theoretical knowledge" (Sloan Foundation 1976, p. 6). After deliberating, the foundation decided to embark on a five-to-seven-year program, involving commitments of up to fifteen million dollars. (This commitment was ultimately increased to twenty million dollars.) The investment took the form, initially, of small grants to many research institutions and, ultimately, of a few large-scale grants to major universities.

Like the spur provided by the Macy Foundation a generation earlier, the Sloan Foundation's initiative had a catalytic effect on the field. As more than one person quipped, "Suddenly I woke up and discovered that I had been a cognitive scientist all of my life." In short order the journal *Cognitive Science* was founded—its first issue appearing in January 1977; and soon thereafter, in 1979, a society of the same name was founded. Donald Norman of the University of California in San Diego was instrumental in both endeavors. The society held its first annual meeting, amid great fanfare, in La Jolla, California, in August 1979. Programs, courses, newsletters, and allied scholarly paraphernalia arose around the country and abroad. There were even books about the cognitive sciences, including a popular account, *The Universe Within,* by Morton Hunt (1982) and my own historical essay, also supported by the Sloan Foundation.

Declaring the birth of a field had a bracing effect on those who discovered that they were in it, either centrally or peripherally, but by no means ensured any consensus, let alone appreciable scientific progress. Patrons are almost always necessary, though they do not necessarily suffice, to found a field or create a consensus. Indeed, tensions about what the field is, who understands it, who threatens it, and in what direction it ought to go were encountered at every phase of the Sloan Foundation's involvement (and have continued to be to this day).

Symptomatic of the controversy engendered by the Sloan Foundation's support of research in cognitive science was the reaction to a report commissioned by the foundation in 1978. This State of the Art Report (soon dubbed "SOAP" for short) was drafted by a dozen leading scholars in the field, with input from another score of advisers. In the view of the authors, "What has brought the field into existence is a common research objective: to discover the representational and computational capacities of the mind and their structural and functional representation in the brain" (1978, p. 6). The authors prepared a sketch of the interrelations among the six constituent fields—the cognitive hexagon, as it was labeled. Through the use of unbroken and broken lines, an effort was made to indicate the connections between fields which had already been forged, and to suggest the kinds of connection which could be but had not yet been effected.

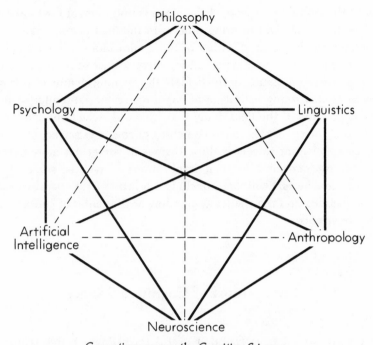

Connections among the Cognitive Sciences
KEY: Unbroken lines = strong interdisciplinary ties
Broken lines = weak interdisciplinary ties

In my view, the authors of the SOAP document made a serious effort to survey principal lines of research and to provide a general charter for work in cognitive science, setting forth its principal assumptions. Then, using the example of how individuals from different cultures give names to colors, these authors illustrated how different disciplines combine their insights. (I'll flesh out this example of color naming in chapter 12.) However, the community-at-large adopted a distinctly negative view of the report. In fact, such virulent opposition was expressed by so many readers that, counter to original plans, the document was never published. I think this negative reaction came from the fact that each reader approached the document from the perspective of his or her own discipline and research program. In an effort to be reasonably ecumenical, the authors simply ensured that most readers would find their own work slighted. Moreover, there is as yet no agreed-upon research paradigm—no consensual set of assumptions or methods—and so cognitive scientists tend to project their own favorite paradigms onto the field as a whole. In view of these factors, it was probably not possible in 1978 to write a document that would have won the support of a majority of cognitive scientists.

It would be desirable, of course, for a consensus mysteriously to emerge, thanks to the largesse of the Sloan Foundation, or for some latter-day Newton or Darwin to bring order into the field of cognitive science. In the absence, however, of either of these miraculous events, it is left to those of us who wish to understand cognitive science to come up with our own tentative formulation of the field. In the opening chapter of this book, I presented a working definition of cognitive science and alluded to five key components of the field. Now that I have sketched out some of the intellectual forces that led to the launching of cognitive science some three decades ago, I want to revisit these themes in somewhat more detail, in order to consider some of their implications as well as some of their problematic aspects. I will then conclude this introductory part by describing the paradox and the challenge standing at the center of contemporary cognitive science.

Key Features of Cognitive Science

In my own work I have found it useful to distinguish five features or "symptoms" of cognitive science: the first two of these represent the "core assumptions" of the field, while the latter three represent methodological or strategic features. Not only are these ideas common to most "strong versions" of cognitive science, but they also serve as specific points of contention for its critics. I shall list each of these characteristics and then indicate certain lines of criticism put forth by those most antagonistic to cognitive science. These criticisms (as voiced by their most vocal adherents) will be expanded upon at appropriate points in the book and reviewed in my concluding chapter.

Representations

Cognitive science is predicated on the belief that it is legitimate—in fact, necessary—to posit a separate level of analysis which can be called the "level of representation." When working at this level, a scientist traffics in such representational entities as symbols, rules, images—the stuff of representation which is found between input and output—and in addition, explores the ways in which these representational entities are joined, transformed, or contrasted with one another. This level is necessary in order to explain the variety of human behavior, action, and thought.

In opting for a representational level, the cognitive scientist is claiming that certain traditional ways of accounting for human thought are inadequate. The neuroscientist may choose to talk in terms of nerve cells, the historian or anthropologist in terms of cultural influences, the ordinary person or the writer of fiction in terms of the experiential or phenomenological level. While not questioning the utility of these levels for various purposes, the cognitive scientist rests his discipline on the assumption that, for scientific purposes, human cognitive activity must be described in terms of symbols, schemas, images, ideas, and other forms of mental representation.

In terms of ordinary language, it seems unremarkable to talk of human beings as having ideas, as forming images, as manipulating symbols, images, or languages in the mind. However, there is a huge gap between the use of such concepts in ordinary language and their elevation to the level of acceptable scientific constructs. Cautious theorists want to avoid positing elements or levels of explanation except when absolutely necessary; and they also want to be able to describe the structure and the mechanisms employed at a level before "going public" with its existence. While talk about the structure and mechanisms of the nervous system is relatively unproblematic—since its constituent units can (at least in principle) be seen and probed—agreement to talk of structure and processes at the level of mental representation has proved far more problematic.

Critics of the representational view are generally drawn from behaviorist ranks. Wielders of Ockham's razor, they believe that the construct of mind does more harm than good; that it makes more sense to talk about neurological structures or about overt behaviors, than about ideas, concepts, or rules; and that dwelling on a representational level is unnecessary, misleading, or incoherent.

Another line of criticism, less extreme but ultimately as crippling, accepts the need for common-sense talk about plans, intentions, beliefs, and the like but sees no need for a separate scientific language and level of analysis concerned with their mental representation: on this point of view, one should be able to go directly from plans to the nervous system, because it is *there,* ultimately, that all plans or intentions must be represented. Put in a formula, ordinary language plus neurology eliminate the need for talk of mental representations.

Of course, among scholars who accept the need for a level of representation, debates still rage. Indeed, contemporary theoretical talk among "card-carrying" cognitive scientists amounts, in a sense, to a discussion of the best ways of conceptualizing mental representations. Some investigators favor the view that there is but a single form of mental representation (usually, one that features propositions or statements); some believe in at least two forms of mental representation—one more like a picture (or image), the other closer to propositions; still others believe that it is possible to posit multiple forms of mental representation and that it is impossible to determine which is the correct one.

All cognitive scientists accept the truism that mental processes are ultimately represented in the central nervous system. But there is deep disagreement about the relevance of brain science to current work on cognition. Until recently, the majority viewpoint has held that cognitive science is best pursued apart from detailed knowledge of the nervous system—both because such knowledge has not yet been forthcoming and out of a desire to ensure the legitimacy of a separate level of mental representation. As the cognitive level becomes more secure, and as more discoveries are made in the brain sciences, this self-styled distancing may be reduced. Not surprisingly, neuroscientists (as a group) have shown the least enthusiasm for a representational account, whereas such an account is an article of faith among most psychologists, linguists, and computer scientists.

Computers

While not all cognitive scientists make the computer central to their daily work, nearly all have been strongly influenced by it. The computer serves, in the first place, as an "existence-proof": if a man-made machine can be said to reason, have goals, revise its behavior, transform information, and the like, human beings certainly deserve to be characterized in the same way. There is little doubt that the invention of computers in the 1930s and 1940s, and demonstrations of "thinking" in the computer in the 1950s, were powerfully liberating to scholars concerned with explaining the human mind.

In addition to serving as a model of human thought, the computer also serves as a valuable tool to cognitive scientific work: most cognitive scientists use it to analyze their data, and an increasing number attempt to simulate cognitive processes on it. Indeed, artificial intelligence, the science built around computer simulation, is considered by many the central discipline in cognitive science and the one most likely to crowd out, or render superfluous, other older fields of study.

In principle, it is possible to be a cognitive scientist without loving the computer; but in practice, skepticism about computers generally leads to skepticism about cognitive science. To some critics, computers are just the latest of a long series of inadequate models of human cognition (remember the switchboard, the hydraulic pump, or the hologram) and there is no reason to think that today's "buzz-model" will meet a happier fate. Viewing active organisms as "information-processing systems" seems a radical mistake to such critics. Computers are seen by others as mere playthings which interfere with, rather than speed up, efforts to understand human thought. The fact that one can simulate any behavior in numerous ways may actually impede the search for the correct description of *human* behavior and thought. The excessive claims made by proponents of artificial intelligence are often quoted maliciously by those with little faith in man-made machines and programs.

Involvement with computers, and belief in their relevance as a model of human thought, is pervasive in cognitive science; but again, there are differences across disciplines. Intrinsic involvement with computers is a reliable gauge of the extent of a discipline's involvement with cognitive science. Computers are central in artificial intelligence, and only a few disgruntled computer scientists question the utility of the computer as a model for human cognition. In the fields of linguistics and psychology, one will encounter some reservations about a computational approach; and yet most practitioners of these disciplines do not bother to pick a feud with computerphiles.

When it comes to the remaining cognitive sciences, however, the relationship to the computer becomes increasingly problematic. Many anthropologists and many neuroscientists, irrespective of whether they happen to use computers in their own research, have yet to be convinced that the computer serves as a viable model of those aspects of cognition in which they are interested. Many neuroscientists feel that the brain will provide the answer in its own terms, without the need for an intervening computer model; many anthropologists feel that the key to human thought lies in historical and cultural forces that lie external to the human head and are difficult to conceptualize in computational terms. As for philosophers, their attitudes toward computers range from unabashed enthusiasm to virulent skepticism—which makes them a particularly interesting and important set of informants in any examination of cognitive science.

De-Emphasis on Affect, Context, Culture, and History

Though mainstream cognitive scientists do not necessarily bear any animus against the affective realm, against the context that surrounds any action or thought, or against historical or cultural analyses, in practice they attempt to factor out these elements to the maximum extent possible. So even do anthropologists when wearing their cognitive science hats. This may be a question of practicality: if one were to take into account these individualizing and phenomenalistic elements, cognitive science might become impossible. In an effort to explain everything, one ends up explaining nothing. And so, at least provisionally, most cognitive scientists attempt to so define and investigate problems that an adequate account can be given without resorting to these murky concepts.

Critics of cognitivism have responded in two principal ways. Some critics hold that factors like affect, history, or context will *never* be explicable by science: they are inherently humanistic or aesthetic dimensions, destined to fall within the province of other disciplines or practices. Since these factors are central to human experience, any science that attempts to exclude them is doomed from the start. Other critics agree that some or all of these features are of the essence in human experience, but do not feel that they are insusceptible to scientific explanation. Their quarrel with an antiseptic cognitive science is that it is wrong to bracket these dimensions artificially. Instead, cognitive scientists should from the first put their noses to the grindstone and incorporate such dimensions fully into their models of thought and behavior.

Belief in Interdisciplinary Studies

While there may eventually be a single cognitive science, all agree that it remains far off. Investigators drawn from a given discipline place their faith in productive interactions with practitioners from other disciplines: in the tradition of the Hixon and Macy symposiasts, they hope that, working together, they can achieve more powerful insights than have been obtained from the perspective of a single discipline. As examples, they point to current work in visual perception and in linguistic processing which has come to draw quite naturally on evidence from psychology, neuroscience, and artificial intelligence—so much so that disciplinary lines are beginning to blur.

Skeptics feel that you cannot make progress by compounding disciplines, and that it is more prudent to place each individual disciplinary house in order. Since it is also unclear *which* of the relevant disciplines will ultimately contribute to a cognitive science, and in which way, much valuable time may be wasted in ill-considered collaborations. From their vantage point, it is perfectly all right to have individual cognitive sciences but ill-considered to legislate a single seamless discipline. At most, there should be cooperation among disciplines—and never total fusion.

Rootedness in Classical Philosophical Problems

As already indicated, I consider classical philosophical problems to be a key ingredient in contemporary cognitive science and, in fact, find it difficult to conceive of cognitive science apart from them. The debates of the Greek philosophers, as well as of their successors in the Enlightenment, stand out in many pages of cognitive scientific writing. I do not mean that these traditional questions have necessarily been phrased in the best way, or even that they can be answered, but rather that they serve as a logical point of departure for investigations in cognitive science.

In my discussions with cognitive scientists, however, I have found this precept to be contentious. Nor is it predictable which scientists, or which science, will agree with a philosophically based formulation of the new field. Some cognitive scientists from each discipline readily assent to the importance—indeed, the inevitability—of a philosophical grounding; while others find the whole philosophical enterprise of the past irrelevant to their concerns or even damaging to the cognitive scientific effort. We may well be dealing here with personal views about the utility of reading and debating classical authorities rather than with fundamental methodological aspects of cognitive science. But whatever the reason, cognitive scientists are scarcely of a single mind when it comes to the importance of the *Meno,* of Descartes's *Cogito,* or of Kant's *Critique.*

Precisely because the role of philosophy is controversial in the cognitive sciences, it is useful to explore the earlier history of philosophy. Only such a survey can prove that cognitive scientists—whether or not they are fully aware of it—are engaged in tackling those issues first identified by philosophers many decades or even many centuries ago. Scientists will differ on whether these questions were properly formulated, on whether philosophers made any significant progress in answering them, and on whether philosophers today have any proper role in a scientific enterprise. Indeed, even philosophers are divided on these issues. Still, it is worth reviewing their positions on these issues, for philosophers have, since classical times, taken as their special province the definition of human knowledge. Moreover, they have also pondered the nature and scope of the cognitive-scientific enterprise, and their conclusions merit serious examination.

In my own view, each of these symptoms or features of cognitive science were already discernible in the discussions of the 1940s and were widespread by the middle 1950s. A cognitive-science text will not necessarily exhibit or illustrate each of the symptoms, but few texts will be devoid of most of them. What legitimizes talk of cognitive science is the fact that these features were not in evidence a half-century ago; and to the extent that they once again pass from the scene, the era of cognitive science will be at an end.

Comments on the ultimate fate of cognitive science are most properly left to the conclusion of this study; but as a kind of guidepost to succeeding chapters, it may be useful to anticipate my principal conclusions. In my view, the initial intoxication with cognitive science was based on a shrewd hunch: that human thought would turn out to resemble in significant respects the operations of the computer, and particularly the electronic serial digital computer which was becoming widespread in the middle of the century. It is still too early to say to what extent human thought processes are computational in this sense. Still, if I read the signs right, one of the chief results of the last few decades has been to call into question the extent to which higher human thought processes—those which we might consider most distinctively human—can be adequately approached in terms of this particular computational model.

Which leads to what I have termed the *computational paradox.* Paradoxically, the rigorous application of methods and models drawn from the computational realm has helped scientists to understand the ways in which human beings are not very much like these prototypical computers. This is not to say that no cognitive processes are computerlike—indeed, some very much resemble the computer. Even less is it to contend that cognitive processes cannot be modeled on a computer (after all, *anything* that can be clearly laid out can be so modeled). It is rather to report that the kind of systematic, logical, rational view of human cognition that pervaded the early literature of cognitive science does not adequately describe much of human thought and behavior. Cognitive science can still go on, but the question arises about whether one ought to remain on the lookout for more veridical models of human thought.

Even as cognitive science has spawned a paradox, it has also encountered a challenge. It seems clear from my investigation that mainstream cognitive science comfortably encompasses the disciplines of cognitive psychology, artificial intelligence, and large sections of philosophy and linguistics. But it seems equally clear that other disciplines mark a boundary for cognitive science. Much of neuroscience proceeds at a level of study where issues of representation and of the computer-as-model are not encountered. On the opposite end of the spectrum, much of anthropology has become disaffected with methods drawn from cognitive science, and there is a widespread (and possibly growing) belief that the issues most central to anthropology are better handled from a historical or a cultural or even a literary perspective.

And here inheres the challenge to cognitive science. It is important for cognitive science to establish its own autonomy and to demonstrate terrains in which computational and representational approaches are valid. I believe that cognitive science has already succeeded in this endeavor, though the scope of its enterprise may not be so wide as one would have wished.

If cognitive scientists want to give a complete account of the most central features of cognition, however, they (or other scientists) will have to discover or construct the bridges connecting their discipline to neighboring areas of study—and, specifically, to neuroscience at the lower bound, so to speak, and to cultural studies at the upper. How to do this (or whether it can be done at all) is far from clear at this point: but unless the cognitive aspects of language or perception or problem solving can be joined to the neuroscientific and anthropological aspects, we will be left with a disembodied and incomplete discipline. Put differently, no one challenges the autonomy of biology, chemistry, and physics; but unless a single narrative can be woven from the components of atomic, molecular, and organic knowledge, the full nature of organic and inorganic matter will remain obscure.

All this risks getting ahead of our story, however. We have seen in the preceding pages how different factors present early in the century came together to form the bedrock of a new discipline. Ultimately, I want to take a close look at some of the best work in the discipline, so that I can properly evaluate its current status and its future prospects. To achieve this overview, however, it is necessary to consider how the very framing of questions within cognitive science grows out of philosophical writings of the past. By the same token, it is necessary to understand the particular histories, methods, and problems that have characterized the component cognitive sciences. Ultimately this philosophical and historical background has determined in large measure the nature and scope of current interdisciplinary cognitive-scientific efforts. In part II of this book, I shall take a careful look at the several disciplines whose existence made possible the idea of cognitive science and whose practitioners will determine the success of this enterprise.

PART II

THE COGNITIVE

SCIENCES:

A HISTORICAL

PERSPECTIVE

4

Reason, Experience, and the Status of Philosophy

Philosophy always buries its undertakers.
—Etienne Gilson

There is no department of knowledge in which so little progress has been made as in that of mental philosophy. The human mind has been studied as if it were independent of the body, and, generally speaking, by philosophers who possessed a comparatively small share of physical knowledge. No attempt, indeed, has been made to examine its phenomena by the light of experiment and observation, or to analyze them in their abnormal phases. . . . Without data, without axioms, without definitions, [the science of mind] proposes problems which it cannot solve. . . . The human mind escapes from the cognizance of sense and reason, and lies, a waste field with a northern exposure, upon which every passing speculator casts his mental tares, choking any of the good seed that may have sprung up towards maturity.
—David Brewster (1854)

Descartes's Mind

In this chapter I begin my survey of the cognitive sciences by examining the history and the current status of philosophy. This choice is appropriate. Not only is philosophy the oldest of the cognitive sciences, but its epistemological branch has supplied the initial agenda—the list of issues and topics upon which empirically oriented cognitive scientists are working today. Indeed, philosophers have wrestled for centuries with such currently fashionable issues as the nature of mental representation, the extent to which human thought is merely a mechanical (as opposed to a spiritual) process, and the relationship between reason and feeling.

René Descartes is perhaps the prototypical philosophical antecedent of cognitive science. Writing at the very start of the modern era (which, in part, he helped to define and launch), he is in some ways a throwback to that confident reliance on one's own intuitions, that commitment to the centrality of mathematical thinking, that belief in innate ideas which we associate with the Greeks. At the same time, in his curiosity about the operation of the sensory system, the nature of brain processes, and the automaton as a possible model of human nature, he is virtually a contemporary figure.

When, in 1623, he sequestered himself in a small farmhouse in Bavaria, he was embarking on a program of reflection that was to exert profound effects on subsequent Western thought. Descartes had become disenchanted with the systems spun by previous thinkers: "[Philosophy] has been cultivated for many centuries by the best minds that have ever lived and nevertheless no single thing is to be found in it which is not the subject of dispute" (quoted in Wilson 1969, p. 111). To cope with this uncertainty, Descartes evolved a method of systematic doubt. He determined to call into question any evidence of which he was not certain, and found that all he was left with then were his own states of consciousness, his own doubts. Upon his capacity to doubt and, therefore, to think, Descartes discerned a secure foundation on which to build a new philosophy.

The centerpiece of Descartes's philosophy was his own mind and, by extension, the minds of individuals in general. Through examination of the contents of his own mind, Descartes felt that he could establish the knowledge that was most valid, least subject to challenge. He searched for thoughts that were clear and distinct, hence indubitable. A privileged position was reserved for the ideas of arithmetic and geometry, which seemed least fettered by doubt, so evident that they must be true. Moreover, these ideas had not arrived at his mind from external sources: rather, it made sense to think of them as generated by the mind itself:

And what I believe to be more important here is that I find in myself an infinity of ideas of certain things which cannot be assumed to be pure nothingness, even though they may have perhaps no existence outside of my thought. These things are not figments of my imagination, even though it is within my power to think of them or not to think of them; on the contrary, they have their own true and immutable natures. Thus, for example, when I imagine a triangle, even though there may perhaps be no such figure anywhere in the world outside of my thought, nor ever have been, nevertheless the figure cannot help having a certain determinate nature . . . or essence, which is immutable and eternal, which I have not invented and which does not in any way depend upon my mind. (1951,* p. 61)

Mind, in Descartes's view, is special, central to human existence, basically reliable. The mind stands apart from and operates independently of the human body, a totally different sort of entity. The body is best thought of as an automaton, which can be compared to the machines made by men. It is divisible into parts, and elements could be removed without altering anything fundamental. But even if one could design an automaton as complex as a human body, that automaton can never resemble the human mind, for the mind is unified and not decomposable. Moreover, unlike a human mind, a bodily machine could never use speech or other signs in placing its thoughts before other individuals. An automaton might parrot information, but "it never happens that it arranges its speech in various ways, in order to reply appropriately to everything that may be said in its presence, as even the lowest type of man can do" (quoted in Wilson 1969, p. 138).

Descartes was aware that the positing of two distinct entities—a rational mind and a mechanical body—made implausible any explanation of their interaction. How can an immaterial entity control, interact with, or react to a mechanical substance? He made various stabs at solving this problem, none of them (as he knew) totally convincing. But in the process of trying to explain the interaction of mind and body, Descartes became in effect a physiologically oriented psychologist: he devised models of how mental states could exist in a world of sensory experience—models featuring physical objects that had to be perceived and handled. He asked:

What must be the fabric of the nerves and muscles of the human body in order that the animal spirits therein contained should have the power to move the members . . . what changes are necessary in the brain to cause wakefulness, sleep and dream; how light, sounds, smells, tastes, and all other qualities pertaining to external objects are able to imprint on it various ideas by the intervention of the senses. (Quoted in Wilson 1969, p. 137)

And he even proposed one of the first "information-processing" devices: Descartes's diagram showed how visual sensations are conveyed, through the retinas, along nerve filaments, into the brain, with signals from the two eyes being reinverted and fused into a single image on the pineal gland. There, at an all-crucial juncture, the mind (or soul) could interact with the body, yielding a complete representation of external reality. The mind

*When relevant, original publication dates are listed in the References (p. 393).

could now consciously perceive the image and play upon the brain, somewhat as a musician plays upon an instrument (Fancher 1979, pp. 133–34).

Like many who have reflected on the sources of knowledge, Descartes had once thought that all experiences and thoughts arise through the senses. But through his meditations, he had come to devalue the senses and to attribute all thought and creativity to the mind. While he had to admit that there were sources for the experiences of his senses, he minimized their significance:

> I cannot doubt that there is in me a certain passive faculty of perceiving, that is, of receiving and recognizing the ideas of sensible objects; but it would be valueless to me and I could in no way use it if there were not also in me or in something else, another active faculty capable of forming and producing these ideas. (1951, p. 75)

Even as Plato had placed his faith in a mind that could possess (or remember) all manner of things, Descartes determined that the mind, an active reasoning entity, was the ultimate arbiter of truth. And he ultimately attributed ideas to innate rather than to experiential causes:

> no ideas of things, in the shape in which we envisage them by thought, are presented to us by the senses. So much so that in our ideas there is nothing which was not innate in the mind, or faculty of thinking, except only these circumstances which point to experience. . . . They transmitted something which gave the mind occasion to form these ideas, by means of an innate faculty, at this time rather than another. (Quoted in Chomsky 1966, p. 67)

If Descartes could have dispensed with external experience altogether, he would have been pleased to do so; again, like Plato, he attributed human error and inconstancy to the vagaries of experience, and our rationality, understanding, and genuine knowledge to the mind reflecting upon its own ideas. And in so doing, he hurled the strongest possible challenge to future empiricist philosophers, whose thinking he would provoke.

In his discussion of ideas and the mind, sensory experience and the body, the power of language and the centrality of an organizing, doubting self, Descartes formulated an agenda that would dominate philosophical discussions and affect experimental science in the decades and centuries that followed. Furthermore, he proposed the vivid and controversial image of the mind as a rational instrument which, however, cannot be simulated by any imaginable machine—an image still debated in cognitive science today. By creating such images and adopting such stances, Descartes helped launch a period that turned out to be the richest ever in philosophy. As Alfred North Whitehead was to note, "A brief, and sufficiently accurate, description of the intellectual life of the European races during the succeeding two centuries and a quarter up to our own times is that they have been living upon the accumulated capital of ideas provided for them by the genius of the seventeenth century" (1925, p. 42).

The agenda initially posed by the Greeks, and carried forward during the seventeenth century by Descartes, came to be fervently debated among the group of philosophers who earned Whitehead's admiration. The initial empirical responses by Locke, Hume, and Berkeley, the bold synthesis put forth by Kant, and the eventual challenge to the Kantian tradition were principal milestones in the philosophical debates about knowledge. Then, at the very time when the epistemological tradition associated with these earlier writers was undergoing the most severe criticism, the computer came on the scene. Very soon newly discovered philosophical perspectives, which go by such names as "functionalism," and "intentionality," raised once again the possibility of a respectable epistemology: a cooperative scientific effort in which the representational nature of thought could be countenanced, and where traditional philosophical concerns merged with the work of cognitively oriented scientists.

Two important themes have recurred in philosophy over the past few centuries. The first involves the tension between rationalists and empiricists. Those of a rationalist persuasion believe that the mind exhibits powers of reasoning which it imposes upon the world of sensory experience; empiricists believe that mental processes either reflect, or are constructed on the basis of, external sensory impressions. Both Plato and Descartes embraced the rationalist pole, while many succeeding empiricists reacted to it. In our own era, behaviorists have clung to empiricism, while cognitivists are likely to embrace some form of rationalism or a rationalist-empiricist mix.

A second, discipline-oriented theme concerns the actual status of philosophy within the world of scholarly disciplines and, in particular, its relation to science. Once again, Descartes and Plato share a common perspective: from their confident stance, philosophical reflection is the primary pursuit, while the observations of more empirically oriented scholars are given less credence. (Although science was only beginning to be established in Descartes's time, he carried out scientific investigations and surely thought of himself as a scientific worker.) In succeeding generations, the findings and laws of science became increasingly visible: indeed, some issues (for example, the essential nature of matter) were so adequately resolved by the physical sciences that they dropped outside the purview of philosophy. Eventually many, if not most, philosophers felt the need both to keep up with scientific discoveries and to justify their activities in a scientifically respectable manner. In recent decades, as the dominance of science continues to grow, the value of philosophical investigations has again been challenged.

From the perspective of some cognitivists, the rise of empirically oriented investigation renders philosophy unnecessary. With science to answer the philosophical agenda, what is left for philosophers to do? I shall argue, however, that this conclusion is wrong. I see at work a dialectic process, where philosophers propose certain issues, empirical disciplines arise in an attempt to answer them, and then philosophers cooperate with empirical scientists in interpreting the results and in proposing new lines for work. The issues raised by Descartes and his contemporaries ultimately became the concerns of psychologists, linguists, and neuroscientists a few centuries later; and indeed, Descartes's reflections on the human as a possible automaton are central to artificial intelligence today. In the light of empirical results, philosophers have sometimes fundamentally reconceptualized the issues on which they were working; and these reconceptualizations, in turn, have sustained and directed empirical work and aided in its interpretations. Rather than being the ultimate arbiters, or the ultimate victims, of scientific work, philosophers have been (and will continue to be) important handmaidens in the scientific study of cognition.

Empiricist Responses to Descartes

Locke's Competing Model

Descartes's views were soon challenged by a group of British empiricist philosophers, chief among them John Locke, George Berkeley, and David Hume. Locke began by questioning whether one could accept any knowledge on the basis of introspective evidence; he looked instead to sensory experience as the only reliable source of knowledge. He challenged the belief in innate ideas as being useless and misleading. "The knowledge of the existence of *any other thing* we can have only by *sensation,*" he declared. "For the *having the idea* of anything in our mind, no more proves the existence of that thing, than the picture of a man evidences his being in the world, or the visions of a dream make thereby a true history" (quoted in Hanfling 1972, p. 356). And in a famous passage he issued his ultimate answer to the origins of knowledge:

Let us then suppose the mind to be, as we say, white Paper, void of all Characters, without any *Ideas:* How comes it to be furnished? Whence comes it by that vast store, which the busy and boundless Fancy of Man has painted on it, with an almost endless variety? Whence has it all the materials of Reason and Knowledge? To this I answer, in one word, From *Experience.* (Quoted in Herrnstein and Boring 1965, p. 584)

These words sum up the empiricist worldview.

While (on the empiricist account) the experience of the world begins with perception, it assuredly does not end there. Locke devoted considerable effort to distinguishing among various external qualities (which he called "primary" and "secondary," "simple" and "complex"). He stressed how complex ideas grow out of simple ones and the various ways in which ideas come to be associated with one another. He described the process by which words come to stand for ideas and make possible abstract or general ideas—for example, the notion of the general idea of a triangle (as opposed to a specific triangle with its unique sides and angles). And, in the end, he posited a person or self able to appreciate these ideas, "a thinking intelligent being, that has reason and reflection and can consider itself as itself, the same thinking thing in different time and places" (Copleston 1964, p. 111).

Locke's epistemology focused on the opposite end of the universe from Descartes's—on the experience of objects in the external world. Yet, Locke was able in the end to construct an organism capable of abstraction and generalization, one deriving knowledge of a certain kind from the interplay of these ideas (rather than from a simple comparison with experience) and culminating in a rational, conscious self. It is not fanciful to suggest that the Lockean individual bears a strong family resemblance to the Cartesian individual. But they differ profoundly in the methods by which each has been achieved.

Berkeley's and Hume's Skeptical Tones

Locke's successors voiced skepticism about certain aspects of his model of man. Berkeley (1929) became so solipsistic that he ultimately denied the existence of the material world, apart from one's perception of it. He ridiculed the notion of a "general idea" and challenged the privileged status of mathematics. He saw language as a barrier to communication, as fostering belief in entities that do not exist, as causing imprecision in thought, and as arousing passions rather than reflection. He placed his faith in the primacy of the experiencing self, the perceiving mind, which alone makes it possible to have sensations or to conceive of ideas.

Hume's skepticism proceeded in a different but equally devastating direction. His particular bugbear was the idea of causality as a privileged link between two events that regularly succeed one another. Hume demonstrated persuasively that there is no license for inferring from particular correlations of past events the generalization that one event causes another. The most that one can assume is that nature will perform the same in the future as in the past: this assumption involves a customary or habitual way of thinking on our part, not a necessary, given link. Hume thus undermined confidence in a rational order, in scientific explanations of causal appearances.

He was equally brutal toward the Cartesian belief in the centrality of the mind, questioning the existence of a substance or locale called "the mind," in which perceptions inhere. To Hume, we know the mind only as we know matter—by perception. In fact, the mind is best thought of as an abstract name for a series of ideas—as a kind of theater where several perceptions successively make their appearance: there is no observing or controlling soul behind the processes of thought (Wolff 1967, p. 92). As the historian Will Durant once quipped (1926), Hume destroyed the mind as quickly as Berkeley destroyed matter.

Despite the rampant skeptical strain among these latter British empiricists, they produced a set of interlocking issues—the nature of sensory experience, the classification of objects, the role of language, the status of the individual conscious self—which budding philosophers were expected to ponder (issues also that are presented to today's fledgling cognitive scientists).

Before long, while individual positions continued to change, the belief that these were the central issues was assumed by all participants in the debate. In fact, the belief that our conceptual apparatus is built up from qualities perceived in the external world became so entrenched that for many years researchers, no less than laypersons, had difficulty in coming up with rival accounts of why we perceive the world in the way we do. But, with all that, the nature of mind continued to dominate discussion. Even Hume, the most skeptical of all, adhered to this central agenda:

> It becomes, therefore, no inconsiderable part of science . . . to know the different operations of the mind, to separate them from each other, to class them under their proper heads, and to correct all that seeming disorder in which they lie involved when made the object of reflection and inquiry. . . . It cannot be doubted that the mind is endowed with several powers and faculties, that these powers are distinct from one another, and that what is really distinct to the immediate perception may be distinguished by reflection and, consequently, that there is a truth and falsehood in all propositions on this subject, and a truth and falsehood which lie not beyond the compass of human understanding. (1955, p. 22)

Kant and Foundational Philosophy

By the late eighteenth century, the German scholar Immanuel Kant was faced with rival alternatives: one, favored by the British empiricists, viewed thought as merely an instrument to reflect or build upon mundane experience; the other, favored by Descartes, Leibnitz, and others in the Continental tradition, stressed the universal province of thought as the organizer and revealer of all possibilities. Indeed, the German Gottfried Leibnitz had directly answered the empiricists: addressing Locke's statement that there is nothing in the mind that has not been in the senses, Leibnitz added the telling Cartesian rejoinder, "Nothing but the mind [intellect] itself." The empiricists were suspicious of *a priori* statements and proofs (which they dismissed as unrevealing tautologies), while the rationalists searched for universal principles embodied in pure thought.

In his monumental *Critique of Pure Reason,* first published in 1781, Kant strove to synthesize these rationalist and empiricist points of view. To accomplish this task, he had to confront the question whether there might exist knowledge that is necessarily so—hence, *a priori*—but is also in some sense dependent upon experience, not just conjured up tautologically in the mind. He had to apply the systematic analysis of the Leibnitz and Cartesian tradition to the vagaries of daily experience, which had seemed regnant to Locke, Hume, and Berkeley. Kant chose to examine both ends of this polarity: to understand the nature of experience and, even more important, to dissect the nature of mind.

In what was probably the crucial step in this process, Kant had to understand what permits the mind to apprehend experience in the way it does, and to yield necessary knowledge. In analyzing what he called the *synthetic a priori,* Kant had to show how knowledge begins with experience (thus not being purely analytic) and yet does not arise out of, or come from, it (thus not being purely *a posteriori*). He had to explain the sources of arithmetic, geometry, Newtonian physics, traditional logic—those ultimate achievements of human minds, which seemed beyond dispute—that is, necessary—once they had been discovered.

A point of departure for Kant was the individual ego—the individual with his own awareness and judgment. In this sense, Kant was a Cartesian: he began with the knowledge of the ego—the transcendental self. "I think" must be capable of accompanying all propositions. Nor was this transcending self a passive instrument: Kant, more than did his predecessors, saw the mind as an active organ of understanding which molds and coordinates sensations and ideas, transforming the chaotic multiplicity of experience into the ordered unity of thought. The transcendental self is always the active subject: unknown in itself, following rules built into its own operation, it makes our experience possible.

Nonetheless, this self, this organizing mental entity, does not operate in autistic fashion. It depends upon and is stimulated by the outside world. The closest we can get to truth are the assertions we can make about information that arises under optimal conditions through our sensible natures. On these assumptions Kant developed a framework detailing how knowledge proceeds from and builds out of the "raw" materials of sensory experience.

Kant's model can be parsed into several parts. Initially, there is the concrete sensory world—the sensory manifold—which exists external to the subject and from which one's knowledge must begin. But this sensory world cannot be perceived directly: there is no privileged access to the thing itself *(das Ding an sich)*. We must deal always with phenomena—appearances—and not with noumena—the unknowable external world. Any phenomenon consists of sensations, which are caused by particular objects themselves: the form of the phenomenon is due to our subjective apparatus which orders the manifold in certain ways. The actual forms of intuition which we use as human beings in apprehending the world are our "spectacles." For instance, we must see things in terms of their embedded-ness in space and in time: we have no choice.

But over and above the immanent properties of space and time, our understanding brings to bear a set of what Kant (following Aristotle) called "categories of thought." These elementary concepts of the pure under-standing—such as *quantity* (unity, plurality, and totality); *quality* (reality, negation, and limitation); *relation* (substance and accident, cause-and-effect, and reciprocity); *modality* (possibility, existence, and necessity)—constitute the mental equipment, the pure synthesizing concepts with which human understanding is endowed. These alone allow the individual to make sense of his experiences.

These categories seem remote from bright red patches or fresh red cherries—examples that have dominated empiricists' accounts of sensory experience. Kant may have thought so as well, because he devised yet another level of analysis—that of the *schemas*, or *schemata*—interposed be-tween the raw sensory information and the abstract *a priori* categories. As he put it, with characteristic obscurity, "This representation of a universal procedure of the imagination in providing an image for a concept, I entitle the schema of this concept" (quoted in Wolff 1967, p. 76). In devising this explanatory apparatus, Kant sought to determine the circumstances under which the categories can find concrete employment. A schema serves as a mediating representation which is intellectual in one sense, sensible in another. Thus, a schema is directly activated in terms of sensory experience and yet can be plausibly thought to provide an interpretation of that experience. As a cognitive scientist might put it today, Kant had entered the world of "mental representation."

While the nature and the operation of the schemas pose difficulties even for Kantian scholars, epistemologists need such a level of analysis to deal with particular instances while mobilizing the abstract categories. The schemas are in part *rules* and thereby are linked to pure understanding; but they are also in part *images* and so are linked to empirical perception. The schema of each category determines the condition by which it is applicable to the objects of experience in general. Thus, the schema for the category of quantity is number; the schema for quality is degree of intensity; the schema for relation is permanence in time; and so on. Moreover, the schemas are also found at the level of concrete experience. Because we can apply the concept of *dog* to Fido, we must be able to produce in our imagination the schematic representation of a dog—the schema of the concept here being distinguishable from the concept itself. Schematic theory thus demonstrates how the categories can have empirical consequences.

While Kant did not publish empirical results of any kind, and his writing on these topics is notorious for its difficulty, his thinking has left its mark on most theoretical writings in cognitive science today. What Kant was groping for (in my view) was a way of describing the level of representation, for a terminology that might account for the way in which knowledge *must* be represented in any entity so as to relate to the physical world, on the one hand, and to the world of the inborn mental architecture, on the other. And while we may use less tortuous language nowadays for addressing these issues, I think that no one has gone beyond Kant in sketching the nature of the problem and in proposing a plausible solution, on the conceptual level, for how knowledge is possible—or, as he would have put it, for the conditions for the possibility of knowledge.

Kant had no illusions about the enormousness of the task—but he had a good deal of confidence about his capacity to negotiate it. He declared in the preface to the first edition of the *Critique of Pure Reason,* "I venture to assert that there is not a single metaphysical problem which has not been solved, or for the solution of which the key at least has not been supplied" (quoted in Russell 1961, p. 680). In the preface to the second edition, he compared himself to Copernicus and opined that, by placing knowledge in the mind of the active thinker, he had effected a Copernican revolution in philosophy.

Kant's belief in his own powers eventually proved contagious, and many philosophically oriented scholars came to believe that he had delimited the domain within which the acquisition of knowledge is possible. Kant's charting of territory included three reasons why a science of psychology was not possible: the fact that the mind is affected while studying itself; the lack of spatial extent essential for any experimentation; and the absence of a mathematical basis, necessary for all science. Kant concluded that "psychology can, therefore, never become anything more than a historical (and, as such, as much as possible) systematic natural doctrine of the internal sense, i.e., a natural description of the soul, but not a science of the soul, nor even a psychological experimental doctrine" (quoted in Watson 1979, p. 88). For many years this warning inhibited researchers interested in cognitive matters.

The Logical-Empiricist Program

Kant's program, his conclusions, and even his warnings exerted an unparalleled effect on ensuing research. Whereas each of the earlier epistemologists had soon aroused a formidable opponent, Kant's epistemology remained without major competition for years. He had apparently reconciled the two competing strands in philosophical writing—the primacy of thought *and* the primacy of experience; and his argument was sufficiently difficult, his critiques of standard rationalist and empiricist positions sufficiently powerful, his examination of the nature of mentation sufficiently revolutionary, his view of philosophy sufficiently reassuring, that it was many years before the weaknesses in his formulation became apparent.

Thanks to Kant, philosophy for a time occupied a special place in the firmament of scholarly disciplines. In light of his supposed demonstration of what knowledge was, of how its attainment was possible, and of why Newtonian science was necessary, Kant conferred upon philosophy the status of a "super" or "meta" discipline. Every scholar was expected to study this foundational subject, which dealt with the most fundamental aspects of knowledge; and no educated person would admit to not having read Kant. Anyone who entertained grave doubts about the utility of philosophical analysis usually kept silent. And it continued to be assumed that science and philosophy could march onward together.

It was not the philosophers who adopted Kant's speculative mode, but rather logicians, who eventually challenged Kantian epistemology. Kant had declared that, since Aristotle, logic "has not been able to advance a single step and is to all appearances a closed and completed body of doctrine" (quoted in Abel 1976, p. 52). In fact, however, in the century and a quarter following Kant, thinkers like George Boole, Gottlob Frege, Giuseppe Peano, Charles Sanders Peirce, and, ultimately Bertrand Russell and Alfred North Whitehead had effected many reformulations in logic. Indeed, rather than being a set of approximate procedures, logic became a non-empirical science, into which new findings could be regularly absorbed. There were equally dramatic advances in mathematics and physics, as scholars like Niels Bohr, George Cantor, Albert Einstein, and Max Planck rewrote our understanding both of the world of mathematics and of the physical universe. Eventually, progress in the fields that Kant held in highest regard called into question many of his fundamental assumptions: the given nature of time and space, the source of mathematical propositions, the unmodifiable rules of logic, the impossibility of psychology.

The work that had the greatest effect on the mainstream of epistemology was carried out in Cambridge, England, at the beginning of the twentieth century by Alfred North Whitehead and Bertrand Russell. These mathematically oriented logicians had been impressed by the work of the German logician Gottlob Frege who had undertaken to show that arithmetic could be reduced to logic. As Frege had written, "Even an inference like that from n to n + 1, which on the face of it is peculiar to mathematics, is based on the general laws of logic" (quoted in Hanfling 1972, p. 103). Building on Frege's insights, Whitehead and Russell sought to derive all of mathematics from the basic laws of logic, as these laws had been reformulated in the century since Kant's time. Indeed, this program was in part explicitly anti-Kantian, for the philosophers wanted to discredit the synthetic *a priori* notion of mathematical knowledge as being dependent upon experience. With respect to this part of their program, they were largely successful.

But Whitehead and Russell's overall program exerted its most revolutionary effect on philosophy. Their work led to much closer ties among empirical science, logic, and mathematics, so that the boundaries between these pursuits could no longer be sharply delineated. Whereas Kant saw philosophy as the ultimate foundational discipline, the standard by which other sciences had to be judged, Whitehead and Russell saw all of these disciplinary forays as part of the same larger enterprise. Indeed, Russell believed that many—if not most—traditional philosophical questions could be expressed in logical terms and either solved in these terms, or shown to be insoluble. As he confidently declared:

> Modern analytical empiricism . . . differs from that of Locke, Berkeley, and Hume by its incorporation of mathematics and its development of a powerful logical technique. It is thus able, in regard to certain problems, to achieve definite answers, which have the quality of science rather than of philosophy. It has the advantage, as compared with the philosophies of the system-builders, of being able to tackle its problems one at a time, instead of having to invent at one stroke a block theory of the whole universe. Its methods, in this respect, resemble those of science. I have no doubt that, in so far as philosophical knowledge is possible, it is by such methods that it must be sought: I have also no doubt that, by these methods, many ancient problems are completely soluble. . . . Take such questions as: What is number? What are space and time? What is mind, and what is matter? I do not say that we can here and now give definitive answers to all these ancient questions, but I do say that a method has been discovered by which, as in science,

we can make successive approximations to the truth, in which each new stage results from an improvement, not a rejection, of what has gone before. (Russell 1961, pp. 788, 789)

As contributors to the scientific enterprise, Whitehead and Russell began with an acceptance of the world of sensory experience, which any individual initially has to confront. They sought to close the gap between what is immediately known and what can be known through inference by using the tools of logic: it should be possible eventually to give an account of the external world by means of a logical construction from sensory data. In their own way, the two Englishmen had put forth a program as ambitious as the ones propounded by those "system-builders" whom Russell had challenged. At the same time, his expressed belief that his approach could ultimately provide empirically valid answers to long-standing philosophical questions—questions dating back to the time of Socrates—puts him within the ranks of cognitive science.

Just as the epistemological agenda of the last century had been dictated by Kant's monumental treatise, much of the philosophical program of this century—particularly in the Anglo-American world with which I am most concerned—can be seen as an effort to pursue Russell and Whitehead's program. As we shall see, their blend of scientific philosophy has been found seriously deficient. Nonetheless, many observers feel that much was gained by the effort to approach human sensory experience with the methods of logical empiricism. Even more important for present purposes, the logical-empiricist school strongly influenced many pioneering cognitive scientists.

One of the first thinkers inspired by the Whitehead-Russell program was the young Austrian philosopher Ludwig Wittgenstein. In his *Tractatus* (1961), which he sent to Russell for a first reading in 1918, Wittgenstein attempted to demonstrate a logical structure implicit in language. As he saw it, language provides, in a sense, a picture of the structure of facts —indeed, a picture of the world. More specifically, the propositions of language are the perceptual expression of thoughts, and thoughts are logical pictures of facts. Wittgenstein thus posited a formal correspondence between configurations of objects in the world, thoughts in the mind, and words in language.

It has been said of necessity that Aristotle thought of it as arising from things; that to Kant it derived from the structure of our minds; while the Wittgenstein of the *Tractatus* saw it as arising from language. Wittgenstein injected language into Russell and Whitehead's program. In Wittgenstein's program, philosophy becomes the activity of clarifying propositions, though the propositions clarified by philosophical analysis are not themselves propositions of philosophy but rather are nonphilosophical propositions about the world (Kenny 1973). At the same time that it clarifies the propositions of natural science, philosophy can also expose as nonsense metaphysical questions about existence.

As is well known, Wittgenstein himself came first to doubt and then to renounce virtually completely his "picture theory" of language and the world (Wittgenstein 1968). But his program of analyzing language logically and trying to relate that analysis to the perceived world became a pivotal ingredient of the program of philosophy adopted by the "Vienna circle" of logical empiricists in the period between the world wars. Scholars like Herbert Feigl, Otto Neurath, Morris Schlick, and especially Rudolf Carnap tried in earnest to tie together what A. J. Ayer called "language, truth, and logic" (1936). The general goal of the circle was to see which traditional philosophical questions could be rephrased in formal terms and which could not be. Those that could not be (for instance, issues about celestial angels) were branded as metaphysical and banned forthwith from further discussion. Those propositions that lent themselves to treatment in logical terms (for instance, ones about geometric angles) would then be examined to see whether they could be verified and thus added to our storehouse of what is true.

One major ingredient of the program of the logical empiricists was *verificationism,* a doctrine that assumed that empirical (nonlogical) statements can be verified under ideal conditions of inquiry. All that is needed is a way of measuring and verifying what is being talked about. As Carnap put it, one must observe the circumstance under which people use a proposition in order to determine the truth of that proposition. Indeed, the meaning of a proposition *is* its method of verification. Another doctrine of the program was *physicalism.* The Vienna circle believed that propositions ordinarily construed as referring to mental states turn out to be logically equivalent to those referring to overt behavior. Indeed, every sentence of psychology could be reformulated as a description of the physical behavior of humans or other animals. Finally, the Vienna circle rejected the notion of philosophy as a special or foundational area of study: as far as these philosophers were concerned, there was just one empirical science, of which philosophy was part (Ayer 1982, p. 128); its role was to describe and criticize the language of science.

Armed with this set of ideas, Rudolf Carnap determined to put into practice the logical-empiricist beliefs. Russell had talked about defining the world from experience, through logical construction; and Carnap sought to translate, into the language of sensory data, all sentences pertaining to the world. For every sentence about material objects, a corresponding sentence about sensory data can express the basic phenomenal elements of the experience of the object.

Having devised sensory-centered sentences of this sort, the next step in the Carnap program was to examine the relationship among sentences. In Carnap's view, traditional philosophical problems had best be considered by examining the theoretical relations between whole systems of sentences: the nature of an entity is determined once one has ascertained the inferential relationships between sentences using that term and other sentences in that language. Ultimately, Carnap believed that much of philosophy could be reduced to such issues of logical syntax: when errors in syntax are avoided (through the use of logical analysis), a philosophical problem can either be solved or be shown to be insoluble.

As I have already suggested, Carnap's program (and that of the Vienna circle) did not work out at all; yet the attempt has been considered significant. Thus, Nelson Goodman, an influential American philosopher who has criticized the Vienna program, says of Carnap's magnum opus:

> The *Aufbau* [the logical construction of the world] brings to philosophy the powerful techniques of modern logic, along with unprecedented standards of explicitness, coherence, and rigor. It applies to [philosophy] the new methods and principles [which had been brought to bear] upon mathematics. . . . The potential importance to philosophy is comparable to the importance of the Euclidean deductive method into geometry. . . . [It] is still one of the fullest examples we have of the logical treatment of problems in nonmathematical philosophy. (1972, p. 22)

Thus, with Russell and Carnap, Goodman believes that the techniques from logical analysis have the potential to solve many—even if not all—existing philosophical problems, and that attacking the problems one at a time is the best means for achieving success.

There is another reason the saga of logical empiricism is highly relevant to a history of cognitive science. Inspired by the Whitehead-Russell tradition, Carnap and his colleagues sought to express everyday scientific findings in terms of the basic elements of logic. Loosely speaking, we might see this effort as a ferreting out of the logical structure of science and, more especially, of the language used in science—as a study of the syntax of science. As I see it, a major ingredient in ongoing work in the cognitive sciences has been cast in the image of logical empiricism: that is, the vision of a *syntax*—a set of symbols and the rules for their concatenation—that might underline the operations of the mind (and a correlative discomfort with issues of mental *content*). Thus, when Noam Chomsky (1965) posits the basic operations of a grammar, when Richard Montague (Thomason 1974) examines the logic of semantics, when Allen Newell and Herbert Simon (1972) simulate human reasoning on a computer, or when Jerome Bruner (1973) and George Miller (1956) seek to decipher the rules of classification, or "chunking," they are trying to decipher a logic—perhaps *the* logic—of the mind. This vision comes through even more clearly in the writings of Jerry Fodor, who explicitly searches for a "language of thought" and even appropriates certain of Carnap's methods. Thus, a model that proved inadequate for the scientific enterprise as a whole still motivates research in circumscribed cognitive domains.

In applying logical methods to the world of empirical experience, the members of the Vienna circle combined the spirit of rationalism and empiricism. They also sought to establish a place for philosophy within the world of laboratory science by providing the tools for analyzing scientific statements and practices. In hindsight, their procedures were too artificially constrained, and their idea of theory too tied to behaviorist and positivist strictures. And yet even those cognitivists who see themselves as doctrinarily opposed to the letter of the Vienna program often partake of the spirit of their approach.

The Unraveling of Logical Empiricism and the Revised Roles of Philosophy

During the late 1930s and early 1940s, a group of philosophers met regularly at Harvard. Among them were the Harvard philosophers Nelson Goodman and W. V. O. Quine, as well as such frequent visitors as Rudolf Carnap, Bertrand Russell, and Alfred Tarski, all three from war-torn Europe. These philosophers had all been involved with logical empiricism but now subjected nearly all of its assumptions to increasingly severe criticism. First of all, they questioned whether it is possible to talk about "raw information": that is, pure sensory data which can be inspected and built upon. Knowledge came to be seen increasingly as a matter of using propositions, and it was now dubious practice to talk about knowing the pure, the immediate, the given. Even more tellingly, the whole logical apparatus devised to analyze "meaning" and "truth" came to be challenged. While the distinction between analytic and synthetic truths had been cherished since the time of Kant, Quine (1953) showed that it is ultimately untenable: the notion of meaning itself is not clear enough to justify the attribution to certain statements of "true by virtue of meaning alone" or "true by definition." Moreover, the logical (or analytic) components of a scientific theory cannot be sufficiently disentangled from the empirical components to allow them to be regarded as subject to different criteria of truth. After all, Euclid's principles would certainly seem to have been *a priori* truths; and yet their truth was ultimately undermined by non-Euclidean geometries. Indeed, once one is confronted by others who do not share one's intuitions, there is no way to establish which truths are due to language, which to common experience. Ultimately, there are as many ways to relate language to the world as there are languages, as many logical syntaxes as there are language systems.

As a result of these and other criticisms, the major American philosopher Hilary Putnam concluded:

> Not a single one of the great positive theses of Logical Empiricism (that Meaning is Method of Verification; that metaphysical propositions are literally without sense; that Mathematics is True by Convention) has turned out to be correct. It detracts from the excitement of the fact that, by turning philosophical theses into linguistic ones [as Carnap had tried to do] . . . one can make philosophy more scientific and settle the truth value of philosophical propositions by hard scientific research, if the results one obtains are uniformly *negative*. (1975a, p. 20)

Still, he softened this verdict, in ways revealing for this history, by declaring, "Even if [logical empiricism] failed, modern symbolic logic, a good deal of modern language theory, and part of contemporary cognitive science were all off-shoots of these attempts" (1984, p. 274).

Critics like Quine and Putnam regretted the collapse of logical empiricism and have been sympathetic toward cognitive science, perhaps sensing that this movement shares at least some of the methods and aspirations of earlier philosophical work. But by the end of the 1940s, far more strident voices were being raised about the tradition that had begun with Descartes and was, after many twists and turns, still discernible in the logical-empiricist camp. The trio of names most vividly associated with this criticism are Gilbert Ryle, Ludwig Wittgenstein (in his later writings), and J. L. Austin.

Gilbert Ryle

In his justly celebrated *The Concept of Mind* (1949), Ryle explicitly confronted the "official doctrine" of mentalism that had begun with Descartes. As Ryle described this doctrine, it entailed the belief that everyone has a mind and a body; minds are not in space and their operations are not subject to mechanical laws; the workings of the mind are private and are accessible only to the person alone; there are, in fact, two different kinds of existence or status—whatever happens may have a physical *or* a mental existence. "Mental happenings occur in insulated fields, known as 'minds' and there is . . . no direct causal connection between what happens in one mind and what happens in another" (1949, p. 13). Ryle dubbed this doctrine, with its many associated assumptions and linguistic turns, as the "dogma of the Ghost in the Machine." He declared, "I hope to prove that it is entirely false, and false not in detail but in principle" (p. 16), and devoted a 330-page book to justifying that hope.

Ryle's basic claim was that talk of mind involves a category mistake. It is perfectly all right to speak about "minds"; but we must not fall into the trap of thinking that there is a place called "the mind," with its own locations, events, and so on, any more than we assume that there is a place called "the university" apart and separate from buildings, roads, lawns, persons, and other physically specifiable entities. To talk of mind as if it has a separate existence, was, to Ryle, mistakenly to treat an entity of one sort (an abstract characterization of a set of dispositions) as if it were itself another of those dispositions. "The theoretically interesting category-mistakes," Ryle pointed out, "are those made by people who are perfectly competent to apply concepts, at least in the situations in which they are familiar, but are still liable in their abstract thinking to allocate those concepts to logical types to which they do not belong" (1949, p. 17). And the mind becomes such a theoretically interesting mistake because Descartes posited a substance, parallel to body but apart from it, that controls and is the scene of our mental life.

Having exposed the flaw in the Cartesian position, Ryle proceeded to show how one can talk, in ways that do not involve category mistakes or violate the actual state of affairs, about those entities and experiences that are generally termed "mental." In general, he took a behaviorist stance: when we talk about a person as having "traits" or inner volitional capacities, we are simply indicating that people are disposed to behave in certain ways and are likely to do so in the presence of the appropriate eliciting circumstances. Ryle questioned whether there are actually happenings in the mind to which each person has privileged access. Instead, he insisted, what we can find out about ourselves is in principle no different from the sorts of things we can find out from other people through observation and through questioning. To speak of a person's mind is simply to talk of certain ways in which the incidents of one's life are ordered.

Ryle declared that he was not interested in the issues of how one sees or understands something if those seeings or understandings involve the positing of some internal understanding or perceptual mechanisms. The most that we can do as philosophical analysts is to try to understand the circumstances under which an individual would *report* having seen or understood something; and these circumstances should be accessible across the full range of reporting individuals. Ryle objected to answers invoking internal mechanisms ("I understand something because I process certain information in certain ways") to conceptual questions ("What are the circumstances under which an individual is likely to report having understood something?"). In his view, the positing of internal mechanisms (à *la* Descartes or Kant) adds nothing to our understanding. Ryle would have seen little reason to embrace a "representational level"; nor would he have been sympathetic with contemporary efforts to found a whole science upon "internal entities" like schemas, rules, or representations whose very positing he found problematic.

Ludwig Wittgenstein

Wittgenstein saw that many philosophical conundrums might be solved by careful attention to the ways in which people use words. In his earlier writings, he had treated language as a means of understanding the world—as a privileged means of looking through to the structure of the world. Now, however, he saw language itself as the spawner of problematic issues, and the exercise of coming to understand how we use language as the therapy for philosophical problems. In his later work, Wittgenstein did not try to solve problems but tried rather to show that they arise from a network of terms that have evolved in such a way as to make their disentanglement extremely difficult. As he once commented, his aim in philosophy was to show the fly the way out of the fly-bottle.

Wittgenstein came to view language as an inherently public or communal activity. One is introduced into language by others in the community, and thus one comes to know how to use words. One certainly has a private experience, for example, of pain, but the use of the word *pain* comes from the ways in which, and the circumstances under which, it is regularly employed by other people. We do not first use the word *pain* by naming something we feel; rather, the word is embedded in various activities that people carry out and in various sorts of things others say in connection with being hurt.

More generally, Wittgenstein believed, it is instructive to think of language as a set of games: we proceed from the fact that we are always involved in many language games—interactions with other individuals in which we move around sets of linguistic counters; and, like a set of games, each of these little encounters has its own set of rules. But it is not easy to ferret out these rules because they overlap with one another: the language games constantly mesh. To add to this tangled state of affairs, words do not have clear and unambiguous meanings. The word *game* itself has a family of meanings, with no definition ever sufficient to account for all, and only all, games. Given the numerous language games occurring at any one time, and their inherently overlapping nature, it is no wonder that Wittgenstein despaired of ever solving philosophical problems in the rigorous way that he and his Viennese peers had once hoped. It made more sense to try to dissolve the problems altogether, by showing that they had been deceptively phrased.

Wittgenstein's attitude toward traditional problems can be gleaned from his comments about psychology, particularly the version that he had encountered during his early studies in Vienna. As he saw it, psychologists were trying to solve problems they did not understand: rather than being genuinely scientific, these problems were in fact embedded in certain uses of language. Wittgenstein illustrated the complex and overlapping manner in which many mentalistic words—*believe, imagine, desire*—are actually used. Instead of trying to explain how each of these putative mental operations actually "works," it would make more sense for psychologists (*à la* Ryle) to study the relations among such ways of talking about behavior and experience. In a pessimistic assessment, Wittgenstein asserted:

> The confusion and barrenness of psychology is not to be explained by calling it a young science—the existence of experimental methods makes us think we have the means of solving the problems that trouble us: though problems and methods pass one another by. . . . Not to explain but to *accept* the psychological phenomena —that is what is so difficult. (Quoted in Hacking 1982, p. 43)

Wittgenstein felt that investigators interested in questions of psychology ought to ponder the phenomena in which they are interested and, most especially, the use of terms in these areas, rather than trying to set up experiments to answer putatively crucial questions. He drew a sharp analogy: "People who are constantly asking 'why' are like tourists who stand in front of a building reading Baedeker [a guide book] and are so busy reading the history of its construction that they are prevented from *seeing* the building. The tendency to explain instead of merely describing [is what yields] bad philosophy" (p. 43).

J. L. Austin

As if one were needed—a final nail was sunk into the coffin of logical empiricist philosophy by J. L. Austin, another British philosopher interested in language. Austin demonstrated convincingly that one cannot simply accept a sentence at face value, as the logical empiricists wanted to do. Many, if not most, sentences need to be thought of not only in terms of their literal meaning *(utterance meaning)* but also with respect to the use to which they are put by the deliverer of the utterance *(speaker meaning)*. As Austin explained in his William James lectures, *How to Do Things with Words:*

> it has come to be commonly held that many utterances which look like statements are either not intended at all, or only intended in part, to record or

impart straightforward information about the facts. . . . Many traditional philosophical perplexities have arisen through a mistake—the mistake of taking as straightforward statements of fact utterances which are *either* (in interesting non-grammatical ways) nonsensical *or else* intended as something quite different. (1962, pp. 2–3)

Thus, "It is very hot here" is as likely to be a request to open a window, or a comment on a tense discussion, as a statement concerning the temperature in a room. Once it had been established that any statement might have quite different effects depending upon who uttered it, in what context, and for what reason, the notion of a neutral evaluation of sentences had to be abandoned. Isaiah Berlin recalls hearing Austin present his ideas at Oxford in the early 1950s:

Freddy [A. J.] Ayer was there, still very keen on the Vienna circle. We all knew by the time the evening was half-done that Carnap and Vienna were finished. Austin made the distinction between analytic and synthetic propositions a special case of his more general way of classifying propositions by their illocutionary* force. It was stunning. (Quoted in Bruner 1982, p. 41)

In urging a focus on the ordinary uses of language, Austin, Ryle, and Wittgenstein were cautioning against the notion of "philosophy as-a-super-discipline" which could legislate topics like knowledge, truth, and science. Perhaps some of these questions might be approached in the manner of empirical science, but certainly philosophers had no privileged means for attacking or solving them. If philosophy had any special mission (and these analysts were skeptical), it was to call attention to the habits of language that often dominate human thinking and to help unravel some obscure modes of discussion (including those exhibited by some scientists).

Could anything of the program of traditional philosophy be salvaged? W. V. O. Quine, himself one of the master architects of the initial critique, thinks so. While pointing out that the dream of epistemology as a kind of "first philosophy" has failed, he insists that there remains a legitimate role for this activity:

But I think that at this point it may be more useful to say rather that epistemology still goes on, though in a new setting and a clarified status. Epistemology, or something like it, simply falls into place as a chapter of psychology and hence of natural science. It studies a natural phenomenon, viz, a physical human subject. This human subject is accorded a certain experimentally controlled input—certain patterns of irradiation in assorted frequencies, for instance—and in the fullness of

Illocution refers to the ends for which a statement is uttered—for example, to give an answer, to make an announcement, or to make a request.

time the subject delivers as output a description of the three-dimensional external world and its history. The relation between the meager input and the torrential output is a relation that we are prompted to study for somewhat the same reasons that always prompted epistemology; namely, in order to see how evidence relates to theory, and in what ways one's theory of nature transcends any available evidence. (Quoted in Royce and Rozeboom 1972, p. 18)

Quine is proposing a substitute. Classically, a philosopher considered how he—or any person—could have a theory, and an understanding of the world, based on the evidence picked up via his senses. Accumulated critiques of the last fifty years had shown that there was no way in which this endeavor could provide an independent justification of our knowledge of the world. There is no pure sense experience, no clear-cut meaning, no unambiguous use of language, no privileged syntax, no "prior" philosophical problem. However, the field of empirical psychology does offer a way of approaching these issues. As Quine sees it, we no longer dream of deducing science from sense data: the scientist (whether philosopher or psychologist) now conducts research in which experimental subjects become the preferred route to discovering how any individual makes sense of his experiences. Locke and Kant are not completely irrelevant but are supplanted by experimental investigators of particular regulated interactions between a subject and the world. Quine quotes a metaphor of which he is fond: that is, the construction and reconstruction of science places each of us in the position of the mariner who must rebuild his boat, plank by plank, while staying afloat on it. On this view, cognitive scientists can be seen as rebuilding the traditional structure of epistemological inquiry.

Richard Rorty: Is Epistemology Necessary?

Surveying the same scene as Quine, Richard Rorty reaches a far less sanguine conclusion. In his much-discussed *Philosophy and the Mirror of Nature* (1979), Rorty questions the whole enterprise of epistemology. He suggests a radically different and far more modest view of philosophy, one that might even undermine the programs pursued by Wittgenstein, Ryle, and Austin, and certainly one much less ambitious and far less optimistic than Quine's. Rorty's impressive critique of all of philosophy since the Greek times not only has intrinsic interest but also raises profound questions about the enterprise called cognitive science, at least as I have characterized it here.

According to Rorty, philosophers have thought of their discipline as confronting perennial questions, enigmas that arise as soon as one begins to reflect. Among these familiar chestnuts are: How does a person come to know anything? And, what are the limitations of knowledge? To delve into these foundational issues is to discover something about the mind:

[Philosophy] understands the foundations of knowledge and it finds these foundations in a study of man-as-knower, of the "mental processes" or the "activity of representation" which make knowledge possible. To know is to represent accurately what is outside the mind; so to understand the possibility and nature of knowledge is to understand the way in which the mind is able to construct such representations. Philosophy's central concern is to be a general theory of representation. . . . We owe the notion of a "theory of knowledge" based on an understanding of "mental processes" to the seventeenth century, and especially to Locke. We owe the notion of "the mind" as a separate entity in which "processes" occur to the same period, and especially to Descartes. We owe the notion of philosophy as a tribunal of pure reason, upholding or denying the claims of the rest of culture, to the eighteenth century and especially to Kant, but this Kantian notion presupposed general assent to Lockean notions of mental processes and Cartesian notions of mental substance. (1979, pp. 3–4)

Rorty considers this habit of analysis—this invocation of certain images for thinking about mind—as pernicious an endeavor as does Ryle. In fact, elsewhere he goes further:

I want to suggest that the concept of mind is the blur with which Western intellectuals became obsessed when they finally gave up on the blur which was the theologian's concept of God. The ineffability of the mental serves the same cultural function as the ineffability of the divine—it vaguely suggests that science does not have the last word. (Rorty 1982b, p. 31)

In Rorty's view, this set of beliefs is the culmination of a long history of thinking in misguided ways about certain kinds of activity. It is all right to label these activities misguided—as Ryle has done: but the only way to exorcise this "ghost" completely is to review its history, much as a therapist helps a patient relive the history of past activities and blunders. Thus, a major part of Rorty's effort involves a reconstruction, or deconstruction, of Western philosophical thinking in an effort to show the various ways in which Philosophy Went Wrong.

The developmental sequence expounded by Rorty can be summarized as follows: In Greek times, beliefs were determined through face-to-face confrontation with the object of belief. Thus the slave boy in the *Meno* discovered the truths of geometry through examination of a triangle. Knowledge was a matter of having accurate representations of ideal forms that could not be directly observed.

The next stage, courtesy of Descartes, held that our knowledge depends upon the activity of a quasi-visual faculty—which Rorty dubs the Mirror of Nature—and consists of an assembly of accurate representations. These representations are in the mind; and an "inner eye" surveys them hoping to find some mark that will testify to their fidelity. Though the empiricists differed with Descartes in many respects, they preserved his mentalistic notion of the mind as a separate region which inspects ideas. Locke introduced a fatal confusion when he confounded an explanation of *how* information gets into our consciousness—a classical psychological question—with a justification of *why* we believe what we believe—a classical philosophical question.

Unlike his predecessors, Immanuel Kant understood the impossibility of anyone's having direct access to things: that is, one has knowledge of propositions about objects not about objects themselves. But, in an effort to locate the most accurate representations, Kant ultimately posited a special privileged set of representations that cannot be doubted. According to Rorty's revisionist account, these representations came to be considered the foundation of all knowledge; and thus Kant granted to philosophers the pre-eminent position for making statements about the world and for regulating inquiry.

In Rorty's view, in the years since Kant's time much of philosophy has sought to retain this vision. But the vision has undergone severe jolts, thanks to a series of compelling critiques of traditional epistemology. There was Wittgenstein's attack on the centrality and legitimacy of classical philosophical problems. There was the pragmatist John Dewey, who insisted that one should try to use knowledge in a practical way rather than to strive after the chimera of objective knowledge. There was the phenomenologist Martin Heidegger, who dissected the various images and metaphors that have obsessed Western philosophy since Greek times. And perhaps most tellingly, there were the failures of both the Russell-Whitehead program and the Vienna circle to arrive at secure knowledge through a logical construction from sense data.

Rorty's own interpretation of recent philosophical history relies especially heavily on criticisms to which I have already alluded. He arrives at the following conclusion: There is no way to account for the validity of our beliefs by examining the relation between ideas and their objects: rather, justification is a social process, an extended conversation, whereby we try to convince others of what we believe. We understand the nature of knowledge when we understand that knowledge amounts to justification of our belief, and not to an increasingly accurate representation of reality. As Rorty concludes, "If assertions are justified by society rather than by the character of the inner representation they express, there is no point in attempting to isolate *privileged* representations" (1979, p. 174).

Perhaps because he did not fully appreciate the radical implications of his own (and others') demonstrations, Quine continued to believe that epistemology can endure through the good offices of the psychologist studying his "knowing subject." But in Rorty's opinion, psychology can in no way succeed in doing what epistemology has failed to do. In an intriguing chapter, Rorty attempts to save psychology from the excessive claims made by thinkers like Quine who see it as a next best attempt to answer the very philosophical questions that have turned out to be ill conceived and outmoded. Rorty asserts that he has no objection to the idea of ideas *per se*—what he calls the "idea idea." As the constructs of scientists, ideas in the mind are no more or less reputable than neurons in the brain. The damage done by the "idea idea" was done by the pseudo explanation of epistemological authority: by the claim that the eyes of the mind have direct acquaintance with special entities like meanings and sense data (1979, p. 209).

Rorty chides critics like Wittgenstein and his disciple Norman Malcolm for being too severe on psychology. Indeed, Rorty does not object to the psychologist Peter Dodwell's (1971) contention that psychologists are in the best position to decide which issues to investigate, and to investigate them in the manner, and with the concepts, that make most sense to them —so long, that is, as psychologists do not suggest that these investigations provide answers to questions like, "How is abstraction, or recognition, or constancy possible?" or, "Where in the nervous system does information begin to be processed?"

But it would be a severe misreading of Rorty, I submit, to conclude that psychology receives a clean bill of health. In another section of his book, Rorty imagines the Antipodeans emanating from a society where one talks not about ideas or feelings or beliefs but just about the stimulation of various fibers in the brain. Moreover, the Antipodeans cannot understand why we earthlings insist on such mentalistic talk: for them, the only thing that gives rise to experience is the stimulation of parts of the brain. Rorty seems entirely in sympathy with this materialist position, where psychological experience is equated with neurology. Consider these various remarks in his book:

Psychologists should be *more* mechanistic rather than less. . . . They should cut straight through the mental to the neurophysiological. (1979, p. 217)

This is to say that if physiology were simpler and more obvious than it is, nobody would have felt the need for psychology. (p. 237)

We can imagine machines in which it would be easier to find out what the machine was up to by opening it up and looking than by reading the program. (p. 238)

If we have psychophysiology to cover causal mechanisms, and the sociology and history of science to note the occasions on which observation sentences are invoked or dodged in constructing and dismantling theories, then epistemology has nothing to do. We would think that this result would be congenial to Quine, but in fact he resists it. (p. 225)

And, in the context of discussing the effect that his Antipodeans might have on philosophy, Rorty adds, "The disappearance of psychology as a discipline distinct from neurology, and similar cultural developments, might eventually free us from the image of the Mirror of Nature much more effectively than philosophers' identity theories" (p. 121).

To summarize, Rorty is unable or unmotivated to come up with any arguments in principle against psychology, but feels that the discipline might well never have been invented, and that it may well at some time disappear, to the regret of few. Neurophysiology seems a much more secure science on which to base one's hope. The issue of an interdisciplinary cognitive science is not addressed directly by Rorty, but some of his thoughts on this matter can be gleaned from this telltale aside:

Only the assumption, that one day the various taxonomies put together by, for example, Chomsky, Piaget, Lévi-Strauss, Marx, and Freud will all flow together and spell out one great Universal Language of Nature—an assumption sometimes attributed to structuralism—would suggest that cognitive psychology had epistemological import. But that suggestion would still be as misguided as the suggestion that, since we may predict everything by knowing enough about matter in motion, a completed neurophysiology will help us demonstrate Galileo's superiority to his contemporaries. The gap between explaining ourselves and justifying ourselves is just as great whether a programming language or a hardware language is used in the explanations. (1979, p. 249)

Rorty believes that the particular course followed by Western philosophy is a matter of history, not of necessity. The history of this field—or even its existence—would have been entirely different if, for example, the Greeks had not modeled knowledge upon vision; if Descartes had not effectively invented the mind by putting feelings and beliefs into a single organ; or if Kant had not set up a tribunal of knowledge and placed his own philosophical synthesis upon the judge's bench.

Rorty proposes a rather sensational prescription for philosophy. He believes that epistemology has served its purposes—mostly evil rather than good—and should now be gently retired from the circle of disciplines. Moreover, philosophy as a whole should radically reduce its claims to specialness. Rorty rejects the need for ambitious philosophers like Kant or Russell who would systematize all knowledge, and plumps instead for "edifiers" like Wittgenstein and Dewey, who are content to react and to interpret. Rorty looks to a more humanistic philosophy in which one investigates the ideas of philosophers in order better to understand the nature and limitations of favored ideas. He wants to abandon the belief (dating back to Kant, if not to Plato) that the philosopher is someone who knows something special or especially well, or that there is a special philosophical method, technique, or point of view. He seeks to halt philosophical debates—for instance, between empiricists and rationalists—as based on faulty premises and of no consequence for either the humanities or the sciences. In his renegotiated disciplinary terrain, physics can explain the structure of the external world, neurophysiology can delineate the processes whereby we experience ideas and feelings, and sociology and history will account for the shape of our current beliefs.

And what of cognitive science? So long as it steers clear of philosophical questions that permit no answer, this new field can presumably continue its quest for the reasons that we humans experience and process the world in the way we do. Rorty seems skeptical that answers of scientific consequence will come from such efforts, at least as they are now being pursued.

Preserving Philosophy's Purview

In the academic year 1946–47, Karl Popper, a sometime member of the Vienna circle, was invited by the secretary of the Moral Sciences Club at Cambridge to read a paper about "some philosophical puzzles." As Popper recalls, "It was of course clear that this was Wittgenstein's formulation and that behind it was Wittgenstein's philosophical thesis that there are no genuine problems in philosophy, only linguistic puzzles. Since this thesis was among my pet aversions, I decided to speak on 'Are there Philosophical Problems?' " (1974, p. 122).

Popper began his lecture by expressing his surprise at the initial invitation since, he pointed out, by implicitly denying that philosophical problems exist, the inviter had taken sides in what was actually a genuine philosophical problem. This teasing remark aroused Wittgenstein, who immediately jumped up and exclaimed loudly and angrily, "The Secretary did exactly as he was told to do. He acted on my own instruction." Popper ignored the interruption and went on; but repeatedly through the talk, Wittgenstein "jumped up again, interrupting me, and spoke at length about puzzles and the nonexistence of philosophical problems" (1974, p. 123). The exchange became increasingly heated until eventually Wittgenstein left the room in anger or disgust.

Reflecting on this incident some twenty years later, Popper repeated his claim that there are indeed philosophical problems, and that he may have even solved some of them. Yet he went on to add, "Nothing seems less wanted than a simple solution to an age-old philosophical problem. The view of many philosophers, and, especially, it seems, of Wittgensteinians, is that if a problem is soluble, it cannot have been philosophical" (1974, p. 124).

This confrontation between Popper and Wittgenstein helps to convey the atmosphere in philosophical circles at the middle of this century. In the background stood the great figures of the past—Popper's heroes—who believed that there are genuine philosophical problems, and that if one ponders them systematically, one should eventually solve them, or at least make progress toward solving them. Rorty also recognized this group but believed that these "systematizers" (as he termed them) have been embarked on a hopeless and wrong-headed task. Instead, Rorty reserved his praise for individuals whom he labels "edifiers," who are deeply skeptical about the legitimacy of such questions and would rather assume a soft, even teasing approach toward the whole philosophical enterprise. Among scholars in the edifying camp were those who criticized the logical empiricist approach, including Wittgenstein, Dewey, Austin, and Rorty himself.

As far as I can tell, the systematizers are not about to relinquish their calling. Thus, a sympathetic reviewer of Rorty's book remarks:

> If "epistemology" means the search for such foundation, then its end is in sight, an end foreseen by Dewey. But if "epistemology" denotes an attempt to understand the possibility and nature of the various kinds of knowledge and styles of reasoning, then Plato, Locke, and Dewey are part of a persistent tradition that has to do with one of the essential characteristics of our civilization. (Hacking 1980, p. 586)

And Hilary Putnam, a contemporary of Rorty, offers a harsher indictment. Putnam is particularly disturbed by Rorty's assertion, from the perspective of cultural relativism, that epistemology is just a particular hang-up of the Western intellectual tradition:

> Cultural relativism is a denial of the possibility of *thinking* . . . [and a] suggestion . . . that philosophy . . . is a *silly* enterprise. But the questions *are* deep and it is the easy answers that are silly. Even seeing that relativism is inconsistent is, if the knowledge is taken seriously, seeing something important about a deep question. Philosophers *are* beginning to talk about the great issues again, and to feel that something can be *said* about them, even if there are no grand or ultimate solutions. There is an excitement in the air. And if I react to Professor Rorty's book with a certain sharpness, it is because one more "deflationary" book, one more book telling us that the deep issues aren't deep and the whole enterprise was a mistake, is just what we *don't* need right now. (Putnam 1981, p. 236)

Putnam is adverting to the belief (or faith) among several philosophers that epistemology is not dead. In fact, in light of cognitive-scientific events occurring at mid-century, new life was breathed into epistemology. Thanks especially to the invention and dissemination of the computer, but also to techniques and findings in a host of allied fields, it is now possible to revisit some classical issues of philosophy and to conceptualize mental processes in new and fruitful ways.

Fresh Approaches to Epistemology

Functionalism

One major contributor to the discussion is Hilary Putnam himself. A mathematically trained philosopher, Putnam has had a long-standing interest in the nature of computers and their implications for thinking. As he himself recalls, the invention of computing machines was an important event in the philosophy of mind because it led to the idea of functional organization (1973, p. 299). This functionalist idea challenges the assertion that thinking and other "intelligent functions" need to be carried out by means of the same specified machinery in order to reflect the same kinds of process. To be sure, before the advent of computing machines, it might have been tenable to hold that thinking can only occur in human beings, or in entities with the kind of brain structure that we have. But computers demonstrated that many of the processes we would once have termed "thinking" can indeed be realized by mechanisms that are constituted of entirely different components—transistors or vacuum tubes—rather than nerves, blood, and tissues.

If there was to be an identity, it obviously could not reside in the hardware but, as Putnam pointed out, might well occur in the software: that is, both human beings and machines—and any other form of intelligent life, from anteaters to Antipodeans—could be capable of realizing the same kinds of program. Thus, the equation occurs at a much higher level of abstraction—a level that focuses on the goals of a cognitive activity, the means of processing at one's disposal, the steps that would have to be taken, the evaluation of the steps, and kindred features.

Indeed, functionalism purported to address one of the most classic philosophical dilemmas—the mind-body problem. Thought can indeed occur in a physical apparatus and can be correlated with certain behavior and yet not *have* to be identified with the precise class of activities that happen to be produced (Matthews 1982). It is perfectly legitimate to talk of mental events, to posit one mental event as causing another, and to do so without taking a position on whether only brain events have the properties to define mental states. Of course, in human beings, mental events are identical to physiological ones, but there is no need to reduce psychological explanations to the neuro-physiological level. Rather one may countenance a level of explanation that connects psychology to neurology, a second level that connects it to social factors, and even a third free-standing level, which is representational.

Intentional Systems

Building on Putnam's pioneering attempt to tackle the issues of knowledge in an idiom that makes sense in the contemporary cognitive milieu, certain philosophers in more recent times have put forth their own analytic schemes. Daniel Dennett begins by distinguishing his own theories from earlier efforts (Dennett 1978). He does not wish to embrace a kind of physicalism in which, for every type of mental event, there is a particular type of physical event in the brain. Nor does he want to adopt a so-called Turing-machine functionalism, which would imply that all individuals have the same program. He thus searches for a level of explanation where it is possible to talk about what two individuals or two entities have in common psychologically without both being the realization of some single Turing machine.

Enter the intentional system. This concept is designed to play a role in the legitimation of mental descriptions parallel to the role played by the abstract notion of a Turing machine in setting down the rules for interpreting an artifact like a computer. Intentionality is seen as the mark of the mental, and Dennett claims that every mental phenomenon can be described in terms of intentional systems.

As Dennett phrases it, one may consider both human beings and a computer and its programs as agents whose acts one is trying to explain. Though one can talk about the computer in terms of its physical design or its actual physical states, it often makes more sense to treat the machine as if it were significantly like an intelligent human being. In other words, one attributes rationality and purpose to an intentional system. And so, if, for example, you are playing a game of chess with a computer, you think of the program as having at its disposal certain goals, procedures, strategies; and you try to outwit the program just as you would try to outwit that more conventional kind of intentional system—another person.

The notion of an intentional system, Dennett argues, is relatively uncluttered and unmetaphysical. It does not touch the issue of the composition, quality, morality, or divinity of any of its instantiations. Intentional systems serve as a bridge from the common-sense world of persons and actions to the non-intentional domain of the standard physical sciences. Artificial intelligence is a handmaiden in this enterprise, because this discipline builds a system that is in fact knowledgeable, and thus provides one answer to the question of how knowledge is possible.

Intentional systems emerge at a certain level of complexity. One can break down an intentional system into subsystems, each one of which is itself viewable as an intentional system, and then break it down in terms of even finer systems. These subsystems can be thought of as little homunculi which communicate with one another. Ultimately, however, one wants to reach a level where these various homunculi are "discharged," where there is no need to adopt the intentionalist stance. As Dennett puts it:

> If one can get a team or committee of *relatively* ignorant, narrow-minded, blind homunculi to produce the intelligent behavior of the whole, this is progress. . . . Eventually this . . . lands you with homunculi so stupid (all they have to do is remember whether to say yes or no when asked) that they can be, as one says, "replaced by a machine." One *discharges* fancy homunculi from one's scheme by organizing armies of such idiots to do the work. (Dennett 1978, pp. 123–24)

Which touches upon the hedge in Dennett's formulation. While he finds it useful to involve "intentional system talk" for the machines of artificial intelligence, he asserts, at the same time, that this is just a manner of speaking:

> [T]he definition of intentional systems I have given does not say that intentional systems *really* have beliefs and desires but that one can explain and predict their behavior by *ascribing* beliefs and desires to them, and whether one calls what one ascribes to the computer beliefs or belief-analogues or information complexes or intentional whatnots makes no difference to the nature of the calculation one makes on the basis of the ascriptions. (1978, p. 7)

But if this is only a manner of talking, what has been gained by this apparently daring move? It is likely that Dennett, a student of Ryle's, would really rather dispense with this mentalistic line altogether and fall back on a more trustworthy behaviorist mode of discussion. Still, Dennett concedes that such discussion really is no longer adequate for scientific purposes. As he comments in a critical piece on the behaviorist B. F. Skinner, "There is no reason why intentional terms can't be used provisionally in the effort to map out the function of the behavioral control system of men and animals just as long as a way is found to 'cash them out' by designing a mechanism to function as specified" (Dennett 1978, p. 62).

In developing their notions, Putnam and Dennett have exemplified the contribution of philosophy to cognitive science. Responding to the various issues raised by the advent of the computer, while drawing on long-standing discussion about the mind's relation to the body and an agent's sense of purpose, these authorities have helped to clarify issues raised in the contemporary science of mind. Still, I think it would be fair to state that both of these philosophers have entered the terrain of cognitive science with considerable caution. And, as we shall see in later chapters, more vexing issues have been raised, by philosophical critics of artificial intelligence, such as John Searle and Hubert Dreyfus. For these reasons, it is salutary to consider the work of Jerry A. Fodor, a full-scale cognitivist—one philosopher who seemingly has no reservations whatsoever about the common fate of philosophers and empirical scientists interested in issues of mind.

The Complete Cognitivist: Jerry Fodor

To read Fodor (1975, 1981*b*) is to feel that the tables of epistemology have been suddenly and radically turned: the "bad guys" have been propelled to the position of heroes and some widely heralded common heroes have been demoted. Following his one-time mentor and present colleague Noam Chomsky, Fodor finds much to admire in the analysis put forth by Descartes over three hundred years ago. For Fodor, the Cartesian tradition has the merit that it recognized the existence of mental states and freely permitted mental events to have causal power. Furthermore, it countenanced the positing of innate ideas—informational content, mechanisms, or principles with which the individual is born and which allow the individual to make sense of experience. As part of his own version of epistemology, Fodor is vociferously critical of the empiricist tradition. He feels that three hundred years of empiricist efforts, from Hume to the logical positivists, have resulted in failure. On Fodor's reading, both empiricists and rationalists had accepted that some concepts must be innate, but he sides with the rationalists in their belief that the human being is born with the knowledge of *many* concepts, which, at most, must simply be triggered by the environment. Fodor also excoriates the Rylean behaviorist position: he, in fact, wants to claim that the kinds of explanations Ryle rejected are just those that are needed. In Fodor's view, it is quite a different matter to explain the circumstances under which an utterance is made from the reasons it is made; and, in defiance of Ryle, it is part of Fodor's project to invade the mental space: to figure out just why and how we make the statements we make, given the mental equipment with which we are endowed.

But Fodor's rejection of much past philosophical work should by no means be interpreted as an uncritical return to the tenets of Cartesianism. First of all, he stresses that mentalism is not equivalent to dualism. One can believe in the existence of mental states and in their causal efficacy without believing that there are two substances—mind and matter—which must somehow interact with one another. In this case, he is putting forth a materialistic variant of mind, which nonetheless allows the existence of mental causes and the interaction of mental states with one another.

Indeed, Fodor accepts much of the functionalist perspective as first introduced by his teacher, Hilary Putnam. On this view, the psychological constitution of a system depends not on its hardware (or its physical realization) but on its software: thus, Martians can have pains, and computers can have beliefs. Fodor goes on to embrace the general information-processing approach of the cognitive sciences: it is in the manipulation of symbols, or mental representations, that cognitive activities are realized and, in fact, constituted. Consistent with many contemporary philosophers of mind, and in direct opposition to those earlier philosophers who saw mind as a mirror of nature, Fodor rejects resemblance as a property of mental representation: the symbols of the mind are abstract entities which need bear no configurational relationship to the entities they denote.

Finally, Fodor's functionalism in no sense reflects a reductionist approach. Intelligence and mental states can be realized in many systems and entities, and there is no priority given to explanation in terms of the biochemical or the neurological. Indeed, Fodor voices his strong reservations that the "natural kinds" of the nervous system will map in any interesting way onto the "natural kinds" of psychological or mentalistic explanations. If anything, the tie between mind and computer is likely to be more intimate than the tie between mind and brain. Throughout, there is a strong "intentionalist flavor" to the discussion: Fodor injects an idiom of beliefs, desires, goals, and the like entering into the very center of discussions about various kinds of cognitive systems.

Until this point it may seem that, while Fodor features a different cast of heroes and villains, his approach is consistent with those of other cognitively oriented epistemologists, such as Putnam and Dennett. And, indeed, viewed from afar, and compared with skeptics like Rorty or Ryle, these philosophers can all be seen as enthusiasts of the computational metaphor in the world of cognitive processes. But Fodor has gone well beyond his contemporaries in his willingness to think about what mental representation might be like. Here his Cartesian allegiance becomes most patent.

In a word, Fodor believes that there must be a language of thought. If cognitive systems involve representations, if cognitive operations involve the manipulation of symbol-like representations, then these representations must exist somewhere and be manipulated in some way. Accordingly, Fodor feels that a commitment to attributing a representational system to organisms must entail a characterization of this mentalistic system. He asserts, "I am proposing . . . to resurrect the traditional notion that there is a 'language of thought' and that characterizing it is in good part what a theory of the mind needs to do" (1975, p. 33). Fodor feels that acknowledgment of some kind of medium, or language, within which thinking takes place is an implicit part of nearly every contemporary cognitive theory. It has become his burden to try to spell out what that language might be.

And so to Fodor's long and highly stimulating essay *The Language of Thought* (1975), seen by some commentators as a "great divide" in twentieth-century philosophy (Piattelli-Palmarini 1983). In this work, Fodor claims that the language of thought must be an extremely rich vehicle if it is to carry out the many cognitive processes—perception, reasoning, language-learning, and the like—of which human beings are capable. Indeed, if mental processes are computational, there *must* be representations upon which computations can be performed. Moreover, he puts forth his radical view that this language of thought is innate: that people are born with a full set of representations, onto which they can then map any new forms of information that happen to emerge from their experiences in the world. Furthermore, "the language of thought may be very [much] like a natural language. It may be that the resources of the inner code are rather directly represented in the resources of the codes we use for communication. . . . [This is] why natural languages are so easy to learn" (1975, p. 156).

Fodor's claim that individuals are born with knowledge of a language —an innate language similar to a natural language—is astonishing, and it is not certain just how seriously he means it to be taken. But his challenges to competing accounts are deadly serious. Take, for example, his critique of Jean Piaget's theory of concept acquisition, according to which the child comes to possess new and more powerful concepts at each subsequent stage of development. Fodor parades the difficulty he has in understanding how one can ever learn a new concept unless one already has the ability to hypothesize that concept—in which case, one already possesses it. Shades of the *Meno*! Similarly, in his critique of the claim that complex concepts are built out of simple ones, Fodor argues strenuously that all attempts *à la* Locke to identify the building blocks of larger concepts have failed, and that this failure is putative evidence that this particular "empiricist" maneuver was ill conceived from the start. The fact that the operations that individuals can carry out, even early in life, are highly abstract, gives further weight to Fodor's (and Chomsky's) claims that the initial intellectual apparatus with which individuals are equipped must be sharply specified, constructed so as to expect particular experiences and information. Even though the exact claims put forth by Fodor have failed to persuade most of his colleagues, the issues he raises about the need for some kind of "mentalese," and the kinds of constraints this mentalese may have to exhibit, have proved difficult to undermine. Thus, his position passes one of the most critical tests for any philosophical claim.

From Fodor's point of view, it is inadequate to conceive of the language of thought as simply a formal medium of symbol manipulation (see Stich 1983). There must be some way in which the contents of the world are represented mentally, for we do not just think, we think *about* certain things, and those certain things surely exist in the world. Yet at the same time, Fodor expresses pessimism about the likelihood that we will ever be able to understand how *content* is dealt with by our computational systems. We may be restricted, as investigators, simply to describing the kinds of "syntactic" operation that are carried out, while remaining ignorant of the ways in which these operations refer to the external world so as to lead to different mental concepts. As Fodor puts it, it may be impossible for the cognitivist to do semantics, even though "to deny that mental operations have access to semantic properties of mental representations is *not* to deny that mental representations *have* semantic properties" (1981*b*, p. 244). Fodor does fear that these properties may be inaccessible to scientific investigation. The machine of our minds does not know what it is talking about, and does not care about a semantic relation. While so-called naturalistic psychology wants to be able to explain how we learn to know about the particular things of the world and what they are like, computational psychology—a psychology of formal mental operations—may be the only kind of psychology we can ever hope to get. On such "content-blind" sentiments the historically oriented student of philosophy can discern links between Fodor's enterprise and that of Carnap and the logical empiricists: indeed, Fodor even adopts Carnap's term *methodological solipsism* to characterize a syntactic approach to cognition.

In sum, then, Fodor believes that any attempt to understand cognition must involve a full-fledged embracing of a mentalistic point of view. He believes that mental states really exist, that they can interact with one another, and that it is possible to study them. Methods of study involve the empirical methods of psychology, linguistics, and other cognitive sciences; and chances of making advances on these issues are tied closely to an informed collaboration among experts in these different areas. Fodor's own guess is that those mental operations that occur in a relatively rapid and automatic fashion—like the syntactic parsing of a sentence or the detection of forms in the visual world—are most likely to be elucidated by current cognitive scientific methods. He is correspondingly pessimistic that those capacities involving sustained judgment and reasoning—such as the development of scientific theories or the making of decisions about ordinary life—will lend themselves to the kind of syntactic (or formal) analysis for which cognitive science has proved suited.

It might be thought that such a reversion to Cartesian notions, such bold talk of a language of thought, would prove anathema to many of the authorities I have discussed. In particular, it might be thought that Richard Rorty would see Fodor's move as exactly the kind of tack a sophisticated cognitive researcher ought to avoid. It is surprising, therefore, but also illuminating, that while Fodor's work is reviewed critically in Rorty's book, it is not by any means dismissed.

Rorty, it will be recalled, saves his harshest criticism for those who believe in the Mirror of Nature—in a mental apparatus that in some way can tell about what the world is like and help us judge it in the most accurate possible way—to give us "right opinions," as he might put it. Rorty notes that Fodor is interested in constructing a mechanistic model of mental processes and is willing to posit all kinds of internal states for doing so, but that his ultimate criteria call only for the kinds of description that may yield a fruitful theory of cognitive processing—an avowedly psychological non-epistemological program like Dodwell's. Rorty stresses that the question, "How do we recognize bottles?," is entirely different from the question, "What is indubitably given to the mind, such as to serve as an infallible touchstone for inference?" (1979, p. 245). And so Rorty and Fodor concur on the importance of separating out two questions: how the organism interacts with the world—a legitimate psychological question; and whether the organism's views about the world are in fact true—the traditional (and, to Rorty's mind, the untenable) question. We now see, Rorty points out, "that Fodor's picture of the mind as a system of inner representations has nothing to do with the image of the Mirror of Nature I have been criticizing. The crucial point is that there is no way to raise the skeptical question 'How well do the subject's internal representations represent reality?' about Fodor's 'language of thought' " (p. 246).

Whatever Fodor's and Rorty's particular points of agreement may be, Fodor, Chomsky, and others in the cognitive camp clearly wear the mantle of Rorty's systematizers: they believe that the traditional questions are important, and they want to try to solve them as best they can, though they may retain rather more skepticism about what is possible than did the great systematizers of a few centuries past. Rorty, on the other hand, as a self-styled edifier believes that philosophy has, at most, puzzles, and that the whole agenda of epistemological questions had better be scuttled. And however little he criticizes the kind of psychology in which Dodwell or Fodor are engaged, he apparently thinks that psychology has thus far not accomplished much, and believes that eventually only neurological and humanistic approaches to mental phenomena will be left (Rorty 1982a). The very fact that Fodor and Chomsky revert to the Cartesian tradition and see themselves as providing answers relevant to the rationalist and empirical disputes exemplifies for me the deep gap between these two strands of current philosophical thinking.

Conclusion: The Dialectic Role of Philosophy

When it comes to our major issue of philosophical content—the question whether the empiricist or the rationalist account has carried the day—the pendulum has swung back and forth. For a brief period around 1800, it appeared that Kant's synthesis had solved the problems once and for all; but 130 years later, in the height of the behaviorist era, the empiricists were in the ascendancy. Now, thanks to the cognitive revolution, and in the wake of the influential writings of theorists like Fodor, rationalism is being taken more seriously than it has been for decades. It is probably fair to say that most cognitive scientists no longer care about which perspective "wins" in this debate, and that the purpose of the Fodor critique is less to resurrect Cartesian rationalism than to demonstrate the bankruptcy of the empiricist position. Still, to the extent that cognitive science continues to gain adherents, the rationalist position will emerge as essentially more credible. The primacy of the knowledgeable subject—one who acquires knowledge only by virtue of prior cognitive structuring (if not innate ideas!)—is now accepted widely. In that sense at least, the trend of philosophy is toward a rationalistic stance, one supported by empirical work in several disciplines.

The role of philosophy as a discipline in its own right—and as a continuing valid contributor to the cognitive sciences—is vexed. Several reservations have been raised about philosophy from both within and without the discipline. As we have seen, critics of logical empiricism—most especially Richard Rorty—question the need for philosophy, at least in its epistemological guise. From their perspective, the questions that once motivated philosophers—from Plato through Kant—were actually misconceived and are not susceptible to the kind of systematic answers their predecessors had sought. It would be preferable for philosophers to abandon these issues—leaving them to empirical scientists to work out if they so choose—and instead become informed commentators about culture—which in the case of our culture would include commenting on the great philosophers of the past. A different argument is put forth by researchers in the mainstream of cognitive science, for example, in artificial intelligence. From their perspective, once one has provided computational accounts of knowledge, understanding, representation, and the like, the need for philosophical analyses will evaporate. After all, philosophy had once helped set the agenda for physics; but now that physics has made such tremendous strides, few physicists any longer care about the musings of philosophers (Holton 1984).

I am not convinced by either of these critiques. On my analysis, philosophy has been crucial from the first in formulating a set of questions worthy of study and in monitoring the course of these questions over the millennia. There is progress in philosophy—not perhaps as linear in the physical sciences—but clear progress nonetheless. This progress comes about because of the debates that take place among philosophers—for example, when Locke criticized certain concepts of Descartes, and Berkeley and Hume in turn criticized Locke; and it occurs with equal impact through interaction between philosophers and empirical scientists, such as those discussions in which physicists and logical empiricists were involved in the early part of this century.

I suggest, then, that philosophy participates in the disciplinary matrix by virtue of its dialectical role: a dialectic within the discipline and a dialectic between the analysis put forth by philosophers, on the one hand, and the empirical findings and theories put forth by scientists, on the other. This has happened dramatically in recent years. Just at the time when philosophy seemed at low ebb, when the program of logical empiricism has been thoroughly discredited, the invention of the computer and the beginning of cognitive science suddenly underscored the need for sophisticated analysis. It was thinkers acquainted with the long-standing philosophical tradition—with Kant's notions about representations, Descartes's claims about the mind-body problem, Locke's skepticism about innate ideas—who could bring to bear the appropriate conceptual framework and then revise it in the light of new scientific discoveries.

All this is not to claim that the traditional questions of philosophy have inherent superiority. While Rorty's critique of traditional epistemology seems like "overkill" to me, the kinds of questions pondered by philosophers have changed over the millennia: some issues, such as the nature of visual perception, which exercised the Greeks, become the exclusive province of empirical science; some issues, such as the nature of "raw" sensory experience, come to be seen as ill conceived; and some issues, like the nature of intention and purpose, gain new urgency because of inventions like the computer.

I see the invention of cognitive science as a wonderful stimulus for philosophy, on the one hand, and philosophy as an indispensable handmaiden for the empirical scientists, on the other. Philosophy enables us to define fundamental cognitive scientific questions in a coherent way, and assures the proper integration of work in disparate fields. But, by the same token, philosophy must attend assiduously to empirical findings in order to avoid becoming a barren discipline or one irrelevant to scientific work. It is thus fitting that the field of philosophy, whose initial agenda helped to stimulate the rise of cognitive science, has been fueled by that new discipline, even as philosophy can, in turn, help to inform and interpret work spawned by its recent intellectual offspring.

Hilary Putnam, a veteran of many of these discussions, has reflected on the role of philosophy in the contemporary scientific scene. His prudent comments take seriously the various critiques of "grand" philosophy, while recognizing the important role philosophy should continue to play in discussions of new scientific endeavors:

> I have not attempted . . . to put forward any grand view of the nature of philosophy; nor do I have any such grand view to put forth if I would. It will be obvious that I do not agree with those who see philosophy as the history of "howlers" and progress in philosophy as the debunking of howlers. It will also be obvious that I do not agree with those who see philosophy as the enterprise of putting forward *a priori* truths about the real world. . . . I see philosophy as a field which has certain central questions, for example, the relation between thought and reality. . . . It seems obvious that in dealing with these questions philosophers have formulated rival research programs, that they have put forward general hypotheses, and that philosophers within each major research program have modified their hypotheses by trial and error, even if they sometimes refuse to admit that that is what they are doing. To that extent philosophy is a "science." To argue about whether philosophy is a science in any more serious sense seems to me to be hardly a useful occupation. . . . It does not seem to me important to decide whether science is philosophy or philosophy is science as long as one has a conception of both that makes both essential to a responsible view of the real world and of man's place in it. (Putnam 1975a, p. *xvii*)

5

Psychology: The Wedding of Methods to Substance

Three Pivotal Lines of Research from the 1950s

George Miller's Magic Number 7

In 1956, George Miller published, in the *Psychological Review,* an artfully presented essay—"The Magical Number Seven, Plus or Minus Two: Some Limits on Our Capacity for Processing Information." More of a synthesis than a report of a crucial experiment or a presentation of a formal theory, Miller's opening statement was backed by considerable empirical evidence: "My problem is that I have been persecuted by an integer. For seven years this number has followed me around, has intruded in my most private data, and has assaulted me from the pages of our most public journals" (p. 81). Miller showed that the individual's ability to make absolute distinctions among stimuli, to distinguish phonemes from one another, to estimate numbers accurately, and to remember a number of discrete items all seemed to undergo a crucial change at about the level of seven items. Below that number, individuals could readily handle such tasks: above it, individuals were likely to fail. Nor did this discontinuity seem accidental. In Miller's view:

There seems to be some limitation built into us either by learning or by the design of our nervous systems, a limit that keeps our channel capacities in this general range. On the basis of the present evidence it seems safe to say that we possess a finite and rather small capacity for making such . . . [judgments] and that this capacity does not vary a great deal from one simple sensory attribute to another. (P. 86)

Humans, however—as Miller reassured his audience—have ways of getting around these constraints. Processing or coding entities in terms of their various dimensions can enlarge the number of elements that can be distinguished from one another. One can chunk, or group together, a number of elements (for example, a set of numbers or letters) and then treat the assemblage as a unit. One can make relative rather than absolute judgments. The capacity to recode information into language and to re-member this more abstract symbolism is especially important. As Miller notes, "This kind of linguistic recoding that people do, seems to me to be the very lifeblood of the thought processes" (1956, p. 95). Indeed, he once described the potential efficiency of this recoding process in this manner, "To use a rather farfetched analogy, it is as if we had to carry all our money in a purse that could contain only seven coins. It doesn't matter to the purse, however, whether these coins are pennies or silver dollars" (Miller, Galanter, and Pribram 1960, p. 132).

Why did this apparently simple point have a decidedly major impact within cognitively oriented communities? First Miller's essay brought to-gether a large amount of hitherto dispersed data and suggested that they pointed to a common conclusion. A valuable synthesis, to begin with. Second, it suggested that the number 7 was no mere accident: it designated genuine limitations in human information-processing capacities. While such "built-in" limitations might be anathema to radical empiricists, they helped signal a shift toward exploring the nature and structure of a central cognitive processing mechanism. The point about strict processing limits, not coincidentally, was made in terms of the theory of information, which Miller explained early in the paper: thus, he introduced a method whereby researchers could examine other sensory modalities or tasks and ascertain whether this apparent limitation in fact obtains. (Much ensuing contro-versy centered on how to make such translations and whether, when made, they did in fact yield the magic number 7.) Third, as indicated, the message in the paper was not without hope, for Miller indicated ways by which humans ingeniously transcend this limitation.

There may have been another reason for the impact of this essay. Psychologists had been trying for approximately a century to discover the basic laws of the human mental system. Many promising avenues had been launched, but most of them—including, most recently, the behaviorist approach—had eventually foundered. In recent years, the most exciting new work in the human sciences had come from two connected areas: information theory, which posited principles of transmission applicable to any kind of channel; and computer science, which now featured machines engaged in symbol manipulation. Miller was holding out hope of marriage between the quantities of data collected by psychologists over the years and the rigorous new approaches of the engineering-oriented scientists. The result might be a genuine science of psychology with its own set of immutable laws. No one thought to question whether all contents, or bits, can in fact be treated (and then counted) as equivalent.

The British Approach to the Processing of Information

Just as Miller and his colleagues were applying concepts from communication science to psychology, a parallel movement was getting under way in Great Britain. This movement grew directly out of the applied psychological work that had been carried out in Britain during the Second World War when psychologists joined other scientists in efforts to crack enemy codes, understand night vision, plan air-raid alerts, assist in spotting of enemy aircraft, and meet sundry other needs of war. Two men who had been involved in this applied effort were Colin Cherry and Donald Broadbent; their studies in the 1950s inspired the British approach to information-processing psychology.

A follower of information theory, Cherry (1953) focused on the capacities of individuals to attend to and obtain information from noisy channels. He instructed subjects to follow a message, delivered to one ear, by the method of shadowing: that is, by repeating each word as soon after its initial presentation as possible. Cherry found subjects unable to report much of what had come into the opposite (unattended) ear. More precisely, they could report gross characteristics of the signal, such as whether it was music or speech, but not shifts of content or tongue. Broadbent (1954) refined this procedure by presenting sets of digits simultaneously, in strings of three, to both ears. He found that subjects had the easiest time and achieved the highest score when they reported all the digits presented to one ear first, and then all the digits presented (at the same time) to the other ear.

For our purposes, the important part of the Broadbent-Cherry work is the model of human thought processes to which it gave rise. The model conformed to the tradition of British empiricism. It began with information taken in from the senses, but focused on a new and important feature: that the individual has a limited capacity for the intake *and* storage of information. (In this stress on limits of information processing, the model was intimately linked to George Miller's studies of the magic number 7.) There was an important added twist: rather than simply speaking of structural limits in a static way, the British researchers sought to determine precisely what *happens* to this information from the moment one first apprehends it. Given this "engineering" approach, it became a natural step to draw a flow chart of what happens, as the perceptual system operates upon new information. In fact, according to a recent textbook, Broadbent was the first psychologist in modern times to describe cognitive functioning with a flow chart (Lachman, Lachman, and Butterfield 1979, p. 188).

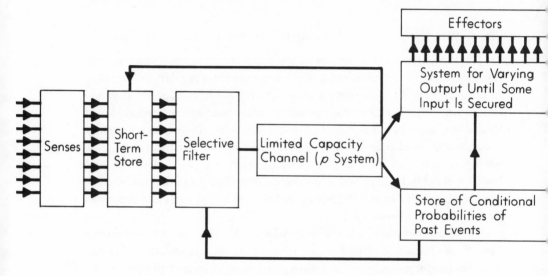

One of the first information-processing diagrams.
SOURCE: From D. E. Broadbent, *Perception and Communication* (Elmsford, N.Y.: Pergamon Press, 1958). Reproduced by permission.

What was this early flow chart like? It featured information coming in through the senses, being placed in a short-term store, and then being selectively filtered before entering into a limited-capacity perceptual system. While a sense organ can take in a lot of information in parallel and retain it momentarily, the job of the selective filter is to block unwanted messages, thereby letting in only those that merit additional analysis. A further property of the selective filter is that it can be so tuned that, at any one time, it allows in only those messages that fulfill certain requirements. The buffer can hold unanalyzed information briefly and thus allows one to report the contents of the second ear, after having spewed out the three digits apprehended by the first ear. According to Broadbent's early model, only information that becomes conscious—that passes through the limited-capacity channel—can enter into long-term memory and thus become part of active knowledge. Information present on an unattended channel, or in an unattended signal, is assumed to decay in a few seconds and to receive no processing beyond the initial "pre-attentive" analysis.

While few, if any, investigators believed that perception or thinking takes place simultaneously or without a series of steps, the option of tracing the stages of information processing had rarely been followed before Broadbent's time. Again, this option became a probability when communication engineering began to impinge on the perceptual and attentional issues that had long interested psychologists. But the model of "flow charting" put forth by Broadbent and his associates and their evidence relevant to specific stages of information processing opened up many productive possibilities. One could now examine the temporal dimensions of diverse psychological processes, and avid experimenters lost little time in pursuing just that course. The lack of attention to the particular *content* being processed, or to the *kinds* of transformation imposed, did not trouble those excited by the Broadbent-Cherry demonstrations.

Jerome Bruner's Strategic Approach

With the collaboration of Jacqueline Goodnow and George Austin, Jerome Bruner published in 1956 a book called *A Study of Thinking.* This volume grew out of the Cognition Project, which Bruner had been directing for several years at Harvard. The subject, well known to psychologists, was classification, categorization, or (as it was commonly called in the trade) concept formation or concept acquisition. And the problem was a classic one: How does a person, confronted with a set of elements, come to group them together reliably into categories—be they all chairs, all atoms, or all large blue triangles?

As psychologists, Bruner and his colleagues followed the tradition of examining abstract forms of categorization, such as those involved in figuring out which of a set of cards, each featuring a different geometric form, belongs to a particular category. The experimenter would target a concept —say, the class of all cards with one red figure, the class of all cards featuring red squares, or, when being particularly diabolical, the class of all cards containing two figures and/or circles. The subject was exposed to one card at a time, asked in each case whether that card belonged to the preordained concept, and then told whether his response was correct. The subject's task, of course, was to figure out the properties of the targeted concept, so as to be able to select all, and only, those cards that exhibited its defining features.

While superficially similar to work carried out in years past, Bruner's approach actually diverged from that undertaken by earlier students of categorization. First of all, rather than treating subjects as deaf and mute animals, Bruner and his colleagues simply told the subjects what to do and relied heavily on their comments as an aid in analyzing the results. Flying in the face of established behaviorist methodology, the subjects were treated as active, constructive problem solvers, rather than as simple reactors to the stimuli presented to them. Their introspections actually mattered.

Reflecting the information-theoretical winds of the day, Bruner and his associates had begun by looking at the bits of information assimilated in subjects' encounters with such simple stimuli. But in another departure from standard operating procedures, they ended up analyzing the informational properties of long sequences of acts called "strategies." It had turned out that the best way to account for individual performances was in terms of these overall patterns of responding over many trials rather than of particular responses to a particular stimulus configuration. This was the most iconoclastic—and the most influential—aspect of the work.

The researchers went on to consider what each strategy accomplished in light of the goals of the organism, such as minimizing risk or conserving storage capacity. Singled out were the strategy of *successive scanning*, where the subject has a single hypothesis (like all red objects) and limits his choices to those instances that directly test this hypothesis; the approach of *conservative focusing*, where one finds a positive instance and then makes a sequence of choices, each of which alters but a single attribute value of the first "focus" card and tests whether the change yields a positive or a negative instance; and the tack of *focus gambling*, where the subject uses a positive instance as a focus but then takes the calculated risk of changing more than one attribute at a time. Focus gambling offers the possibility of attaining a concept far more rapidly than does conservative focusing, but also may necessitate extra trials if one's choices happen to be unrevealing. Conservative focusing is the most foolproof method since it limits the burden on memory and allows steady progress toward a solution. However, in case of a time limit or some other pressure, the respondent may adopt the riskier course of changing several attributes simultaneously.

Perhaps not surprisingly for a work published in the pivotal year of 1956, the Bruner book presented itself as an innovation in psychology. The authors comment:

the past few years have witnessed a notable increase in interest in and investigation of the cognitive processes. . . . It has resulted from a recognition of the complex processes that mediate between the classical "stimuli" and "responses" out of which stimulus-response learning theories hoped to fashion a psychology that would by-pass anything smacking of the "mental." The impeccable peripheralism of such theories could not last. . . . One might do well to have a closer look at these intervening "cognitive maps." (P. *vii*)

The importance of Bruner's book was signaled by praise from the distinguished physicist J. Robert Oppenheimer: *"A Study of Thinking* has in many ways the flavor of the opening of a new science. . . . The book has a unity of view and a fervor of conviction which makes it point to the future" (quoted in Bruner 1983, p. 121). The possibility that the use of such artificial concepts might invalidate the findings was far from anyone's mind at that time.

The Program of Cognitive Psychology

The lines of research inaugurated by Miller, Broadbent and Cherry, and Bruner, energized the psychology of the late 1950s and the 1960s. In the face of the artificially tough strictures that had been imposed by behaviorism on issues of cognition, these young psychologists were willing to introduce notions that had long been ruled "out of court." Talk of built-in limitations to the amount of information that could be taken in, attempts to trace the steps involved in processing such information, and positing of overall strategies employed to solve a problem—all of these signaled a greater willingness to discuss issues of mind directly, without attempting to explain them away in terms of long series of publicly verifiable stimuli and responses.

Such a change cannot be attributed to a single factor, but it is clear that the advent of the computer, as well as the information-theoretical language by which it was commonly characterized, helped to legitimize such approaches. No longer were psychologists restricted in their explanatory accounts to events that could either be imposed on a subject or observed in one's behavior; psychologists were now willing to consider the representation of information within the mind. To be sure, this willingness to deal with mental representation took different forms in the writings of different psychologists. Miller looked at the structural properties and limitations built into the representational system; Broadbent and Cherry examined the transformations on the information as it came in from the senses and was stored in memory; Bruner attributed to subjects a variety of approaches or strategies which governed performance on a task. While the issues being probed—memory for isolated units, processing of words or tones, sorting of concepts—were scarcely new to psychology, the prospect of applying concepts from information theory, of building on the model of a computer, of countenancing various forms of mental representation, and of allowing subjects to use their full reflective powers was bracing and freeing.

Psychology is a discipline central to any study of cognition. Yet it is also a difficult discipline to pursue and one where genuine progress has been hard to achieve. Nearly every conceivable element is relevant to a subject's performance, and few issues having to do with human nature and behavior can be excluded from the laboratory *a priori*. Thus, choosing a problem, and screening out all competing ones, becomes an especially vexing task.

Psychology also poses special problems for the historian of cognitive science—a problem in no way minimized when the historian is also a psychologist. It is an enormous field—there are many more psychologists than there are representatives of the other fields—and there are consequently more programs of research to survey. While it is oversimplification to organize any field around one or two themes, it is especially difficult to select key issues in psychology. Should one, thus, pay attention to the particular content of information (auditory or visual, musical or linguistic) or instead treat all contents as if they were interchangeable? Does one approach research in order to illuminate those processes that are true of all individuals, or look instead at pertinent individual differences—child versus adult, male versus female, naïve versus trained in experimental tasks? Does one examine behavior in its natural context or try to strip away all everyday accouterments and resort to artificial laboratory conditions? Does one assume that the individual approaches tasks by building up larger elements of meaning from small, isolated units? Or does it make more sense to assume that one comes to tasks with general strategies or scripts, which one simply imposes upon a task, irrespective of its particular dimensions, details, and demands?

I have elected to organize this chapter in terms of a distinction that touches upon some of the aforementioned ones but is perhaps better phrased in somewhat different terms: that is, the distinction between *molecular* or small-scale units of analysis and *molar* or large-scale units of analysis. For reasons of scientific strategy or simple personal preference, it seems possible to classify most psychological research programs along this dimension. Some programs, such as those of traditional psychophysics and contemporary information processing, show a penchant for small-scale units (bits, individual percepts, single associations examined in brief periods of time) on the assumption that a thorough understanding of these elementary units and processes is the surest path toward the ultimate explanation of complex units and entities. A contrasting faith is found among proponents of the molar approach—those who look at large-scale problems tackled over a long period of time and invoke analytic concepts like schemas, frames, or strategies. According to these researchers, these large-scale properties are most salient in human cognition and thus serve as a logical point of departure. Why gamble that an elementaristic approach will eventually yield larger units, when one has the option of *beginning* instead with these larger units, which seem closer to the data and the experiences of everyday life?

The contrast between molecular and molar approaches resembles, but is by no means identical to, the distinction between the *top-down* and the *bottom-up* approaches. In a top-down approach, which has rationalist overtones, the subject is assumed to bring to the task his own schemes, strategies, or frames which strongly color his performance. In a bottom-up approach, more allied to the empiricist camp, the actual details of a focal task or situation are assumed to exert primary influence on a subject's performance. In what follows, I shall often identify *molar* with "top-down" and *molecular* with "bottom-up"—not because each is logically bound to the other but because they often, and perhaps typically, occur together.

Like all dichotomies, this one is easily exaggerated, with subsequent distortion of the field. Nearly all psychologists have some sympathy for each tack, and many move from a molecular to a molar approach (and back again). For example, George Miller favored a molecular hat when pondering the number 7 but readily shifted to a molar one when discussing plans and goals in the 1960 volume. Indeed, when the computer is used as a model, it is equally justifiable to focus on the most molecular level (individual bits, symbols, "on-off" circuits) or the most high-level programming concepts (goals, means, and routines). Also, one can embrace a molecular (or a molar) approach for different reasons: some psychologists begin with a molecular approach in the hope of being able to adapt their methods to molar entities; while others believe that ultimately all behavior can be reduced to, and explained by, molecular entities. Thus, in embracing this dichotomy, I seek to convey an ongoing tension or struggle for the soul of psychology—not to label two bins into which one can readily and reliably sort all experiments, concepts, and psychologists.

Two other trends must be mentioned as well in any thumbnail sketch of psychology's first one hundred years. The first trend is the increasing splintering of the field. The American Psychological Association alone has over fifty thousand members (including several thousand active researchers) who spread themselves over forty divisions and several hundred special interest groups, many of which are completely ignorant of what is going on elsewhere in their association and their discipline. In this climate, efforts to find unifying concepts are vital but by no means easy to sustain.

The second is the trend toward methodological perfection. With the passage of time, the invention of new instruments, and the increased sophistication of statistical techniques, the design of individual studies and sets of studies has become increasingly elegant. No one would deplore this situation, but the question must be raised whether (in comparison, say, with molecular biology) this increasing methodological sophistication has deepened our understanding of psychological phenomena. In other words, have we obtained more penetrating knowledge about human cognition, or are we simply using more convincing experimental demonstrations to reaffirm knowledge that has long since been established?

In my view, its methodological sophistication is among psychology's proudest achievements, but it is an attainment that has not yet been fully integrated with the substance of the field. Many of psychology's most important issues need to be approached from a molar perspective and entail a top-down perspective. And yet the most rigorous psychological methods often are not appropriate for these large-scale issues. As I see it, the challenge currently faced by psychology involves a wedding of its sophisticated methodological armamentarium to issues and questions of unmistakable consequence. Since many of these questions arise from the philosophical tradition out of which psychology directly grew, it is appropriate to begin this survey of the course of cognitive psychology with a brief consideration of the Kantian legacy to nineteenth-century psychological studies.

Scientific Psychology in the Nineteenth Century

Coping with the Kantian Legacy

Immanuel Kant had severe doubts about the possibility of a science of psychology—a skepticism that, as I noted in the last chapter, arose from several causes. He believed that a science has to apply mathematical laws to empirical data, and that such data have to be collected in real experiments, but because psychology deals with elements that putatively have no spatial dimensions—pure thoughts—such experimentation was not possible. A second problem was that psychology would have to consider the instrument of knowing—the self; but it is not possible for the self to examine its own workings, let alone to do so in a disinterested way. There was, in addition, the problem of the level of abstraction. To conduct scientific research, one has to be able to strip away accidental factors so as to focus on the variables crucial to a theory—a radical manipulation of the subject matter difficult, if not impossible, to bring to bear on complex and all-pervasive human interaction.

Kant's most severe objections derived from his overall conception of the domain of knowledge. In his "foundational" view, it was the province of philosophy to lay out the nature of thinking—to chart the relations among the various sciences and to designate their foundations and limitations; psychology was seen as a second-rate poacher upon such a program. Psychology should be content to look at the social and historical contexts in which thinking occurs but should not attempt to crack the nature of thought itself.

Such was the authority of Kant—and the surface persuasiveness of his arguments—that many scholars of his time shied away from the empirical investigation of psychological issues. Fortunately, however, at least some individuals were spurred by Kant's skepticism to seek a more positive role for psychology. According to the historian of psychology, David Leary (1978), a trio of German thinkers—Jakob Friedrich Fries, Johann Friedrich Herbart, and Friedrich Eduard Beneke—directed their energies, in the early part of the nineteenth century, to the conceptualization of a scientific psychology. Each of these scholars believed that mental processes could be measured by experiment and that studies could be carried out that actually provided information on the operations of the mind. In particular, Herbart claimed that ideas exhibit the variables of time, intensity, and quality, and that one should be able to measure quantitatively each of these aspects of ideation and even to write equations mapping their relations one onto another. While the work of Herbart and his colleagues was basically restricted to armchair speculation, these scholars kept alive the possibility of a scientific psychology during an era where Kant's strictures remained a formidable obstacle.

By the middle of the nineteenth century, scientists came to have fewer reservations about empirical investigations bearing directly on psychological issues. Less under the shadow of Kant and other philosophers, more willing to carry out experiments and simply see what would turn up, these scholars directly anticipated the founding of scientific psychology toward the end of the century and set up ripples that can still be detected in the laboratories of today. Moreover, in each case, they made specific contributions that remain pertinent to psychological discussions.

Laying the Groundwork: Helmholtz, Fechner, Donders, and Brentano

Of the many empirically oriented researchers who displayed an interest in psychological issues, probably the most outstanding was the German physicist and physiologist Hermann von Helmholtz. Helmholtz wanted to show that much of what Kant had speculated about could be subjected to empirical study. Skeptical of various competing claims about the astounding speed of thought, Helmholtz actually undertook to measure the length of time it takes to transmit impulses along a nerve. Using an ingenious instrument, adapted from his laboratory galvanometer, Helmholtz was able to measure the time that it took for a nerve impulse to pass through the severed leg of a frog. He then succeeded in adapting the method for human subjects, who were asked to respond by pushing a button whenever a stimulus was applied to their legs. This allowed him to ascertain the speed of the impulse in human sensory nerves: it turned out to be between 165 and 330 feet per second (Fancher 1979, pp. 100–101). Human behavioral reactions could be measured, after all.

Having successfully challenged the belief that thought is essentially instantaneous or inherently unmeasurable, Helmholtz went on to call into question Kant's beliefs in innate ideas of space. According to Helmholtz's rival position, individuals build up knowledge of space, just as they construct the facts of their physical world. By having subjects wear prisms which distorted their world, Helmholtz showed that individuals could readily adjust or adapt to these distortions and were soon seeing the world again in essentially undistorted fashion. In a complementary investigation, he studied individuals who had once been blind but could now see, and documented the considerable time that elapsed before they learned to perceive the world of objects in the manner of the sighted.

From such demonstrations, Helmholtz developed the still-influential idea of *unconscious inference:* rather than simply reading off percepts from the world of external stimulation, we unconsciously draw on our past knowledge in order to effect accurate interpretations of what we perceive. The experience of one's past perception is unconsciously added to one's present reaction to a stimulus—as happens when, defying the evidence of the senses, one succumbs to an optical illusion. Helmholtz used the word *inference* deliberately. He believed that the visual system was implicitly reasoning about its experiences: for example, in order to figure out the actual sizes of objects, the visual system had to make inferences based on the images formed on an individual's retina. Unlike syllogistic inferences, of course, these processes occurred without conscious awareness.

In forging ahead with his research, and in introducing certain conceptual distinctions, Helmholtz made three major contributions. First of all, he indicated that Kant's philosophical dicta did not have absolute validity: it was indeed possible to illuminate aspects of human mental functioning in an empirical fashion. Second, Helmholtz cleared places for molecular forms of analysis (the speed of an impulse traveling along a nerve fiber) as well as molar investigations (the ways in which complex spatial arrays are seen under both normal and distorted conditions). Finally, by stressing the perceiving subject's contribution to perception, Helmholtz became an early contributor to the ideology of cognitive science.

It now became possible for scientists of a less overpowering status to contribute to the incipient science of psychology. The pioneering psycho-physicist Gustav Fechner (1912) was able to show that, within limits, the intensity of a perceived sensation varies as a logarithmic function of objective features of the stimulus. Thus it seemed that the most personal aspects of a psychological experience—how loud a sound seems, how bright a light appears, how sweet an object tastes—could bear a quantitative relation to a measurable characteristic of an object in the world.

Building on Helmholtz's documentation of the speed of neural events, F. C. Donders proposed in 1868 that one could also measure the time that it takes for higher mental operations to be carried out. For instance, in order to measure how long it takes to effect discrimination between two stimuli, one would subtract the time that it takes to detect a single event in isolation from the time it takes to respond to only a single event when two events are presented. By subtracting the time needed to detect a single event in isolation from the time needed to respond when given two stimuli, one could infer the exact time required for the *operation of discrimination*. Like Fechner, Donders worked with relatively molecular materials: but, in principle, their methods could be applied to molar tasks.

While Helmholtz, Fechner, and Donders were all concerned to demonstrate that psychological issues could yield quantitative results in the experimental laboratory, a priest-philosopher named Franz Brentano was approaching questions of psychology from a different standpoint. Brentano's writing was directed against the molecular notion that one can break psychology down into elements and examine the elements of experiences or consciousness in isolation, as well as the notion that one can conceive of thought processes or consciousness in a purely mechanistic way. For Brentano, psychology starts with the mind—an active, creative entity which has intentions, for it implies and demands an object. The true subject matter of psychology is the mental act—such as judging, sensing, imagining, or hearing, each of which reflects a sense of direction and purpose. One cannot simply *see*; one must see *something*; and the *act* of seeing something is psychological or mental.

Given this viewpoint, the task of empirical psychology is to study the mind of the agent at work, dealing with objects, purposes, and goals. Brentano stressed the phenomenological aspects of the psychological endeavor: one cannot conceive of thoughts and judgment, let alone study them, except by taking into account one's inner phenomenal experience. And this can be accessed not by prompted introspection—for one cannot observe at the same time that one experiences—but rather by simple phenomenal experience of one's inner mental life (Brentano 1874).

The words of Brentano would be stilled temporarily during the first years of the discipline of psychology, when an obsession with studying the elements of sensations, and the basic constituent mental states, came to the fore. The laboratories of Leipzig had little place for such high-flown sentiments as act, purpose, intention, and phenomenal experience. Yet the kinds of top-down or molar concern that Brentano had raised could not forever be ignored. They were to re-emerge, in different forms, in the rebellion in Würzburg, in the platform of the Gestalt psychologist, and, once again, in the view of the computer as an agent with plans, intentions, and goals. In not a few ways, Brentano has had profound influence on the course of psychology and has affected many experimenters who have never heard his name.

Wundt's Program

In a sense, psychology was well under way by the latter part of the nineteenth century. With the pioneering work of Helmholtz, and the considerable efforts by Donders, Fechner, and Brentano, who devoted themselves chiefly to psychological matters, there was already a minor industry of psychological thinking and research. And yet, as I shall note repeatedly in this history, the flowering of a discipline depends heavily upon the founding of institutions and organizations. The efforts of the earlier nineteenth-century pioneers might never have coalesced and become cumulative had it not been for Wilhelm Wundt, who took it upon himself in the latter part of the century to establish psychology as a separate experimental discipline. More than any other individual—perhaps than any collection of individuals—Wundt is responsible for the emergence of psychology as a separate scientific discipline with its own methods, programs, and institutions. Psychology has grown from its original establishment in a single university—Leipzig in 1879—to a field with representatives in virtually every institution of higher learning. Its spectacular success can be attributed in no small measure to the labors—if not always to the ideas—of Wundt (Boring 1950; Fancher 1979; Watson 1979).

According to Wundt, physics studies the objects of the external world: while this investigation is necessarily mediated by experience, physics is still not the study of experience itself. Psychology, in contrast, is the study of conscious experience as experience. It must be approached through internal observation, through introspection. While all individuals have such experiences, not all are necessarily qualified as *expert* witnesses on the nature of their experience. Thus Wundt embraced the method of *introspection*—a method whereby one attends carefully to one's own sensations and reports them as objectively as possible. Such objectivity here means that one describes the sensations felt, rather than the stimulus giving rise to them; and that one reports thoughts (or images) without reference to their meaning or context of presentation. Wundt's program hinged on the possibility of introspecting in this fashion.

Just as it was important to separate psychology from physics, it was also important to effect its divorce from physiology. Physiology has as its special province the study of mental processes that are not conscious—not susceptible to introspective examination—while psychology appropriates those higher mental processes that could be subjected to personal examination. Physiology explains how we have sensations, but psychology covers the description and analysis of sensory experience. Recognizing that some aspects of human experience prove less hospitable to examination in terms of introspection, Wundt made a further discrimination within psychology between those individual experiences that are susceptible to introspection and those aspects of human experience that are by their nature social or communal. In Wundt's division of labor, it fell to ethnic or folk psychologists to study these complex and large-scale human activities, such as customs, rituals, and, perhaps, certain features of language and thought. Ultimately, he contributed ten volumes to this effort at constructing folk psychology.

As George Miller has put it, Wundt looked at the agenda of British empirical psychology with an eye of a man trained in the traditions of German physiology (Johnson-Laird and Wason 1977, p. 2). Like Helmholtz and Donders, Wundt devised simple tasks—but asked subjects to introspect about them during the course of their participation. In one sample task, subjects were asked to press a button whenever they heard a tone. On some trials, the subjects' attention was directed to the tone; while on others, their attention was directed to the movement of their fingers on the button. It turned out that reaction times were *longer* when a subject had to attend to the sound, shorter when one attended to the movement. Wundt inferred that this greater time was due to *apperception*—the process of making one's experience clear in one's consciousness. Apparently, when one is concentrating on a stimulus, the stimulus first has to be perceived and then apperceived, or consciously interpreted, in the light of the response associated with it. Even further complications resulted when several different stimuli were presented, only one of which was targeted for response. This process took even longer, because, according to Wundt, "cognition" has to occur: the stimulus has not only to be perceived and apperceived but also differentiated from other stimuli that are not to elicit responses (Fancher 1979, p. 139).

Wundt revealed his ties to the British philosophical tradition in the way in which he made sense of such findings. He came to think of experience as composed of simple basic elements—raw sensory content devoid of any meaning; and all conscious thoughts were accordingly assumed to be *combinations* of these sensations which can be analyzed in terms of quality, mode, duration, intensity, and the like. Elements can be fused into complexes in any number of ways, so that one element arouses several others. In the experiment just described, the subject would reveal through introspection his awareness of the impact of tones, the feelings of pressing the button, and any connections perceived between these sensations. The various images passing through the subject's consciousness would be crucial contributors to the subsequent analysis. Wundt's interest lay in identifying the various laws of association occurring during an experimental subject's experience; he sought to understand how the laws came to unfold while individuals were generating ideas, and how they attained different degrees of clarity.

It is important to stress that Wundt was neither a simple-minded atomist nor a person ignorant of the effects of context or cultural influences. Indeed, in many studies, he paid attention to molar issues and top-down effects. In his writings on language, for example, he anticipated some of the ideas of modern psycholinguistics—such as the role of prior intentions in governing speech output and the effects of syntactic structure on the production of messages. Still, a scientist must be judged by the major thrust of his work; and, in the aggregate, Wundt's psychology emerges as a kind of mental chemistry, focused principally on the discovery of the pure elements of thought, through whose combination complexes of mental activity come to be formed.

This, then, in outline, was Wundt's program. I must stress that this program was not simply enunciated once and then forgotten. Rather, Wundt worked tirelessly for fifty years to promulgate it, to train individuals in its practice, and to make sure that there existed the appropriate laboratories, handbooks, journals, and conferences through which to put it into practice. Wundt trained many, if not most, of the leading researchers around the turn of the century. He set a high standard for the conduct of experiments, insisting on careful selection and training of subjects, on the administration of relevant controls, and on the replication of experiments to make sure that findings were not accidental. He himself systematized findings in encyclopedias, handbooks, and textbooks, revising them with awe-inspiring regularity. Indeed, his literary output in psychology stretching over a period of sixty-three years has never been equaled.

Innovative Methods: Hermann Ebbinghaus

Everyone marveled at Wundt's scholarly productivity, but not all embraced his view of psychology. Some of his colleagues—for example,

Hermann Ebbinghaus (1913)—simply went their own way. Inspired with the fertile idea of ferreting out principles of memory through the use of materials that could not be contaminated by earlier experiences and associations, Ebbinghaus generated over two thousand nonsense syllables and measured his own skill at learning sets of them. Practicing them either at one sitting or over a series of sessions, Ebbinghaus probed the effects of drill time between presentations, backward and forward interference, and other "independent variables." His stimuli were no more meaningful than Wundt's; but, by breaking away from introspection as the sole source of information, and by instructing novel methods of statistical analysis, Ebbinghaus succeeded in reorienting psychology in a very productive manner. It was one's actual skill at a task—not one's introspections about what one senses or feels—that became the object of study and measure. Ebbinghaus's methods have exerted far more of an impact on experimental psychology than has Wundt's introspective tack. Yet, influential as this work has been, the question must be raised whether the immaculate, content- and context-free approach of Ebbinghaus ultimately accomplished more harm than good; for we now know that methods used to remember ordinary events differ in important particulars from methods used to remember meaningless arrangements of letters or organized material.

The Early Twentieth Century

The Attack on the Wundtians

For a while Wilhelm Wundt and his followers held sway over the growing band of psychological researchers. But within two decades, the program of systematic introspection underwent severe attacks from some one-time students of the master of Leipzig. Around 1900, there began in Germany a modern-day incarnation of the debate between Locke—who believed in abstract ideas, devoid of imagery—and Berkeley who, skeptical of the existence of abstract ideas, believed only in the utility of specific imagery. The renegade, Lockean view was defended by a group of psychologists housed in the small city of Würzburg, and ultimately known to historians of psychology as the "Würzburg school." Headed by Oswald Külpe, a psychologist influenced by Franz Brentano, this school became embroiled with Wundt and his devoted American follower Edward Bradford Titchener in a notorious controversy over "imageless thought." In its specific form, this controversy simply re-created a classic empiricist debate.

But in its more general form, Würzburg had launched a severe critique of the entire manner in which Leipzig went about its investigations and drew its conclusions.

The story begins innocently enough in 1901, when the young psychologist Karl Marbe asked his subjects to compare weights with one another—a familiar procedure, dating back to Fechner's first reveries. Marbe found that, in judging weights, subjects reported no imaginal concepts as the basis of judgment: in other words, no images flitted through their introspecting minds. Instead, counter to the Wundtian expectation, subjects reported that various vague attitudes passed through consciousness—attitudes like hesitation, doubt, waiting for an answer, feeling that the answer had arrived. Marbe was forced to conclude, "The present data are quite sufficient to draw the conclusion that no psychological conditions of judgments exist. . . . Even . . . the observers concerned . . . were extremely surprised to note the paucity of experiences that were connected with the judgmental process" (Mandler and Mandler 1964, p. 143).

That some subjects failed to report imagery while rendering a judgment may hardly seem like headline news in the scientific community, but it ran against the widespread dictum that all thought features imagery accessible to consciousness. Then, in the following years, a whole raft of studies emanating from Würzburg repeated and elaborated upon this initial negative report (see Boring 1950; Humphrey 1951; Mandler and Mandler 1964). There was Henry Watt who reported that the conscious task (or *Aufgabe*) that a subject was posed had an important effect on the kinds of associations one made. There was Narziss Ach who reported the operation of a *determining tendency:* the task had the effect of orchestrating various associations and skills into a purposeful orderly sequence—a kind of "directing" will—which led smoothly to its final execution. There was August Messer who saw consciousness as the visible portion of an iceberg, with most thought processes occurring beneath the surface, and with conscious processes themselves exhibiting varying degrees of clarity. And there was Karl Bühler, one of the seminal figures of psychology, who dismissed the simple problems posed by the Leipzigers and posed truly complex tasks to his subjects—for example, the discussion of philosophical problems. Like his Würzburg colleagues, Bühler uncovered peculiar varieties of consciousness like doubt, astonishment, and even consciousness of consciousness.

Oswald Külpe sought to put these different demonstrations together. In a critique of the Wundt-Leipzig program, he pointed out that it was not enough merely to pose problems to individuals and let them introspect as they wished. It was necessary to pose problems making different kinds of demand and to monitor their varying effects. One could not simply assume that all important aspects of mental processes are conscious, that images always guide thinking, and that mental contents (like sensations) are necessarily the constituent elements of thought. There was a more positive aspect to the critique as well. Thanks to the work of Külpe and his associates, mental acts like attending, recognizing, willing, comparing, and differentiating came to constitute a proper sphere of psychology. While, to be sure, these acts lack vivid perceptual characteristics of sensations, images, and feelings, they are no less important on that account. Most generally, there was an increased willingness to recognize top-down "structuring tendencies" in the solution of these problems and to use problems that truly engaged a subject's ratiocinative capacities. Here is a harbinger of the molar concerns of many contemporary cognitive scientists.

The Wundtians did not accept such criticism without a rejoinder. Points were scored on both sides—Wundt's more methodological, Würzburg's (to my mind) more substantive; but in the end, this disagreement had a radical consequence. It called into question the merits of *any* psychology that relies heavily on introspection, and particularly on the introspections of trained subjects, an uncomfortably high proportion of whom are drawn from the ranks of the experimenters themselves. As vast an enterprise as a new science could not countenance so vague and subjective a set of basic procedures.

Functionalism: William James

The programs of Wundt and the Leipzig school at first had a significant impact on the other side of the Atlantic. Most young American scholars interested in psychology served an apprenticeship in Wundt's laboratory; and some, like the transplanted Englishman Edward Titchener, became lifelong adherents to the introspectionist program. But the dean of American psychologists of the period, William James, soon became disenchanted with Wundt. He saw Wundt as a classic German professor, who had to have an opinion on every issue, but who, in his dogged pursuit of the elements of thought, missed many of the most exciting and important issues in psychology. In his landmark textbook, James wrote, with ill-conceived contempt, that Wundt's experimental psychology "could hardly have arisen in a country whose natives could be *bored*. . . . There is little of the grand style about these new prism, pendulum, and chronograph-philosophers. They mean business not chivalry" (James 1890, vol. I, p. 193).

There was plenty of style in William James's writings. Indeed, juxtaposed to the involuted sentences and turgid experimental details of the Leipzig-Würzburg schools, his words are like a gust of fresh air. James took his methods where he found them and had little interest in starting a program or launching an institution. Instead, he was fascinated by the questions of psychology, as encountered in daily life, and sought illumination from literature and history as well as from experimental science. He allowed his lively imagination to frolic over the full playing field of psychological phenomena—from brain processes to the will, from the sensory organs to the study of attention, from an investigation of habit to the description of the momentary stream of consciousness. In his *Principles of Psychology,* he took a characteristically American pragmatic approach, which he himself was to propound in philosophical writings. He suggested that psychological mechanisms exist because they are useful and help individuals to survive and carry out important activities of living. As he declared, "Our various ways of feeling and thinking have grown to be what they are because of their utility in shaping our reactions to the outer world." Without hesitation, he assumed *purpose* to be the mark of mentality —Romeo wants Juliet as filings want a magnet, he asserted. "The pursuance of future ends and the choice of means for their attainment are thus the mark and criterion of the presence of mentality in a phenomenon" (quoted in Herrnstein and Boring 1965, p. 610).

The mood permeating James's writings may well have had more of an effect on subsequent generations of American psychologists than did any of his particular claims. For he was signaling an impatience with the whole tone of German psychology, with its inconclusive introspection. Instead of trying to figure out the contents of mental life, and how they were structured, James directed attention to the various functions carried out by mental activity—to the active exploring nature of mind in the positing of problems and the attainment of goals, and to the perennial dialectic between means and ends. James stood at the vanguard of a new American movement which opposed Wundt-Titchener structuralism—a movement that came to be known, appropriately enough, as "functionalism."* As against the structuralist attempt to ferret out the elementary components of experience, the functionalist psychologist sought to investigate the operations of mental activities under actual life conditions.

According to functionalist precepts, it is important to focus on functions or dispositions, like perceiving or recalling or thinking. A function persists and recurs, while the contents of consciousness and specific response patterns occur but once. Science ought to be based on these more enduring and meaningful series of actions.

Functionalism undeniably provided a needed shift in emphasis, and a counterweight to the search for ultimate units of consciousness. But just a few short years after the canons of functionalism had been put forth by

---

*Not to be conflated with the philosophical brand of functionalism described in chapter 4.

William James (and also by James Angell and John Dewey), a far more radical shift was to occur in American psychology. This shift to behaviorism may initially have been necessary in order to put firmly to rest the excesses of structuralism and introspection, whether in their Leipzig or their Würzburg guise. Yet, from the point of view of a history of cognitive science, it is difficult to think of this phase as other than primarily negative and regressive.

The Behaviorist Revolution

In 1913, John B. Watson, scarcely out of graduate school but already a force in American psychology, launched the behaviorist revolution. Watson asserted that the proper subject for psychology was not the operation of the mind but rather the examination of objective, observable behavior. Building on the physiological studies of the operation of the reflex arc, Watson proposed that all concerns of psychology could be explained through understanding the reflexes occurring in the upper portions of the nervous system. This was molecular and bottom-up psychology, pure and simple. As he declared:

> Psychology as the behaviorist views it is a purely objective natural science. Its theoretical goal is the prediction and control of behavior. Introspection forms no essential part of its method nor is the scientific value of its data dependent upon the readiness with which they lend themselves to interpretation in terms of consciousness. The behaviorist, in his efforts to get a unitary scheme of animal response, recognizes no dividing line between man and brute. The behavior of man, with all its refinement and complexity, forms only a part of the behaviorist's total scheme of investigation. (Quoted in Fancher 1979, p. 319)

Watson's dramatic call had far-reaching consequences. He was rejecting much of the program and nearly all of the method of traditional psychology. No more felt sensations or intentions: henceforth, only observation of overt *behavior* was relevant. Description and explanation of states and contents of consciousness were to be replaced by the prediction, and eventually the control, of behavior. Psychology would no longer care about what is putatively on a person's mind because all mentalistic terms themselves were hereby expelled from the psychologist's vocabulary.

It would be difficult to overestimate the extent to which Watson's program came to dominate American psychology and even to exert influence abroad. The old psychology might have collapsed of its own weight, but this disintegration was certainly abetted by Watson's rhetorical vigor and by the efficacy of his demonstrations. On his practically oriented account, it was possible to condition organisms, including humans, to do almost anything one wanted—for example, to fear an object—just by arranging the environment in a certain way. Indeed, he did just this in his famous study of baby Albert, whom he conditioned to fear a white rat (Watson and Rayner 1920).

Such dramatic demonstrations of what psychology could do appeared even more convincing when set alongside the inconclusive debates of the German school. A whole generation of scientists—the leading psychologists of the next generation—were trained in the orbit of Watson; and investigators like Clark Hull, B. F. Skinner, Kenneth Spence, and E. L. Thorndike helped to ensure that the psychology of America between 1920 and 1950 was irremediably behaviorist. Child care, treatment of prisoners, teaching of children, and many other societal activities came to be dominated by behaviorist rhetoric and behaviorist practices. No less an authority than the *New York Times* declared in 1942 that behaviorism marked "a new epoch in the intellectual history of man" (Fancher 1979, p. 322).

Even members of the American psychological community who had fundamental doubts about Watson's program—scholars like Edward C. Tolman at Berkeley and Watson's one-time student Karl Lashley at Harvard—worked primarily with animals and adhered rigidly to the experimental precepts of the behaviorists. To be sure, Lashley ultimately voiced his qualms: at the Hixon Symposium, he called attention to behavior that could not be explained in terms of stimulus-and-response links. For his part, Tolman (1932) found it impossible to explain the ability of animals to find a reward simply through invoking a memorized sequence of actions. Inasmuch as the animals seemed to know where to go, even when the orientation or the cues of a maze had been altered, Tolman found it necessary to posit "cognitive maps" which guide the behavior of animals engaged in problem solving. Moreover, in describing the activities of animals, he found it necessary to invoke an intentionalistic vocabulary, using terms like "expectancies," "purpose," and "meanings." Correlatively, he took the then-daring step of introducing "intervening variables" between stimulus and response. And yet, despite such heterodoxies, these influential scholars remained respectful of the behaviorist canons and, in fact, continued to speak of themselves as behaviorists, if of a somewhat renegade stripe.

As I noted in chapter 2, far too much of consequence in human behavior was denied by the behaviorist approach. By the middle 1950s, its program had begun to come apart; and today the theoretical claims of behaviorism (though not its various applied achievements) are largely of historical interest. The cognitive revolution spawned by psychologists like Miller and Bruner has carried the day, just as surely as the behaviorist revolution did half a century ago. Indeed, somewhat paradoxically, cognitivism has prevailed for some of the reasons behind behaviorism's original success: an exciting and refreshing new approach was seen as supplanting a time-worn tack mired in questions of little interest to anyone outside the field. But despite behaviorism's relatively rapid decline, only a few lines of work in psychology fall largely outside the behaviorist camp. Among these, I shall focus on the most direct link between the cognitively oriented psychology of 1900 and that of today—the school of Gestalt psychology.

Gestalt Psychology: A View from Above

Origins

Gestalt psychology can be introduced as a school rooted in several dramatic demonstrations, which make a vivid point and thereby inspire a certain way of thinking about mental phenomena. The initial demonstration of Gestalt phenomena was made in 1890 by Christoph von Ehrenfels, an Austrian student of Brentano's. Ehrenfels's particular interest was the perception of melody. He argued that the perceptual "form quality" involved in a melody cannot be properly viewed as simply the sum of its several tonal elements: indeed, it is an overall quality, a Gestalt, that transcends its particular elements. As he pointed out, one could take the same set of elements, or tones, and produce an entirely different melody. Conversely, one could select an entirely different set of tones—for instance, those in another key—and produce a figure that would be apprehended as the "same melody" as the original one.

Ehrenfels is generally regarded as a predecessor, rather than the actual founder, of the Gestalt movement. That honor belongs to Max Wertheimer, who in 1912 published a paper on the visual perception of movement. Working with two young assistants, Wolfgang Köhler and Kurt Koffka, Wertheimer carried out a set of studies on apparent motion, or the "Phi" phenomenon—roughly, the perceptual experience of movement which arises when a set of lights or forms appears one right after another (as in neon billboards or, for that matter, motion pictures). Wertheimer did not discover apparent motion—the phenomenon had been recognized for some time; but he showed that the standard psychological account of this phenomenon was untenable.

In particular, Wertheimer ruled out the common hypothesis of the perception of movement being due to eye movements: he showed that movement is perceived even if the interval is too brief to permit a movement and even if the subject maintains a rigid fixation. Wertheimer also made a convincing case that perception of movement is not a sum or an association of different elementary sensations: his subjects—who were simply asked to report, and not to analyze, what they saw—all agreed that they apprehended a movement directly, rather than its being a movement of something, or of something from one place to another. This finding suggested the need for a new way of thinking about such perceptual phenomena.

Wertheimer and his colleagues attributed perceptual experiences like apparent motion to the way in which the brain organizes perceptual input. In their view, a kind of short circuit occurs in the "physiological fields" of the brain. Hence, there was no need to posit a construction from single elements: the patterns of excitation in the brain ensure that movement can be perceived directly.

The Gestalt psychologists examined a whole raft of "form qualities," whose phenomenal appearance could be explained in terms of analogous brain processes, and put forth laws purporting to explain how perception is organized. For instance, they showed that objects that are close together tend to be grouped together (the law of proximity); the more symmetrical a closed region, the more it tends to be seen as a figure (the law of symmetry); and the arrangement of figure and ground seen is the one featuring the fewest changes or interruption in straight or smoothly curved lines (the law of good continuation) (Hochberg 1978). Though usually referring initially to visual demonstrations, versions of these laws also applied to auditory sequences—for example, rhythmic patterns. Pervading their powerful demonstration was the Gestalt psychologists' doctrinaire opposition to atomistic, bottom-up, or purely molecular analysis; they favored a view of perceptual organization in which the way the parts are seen is determined by the configuration of the whole, rather than vice versa.

Köhler's Comprehensive Researches

Perhaps because Gestalt laws could be applied readily to the range of perceptual phenomena with which psychologists were already familiar— such as various illusions and constancies—the Gestalt movement rapidly gained in popularity and influence, particularly in Continental Europe. But the Gestalt psychologists were not content to rest on their perceptual laurels. When Wolfgang Köhler found himself stranded on Tenerife (off North Africa) during the First World War, he undertook a landmark set of investigations with chimpanzees. Köhler's interest centered on the way these apes tackled problems whose solution required some changing or "restructuring" of the elements in a situation. Thus, in order to fetch a banana that was out of reach, an ape would have to move a chair from one site to another, join two sticks together, or engage in some other reorganization of the situation that it beheld. Köhler (1925) found standard trial-and-error accounts inadequate to account for the apes' behavior. Instead, what seemed to happen was far more of a humanlike thought process, where the ape would stop, reflect, and then, as if struck with a sudden flash of insight, reach for the chair or the rope that provided the solution. According to Köhler's analysis, the chimpanzee "restructured" the field that had been presented to it; and did so courtesy of a moment of insight —what the Würzburg school had termed an "A-ha experience."

Köhler also distinguished between bright and stupid apes. While a bright ape would regularly exhibit these moments of insight, the dull ape worked in quite a different fashion. Even when it saw the correct behavior modeled, the ape would not be able to gain the treasure. Instead, in piecemeal fashion, the ape would imitate the component actions without ever apparently appreciating how to link them in order to secure a reward.

According to Gestalt psychology, the most primitive forms of learning can be explained in terms of mere repetition or piecemeal associations. In contrast, what characterizes higher learning or "intelligent" processes, wherever found, is the capacity to grasp the basic fundamental relations in a situation. These are the criteria of insight: "the appearance of a complete solution with reference to the whole layout of the field" (Mandler and Mandler 1964, p. 248).

Other scholars in the Gestalt tradition extended this line of study to problem solving in human beings. Wertheimer (1945) himself examined the solution of geometry problems, arithmetic puzzles, and even the steps through which Einstein allegedly passed in arriving at his theory of relativity. Karl Duncker (1945) focused on the solution of engineering problems —for example, the way in which one can direct X rays to kill a tumor without destroying an unnecessary portion of intervening tissues. Abraham Luchins (1942) examined the phenomenon of functional fixedness: the way that the customary uses to which a material are put can inhibit an individual (ape or professor) from perceiving how to use that same implement in a novel way in order to solve a problem.

Note that the kinds of molar problem posed stood in sharp contrast to those molecular tasks typically posed by the early German structuralists and the American behaviorists. These molar problems are somewhat closer to those posed by the Würzburgers but unencumbered by the weight of introspections and elaborate interpretive terminology, and are forerunners of problems favored today by many researchers in artificial intelligence. The modes of explanation are also of a different order. Wertheimer and the other Gestaltists proposed a far more active, strategic approach to problems, in terms of recognition of structural characteristics: how these structures are initially realized; which gaps are sensed; which elements can be fitted with one another or rearranged; which dynamic operations can then be brought to bear to fill the gaps, leading from "an unclear inadequate relation to a clear transparent, direct confrontation—straight from the heart of the thinker to the heart of his object, of his problem," as Wertheimer rather grandly put it (1945, p. 191).

The Gestaltist saw the best thinking as productive and novel rather than as reproductive. There are regular perceptual reorganizations as one confronts a problem; and sooner or later, a pivotal reorganization is accompanied by insight as elements critical to a solution come to the fore. There was a Kantian undergirding to the belief that the mind is so constructed that certain logical relations are imposed upon the world, rather than being "read off" of one's experience of the world.

In the view of most contemporary observers, the particular theoretical program of Gestalt psychology was not well founded. Principles of perception such as *proximity* and *symmetry* do provide a rough-and-ready guide to how information is organized, but there are too many exceptions or indeterminate cases; speculations about the operation of the brain, and its effects upon phenomenal perception, have been undermined by neurological findings; the major explanatory concepts are too vague to be operationalized. As psychologist Ulric Neisser concludes, in a sympathetic review of Gestalt psychology:

> The gestalt concept of organization plays almost no role in cognitive psychology today. It ran aground on the emerging facts of neuropsychology (the nervous system turned out to be more elementistic than Köhler believed) and it was overtaken by mechanistic computer models that gave plausible alternative accounts of the same facts. . . . The currently popular explanations of motion phenomena in terms of eye movements and specific motion detectors are about as far from the spirit of Gestalt psychology as one could get. (1980, p. 4)

Yet Neisser concludes with a more positive assessment: "Whatever our differences, all of us are still working on the problem Wertheimer set: to see the world 'from above,' as Köhler put it, instead of from below. Because, indeed, the view is better from there" (p. 6). Here is a suggestion that the top-down approach may have time on its side.

Frederic Bartlett's Schematic Approach

As the Gestaltists were sustaining a concern with large-scale problems, holistic methods of solution, and the constructive aspects of thinking, a solitary psychologist working in Britain was also keeping the cognitive faith. In his own explorations of memory, Frederic Bartlett had sought to use, but had found inadequate, the strict experimental methods pioneered by Ebbinghaus. They seemed to miss much of what was central in remembering meaningful content, and Bartlett came to the conclusion that it is not possible to employ totally arbitrary materials and still capture the salient features of memory on the wing. A fundamentally different approach was wanted.

Bartlett had vague intimations that memory was more of a social or cultural phenomenon, and that the "set" accompanying a stimulating experience has a crucial effect on what one remembers and how well one remembers it. Yet, according to his own recollections, Bartlett was stymied for an experimental approach until he had a conversation with his friend Norbert Wiener. In an important moment in the intellectual history of cognitive psychology, Wiener gave Bartlett a crucial idea, as the latter recalls:

> I was fascinated by the variety of interpretations which different people then achieved. . . . One day, when I had been talking about my experiments, and the use I was making of sequences in a study of conventionalization regarded as a process more or less continuous in time, [Wiener] said: "Couldn't you do something with 'Russian Scandal'* as we used to call it?" That was what led to the method which I later called "The Method of Serial Reproduction," one which, in varied form, was to contribute much to the final working out of my experiments. (1958, pp. 139, 144)

In the set of studies that Bartlett eventually launched, subjects heard exotic stories and then were asked to recall them at various subsequent intervals. (In variations of the procedure, they were shown geometrical figures or exposed to logical arguments and asked to retain them for later "debriefing.") Bartlett (1932) found that individuals were not able to recall such input accurately and, more revealing, that the inaccuracies exhibited systematic patterns. Take, for instance, "The War of the Ghosts," an Indian folk tale which (to a modern Western ear) seems to be filled with strange gaps and bizarre causal sequences. Subjects would regularly supply their own causal links, drop difficult-to-assimilate information, and revise the plot until it had come to resemble that of a standard Western tale. Moreover, on subsequent recall, these alterations would come increasingly to the fore until the story reached a relatively stable form—one far closer to a prototypical Western story than to the folk tale originally presented.

Drawing on a term that had been used (in a somewhat different

---

*"Russian Scandal" is a parlor game in which players pass a message from one to another and then observe how it has been transformed.

sense) by Kant and introduced into the psychology of the period by the British neurologist Henry Head, Bartlett tried to make sense of his findings in terms of the notion of *schemas* (sometimes called "schemata"). Bartlett claimed that the typical memory system used by humans involves the formation of abstract cognitive structures, or schemas. These schemas arise from prior encounters with the environment, as a result of which certain kinds of information have come to be organized in specified ways. Thus, in listening to "The War of the Ghosts," subjects would draw on their schemas for dealing with daily experience, in general, and for dealing with adventure or ghost stories, in particular. To make sense of this story of a war party proceeding on a canoe in order to kill people, the listeners would use experiences of their own—say, a canoe trip at night on a river—as well as structured information from earlier stories—a typical adventure story involving primitive folks and ghosts. To the extent that the information in Bartlett's story was consistent with these previously constructed schemas, recall would be aided and might turn out quite accurate. On the other hand, divergences between the prior schemas and the details of the present story would cause systematic distortions in the initial recollection of the story and probably introduce even further deviations in subsequent retellings.

Speaking more generally (and no doubt with the Ebbinghaus nonsense-syllable tradition in mind), Bartlett declared:

> Remembering is not the re-excitation of innumerable fixed, lifeless, and fragmentary traces. It is an imaginative reconstruction, or construction, built out of the relation of our attitude towards a whole active mass of past experience. . . . It is thus hardly ever really exact, even the most rudimentary cases of rote recapitulation, and it is not at all important that it should be so. The attitude is literally an effect of the organism's capacity to turn round up upon its own "schemata" and is directly a function of consciousness. (1932, p. 213)

Bartlett did more than keep alive a model for molar studies; he directly anticipated the self-reflective system that cognitive scientists like George Miller view as central to human cognition.

Jean Piaget's Developmental Concerns

Jean Piaget got his start in psychology in a most unusual way. Trained as a biologist, with a particular interest in mollusks, he had taken a job as a tester in the laboratory of Théodore Simon, a former colleague of Alfred Binet, who had invented the IQ test. Never one to accept a task as given, Piaget became interested in the kinds of *errors* children make on intelligence test items. Since Piaget's lifetime goal was to found an epistemology on biological principles, he decided to take a brief detour to study the development of thought in children. As he liked to say, this detour lasted a lifetime.

In the course of a sixty-year career, rivaling Wundt's in productivity and exceeding Wundt's in its influence upon subsequent research, Piaget provided portraits of the developmental course of children's thought, in a variety of domains (see Piaget 1970 for an overview). Nearly always, his work exhibited two hallmarks. On the one hand, conforming closely to my definition of a cognitive scientist, Piaget took as his research agenda the great issues of Western epistemology: the nature of time, space, causality, number, morality, and other Kantian categories. He regarded these categories not as givens in the mind but rather as categories to be constructed, Helmholtz style, over the course of a child's development. On the other hand, Piaget insisted on painstakingly careful observations of children: sometimes as they were engaged in free exploration and play; more often as they were involved in experimental tasks he had cleverly contrived.

It is probably as an inventor of brilliant experimental paradigms and riveting demonstrations that Piaget will be best remembered by both the public and the psychological community. His demonstrations have had profound effects on work in cognitive developmental psychology. Who, before Piaget, suspected that infants believe an object remains in its original location even when it has been moved before their eyes to a new one? Who thought that toddlers cannot appreciate how a collection of objects looks from a perspective different from their own? Who anticipated kindergarteners' beliefs that the amount of liquid changes when it has been poured into a vessel of different shape? Even when Piaget's particular demonstrations have not always stood up in just the way he described them, further knowledge has invariably been built upon his pioneering discoveries.

But in Piaget's mind, he was an epistemologist or, as he preferred to say, a genetic epistemologist—not a child psychologist. He sought to unravel the basic laws of thought: informal tasks with young children were simply his preferred means of securing data about the nature of knowledge. His principal contribution to psychology, as he saw it, was an unraveling of the basic structures of thought that characterize children at different ages or stages of development, and his suggestion of the mechanisms that enable a child to effect a transition to higher stages of development—from the sensorimotor stage of infancy to the intuitive stage of early childhood, or from the concrete operational stage of middle childhood to the formal operational stage of adolescence. In positing specific stages, Piaget relied heavily on logical formalisms; in expounding the rules of transformation from one stage to another, he relied on biological mechanisms, of the sort thought to govern change in any organismic system.

Piaget's grandiose claims have proved less robust than his specific experimental demonstrations. The logical formalisms underlying specific stages are invalid, the stages themselves are under attack, and his descriptions of the biological processes of stage transformation have eluded even sympathetic scholars (see Brainerd 1978). Even his impressive program of genetic epistemology has fallen into disuse—apparently too daunting a challenge for most investigators to pick up. But Piaget did more than simply help to keep alive the cognitive flame during the behaviorist hegemony. More than nearly any of his predecessors, he launched an entire field of psychology—that concerned with human cognitive development—and provided the research agenda that keeps it occupied until this day. Even disproofs of his specific claims are a tribute to his general influence.

Thanks to research programs like Piaget's, to lines of study like Bartlett's, and to molar concepts like schemas, operations, and strategies, the concerns of the Gestalt psychologists and of their Würzburg predecessors remained alive in the English-speaking world during the height of the behaviorist era. Among the few other similarly minded scholars were, as I have noted, the comparative psychologists Karl Lashley and Edward Tolman, along with the perceptual psychologist J. J. Gibson, who avoided the vocabulary of stimulus-response psychology and directed his attention instead to the rich lodes of information present in the visual environment (see chapter 10 and references contained therein); and the English social psychologist William McDougall (1961), who insisted on the place of purposeful, goal-striving activity and complex motivations in an otherwise antiteleological environment. But these psychologists, however illustrious, still comprised a small and isolated group during the behaviorist era of the 1930s and 1940s.

The Turn to Cognition

Inspiration from Computers

Defying the warnings of Kant, the first century of psychological research—roughly from 1850 to 1950—demonstrated beyond question that psychological studies were possible. Mental processes could be investigated in the laboratory, many of them could even be timed, and the role of the knowing subject could be adequately controlled. This new psychology took many forms in many places, and there were definite swings of the pendulum between molar and molecular approaches, between an emphasis on the determining role of the environment and one on the contributions of the subject to the task at hand. Excesses of introspectionism at the turn of the century were replaced in turn by excesses of behaviorism in the early part of the twentieth century. In particular, mentalistic constructs were disallowed, and aspects of language and problem solving were either omitted altogether or treated in much attenuated form.

By the late 1940s, at the time of the Hixon Symposium, it was becoming clear that neither the physiological nor the psychological forms of behaviorism were viable. Available as alternative models were Gestalt psychology, as well as the still-isolated efforts to study higher forms of problem solving by Bartlett, Piaget, and a few other investigators. But it took the advent of computers (which could themselves exhibit problem-solving behavior), and the rise of information theory (which provided an objective basis on which to stipulate components of language or concepts) to grant legitimacy to cognitive studies. As Ulric Neisser comments, in a brief sketch of the history of cognitive psychology:

> It was because the activities of the computer itself seemed in some ways akin to cognitive processes. Computers accept information, manipulate symbols, store items in "memory" and retrieve them again, classify inputs, recognize patterns and so on. . . . Indeed the assumptions that underlie most contemporary work on information processing are surprisingly like those of nineteenth century introspective psychology, though without introspection itself. (1976, pp. 5, 7)

As I have already noted, the rise of cognitive psychology in the middle 1950s was a complex matter, reflecting changes in the *Zeitgeist*, new methods in allied sciences, and the enhanced legitimacy of concepts like intention, purpose, goal, and problem solving now that "mere" mechanical gadgets could lay claim to these processes. The particular achievements of innovative psychologists like Donald Broadbent, Jerome Bruner, and George Miller doubtless promoted the turn to cognitive psychology, as did the excitement surrounding the rediscovery of Piaget, Bartlett, and certain works of the Gestalt psychologists. In some cases, high-power informational and mathematical techniques were simply transferred to elementary aspects of learning and problem solving left over from an earlier day; but, at its best, the new technology was solidly concentrated on problems of substance.

Further Stages of Information Processing By and large, the first efforts on both sides of the Atlantic sought to ascertain the details of information-processing. The paradigm pioneered by Donald Broadbent proved an especially popular source for experimentation; and soon experimentalists were finding difficulties of various sorts in his imaginative line of research. Neville Moray (1969) showed that one does obtain information from an unattended message prefaced by one's own name. Anne Treisman (1960, 1964) showed that when identical messages are presented to both ears without the subject being warned, the subject does indeed detect this ploy and so can be said to be detecting informative aspects of the message binaurally after all. This finding led Treisman to argue that the filter serves not as a simple "all or none" switch but rather as a means of attenuating irrelevant or unattended signals: the unattended signal just receives less processing than does the attended signal. Treisman also showed that subjects can shift from one ear to the other if the content of a message itself makes this shift.

In his influential textbook published in the middle 1960s, Ulric Neisser (1967) put forth a much more complex informational account. He argued that a subject comes to understand a signal by synthesizing (producing from scratch) an internal representation that matches that signal. Thus, attention itself is seen as a process of constructing the information presented to the listener (p. 213). Remote or apparently irrelevant streams of speech are analyzed only by passive "pre-attentive" mechanisms and are not themselves synthesized in this manner; but once a message has passed through a pre-attentive scan, the subject concludes that the message is worth attending to, and the process of synthesizing commences. Finally Broadbent (1980) has come to revise his own unidirectional model of attention, and now sees information as going back and forth in either direction. He allows individuals a multiplicity of ways of accomplishing the same task as well as a more active (synthesizing) role in the apprehension of information.

In the United States, shortly after the rebirth of cognitive psychology, several very influential experiments were conducted. In 1960, George Sperling became interested in the question of how much information an individual can take in visually at one time. Sperling (1960) instituted a measure called a "partial report": just moments after the initial presentation of a grid of nine letters (arrayed three by three), subjects were instructed (by a tone) on which row of letters to report. Using this procedure, Sperling showed that individuals are able to recall far more digits than had been predicted. Under normal conditions of "free report," subjects reported only four or five digits of the possible nine—a finding that suggests that only about one half of all the information had been taken in; but under this condition of partial report, the subjects were almost always completely correct. Sperling inferred that information presented to the eye is held in a sensory memory where it decays within a second. Provided that the information can be accessed immediately, twice the suspected intake of information can be documented.

Sperling's clever demonstration helped to kindle interest in the structure of the early information-processing system. Interest in the fine details of stages of processing themselves received a large boost from studies a few years later by Saul Sternberg (1966, 1969). In a typical Sternberg study, a subject is shown a "memory set" of five numbers. After initial presentation, one is presented with a single target number and asked to indicate whether it was in the initial memory set. On succeeding trials, the number of items to be chosen from is systematically varied, and the effect of the size of the memory set on speed and accuracy of recall is assessed.

Sternberg reported two principal findings. First of all, he showed that each additional item of information to be surveyed adds about thirty to forty milliseconds to the search. Apparently, a subject is engaging in serial search, making one comparison after another, rather than in simultaneous or parallel search. Second, a subject engages in exhaustive search. Contrary to intuition, one does not terminate the search, even after having discovered an identity between the target number and one of the numbers in the initial set. Thus, search time increases linearly with the size of the set but does not depend on the position of the target within that set.

Sternberg's demonstrations rekindled the hope that basic human cognitive operations could be timed in the manner suggested by Donders's work nearly a century earlier. In point of fact, Sternberg's technique represented a methodological improvement on Donders's in not requiring the devising of new, possibly incomparable tasks in order to isolate the hypothetical stages. According to Sternberg's analysis, such tasks involve a series of four stages: encoding; search through memory to find a match; selecting a response; and executing the response. He then proposed a model according to which the period between the occurrence of a stimulus and the production of a final solution is taken up by a series of discrete operations, or stages, that sum to the total time. The duration of any particular stage is not affected by the duration of any prior stage.

Using what he called an "additive factors approach," Sternberg sought to uncover the individual effects and the interaction of various factors that might influence this task. If two factors had additive (or cumulative) effects, they would be considered as reflecting different stages of processing; but if they interacted, then they were seen as affecting the same stage. Through this analytic method, a single task could be analyzed in its components, each stage could be thought of as an elementary operation, and a laying out of each factor would ultimately yield a flow chart for the entire task.

A Model of Memory The Sperling and Sternberg studies were concerned only with the brief interval following presentation of stimuli (see Posner

1969 for another set of influential studies). Other cognitive psychologists directed their attention to the properties of the memory system over longer intervals. In the influential model of memory put forth by Richard Atkinson and Richard Shiffrin (1968), memory was viewed as having three "stores." To begin with, there is a store where a stimulus is immediately registered within the appropriate sensory system: this is the locus of Sperling's buffer. Then there is a *short-term store,* a working system in which entering information normally decays and disappears rapidly, but may pass into a *long-term store.* Information decays in the short-term store in fifteen to thirty seconds, but can be placed in a "rehearsal buffer" and remain there for a longer time. The longer it is held there, the greater the probability that it will ultimately be transferred into the long-term store. Short-term memory is viewed as a buffer consisting of about seven slots, each of which can hold a single piece or chunk of information. It is assumed that the processing capacity of short-term memory is fixed and can be devoted only to maintaining a large buffer at the expense of other activities.

Information entering into the long-term store is envisioned as being relatively permanent. There are no limits on amount, even though information housed there can be rendered inaccessible because of the interference of fresh incoming information. Long-term memory consists of several storage mechanisms—such as one that places information in certain loci, according to content—as well as several mechanisms of retrieval, including various searching procedures. Because of its clarity, simplicity, and susceptibility to testing, the Atkinson-Shiffrin model became widely accepted (or *modal*) within experimental psychology. (In some respects, it held the same niche in the 1970s that Broadbent's model had assumed a decade before.) The authors of a widely used text described the fate of this model:

> It was only natural that the modal model became the focus for a generation of memory textbooks. Textbooks guided by the model characteristically follow the perceptual input from the sense organs to the brain. . . . The main problem with this type of textbook organization is that by the end of the 1970s the "sequential stage" model [was] modal no longer. (Glass, Holyoak, and Santa 1979, p. *iv*)

It is difficult to say why the information-processing model described here eventually waned. After all, it was successful in the sense that researchers could readily devise experiments that yielded quantitative information about the number of elements of information processed in a given amount of time or the consequences of various kinds of manipulation of stimulus load. Indeed, thanks to the model, most researchers have tended to think of information processing as a sequential process, where information first enters at one site and then is passed on, or shunted off, until it reaches some central processor, where more complex forms of analysis (including top-down processing) may take place. There has been a correlative tendency to think of an individual's information-processing capacity as being sharply limited—a certain number of chunks, a certain amount of sensory information, a limited short-term buffer, and the like; and this consensus has obtained on both sides of the Atlantic. Both of these tendencies, I should stress, are direct bequests from the Broadbent model of the human being as a vessel that, like a computer, takes in information and handles a certain amount of it in a certain amount of time.

Still this general approach to cognition has come increasingly under critical scrutiny. Some commentators, like Allan Allport (1980) of Oxford, suggest that there are essentially *no* limitations to the amount of information that can come in through various sensory channels: on Allport's account, the primary model of information input should be parallel (multiple entries at multiple points) rather than serial (one bit after another entering at a single point). Scholars like Richard Shiffrin of Indiana University have suggested that certain processes can become automatic and will thereafter exert no significant drain on the organism's ability to take in or filter novel information. On this view, speed and accuracy eventually become independent of the number of elements to be processed (Shiffrin and Schneider 1977). More radical critics, like Benny Shanon (1985) of the Hebrew University in Jerusalem, contend that contextual information affects *any* processing of sensory information: they question whether any bottom-up or any "outward-inward" model, which treats "bits of information" apart from their meaning and context of presentation, can do justice to human cognition. They also challenge the serial, "one operation at a time" logic of the model. While the standard linear information-processing mode of thinking has not yet been abandoned by most researchers, these various chinks in the traditional picture have led many researchers to rely on parallel, top-down, or contextual approaches to the processing of information.

In addition, a closer look at the "modal model" itself pointed up genuine problems, and the rewards of this research became more elusive. The more closely the hypothetical stages were examined, the more they blended into one another; short-term memory could not be readily separated from intermediate memory; pre-attentive processes merged with sensory buffers; processing often did not appear to be strictly serial; the assumption that specific factors affect specific stages of the sequence proved difficult to sustain; an individual's expectations might even affect the early stages of recognition (Glass, Holyoak, and Santa 1979).

Not even the most highly touted experiments withstood close scrutiny. While the Sternberg model proved an elegant description of a particu-

lar experiment, even slight changes in the model affected human performance in significant ways. For example, if the probability of test items in the
memory set is unequal, reaction times are faster to more probable items;
if an item is repeated in the memory set, reaction times to it are usually
short; if the items in the memory set are drawn from different conceptual
categories, subjects search exhaustively within categories, instead of
searching every category in the memory set. It has even turned out that
some findings can be accounted for equally well using a parallel (as opposed to a serial) processing model (Lachman, Lachman, and Butterfield
1979). Because of these disturbing findings, often linked to the content of
items, few strong generalizations of power could be sustained (Glass,
Holyoak, and Santa 1979; Neisser 1976).

But there was an even deeper problem. Even when results held up
reasonably well, there was increasing skepticism about their actual value.
In daily life, one never encounters such meaningless stimuli under such
controlled conditions; meanings, expectations, contextual effects are always present and are, more often than not, the dominant consideration.
Information-processing psychologists in the Donders-Sternberg-Sperling
tradition developed increasingly elegant models about effects which did
not prove robust when they were changed in various ways; nor did these
models clearly add up to a larger, more comprehensive picture of how
information is processed under real-life situations. Eventually many of
these researchers themselves abandoned this tradition and went on to
other lines of study.

Reactions to the Standard Information-Processing Paradigms: The Top-Down Perspective

One line of work has investigated the effects of general (so-called
"real-world") knowledge on approaches to apparently simple linguistic
tasks. In an experimental paradigm pioneered by John Bransford and his
colleagues at Vanderbilt University, a subject hears several sentences. One
is expected to listen carefully because one will be questioned about them.
In an unannounced subsequent part of the study, one is exposed to a new
set of sentences and asked to indicate whether one has heard each particular sentence before and how confident one is in the correctness of one's
judgment. Bransford and his colleagues found that their subjects' responses were little affected by the precise wording of the sentences they
initially heard. They seemed to listen, right through the surface wording
of a sentence, to its meaning; were likely to accept a sentence that made
the same point as one of the initial ones; and even combined the contents
of disparate sentences if they fitted comfortably together. Suppose, for

instance, that a subject heard the separate sentences: "The ants ate the jelly," and, "The ants were in the kitchen." Subjects so stimulated tended to say that they actually heard the sentence, "The ants in the kitchen ate the jelly," or even, "The ants in the kitchen ate the jelly which was on the table" (Bransford and Franks 1971, p. 339).

The Bransford paradigm highlights the inferential and integrative approaches subjects often exhibit in dealing with language, and thus casts doubt on the legitimacy of conclusions drawn from the hundreds of experiments in which individuals are asked to remember nonsense syllables or phrases. Rather than suggesting a passive, rote kind of recall, the Bransford results indicate that subjects are actively and constructively processing information and are inferring meaning rather than recalling sheer strings of words.

A cluster of further studies from the Bransford group fills out this perspective on "organizing schemas" (Bransford and Johnson 1972; Bransford and McCarrell 1975; Bransford et al. 1979; Johnson, Bransford, and Solomon 1973). Researchers have found that subjects' abilities to process a paragraph differ dramatically, depending upon whether they have been provided with a title or a relevant picture to look at beforehand; the title or picture creates a set that strongly influences how a sentence is interpreted. Other studies reveal that subjects inevitably draw inferences about the sentences they hear, and answer questions based on those inferences rather than on the literal contents of the sentences themselves; and that different cues will help an individual remember a given word, depending upon *which* sense of that word has been elicited by the initial sentence in which it was presented. Such supplementing, interpretive, or inferential activities turn out to be common if not automatic in the processing of verbal materials; and, in fact, when meaningful nonverbal materials are used, be they pictures or songs, the same kinds of "organizing schema" can be discerned as well.

Once we move beyond the level of sentences and approach paragraphs, stories, or whole texts, the role of organizing schemas becomes ever more evident. In an influential line of research, David Rumelhart (1975) and his colleagues have investigated how individuals remember stories. Building on some of the ideas in Bartlett's earlier work, and also on Chomsky's analysis of sentences, the Rumelhart circle has put forth the notion of a *story grammar*—an underlying set of assumptions about how the plot of an ordinary story will unfold. A story-grammatical approach posits that a story has an actor who seeks various goals, takes steps to achieve these goals, experiences various reactions in approaching these goals, and eventually fulfills (or fails to fulfill) them. People bring such expectations to stories: the stories that fulfill these expectations will prove easy to remember; but when stories violate these expectations, people are likely either to forget the stories or to regularize them (à la Bartlett) so that they become consistent with usual story-grammar assumptions. Moreover, even when individuals deal with other kinds of experience or text, which are not storylike but feature a regular sequence of specified events, they also draw upon organizing scripts or frames: for example, the customary way in which one changes a tire or visits a restaurant colors one's experience of, and memory for, new instances of such an incident.

Paralleling trends in other cognitive sciences, this interest in schemas, scripts, and other inferential and organizing processes has had a major effect on theory in cognitive psychology. It is not precisely that the belief in bottom-up or in "sequential serial processing" has been abandoned: such models still have their uses and adherents. But researchers have come to appreciate anew that human subjects do not come to tasks as empty slates: they have expectations and well-structured schemata within which they approach diverse materials, even including the apparently colorless and meaningless stimuli of a standard information-processing paradigm. Thus, an influential alternative approach in cognitive psychology focuses instead on how the organism, with its structures already prepared for stimulation, itself manipulates and otherwise reorders the information it freshly encounters—perhaps distorting the information as it is being assimilated, perhaps recoding it into more familiar or convenient form once it has been initially apprehended.

This top-down schematic-based approach stems from earlier efforts in cognitive psychology: from the "determining tendency" of the Würzburgers; from the search for organized structure by Gestalt psychologists; and, most directly, from Bartlett's story schemas. It also exhibits revealing ties to Bruner's work on strategies of concept formation. As it happens, the particular line of work on concept formation undertaken by Bruner, Goodnow, and Austin has rarely been followed up—probably because the view of concepts as arbitrary clusters of features has been as thoroughly rejected in cognitive psychology as have Ebbinghaus's nonsense syllables (more on that in chapter 12). However, interest in the strategies or the organizing schemes that one brings to a task is a robust legacy of the Bruner enterprise.

The adherents of this approach to cognition feel that it is on firm ecological grounds. Where the users of artificial stimuli and arbitrary tasks need to prove the relevance of their approaches to the real world, those who adopt the contextual, top-down approach can point to the fact that, in everyday experience, such highly interpreted and meaningful stimuli are the norm.

Even within the relatively conservative area of memory research, there has been a shift in the perspective of many researchers. Instead of the Ebbinghaus intoxication with meaningless information, researchers use meaningful and even highly elaborated, context-rich materials, like stories (Bower 1976). Attention is now being directed to the "depth" with which the information is processed. On this view, a subject has the option of paying attention only to superficial aspects of the stimulus (say, the sounds of words or the precise syntactic form of phrases) or of assimilating it to various schemata that have already existed: the more information is enveloped in earlier ways of knowing and embedded with rich associations, the deeper the level of processing; and hence, the more likely that the information will be firmly encoded and adequately remembered. Whether the stimulus is processed at a shallow (surface or sensory) level, or at a more semantically integrated level, depends on the nature of the stimulus, the time available for processing, and the subject's own motivation, goals, and knowledge base.

Such a "depth of processing" approach (Craik and Lockhart 1972) has at least partially replaced sequential models of information processing. On this view, the nature of incoming information is determined by the operations performed during its input. Input operations include analysis not only of sensory aspects but of semantic features as well. Thus, memory depends on the nature of the code and the type of analysis undertaken, and not on the properties of particular memory stores. Moreover, one form of encoding is not necessarily superior to another. Ordinarily it is preferable to perform deep processing. However, it turns out that a more superficial mode of processing is recommended if, for example, one is trying to remember which words rhyme with an initial list (Lachman, Lachman, and Butterfield 1979, p. 279). Ultimately, psychology's contemporary memorizer has many options: one can choose to process information at different depths; and one may even find that, for some purposes, a more shallow mode of processing is preferable. We have come a long way from the compulsory stream leading from periphery to long-term memory. Indeed, in this concern with goal-directedness, diverse approaches to information, and highly meaningful contents, psychology is re-embracing parts of the Würzburg program.

An interest in peripheral forms of stimulation and in context-free processing is certainly justifiable, but all too often it seems to leave the heartland of human psychological processing unscathed. Proceeding in a molar and top-down fashion, this work on schemas, stories, and depth of processing strikes many observers (including me) as closer to what psychology ought to focus upon. And yet the question arises whether this strand of psychology has achieved much that was not evident to our predecessors or, indeed, to nonpsychologically trained observers. After all, it hardly takes twentieth-century technology and high-power statistics to demonstrate that individuals bring certain experiences and organizing frameworks to a new activity, or that it is possible to process information with more or less effort for sundry purposes. And if we embrace a twentieth-century approach, the question arises whether we have advanced beyond the Gestaltists and the Würzburgers or are simply rediscovering what they knew (and what the narrow behaviorists and information processors had apparently forgotten).

There is no easy answer to this question. In my view, the major advance over previous work inheres in the better understanding of which structures individuals bring to experience, and of which manipulations are likely to cause a significant change in processing, memory, or inference; in other words, it is in the fine details of how such top-down process works, and not in the fact of its existence, that psychological advances consist. While less exciting than the discovery of an entirely new set of processes, and scarcely counterintuitive, this understanding is, to my way of thinking, no less significant. At times, advances of science occur in the details of understanding, rather than in the promulgation of revolutionary new laws. This may be the fate of psychology in our time.

Mental Representations

As the molar approach continues to struggle with the molecular approach, other lines of investigation bear in critical ways on the classical information-processing model of the 1950s and 1960s. That model was essentially *content-blind*: the assumption was that information of any sort is processed in essentially the same manner. Thus, if short-term memory holds seven slots, these slots are equally capacious for any kind of information, be it verbal, pictorial, or musical, be it dross or gold. By the same token, if a search takes a certain period of time per item and is exhaustive rather than self-terminating, these processes obtain irrespective of what is being searched for and of who is doing the searching.

These assumptions, which were made by all the pioneering cognitivists on both sides of the Atlantic, served as simplifying beginning points. They also reflected the computer model and information-theoretical origins of modern cognitive psychology: with such mechanisms, it is relatively easy to set up experiments so that actual contents are irrelevant. After all, information theory and computers are deliberately constituted to be content-blind.

Recently, however, these assumptions have been called into question. One group of scholars, represented by Roger Shepard of Stanford University, has been exploring the operation in individuals of a form of representation involving visual imagery. Shepard has studied the abilities of individuals to form mental representations of objects—be they familiar or unfamiliar shapes—and to answer questions about their physical similarities. In typical studies, subjects are asked to judge whether two presented geometrical forms are the same when one of them has been rotated, or to answer questions about other kinds of entities, which can be imaged, such as the shapes of the fifty United States (Shepard and Chipman 1970).

With his colleague Jacqueline Metzler, Shepard discovered that reaction times preceding decisions about the identity of forms directly reflect the size of the angle of difference between the orientation of the two forms (1971). In cases where the angle between the figures is close to zero, a response is given almost instantaneously: as the angle climbs toward 180 degrees, a subject's reaction times climb in a linear relation to the size of the angle. The authors interpret such findings as evidence that the subjects are actually effecting the comparison by mentally rotating one or another figure at a constant rate. Such mental imagery mimics the trajectory through which the figures would pass if they were actually in hand and being rotated before one's eyes.

These experiments, as carried out by Roger Shepard and (in recent years) by Stephen Kosslyn, are controversial but I shall postpone discussion of such debate to chapter 11. For now, what is germane is Shepard's belief that cognitive scientists have erred in positing propositional (languagelike) representations as the *lingua franca* of cognitive systems. The fact that computers can—and usually do—transmit information in only one symbolic form is no reason to assume that human beings do the same. Shepard sees mental imagery as a human capacity that has evolved over millions of years to enable the organism to deal with an ever-changing environment whose consequences it must be able to anticipate. Whatever the initial focus, such knowledge has been internalized through evolution so that it is now "pre-wired" in individuals and governs how they apprehend objects in space.

Nor are these capacities limited to the visual modality. Shepard's work with audition suggests that the representation and transformation of musical sounds reflect the same general principles as does visually presented information: principles of conservation, symmetry, proximity, and the like. Thus, Shepard comes to endorse some of the underlying notions of Gestalt psychology while placing them on more rigorous experimental footing (Shepard 1981, 1982; see also Jackendoff 1983).

Though growing out of research on information in a single sensory modality, Shepard's work challenges much of cognitive-psychology mainstream. If he can make a convincing case for more than one mode, the question arises whether there might not be a multiplicity of modes of mental representation, each tied to a particular *content*. In the interests of parsimony, most philosophers and not a few psychologists have voted in favor of a single form. The positing of another form of mental representation complicates the picture—for if two representational modes, why not three, or seven, or three thousand? From Shepard's perspective, however, it is ill-advised to adjust the findings of human experimentation to the demands of the digital computer.

Psychology's Contributions

In my view, cognitive psychology has made impressive progress since the mid-1950s, inventing paradigms that are widely and productively used, and investigating a variety of topics, of which I have named but a few. Cognitive psychologists have identified fascinating phenomena, ranging from the number of units that can be held in mind at any one moment to the manner in which geometric forms "are mentally manipulated" by normal adults; they have initiated many intriguing comparisons, ranging from the difference between concrete and formal operations in children, to the contrast between propositional representation and visual forms of imagery; they have devised a slew of new methods, some technically sophisticated, while also refining techniques that have been around for a century. Certainly, as William Kessen has put it (1981), several interesting new settlements have been founded and are being populated; and researchers have become expert in such areas as mental imagery, conservation of liquid, or the use of schemas for understanding stories.

Perhaps even more important, cognitive psychologists have won the battle on their chosen field within psychology. While behaviorism still has appeal as a method for dealing with various clinical populations, its theoretical superstructure and its experimental strictures no longer exert much influence within the research community. Nearly all researchers accept the need—and the advisability—of positing a level of mental representation. These scholars deal comfortably with concepts like schemas, mental operations, transformations, and images. Disputes center on the best model of representation, not on the need for some such conceptual apparatus.

But while cognitive psychology emerges on these criteria as a singular success, substantial problems remain—some within the field, others having to do with the place of this discipline within a larger cognitive enterprise. A first evident problem is the splintering of the field. There are now many specialties and subspecialties, each proceeding more or less well on its own, but having relatively little contact with neighboring work. Research on visual perception makes little contact with research on story understanding or musical memory, and often the concepts used to account for these phenomena are equally remote from one another.

A forthright and ambitious effort to introduce unifying constructs into cognitive psychology comes from the work over the past decade of John Anderson (1983). This psychologist, deeply rooted in the practice of artificial intelligence, has developed the so-called ACT (for "Adaptive Control of Thought") system which is put forth as a general model of the "architecture of cognition."

ACT incorporates a process model that describes the flow of information within the cognitive system. The central notion is a *production system* (see chapter 6 for further discussion). As soon as a node in a network is sufficiently activated, a certain action (or production) is carried out: this construct has been described as a kind of cognitive stimulus-response bond, because whenever the proper stimulating phenomena are present, an action is elicited. The system itself includes different kinds of memory— a *working memory* (consisting of information with which the system can currently work), a *declarative memory* (with propositions in it), and a *production memory* (which involves the actions carried out by the system). There are numerous other mechanisms as well. Encoding processes deposit information about the outside world into working memory. Performance processes convert commands in working memory into behavior. A storage process creates permanent records in declarative memory; a retrieval process retrieves information from declarative memory; and an execution process deposits the action of matched productions into working memory. A match process places data in working memory in correspondence with the conditions of production. Anderson's theoretical work involves specifying the nature of the knowledge structures that reside in working memory, the storage process, the retrieval process, and the various factors that activate productions.

As should be evident from this barrage of mechanisms and concepts, Anderson's system is complex, as is the evidence he has brought to bear. The system is also controversial, with some psychologists putting their faith in the kind of enterprise in which Anderson is engaged, and others suspecting that it is built on a base of sand. As Keith Holyoak, not an unsympathetic critic, has noted:

Some who have offered empirical evidence apparently contradicting [Anderson's] theory have been frustrated in their attempts to hit a moving target. . . . Some have worried that ACT is less a predictive theory than a very general framework that imposes few detailed constraints on the nature of the cognitive system. And the most skeptical critics have claimed that the search for a general theory of cognition is simply a wasteful misdirection of energy. (1983, p. 500)

My own feeling is that it is premature to call off efforts to locate and describe a general cognitive system. Like Piaget and other "systematizers," Anderson is bold enough to attempt such a daunting task; and, even if he fails, we should learn from the kinds of moves (and the mistakes) he makes. I find, however, one telling difference between Piaget and Anderson. Whatever Piaget's theoretical meanderings, he always had a deep involvement with the phenomena of cognition and drew his principles from intensive work with children in a rich clinical setting: these are, in fact, his most lasting contributions to psychology. At times, Anderson seems to have a *second-order* psychology: a psychology based on reading (and sometimes taking too seriously) the psychological treatises of other scholars, and on attempts to do psychology in a way that fits into the digital computer, rather than on wide immersion in the actual phenomena of thinking, remembering, perceiving, and the like. To the extent that this characterization is apt, it suggests that ACT may be internally coherent rather than externally linked to the actual flowing processes of human thought.

There has been a long tradition within psychology which ignores the particular content of information—a tradition that dates back to the work of Donders and that was fully subscribed to in the pioneering researches of Broadbent, Bruner, Miller, and their peers. Anderson's work fits comfortably into this tradition. However, in recent years, several workers, and most especially Jerry Fodor (1983), have suggested that the mind is better construed as a number of largely separate information-processing devices, including ones constructed to deal with language, visual processing, music, and other such specific kinds of content. On this "modular" view, modules have evolved to carry out specific forms of analysis in a hard-wired, rapid, and encapsulated manner; communication between the modules occurs only subsequently, in ways that remain obscure. There is also considerable skepticism among modularists on the need for some kind of central processor or executive function; and even those who (like Fodor) believe in such central systems are skeptical that cognitive science will ever be able to account for them.

The modular point of view, for which I have considerable sympathy (Gardner 1983), stands in contrast to those cognitive theories that are "content blind" as well as to those that subscribe to a belief in "horizontal faculties." On a horizontal view of the sort embraced by Anderson, faculties like learning, memory, and perception are assumed to work in the same or similar fashion, independent of whether the content is verbal, pictorial, musical, gustatory, or the like. But as Fodor and I have attempted to show, there is accumulating evidence that "vertical" psychological mechanisms deal in individual fashion with different contents. It appears probable that the ways we humans deal with, say, syntax in language share few fundamental properties with our transformations of spatial images or our interpretations of musical expressiveness. None of these possibilities were adequately appreciated by the first generation of psychologist-cognitivists, and they have been basically ignored or minimized by those who, like Anderson or Piaget, attempt to produce general cognitive architectures.

If the modularists are on the right track, there is a disturbing possibility for psychology. Rather than being a single coherent discipline—as its leading figures have understandably wished—psychology may turn out to be more of a holding company. In such a vision, there will be separate studies of language, music, visual processing, and the like, without any pretense that they fit into one supradiscipline. (In my concluding chapter, I suggest that this may be a possible fate for cognitive science as a whole.) Since this outcome would fly in the face of the established wisdom within the field, it is important to continue to put forth synthetic accounts as scholars like Anderson are doing.

While current debates pit the generalists against the modularists (see, for example, Piattelli-Palmarini 1980), it may be that both the modularists and the central processors have hit upon important truths. The modularists may be right in thinking that many domains operate by their own laws; the centralists, in believing in another, synthetic intellectual realm where modular processes are inadequate, and where horizontal processes prove necessary. Debate might then come to center on whether any of the modular realms can be subsumed under some aspect of a central-processing view.

Discussions of the modular as against the centralist approach are conducted by those who are generally in sympathy with the current methods and concepts of cognitive psychology. More severe criticisms of the enterprise have also been leveled, however. One school deplores the artificiality of studies in cognitive psychology. In this view, the most convincing models pertain to tasks that have little clear-cut relation to ongoing human activity; in contrast, those studies that do pertain to ongoing human activity take the form of intriguing demonstrations rather than theory-enriching experiments. In its harshest form, this criticism harbors the suggestion that the whole information-processing approach has been misguided; that attempts to model human cognition, in terms of a series of operations upon mental content, is simply a bad model of the human mind; and that some radically different (though perhaps not yet articulated) approach will be needed (Shanon 1984). I shall return to this theme when I consider the computational paradox.

Such skepticism has even been voiced by some of the leading experts in psychology. In his 1967 book *Cognitive Psychology,* Ulric Neisser exuded optimism concerning the promise of the field in which he had been working. But a decade later in *Cognition and Reality* (1976), he was much more sober. Berating his colleagues for both their homage to the computer model and their insistence on artificial laboratory scenarios, he lamented the lack of an ecologically valid psychology—one that speaks to the kinds of issue human beings encounter and resolve in everyday life.

As Neisser described it, such a psychology—lacking ecological validity, indifferent to culture—risks becoming a narrow and uninteresting specialized field. And, in his view, "the villains of the piece are the mechanistic information-processing models, which treat the mind as a fixed-capacity device for converting discrete and meaningless inputs into conscious percepts" (1976, pp. 7, 10). Neisser (1984) calls for a perceptual psychology, which studies how humans see while moving around and interacting with objects (Gibson 1979); for concept-formation research, which features complex objects in the world (Rosch 1973*b*); and for a study of memory which includes autobiographical accounts, eyewitness reports, and memory of childhood friends (Bahrick, Bahrick, and Wittlinger 1975). John Morton, one of the leading information-processing psychologists in Britain, has declared, "Experimental psychology has a disastrous history with respect to its relevance" (1981, p. 232). And Arnold Glass, Keith Holyoak, and John Santa, authors of a well-regarded textbook in cognitive psychology, raise the unsettling possibility that psychology is a "fast race on a short round track." They explain that this remark is meant to imply:

> Cognitive psychology is not getting anywhere; that in spite of our sophisticated methodology, we have not succeeded in making a substantial contribution toward the understanding of the human mind. . . . A short time ago, the information processing approach to cognition was just beginning. Hopes were high that the analysis of information processing into a series of discrete stages would offer profound insights into human cognition. But in only a few short years the vigor of this approach was spent. It was only natural that hopes that had been so high should sink low. (1979, p. *ix*)

While Glass and his colleagues do not themselves endorse this bleak outlook, they correctly note that this view is expressed "with depressing frequency these days," and, as I have suggested, outside as well as within the halls of cognitive psychology.

In my own view, there was understandable but probably excessive excitement about cognitive psychology during the first few years following its birth (or rebirth). Not surprisingly, then, some of those who were jubilant at the demise of behaviorism have been less than ecstatic at the results of the last (or first!) twenty-five years. There is certainly nothing wrong with experiments conducted under artificial conditions per se (see the example of physics!), but there is something bothersome when findings prove fragile once the experimental conditions are altered slightly, applied to more complex phenomena, or moved one step outside the laboratory.

Part of the dissatisfaction at the present time comes, paradoxically, from the perfection of experimental methods within psychology. One of the genuine contributions of behaviorism in psychology was the refinement of experimental methodology; but in this case, the refinements may have reached the point of diminishing returns. As I read the literature, too much emphasis has been placed on having an experimental procedure without any perceptible flaws or ambiguities; and all too often this emphasis takes place at the expense of considering what is an interesting or important problem. By the same token, once an interesting demonstration has been introduced into the psychological literature, dozens of other experimenters devote their attention—and their methodological zeal—toward finding the vulnerabilities in the experiment. And ultimately, nearly all these experiments get shown up (and ultimately abandoned) for their limitations. These trends combine to produce a science that has progressed rather less than it should have, and that still consists more of a set of impressive but isolated findings than of a truly cumulative discipline.

It hardly needs saying that it has been easier to achieve methodological perfection in those studies that deal with molecular phenomena and proceed in a bottom-up fashion. As I have noted, however, there recently has been growing dissatisfaction with experiments in this tradition: and there has been a correlative attraction for psychological investigations that deal with more molar phenomena (like the understanding of a story or the transformation of a mental map) and that do so in a top-down fashion (taking into account schemas, frames, and the surrounding context). The pendulum has definitely been swinging in a molar direction once again.

These two situations—the intoxication with method and the trend toward molarity—provide psychology with an invaluable opportunity. Put simply, it is time for psychology to wed its indubitable methodological sophistication to a concern for problems that are more molar, less artificial, more representative of real-life situations, more substantive. Just how to accomplish this is hardly an easy question to answer—though I have tried to indicate some of the lines of investigation that I personally find most promising. In this context, I strongly believe that psychologists can benefit from studying the example of artificial intelligence. In spite of (or perhaps because of) the presumed rigor of the computer, researchers in the A.I. tradition have been much more ready to deal with molar topics (like problem solving or story understanding) and to do so in a top-down fashion. The partnership that is developing between the two fields—and that will occupy me more fully in the next chapter—may serve as the best model for how to wed methodological sophistication to problems of unquestioned substance.

Discussion of these interdisciplinary matters brings me to the remaining issue of whether, like philosophy, psychology will remain a viable discipline, or whether it will eventually be absorbed into another discipline or set of disciplines. To my mind, psychological methods will always be central in any cognitive science enterprise. Indeed, it is in the perfection of methods for studying individual cognition, for comparing groups, or for tracing processes over time that psychology has probably realized its most outstanding achievements. It is simply inconceivable to me that studies of music, language, or visual spatial abilities will be carried out without the techniques and approaches honed over the past century by psychological researchers.

Psychology is central to any cognitive science and thus is especially likely to be absorbed by a larger field—in contrast to, say, philosophy or neuroscience. Philosophy may contribute an agenda of questions to cognitive science, but it contributes agendas to many other sciences as well and thus should continue to exist whatever good or ill befalls cognitive science. On the other hand, neuroscience with its well-defined domain—the study of the human brain and the nervous system—can also continue irrespective of events in psychology or cognitive science.

To the extent that the mind is indeed a single coherent domain—as Wundt, Piaget, and John Anderson believed—it will make sense for psychologists to continue to practice their calling under the same label and with the same goals in mind. If, however (as I believe is the case), the terrain of cognition is better mapped in terms of certain problems or topics —such as visual perception, object classification, rationality, consciousness, and the like—then cognitive psychology may lack a central subject matter, a "natural domain."

I believe that it is only as part of a research team that cognitive psychology is likely to survive. Psychological methods (observational as well as experimental) need to be brought to bear in the analysis of a field like language (in cooperation with a linguist), or music (in cooperation with a musicologist), or problem solving (in cooperation with a logician, a technician, or a physical scientist). The psychologist can then test the distinctions offered by the domain expert; and programs of artificial intelligence can be devised to indicate whether the models proposed by the psychologist-domain-expert team are actually viable. I anticipate the merger of cognitive psychology and artificial intelligence into the central region of a new unified cognitive science, with fields like linguistics, music theory, or spatial analysis providing the appropriate frameworks for problems that lie within their domain.

While I expect that cognitive psychology will simply, and advantageously, be absorbed into an issue-oriented cognitive science, I do not mean to indicate that psychology as a whole will disappear. (Far be it for me to predict—or wish—the end of my own discipline!) There will always be many practical needs for psychologists in the clinic, in the school, and in industry. Even on the level of theory, some pockets of psychology will endure. I do not anticipate that topics like human personality or motivation will be absorbed by other disciplines: neither neuroscience nor artificial intelligence can gobble them up. By the same token, psychology will continue to be indispensable in illuminating the differences among human beings: between normal and exceptional individuals, between individuals with different kinds of disease, or individuals from different social or cultural settings. The practice of individual or differential psychology should continue and may well yield interesting scientific principles. By the same token, psychology can play an equally valuable role in effecting other kinds of comparison—between one sensory modality and another, between one symbol system and another, between one form of representation and the other—whether or not, in the end, the modularity view is judged as more powerful than the central-processing view.

Psychology has been one of the great disciplinary success stories of this century, and it seems inopportune to be predicting its disappearance into a larger discipline. In fact, however, it is precisely the innovations in psychology of the past few decades which have given rise to a larger cognitive revolution, within which psychology has clearly been a central discipline. In no ways should psychology be considered simply a holding operation until neurology or sociology or anthropology comes along: as much as any scholars, psychologists have successfully made the case for the centrality of the human mind and mental representation within the current scientific milieu. The ultimate merger of psychology with artificial intelligence and other disciplines into a larger cognitive science will be a tribute to its success and its significance.

Perhaps events of the past century have demonstrated that psychology is a difficult science to bring to completion, at least without the aid of other disciplines. But even more clearly, we have come a long way since Kant declared, less than two centuries ago, that a psychological science was impossible.

6

Artificial Intelligence: The Expert Tool

> I am prepared to go so far as to say that within a few years, if there remain any philosophers who are not familiar with some of the main developments in artificial intelligence, it will be fair to accuse them of professional incompetence, and that to teach courses in philosophy of mind, epistemology . . . without discussing . . . aspects of artificial intelligence will be as irresponsible as giving a course in physics which includes no quantum theory.
>
> —Aaron Sloman

The Summer of 1956 at Dartmouth

In the summer of 1956, a group of ten young scholars trained in mathematics and logic gathered on the campus of Dartmouth College in Hanover, New Hampshire. Their purpose: to confer about the possibilities of producing computer programs that could "behave" or "think" intelligently. As they had declared in their grant application to the Rockefeller Foundation: "The study is to proceed on the basis of the conjecture that every aspect of learning or any other feature of intelligence can in principle be so precisely described that a machine can be made to simulate it"* (McCorduck 1979, p. 93).

Of the numerous scholars who attended parts of the summer institute, four in particular came to play crucial roles in the development of a new field called artificial intelligence. First of all, there was John McCarthy, then an assistant professor of mathematics at Dartmouth and eventually

*This historical sketch follows the account given by Pamela McCorduck (1979), a historian of artificial intelligence.

the founder and first director of the A.I. labs at both the Massachusetts Institute of Technology (1957) and Stanford University (1963). McCarthy was the major organizer of the institute and the coiner (according to most accounts) of the term *artificial intelligence*. The remaining three leading figures were Marvin Minsky, then a Junior Fellow in mathematics and neurology at Harvard and eventually the director of the Artificial Intelligence Laboratory at M.I.T.; and Herbert Simon and Allen Newell, then at the Rand Corporation in Santa Monica and also at Carnegie Institute of Technology (now Carnegie-Mellon University) in Pittsburgh, where they have remained until this day.

The summer at Dartmouth gave these and other scholars a chance to exchange views and to arrange to collaborate on future work. Various authorities during the 1940s and early 1950s had expressed the belief that computers should be able to carry out processes resembling human thinking, and it was the job of the present assemblage to put these promises to the test. Alex Bernstein, then a programmer for International Business Machines in New York City, talked about the chess-playing program on which he was working. Arthur Samuel, also of the I.B.M. Corporation, discussed a program that played checkers. Newell and Simon described a program that they had devised to solve theorems in logic. Nathan Rochester of I.B.M. in Poughkeepsie described work on programming a model of neural networks, while Marvin Minsky discussed the use of computers to prove Euclidean theorems.

The meeting at Dartmouth did not fulfill everyone's expectations: there was more competition and less free exchange among the scholars than the planners had wished. Nonetheless, the summer institute is considered pivotal in the history of the cognitive sciences, in general, and in the field of artificial intelligence, in particular. The reason is, I think, chiefly symbolic. The previous decade had seen the brilliant ideas of an older generation—Norbert Wiener, John von Neumann, Warren McCulloch, Alan Turing—all point toward the development of electronic computers which could carry out functions normally associated with the human brain. This senior group had anticipated developments but were uncertain whether they themselves would have the opportunity to explore the promised land.

At Dartmouth, members of a younger generation, who had grown up in an atmosphere seeded with these seminal ideas, were now ready (and in some cases, beyond mere readiness) to devise the machines and write the programs that could do what von Neumann and Wiener had speculated about. These younger scholars were attracted by powerful (if still vague and poorly understood) notions: data being processed by a program and then becoming part of the program in itself; the use of computers to process symbols rather than simply to "crunch numbers"; the proclivity of new languages for bringing out unsuspected potentials in the machine's hardware; the role of computers in testing scientific theories. Perhaps conducted in isolation, the meeting might not have had much of an impact. But it came just weeks before the meeting at M.I.T. (see pages 28–29), where some of the same participants, and such formidable figures from neighboring fields as Noam Chomsky in linguistics and George Miller in psychology, were presenting their own ideas to the emerging world of cognitive science. And, finally, it was the time as well of key publications—not only Simon and Newell's Logic Theorist and Marvin Minsky's widely circulated "Steps toward Artificial Intelligence" (1963), but also important monographs by Bruner, Chomsky, Lévi-Strauss, Piaget, and many other scholars of a cognitive bent. While no single event can lay claim to signaling the "birth" of all of cognitive science, the workshop at Dartmouth is the chief contender within the field of artificial intelligence.

The Ideas of Artificial Intelligence

Since the Dartmouth meeting, artificial intelligence has had a brief but stormy history. Part of the storm swirls around definitions. Nearly all authorities agree that artificial intelligence seeks to produce, on a computer, a pattern of output that would be considered intelligent if displayed by human beings. Most authorities see the computer program as a test of a particular theory of how a cognitive process might work. But thereafter consensus falters. Some definitions stress the devising of programs; others focus on programming languages; others encompass the mechanical hardware and the human conceptual component, as well as the software. Some practitioners want to simulate human thought processes exactly, while others are content with any program that leads to intelligent consequences.

Authorities also disagree on how literally to take the thinking metaphor. Some researchers take what has come to be termed the "weak view," where the devising of "intelligent" programs is simply a means of testing theories about how human beings might carry out cognitive operations. Others, however, put forth much more forceful claims about their field. According to the view of "strong AI," as phrased by philosopher John Searle, "the appropriately programmed computer really *is* a mind, in the sense that computers given the right programs can be literally said to understand and have other cognitive states. In strong AI, because the programmed computer has cognitive states, the programs are not merely tools that enable us to test psychological explanations; rather the programs are themselves the explanations" (1980, p. 417). I shall consider the merits of weak and strong A.I. at the conclusion of this chapter.

But while the tension between weak and strong claims is one of the most momentous debates, it is by no means the only one. As Robert Wilensky, a leading artificial intelligence researcher, recently commented, "Artificial intelligence is a field renowned for its lack of consensus on fundamental issues" (1983, p. *xii*). Indeed, in a recent capsule history of artificial intelligence, Allen Newell (1983) was able to single out no fewer than three dozen issues that have at times divided the field. While some of these are quite technical, and others of only transient interest, two of them seem to me of particular note. The first is the tension between "generalists" and "experts"—a tension recalling the dialectic between the modular and the central-processing perspectives in contemporary psychology. Generalists believe in overarching programs (or families of programs) that can be applied to most any manner of problem: experts place their faith in programs that contain much detailed knowledge about a specific domain but prove relatively restricted in their applicability. A second tension has to do with the scientific status of the field. While some of the founders were prepared to make strong claims for scientific importance (and, indeed, see A.I. as replacing epistemological pursuits), more skeptical commentators have wondered whether artificial intelligence deserves to be considered a scientific discipline at all. From their point of view, A.I. is simply a form of applied engineering—even gimmickry—with no real standing as a theoretically based scientific discipline. To be sure, similar skeptical challenges have been leveled at other of the cognitive sciences; but perhaps because of the dramatic promise of a "thinking machine," the battles about the scientific status of A.I. have been particularly vehement.

In this chapter, I shall observe the wide swings of mood and the diverse viewpoints that have characterized the leading practitioners and commentators during the first three decades of A.I. It is not possible, of course, to touch on every strand of artificial intelligence; for example, except incidentally, I shall not discuss work on robots, retrieving information from data bases, planning optimal combinations or optimal schedules, simulating organizational activities, or writing programs that write programs, even though each of these areas is becoming part of standard reviews of artificial intelligence (Nilsson 1980; Waldrop 1984*a*, 1984*c;* Winston 1977). But I will touch on those lines of work that seem to me to be most relevant to human psychology and, at the conclusion of this chapter, attempt to situate the field of A.I. within the broader framework of cognitive science.

The Dream of Artificial Intelligence

A.I. may have a short history, but the dream of a mechanical mind goes back a long time. Early intimations can be discerned in the work of René Descartes, who was interested in automata that could simulate the human body (he was skeptical about simulating the mind). Whether or not inspired by Descartes, thinkers within the French tradition seem to have been the first to pursue the idea of a machine that can reason. In Paris in 1747, a French physician named Julian Offray de la Mettrie published his book *L'Homme Machine,* in which he argued that "the human body is a machine that winds up its own springs" (quoted in McCorduck 1979, p. 36), and that the brain, as the organ of thought, was subject to study and duplication. As he put it, "thought is so little incompatible with organized matter, that it seems to be one of its properties on a par with electricity, the faculty of motion, and impenetrability" (quoted in Lowry 1971, p. 42).

Pursuing such a train of thought on a more practical level was the craftsman Jacques de Vaucanson, a builder of automata who thrilled Europe during the early part of the eighteenth century with mechanical flute players, ducks, and tabor-pipe players. In a lengthy accompanying document, Vaucanson indicated how each part of the flute player was in fact modeled after comparable components of the human model. According to the historian of psychology John Marshall, Vaucanson "was concerned to formulate and validate—in the most precise and formal language available to him—a theory of the German flute player" (Fryer and Marshall 1979, p. 261).

The scene now shifts to nineteenth-century England, to investigators who pursued the mechanization of thought in ways much closer to our own. One such character was the brilliant and prescient Cambridge mathematician Charles Babbage who devoted many years to devising an automatic table calculator which could carry out the complicated computations needed for navigation and ballistics. Unfortunately the machine that he designed would have required the production of thousands of precision parts; and while scientists of today think that Babbage's machine would have worked, the British government withdrew its support after investing the then large sum of seventeen thousand pounds. Meanwhile, inspired by his collaboration with one Lady Lovelace, Babbage became even more grandiose, conceiving of a machine that could tabulate any function whatever and could, in principle, play chess (McCorduck 1979, pp. 25–27). This "difference machine" (as it was called) was based on the difference tables of the squares of numbers. It would use punched cards of the sort hitherto used to control special weaving looms:

there were operation cards, which directed the operations to be performed, and variable cards, which determined the particular variables on which the operations were to be performed (Dorf 1974). Any arithmetic problem could be set; and, provided that the proper cranks were turned, the right answer should issue forth.

While Babbage was attempting to implement his ambitious mechanical aspirations, another British mathematician, George Boole of Queens College Cork, was involved in a different but equally momentous undertaking: that is, to figure out the basic laws of thought and to found them on principles of logic. In order to eliminate the ambiguities of natural language (which had dominated logic since the time Aristotle had studied the syllogism), Boole used a set of arbitrary symbols (*a, b, x, y,* and so on) to stand for components of thought. As he put it, "a successful attempt to express logical propositions by symbols, the laws of whose combinations should be founded upon the laws of the mental processes which they represent, would, so far, be a step toward the philosophical language" (quoted in Hilton 1963, p. 163). These symbolic elements could be combined or dissociated through operations like adding, subtracting, or multiplying, so as to form new expressions, or new conceptions, involving the same elements. These procedures amounted to a kind of "mental algebra," where reasoning could be carried out in abstract positive or negative terms, unsullied by the particular associations tied to specific contents. And these operations were termed by Boole the "laws of thought." Most important for the future, Boole observed that his logic was a two-valued or true-false system. Any logical expression, no matter how complex, could be expressed either as 1 (standing for "all," or "true"), or as 0 (standing for "nothing," or "false"). The idea that all human reason could be reduced to a series of yes or no discussions was to prove central for the philosophy and the science of the twentieth century.

The significance of Boole's work was finally appreciated a half-century later by Alfred North Whitehead and Bertrand Russell when they produced their *Principia Mathematica* (1910–13). The goal of this work, as I have noted, was to demonstrate that the roots of mathematics lie in the basic laws of logic. Whitehead and Russell relied heavily on the formalism pioneered by Boole. Russell went so far as to declare in his ascetic manner, "Pure mathematics was discovered by Boole in a work he called 'The Laws of Thought'" (quoted in Halacy 1962, p. 106).

The cluster of ideas represented by Babbage's calculating machines, Boole's laws of thought, and Whitehead and Russell's decisive demonstrations were eventually to be integrated by scholars in the 1930s and 1940s. Their work culminated in the first computers and, eventually, the first programs that can be said to display intelligence.

Realizing the Dream

Many individuals set the groundwork for the mid-century explosion which led to Dartmouth and its aftermath. Of tremendous significance was the work of the M.I.T. mathematician Claude Shannon. In 1938, Shannon published "A Symbolic Analysis of Relay and Switching Circuits"—possibly the most important, and also the most famous, master's thesis of the century. In this work, Shannon showed that relay and switching circuits of the type found in an electronic machine could be expressed in terms of equations of a Boolean sort: for the true-false system could parallel "on-off switches," or closed and open states of a circuit. Indeed, any operations that could be described in a finite set of steps could be carried out by such "switching" relays. Shannon's work laid the groundwork for the construction of machines that carried out truth-logic operations, and also suggested new ways in which the circuits could be designed and simplified. At a theoretical level, he also indicated that the programming of a computer (laying out a set of coded instructions to be precisely followed) ought to be thought of as a problem of formal logic rather than of arithmetic, an insight that grew out of Boole's work. In one swoop, Shannon had injected a subject of purely academic interest into the world of practical machinery, including the newly emerging computing machines.

Shannon's insights did not occur in an intellectual vacuum. Alan Turing was then putting forth his idea (1936) that any explicitly stated computational task could be performed by a machine in possession of an appropriate finite set of instructions. He was demonstrating that, in principle, there was only one kind of computer (though, of course, there could be many models built in many ways); and he was beginning to think about the central issues of artificial intelligence: the relationship between human thought and machine thought. This concern manifested itself some time later in the famous Turing test, where a skeptic was challenged to distinguish the answers of a human respondent from those put forth by a computer (see page 17). Vannevar Bush, an engineer at M.I.T., who had suggested to the young Claude Shannon that he explore the analogy between electrical network theory and the propositional calculus, was beginning to build machines that could solve differential equations. Also at this time, as I mentioned earlier, Warren McCulloch and Walter Pitts (1943) were developing their ideas about neural networks, specifically that anything that can be exhaustively and unambiguously put into words can be realized by a suitable finite network of neurons; thus, the brain can be construed as a machine in a more precise way than before and, indeed, be thought of as a Turing machine (McCorduck 1979, p. 15). And Norbert Wiener was weaving together the strands of cybernetics, a new interdisciplinary field which investigated feedback mechanisms in organic matter and in automata.

Finally, there was John von Neumann, in touch with all of these veins of thought, and with perhaps the most sustained interest in the theory of computing machines. He is generally credited with developing the idea of a stored program, where the operations of the computer can be directed or controlled by means of a program or a set of instructions, housed in the computer's internal memory. (It was thus no longer necessary to reprogram for each new task.) He demonstrated how binary logic and arithmetic could work together in forming stored programs. One can encode instructions to the machine in the same language as that used for the data it processes, and thus mix instructions and data in the program and store both in the computers. These conceptual breakthroughs opened the way for adjuncts to programming—such as *assemblers,* which can cull together subroutines into the main program, and *compilers,* which can translate from one language (usually a high-level programming language which is convenient to use) to a more basic language, reflected in the actual electromechanical operations of the computers. Finally, von Neumann pursued with special vigor the analogies (and disanalogies) between the brain and computing machines.

It is not entirely clear whether von Neumann appreciated the potential of programs to attack and solve problems of intellectual depth. Yet he was certainly aware of the nexus of issues in this area and if he had not died of cancer while still relatively young, he might well have become the major figure in the history of artificial intelligence. But this role was shared by four scholars at the Dartmouth meeting in 1956: Herbert Simon and Allen Newell, Marvin Minsky, and John McCarthy.

The Programs of the Dartmouth Tetrad

Programs for Problems: Allen Newell and Herbert Simon

While all the scholars at Dartmouth were actively engaged in thinking about thinking machines, only the team of Newell and Simon had already demonstrated that these ideas "in the air" could be implemented. Their first program, Logic Theorist (LT), could actually prove theorems taken from Whitehead and Russell's *Principia.*

Confident that their discovery marks an important point in the intellectual history of science in this century, Newell and Simon have described their progress in detail. In 1952 the two men had met at the Rand Corporation and had been impressed by the fact that the new electronic computers were more than simply "number crunchers" and could, in fact, manipulate all manners of symbols. Working with Cliff Shaw, a colleague at Rand, Newell and Simon began to explore the kinds of symbol-manipulation task that might be solved by a computer. Among other things, they considered the playing of chess and the solving of geometrical problems and arrived almost as an afterthought at the proof of logical theorems.

Newell and Simon knew it would be difficult to write programs capable of complex forms of information processing directly in the language of computers. What they needed was a "higher-level" language, one more congenial to the human programmer, which could then automatically be translated into the "machine language" of the computer. In 1955 the Newell team began to devise such "information processing languages" (IPL) or "list processing languages." On 15 December of that year, Simon simulated "by hand" a proof from Whitehead and Russell's *Principia;* moreover, the hand simulation was carried out in such detail that his colleagues agreed that the procedure could actually be carried out on an early computer called (after von Neumann) the Johnniac. Simon told his class in mathematical modeling, "Over Christmas Allen Newell and I invented a thinking machine" (quoted in McCorduck 1979, p. 116). And in August 1956, the Logic Theorist program actually produced on Rand's Johnniac computer the first complete proof of a theorem (Whitehead and Russell's theorem 2.01).

List processing was a technique developed to answer the problem of allocating storage in a limited computer memory. Until that time, the allocation of space had been prescribed at the beginning of a program run. But the Logic Theorist ate up memory so rapidly and unpredictably that users could not afford to allocate memory storage permanently. Shaw and Newell solved the problem by labeling each area of storage, having the machine maintain an updated list (including lists of lists) of all available spaces, and simply making the storage space available as needed.

In addition to solving the space-allocation problem, this method of list processing allowed the programmers to create data structures to store information in a way that was readily accessible and that, not coincidentally, may have borne a resemblance to human thought processes.

How does the computer program Logic Theorist actually work? This program discovers proofs for theorems in symbolic logic, of the kind originally presented in Whitehead and Russell's *Principia Mathematica.* The program contains the basic rules of operation—a list of axioms and previously proved theorems. The program then receives a new logical expression and is instructed to discover a proof. From that point on, the program runs through all the operations of which it is capable in an effort to find a proof. If it finds one, the proof is printed out on a long strip of paper. If not, it declares it cannot solve the problem and ceases its operations.

The demonstration that the Logic Theorist could prove theorems was itself remarkable. It actually succeeded in proving thirty-eight of the first fifty-two theorems in chapter 2 of the *Principia*. About half of the proofs were accomplished in less than a minute each; most of the remainder took from one to five minutes; a few took fifteen to forty-five minutes; there was a strong relation between the number of items in the logical expression and the length of the proofs. It turned out that one proof was more elegant than Whitehead and Russell's attempt of fifty years before—as Simon informed Bertrand Russell, who was delighted by this ironic twist. However, the *Journal of Symbolic Logic* declined to publish an article co-authored by the Logic Theorist in which this proof was reported (McCorduck 1979, p. 142).

It was still possible that this demonstration—although intriguing to engineers or logicians—could fall outside the purview of scientists interested in the operation of the human mind. But Newell, Simon, and their colleague Cliff Shaw stressed that they were demonstrating not merely thinking of a generic sort but, rather, *thinking of the kind in which humans engage.* After all, Logic Theorist could in principle have worked by brute force (like the proverbial monkey at the typewriter); but in that case, it would have taken hundreds or even thousands of years to carry out what it actually achieved in a few minutes. Instead, however, LT worked by procedures that, according to the Newell team, were analogous to those used by human problem solvers. Among the methods used by LT are substitution of one kind of expression for another; a detachment method, where the program works backward from something that has already been proved to something that needs to be proved; and a syllogistic form of reasoning, where if *"a* implies *b"* is true, and *"b* implies *c"* is true, then *"a* implies *c"* is also true.

In a further effort to underscore parallels between human and machine problem solving, Newell and Simon performed various experiments with their program. They showed that, if they removed the record of previous theorems (on which solutions to new theorems were constructed), the Logic Theorist could not solve problems it had previously handled in ten seconds. This was perhaps the first attempt ever to perform an experiment with a computer to see if it "responds" in the way that human beings do.

Trying to portray their demonstration in the proper light, the Newell team also stressed the resemblance between human and machine problem solving. They based this claim on some protocols they had gathered on human subjects engaged in the same tasks. In both humans and computing machines, the team found certain staples of human problem solving. For example, they reported certain moments of apparent insight as well as a reliance on an executive process that coordinates the elementary operations of LT (for example, substitution, detaching) and selects the subproblem and theorems upon which the methods operate. In conclusion, they located their work centrally within the new cognitive vogue:

We do not believe that this functional equivalence between brains and computers implies any structural equivalence at a more minute anatomic level (for example, equivalence of neurons with circuits). Discovering what neural mechanisms realize these information processing functions in the human brain is a task for another level of theory construction. Our theory is a theory of the information processes involved in problem-solving and not a theory of neural or electronic mechanisms for information processing. (Newell, Shaw, and Simon 1964, p. 352)

These remarks can be seen as directed at those—for instance, the McCulloch circle—who looked for the secret of the computer's operations (and of thinking in general) in an understanding of how neural circuitry works. The Simon and Newell group bet that this analogy was not helpful, and that it would be more profitable to conceptualize problem solving at a much more macroscopic level. For twenty-five years, this "dry" view has carried the day: as we shall see, it is only in the last few years that an approach that pays closer attention to what is known about the nervous system has begun to gain support within the artificial intelligence community.

By devising and running Logic Theorist, Newell and Simon showed that A.I. was a possibility, if not a reality. While all claims before had, in a sense, been handwaving, two key demonstrations had now been made: (1) computers could engage in behavior that, if exhibited by humans, would unambiguously be considered intelligent; (2) the steps through which the programs pass in the course of proving theorems bear a nontrivial resemblance to the steps observed in human problem solving.

But Newell, Simon, and their colleagues were soon after even bigger game. Their most ambitious project was the devising of the General Problem Solver (GPS), a program whose methods (at least in principle) could be utilized for all manner of problem solving (Newell and Simon 1972). The General Problem Solver was capable of such apparently diverse tasks as solving theorems, playing chess, or solving such puzzles as the missionary-cannibal conundrum, the tower of Hanoi, and cryptarithmetic—a fiendish mind bender where letters stand for numbers and the sums or products of words yield yet other words. But GPS did not just attempt to solve these problems in the most efficient way. Rather, it sought to mimic the processes used by normal human subjects in tackling such problems. Thus, a very important part of this research enterprise was the collection of protocols that recorded the introspections and notations of subjects engaged in problem solving.

The methods used by the General Problem Solver can be readily described. In *means-ends analysis,* one first states the desired form of the solution of a problem, and then compares one's present place in the process of problem solution with the final goal desired. If these two instances coincide, then the problem has been solved. If not, the solver (human or mechanical) clarifies the difference and searches for methods to reduce the difference between where one is and where one wants to go.

The art in the General Problem Solver lies in the methods of reducing this distance. A table is set up that associates the system's goals with operators that may be of use in achieving them. Once the difference has been computed between the present situation and the goal, the system then selects an operator associated with that difference and tests whether the operator is applicable to the current situation. If it can be applied, and if it produces a result that is closer to the desired end state, it is repeated again. If it proves inapplicable, then the system generates a subgoal, whose aim is to reduce the difference between the current situation and the situation where the operator can be applied. This procedure is simply repeated until the goal is achieved or it has been demonstrated that it cannot be achieved with the information given, or with the operators available in the program.

The General Problem Solver also exhibited other features designed to facilitate problem solving. It was possible to decompose the program into subproblems which could be tackled one at a time. It was possible to ignore some of the complicating factors in a situation in order to arrive at a plan of attack. It was possible to omit certain details of a problem as well. For example, in solving a problem in the propositional calculus, the machine can decide to ignore differences among the logical connectives and the order of symbols, only taking into account what the symbols are and how they have been grouped.

While the General Problem Solver was eventually abandoned because its generality was not as great as its creators had wished, and because the field of artificial intelligence moved in different directions, the program can be regarded as the first to simulate a spectrum of human symbolic behavior. GPS also occupied a major role in Simon and Newell's thinking about the enterprise in which they were engaged. As they conceived it, all intelligence involves the use and manipulation of various symbol systems, such as those featured in mathematics or logic. In the past, such manipulation had been done only by the human being within the confines of his own head, or with paper and pencil, but, with the advent of the digital computer, symbol manipulation has become the province of electronic machinery as well. On the Newell-Simon account, the computer is a physical symbol system like the human brain and exhibits many of the same properties as the human being whose behavior it has now been programmed to simulate.

Just as the cell doctrine has proved central in biology, and germ theory is pivotal in the area of disease, so the concept of *physical symbol system* is deemed by Simon and Newell and their colleagues at Carnegie-Mellon as the core doctrine in the area of computer science. Proceeding in Boolean spirit, the job of the theorist is to identify that set of processes which operates on symbolic expressions in order to produce other expressions that create, modify, reproduce, and/or transform symbolic structures. A physical symbol system is necessary and sufficient to carry out intelligent actions; and, conversely, any system that exhibits general intelligence will prove upon analysis to be a physical symbol system. Such a system consists of a control, a memory, a set of operations, and input and output: its input consists of objects in certain locations; its processes are operations upon the input; its output is the modification or re-creation of objects in certain locations.

A key notion in the Newell-Simon scheme is the production system, in which an operation will be carried out if a certain specific condition is met. Programs consist of long sequences of such production systems operating on the data base. As described by the theorists, the production system is kind of a computational stimulus-response link; so long as the stimuli (or conditions) are appropriate, the response (or production) will be executed. In the course of developing the General Problem Solver, Simon and Newell had propounded a perspective on artificial intelligence, a theory of thinking, and an agenda for future research.

The vision of Newell and Simon was formidable. From their perspective, the profound similarities between the human mind engaged in solving a problem, and the computer programmed to solve the same problem, far overrode differences in hardware (an electronic machine versus a parcel of neural tissue). Both are simply systems that process information over time, proceeding in a more or less logical order. Moreover, to the extent that the steps noted by an introspecting individual paralleled the lines of a computer program, one was no longer simply engaging in weak A.I.: it made sense to think of this man-made physical symbol system as actually engaging in problem solving.

Critics of the Newell-Simon effort brought up a number of issues. First of all, all the information in the computer program had been placed inside the program by humans: thus, to put it colloquially, the problem solver was only doing what it was programmed to do. For instance, it was Newell and Simon who structured the problems given to the program and, in some cases, determined the order in which they were presented. Use of terms like insight was but a misleading metaphor. To

Newell and Simon, this criticism appears anachronistic: so long as the program was not simply engaging in rote repetition of steps but actually used rules to solve problems to which it had not previously been exposed, its behavior was as "intelligent" as that of a human being. Simply old-fashioned habits of thought induced critics to withhold the term *intelligent.* Indeed, it was necessary to think of humans as being programmed with rules, just like computers. Not all scholars were convinced by this "democratic response."

Another line of criticism centered on certain differences between human beings and computer programs. For example, human beings can improvise shortcuts or heuristics, whereas computers will repeat the same processes unless they can be programmed to learn from earlier efforts. Recognizing this limitation in the General Problem Solver, Newell and Simon set out to devise programs capable of learning.

A final line of criticism involves the kinds of problem posed to the General Problem Solver. Despite its ambitious name, the problems were all puzzles or logical challenges: these lend themselves to expression in symbolic forms, which in turn can be operated upon. This restriction to "closed" questions was essential since GPS could tackle only mathematical-logical problems. Clearly, many problems confronted by humans (such as finding one's way about a forest or learning to master a dance) are not readily expressed in symbolic logic. Here we encounter a revealing instance of how notions of "thinking" or "problem solving" may be artificially constrained by the programs that currently exist.

Some of these criticisms pertain to other efforts in artificial intelligence as well, but each separate line of inquiry deserves consideration on its own merits. Let me therefore turn more briefly to what other principal investigators were doing in the first decade or so following the Dartmouth conference.

Marvin Minsky and His Students

Marvin Minsky at M.I.T. has not been as active a contributor to the published literature as Newell and Simon, nor is a single line of work particularly associated with his own laboratory. But as a seminal thinker about artificial intelligence, who had arrived independently at some of Newell and Simon's ideas, and as a mentor of an active cadre of talented students, he played a significant role in the progress wrought by artificial intelligence in the 1960s (and thereafter).

Under his inspiration, Minsky's students have led artificial intelligence in directions other than those explored by Newell and Simon. One student, T. G. Evans, devised a program in the late 1960s which solved analogies of a visual sort (1968). Expressed anthropomorphically, the program was shown a pair of figures that bore some relation to one another, and was asked to select another set of figures from a set that completed the visual analogy. Thus, for example, the program is shown "A is to B" and must then pick that picture out of five which indicates the relations that obtain between "C" and "D."

It must be noted that the program does not solve the visual analogy by use of perceptual "pick-up" mechanisms (of the sort humans might use), but converts the description into symbolic forms of the sort that would be used in a numerical analogy problem. The program accomplishes the analogy by describing both A and B as figures, and then characterizing the difference between the descriptions (in terms like *inside, above, left of, rotated,* or *reflected*); next, it applies the identified difference as a transformation rule to C, in order to arrive at a pattern having the same description as one of the five candidate numbered patterns (Boden 1977). Evans's program performs this task at the level of a high school sophomore. To program at that level, Evans had to build one of the most complex programs that had ever been written. The machine had about a million bits of memory, and the program had to use every bit of it.

Another individual working in Minsky's laboratory, Daniel Bobrow, adapted the work on problem solving to a linguistic domain (1968). Bobrow's STUDENT program was designed to solve the kinds of algebra problem which youngsters encounter in high school mathematics books. As an example, one of the problems posed in Bobrow's thesis went like this:

> The gas consumption of my car is 15 miles per gallon. The distance between Boston and New York is 250 miles. What is the number of gallons of gas used on a trip between New York and Boston? (Bernstein 1981, p. 113)

As described by Marvin Minsky, the program assumed that every sentence is an equation; it was given knowledge about certain words to help it locate the equation. For example, the word *is* was coded to mean equal amounts, on both sides of an equation. *Per* meant division. The program was driven by these desired meanings to analyze the syntax. In Minsky's words:

> From the mathematical word "per" in that first sentence's "miles per gallon," it can tell that the number 15 would be obtained by dividing a certain number x of miles, by some other number, y, of gallons. Other than that, it hasn't the slightest idea what miles or gallons are, or, for that matter, what cars are. The second sentence appears to say that something else equals two hundred and fifty miles—hence the phrase "the distance between" is a good candidate to be x. The

third sentence asks something about a number of gallons—so that phrase of "gas to be used on a trip" is a candidate to be y. So it proposes one equation: $x = 250$, and another equation, $x/y = 15$. Then the mathematical part of the program can easily find that $y = 250/15$. (Bernstein 1981, p. 113)

STUDENT illustrates well the powers that were being exhibited by programs in the mid-1960s, as well as certain limitations for which they were criticized. That the programmers were extremely clever, and that the machines could often carry out feats that, if executed by human beings, would unquestionably be considered intelligent, was difficult to dispute (though certainly some critics did [see Arnheim 1969; Dreyfus 1972]). And yet it seemed equally clear that the procedures used were often completely at variance with those ordinarily used by ordinary people. Faced with the preceding problem, a flesh-and-blood student would think about the nature of an automobile trip, the geographic locations of New York and Boston, and what happens when you are using up gas on such a trip. Indeed, the student would almost have to look through these particularities in order to figure out just what the actual mileage per gallon should be (even as he might hazard a plausible guess based simply on his own "real world" experience).

In the case of the computer, however, the procedure was almost the exact opposite. The computer had no idea what the problem was about, and would have performed in exactly the same way had the issue been pennies for peanuts or millions for missiles. The computer's knowledge was purely syntactic. The program is designed to expect certain statements about equalities and to draw the most probable inference about which entities in the problem are likely to constitute the principal components of an equation. It becomes a relatively trivial matter to confuse the program —for example, by including the word *is* in a context where it does not denote an equation but rather forms part of a relative clause or an incidental remark. Similarly, one can wreak havoc by injecting the word *per* as part of an expression, such as *per* capita or *per* chance. The human subject will sometimes be fooled by some extraneous fact which looks relevant (for example, the cost of the gas). The computer's difficulty is that it cannot look through the particular way in which it has been programmed in order to pick up the actual reference of a word or a number. Having no insight about the subject matter of a problem, the computer is consigned to make blunders that, in human beings, would never happen or would be considered extremely stupid.

Indeed, the computer resembles a human being who is asked to solve an algebra problem in a foreign language, of which one knows but a few words: faced with such an enigma, both computer and foreigner gravitate to the few numbers each recognizes, and make the best guess about the mathematical operations that should be carried out on those numbers. While the problems selected by Minsky and students span a wider gamut than those tackled by GPS, they are always reformulated as symbolic expressions of a canonical sort. Nonetheless, it must be stressed that, as with the Newell-Simon efforts, the programs worked. The kinds of exercise expressed in ordinary language, over which schoolchildren have struggled for generations, could be solved by a mechanical process.

Lists and Logics: John McCarthy

While the Simon and Minsky laboratories were busily engaged in fashioning demonstration programs, John McCarthy—first at M.I.T., later at Stanford—was engaged in less flashy but equally important endeavors. One of his major accomplishments was to design LISP (for "*list* processing"), the computer language that became most widely used in the field of artificial intelligence (McCarthy et al. 1962; Foster 1967).

As I have indicated with respect to Newell and Simon's early work, it was important for workers to have a language in which they could think readily about problem solving, and one that mimicked closely the kinds of mental step through which a human problem solver putatively passes. LISP and LISP-like "higher-order" languages came to be considered the mathematics of artificial intelligence, the precise and unambiguous argot in which theories are cast (see also Boden 1977 and Winston 1977). The language is basically concerned with the presentation and manipulation of lists, of items on lists, and of lists of lists, each of which can be named. Both programs and data are structured as lists. LISP's power derives from the fact that it is a recursive programming language, one well suited to the description and manipulation of structures and sets of structures. As a recursive language, it is hierarchical and can be described (and can operate) at several levels of detail. LISP is also very flexible: the program can move among levels that are nested within one another, can refer to and operate upon itself as often as necessary, and can automatically reallocate bits of memory. For these and other reasons, LISP and its descendants have continued to be used by most cognitively oriented workers in the computer sciences.

But McCarthy is more than a mere inventor of a useful language. He also has had strong ideas about the goals of artificial intelligence and how they can best be achieved. McCarthy believes that the route to making machines intelligent is through a rigorous formal approach in which the acts that make up intelligence are reduced to a set of logical relationships or axioms that can be expressed precisely in mathematical terms. With

Patrick Hayes, then of Edinburgh University, McCarthy wrote a seminal article in 1969, in which he argued for the use of a formal predicate calculus substrate embedded within a system designed for understanding language (McCarthy and Hayes 1969). He called for the formalization of concepts like *causality, ability,* and *knowledge.* If such an approach were to be adopted, it would prove possible to use theorem-proving techniques that are not dependent on the details of particular domains. McCarthy's system was based upon a faith in the consistency of a belief system and upon a view that all knowledge is (or can be) thought of in purely logical terms. As we shall see, these assumptions have had relatively few proponents in recent years. Still, McCarthy has adhered to the general program. He has been designing a nonconventional modification of standard logic in order to model common-sense reasoning, and his former associate Hayes (1982) has been trying to formulate in logical terms the thinking processes of "naive physics"—the physics of the man in the street. McCarthy stands as an extreme proponent of one point of view in artificial intelligence—a man who holds high standards for the field and is less willing than others to bend to the practical or to the particular.

Other Programming Milestones

While mainstream scholars in the 1960s were either pursuing logical problem solving or theorizing about the proper course of artificial intelligence, certain other work undertaken during that era held considerable implications for the future. One such line was carried out by Edward Feigenbaum, an early student of Simon's. In collaboration with Joshua Lederberg, a Nobel Laureate in genetics at Stanford, Feigenbaum decided to analyze data from a mass spectrograph (Feigenbaum, Buchanan, and Lederberg 1971). The result was a program named DENDRAL which was designed to figure out (on the basis of a vast amount of data from mass spectrographs) which organic compound was being analyzed. After processing the relevant data, the program formulated hypotheses about the compound's molecular structure and then tested those hypotheses by way of further predictions. The ultimate output was a list of possible molecular compounds ranked in terms of decreasing plausibility. DENDRAL's performance compared favorably with that of expert chemists (Boden 1977).

As a program, DENDRAL departed from Simon and Newell's classical model in two ways. First of all, DENDRAL made use of considerable stored knowledge about chemicals. It was predicated on the assumption that experts have a great deal of knowledge and as much of it as possible ought to be possessed by any program that purports to behave intelligently.

Second, if seemingly at odds with this assumption, was the decision not to try to emulate the ways in which human beings would solve the problem. Feigenbaum was explicitly interested in top-flight performance, and not particularly intent on mimicking the way that a human being would operate when confronted with the same closetful of information. Here we see an early sign of the sharp cleavage that was to ensue between simulation of human behavior and cultivation of intelligent performances by whatever means.

Two other investigative lines in the 1960s attempted to enter into a seemingly elusive area of human performance: meaningful conversation between individuals. In view of Turing's famous challenge (see pages 17–18), this was a tempting goal to pursue. Kenneth Colby, a psychiatrist then working at Stanford, and Joseph Weizenbaum of M.I.T. both wrote programs that modeled two-person dialogues. In Colby's case, he was interested in psychiatric disorders and so produced a program whose answers might be given by a paranoid personality with a particular obsession about the Mafia:

> Why are you in the hospital?
> I SHOULDN'T BE HERE.
> Who brought you here?
> THE POLICE.
> What trouble did you have with the police?
> COPS DON'T DO THEIR JOB.
> What do they do instead?
> COPS ARREST THE WRONG PEOPLE.
> Are you Italian?
> MY BACKGROUND IS BRITISH BUT I WAS BORN IN THIS COUNTRY.
> Do you know any Italian crooks?
> I TRY TO AVOID THE UNDERWORLD.
> (Boden 1977, pp. 100–1; see also Colby 1975)

Weizenbaum sought to reproduce the behavior of a Rogerian therapist, who assumes a nondirective stance toward clients:

> Men are all alike.
> IN WHAT WAY?
> They're always bugging us about something or other.
> CAN YOU THINK OF A SPECIFIC EXAMPLE?
> Well, my boyfriend made me come here.
> YOUR BOYFRIEND MADE YOU COME HERE.
> He says I'm depressed much of the time.
> I AM SORRY TO HEAR THAT YOU ARE DEPRESSED.
> It's true. I am unhappy.

DO YOU THINK COMING HERE WILL HELP YOU NOT TO BE UN-
HAPPY?
I need some help, that much seems certain.
WHAT WOULD IT MEAN TO YOU IF YOU GOT SOME HELP?
Perhaps I could learn to get along with my mother.
TELL ME MORE ABOUT YOUR FAMILY.
(Boden 1977, pp. 106–7; see also Weizenbaum 1966)

Both of the programs were disguised with sufficient artfulness that
they might, for a time, fool an unsuspecting person conversing with the
computer or a naïve witness of an interchange. Yet both devisers concede
that anyone who knew the design of the program, or was able to make the
correct inference, could readily unmask (or "defrock") the program. The
reason is that, as in the case of Bobrow's STUDENT program, the programs
do not in any interesting sense understand the words being used but are
simply constructed in such a way that certain key words will trigger fixed
responses. For example, Weizenbaum's ELIZA depends on pattern-match-
ing techniques. Each sentence in the input text is scanned for key words
like *I, you, like,* and *father:* if one of these words is found, the sentence is
transformed according to a rule associated with that word. In contrast, if
no such key word is found in the input text, ELIZA responds with a
content-free formula, such as "WHY DO YOU THINK THAT?" or with
a neutral referral to some earlier remark. There are some other fiendish
features. For example, suppose that in the absence of a recognizable key
phrase, a decision is made to revert to an earlier topic: the program is so
devised that it will return to a topic that had been prefixed by the term
mine on the not unreasonable assumption that such topics are likely to be
"charged" for the conversant.

It should be noted, not entirely parenthetically, that while the Colby
and the Weizenbaum research programs were developed in similar fash-
ions, and indeed initially involved some collaboration, the two men have
evolved diametrically opposed attitudes toward artificial intelligence. They
also have engaged in a heated personal dispute. Weizenbaum, it seems,
became disaffected with the whole field of artificial intelligence: he was
appalled that some individuals in the clinical professions and in the mass
media took his rather whimsical demonstrations as a serious therapeutic
tool which might actually be used with disturbed human beings. Colby,
on the other hand, is a "true believer," who feels that computers have an
important role to play in research about mental illness and possibly in its
treatment as well. The issues between these two individuals run deep and
touch on the humanistic aspect of the use of computers—a theme that has
come up repeatedly in recent debates about the value, and the values, of
artificial intelligence.

The Phenomenal SHRDLU

While the Weizenbaum and Colby programs make no pretense of actually understanding the utterances to which they are responding (being "dumbly" keyed instead to certain triggering phrases), a different story concerns a program devised around 1970 by an M.I.T. doctoral student, Terry Winograd. Called SHRDLU (after the seventh through the twelfth most frequent letters in a printer's array), this program operates in a way remote from those I have so far described. Rather than being a general problem solver, or a responding mechanism simply activated by key words, SHRDLU purports to be an understanding expert—albeit one working in a very limited domain. Winograd designed for his program a make-believe world of simple blocks which could (if they really existed) be piled and stacked in various ways: his program is sufficiently sophisticated in its linguistic knowledge that it can carry out a complex set of instructions. Moreover, SHRDLU issues signs that these instructions are, in fact, understood—one of the clearest signs of that understanding being that the program asks for clarification in cases where instructions are ambiguous.

What does SHRDLU do? Briefly, it replies to questions about its block world as posed by an interviewer, executes commands on the simulated objects in the block world, and reports the results. Sometimes these are simple actions like *grasp, move,* or *put;* while at other times, they are actions at a higher level of abstraction, like *stack* and *clear top.* Before *stack* can be handled, for example, the tops of both objects that will form the stack must be cleared. The program searches for actions that will achieve each subgoal and for sets of preconditions for each action in turn. This task may involve the construction of a sequence of actions from the goal state back to the state in which all the preconditions of the action necessary to initiate the chain have been satisfied.

Let us eavesdrop on some sample snatches of SHRDLU's expertise:

Pick up a big red block.
OK

. . .

Find a block which is taller than one you are holding and put it into the box.

. . .

OK
What does the box contain?
THE BLUE PYRAMID AND THE BLUE BOX.

What is the pyramid supported by?
THE BOX

. . .

Can a pyramid be supported by a block?
YES

. . .

Will you please stack up both of the red blocks and either a green cube or a pyramid?
OK
Which cube is sitting on the table?
THE LARGE GREEN ONE WHICH SUPPORTS THE RED PYRAMID.
Is there a large block behind a pyramid?
YES, THREE OF THEM: A LARGE RED ONE, A LARGE GREEN CUBE AND THE BLUE ONE.

. . .

When did you pick up [the green pyramid]?
WHILE I WAS STACKING UP THE RED CUBE, A LARGE RED BLOCK, AND A LARGE GREEN CUBE.
Why?
TO GET RID OF IT.
Why did you do that?
TO CLEAN OFF THE RED CUBE.

. . .

Put the blue pyramid on the block in the box.
OK

. . .

Thank you.
YOU'RE WELCOME.
(Winograd 1972, quoted in Boden 1977, pp. 115–22)

Compared with the level of understanding exhibited by other programs, SHRDLU was a major breakthrough. To be sure, its simulated world was small, and the number of actions it could carry out and of questions it could answer, extremely limited. Still, within its particular universe, the program performed in a plausible way, "perceiving" distinctions and "acting out" commands, as if to suggest that it actually understood what was being asked of it. (Whether it can be said to *really* understand is a question of tremendous controversy, as we shall shortly see.)

Winograd's program was more sophisticated than its predecessors owing to its use of a series of expert parsers or specialists: a syntactic specialist which segments the sentence into meaningful word groups; a sentence specialist which determines how the objects described by a noun group relate to the action described by a verb group; and a scenario specialist which understands how individual scenes relate to one another and to the sequential story they must collectively tell. For example, in the block world situation, the scenario specialist must handle pronoun references (no mean task) and the temporal sequence of all actions performed. In addition to these experts which can flexibly interact with one another and share information, the program also has belief systems, knowledge about problem solving (such as the mechanisms of deduction), and specialists that detect whether an utterance is question, command, or comment.

SHRDLU was, for its time, a stunning demonstration of apparent language production and understanding capacities. Yet, according to Daniel Dennett (1978), one of its chief contributions lay in another sphere. Specifically, the SHRDLU experiment explored some of the extensive demands imposed on any system that undertakes to follow directions, plan changes in the world, and then keep track of them. While the ways in which these tasks are done may not simulate the way that a real person would work in a real block world, the procedures devised by Winograd were ingenious and at least suggested the kinds of problem that would have to be confronted by any system seeking truly to understand, rather than simply to mimic understanding.

Certain limitations should be noted, however. SHRDLU does not have adequate semantic information to appreciate the differences in meaning between function words like *and, the,* and *but.* More tellingly, SHRDLU lacks any ability to learn to perform better. Its knowledge suffices for it to know why it does what it does but not enough for it to remember what has gone wrong when a failure occurs, or to learn from error to make more appropriate responses in the future. A later block-world program, designed by Gerald Sussman (1975) and called HACKER, showed that such learning was, in fact, possible.

Winograd's program came into being at a crucial moment in the history of artificial intelligence. There were furious debates going on about that time, both within the artificial intelligence community and between it and its severest critics. In many ways, the Winograd program spoke to these debates, even if it did not singlehandedly resolve them.

Pivotal Issues

The Need for Expert Systems

First, debates within the A.I. community. The 1960s were a time of excitement about general problem solving. Led by the redoubtable Newell and Simon, the search was on for programs that could, at least in principle, deal with every manner of material. But by the late 1960s, the limitations of these programs, which had to be couched in highly general terms, were becoming increasingly evident.

About this time, Edward Feigenbaum returned to Carnegie, his alma mater, to deliver a talk to an audience that included Newell, Simon, and other leading cognitive scientists. Feigenbaum threw out a challenge to his former teachers: "You people are working on toy problems. Chess and logic are toy problems. If you solve them, you'll have solved toy problems. And that's all you'll have done. Get out into the real world and solve real-world problems" (Feigenbaum and McCorduck 1983, p. 63). Feigenbaum had brought along information about DENDRAL, his expert system which incorporated massive amounts of specific knowledge about organic compounds. While DENDRAL was achieving impressive successes, it initially met a skeptical audience. As Joel Moses of M.I.T. has commented:

> The word you look for and you hardly ever see in the early AI literature is the word knowledge. They didn't believe you have to know anything, you could always rework it all. . . . In fact 1967 is the turning point in my mind when there was enough feeling that the old ideas of general principles had to go. . . . I came up with an argument for what I called the primacy of expertise, and at the time I called the other guys the generalists. (Quoted in McCorduck 1979, pp. 228–29)

Moses noted Allen Newell's intense objections to his approach:

> He called my position the big-switch theory, the idea being that you have all these experts working for you and when you have a problem, you decide which expert to call in to solve the problem. That's not AI, you see. . . . I think what finally broke Newell's position was Winograd. (Quoted in McCorduck 1979, p. 229)

And, indeed, shortly after Winograd's program had been completed, even the leaders of the old guard, like Marvin Minsky and Allan Newell, became convinced of the limitations of generalist programs and of the need for systems possessing considerable specialized or expert knowledge. Yet analogous issues were to return in other guises: for example, the question whether there should be a general language for all artificial intelligence programs or many specifically crafted tongues.

Procedural versus Declarative Representation

As for the preferred manner of programming, there was at the same time a vigorous battle between scholars who favored *declarative representation*—knowledge coded essentially as a set of stored facts or declarations —and those who favored *procedural representation*—knowledge coded as a set of procedures or actions to be carried out. In the early 1970s, the respective camps were sharply divided, with those wedded to LISP typically veering in favor of declarative knowledge. In their view, declarative languages are easy for people to understand and use. Moreover, such programs are economical, since a bit of information has to be stored only once and can then be tapped at will. Declarativists felt that intelligence rests on a highly general set of procedures which can be used widely, coupled with a set of specific facts useful for describing particular knowledge domains; they were not convinced that knowledge of a subject matter is necessarily bound up with the procedures entailed in its use in one or another context.

In a manner reminiscent of the functionalists in psychology, the proceduralists felt that human intelligence is best thought of as a set of activities that individuals know how to do; whatever knowledge is necessary can be embedded in the actual procedures for accomplishing things. Many things that we do know how to do are best viewed as procedures; and, indeed, it is difficult to describe them formally in a declarative way. For example, if one wants to build a robot to manipulate a simple world, one does it most naturally by describing these manipulations as procedural programs. Procedural representation has the additional advantages of allowing ready use of higher-order (second-level) control information or knowledge of where one routine in a program has to be triggered by another, and being applicable across several domains (Boden 1977; Cohen 1977; Newell 1983; Winograd 1975).

The debate about procedural versus declarative representation has become somewhat muted in the last several years. There is now increasing recognition that not all computing functions lend themselves better to one mode of representation than to another; and that, in fact, some problems are better handled by one approach, other problems by its rival. Initially Winograd had been a chief proponent of procedural systems; but he himself wrote a paper describing the advantages of these two different modes and, more recently, has collaborated with Daniel Bobrow in devising several Knowledge Representational Languages which incorporate both procedural and declarative components (Bobrow and Winograd 1977).

The Three Sharpest Cuts

Also in the early 1970s, at the same time that these intramural debates were going on among scholars generally in sympathy with the goals of artificial intelligence and at odds only about the optimal means, far more critical examinations of artificial intelligence were also afoot. Joseph Weizenbaum (1976), an early practitioner who had devised the seductive ELIZA, launched a strong attack on A.I. enthusiasts. In his view, many of their claims were excessive, wholly out of line with what had actually been achieved. Moreover, he was critical of the future aspirations of artificial intelligence; he believed that many of the tasks now being assigned to machines had best be left to human beings ("Render unto Johnniac . . ."), and that a dangerous confusion was taking place regarding what was properly the realm of humans and what ought to be ceded to machines. People are entities that are wholly different from machines; such uniquely human experiences as love and morality must remain sacrosanct.

In an even more wide-ranging attack on artificial intelligence, Hubert Dreyfus, a phenomenologically oriented philosopher at the University of California in Berkeley, had published in 1972 a critical book called *What Computers Can't Do: A Critique of Artificial Reason.* Dreyfus made much in this book of the fundamental differences between human beings and computers: he claimed that, unlike computers, human beings have a fringe consciousness; a tolerance for ambiguity; a body that organizes and unifies one's experience of objects and subjective impressions; the potential for boredom, fatigue, or loss of drive; and clear purposes and needs that organize one's situation.

According to the tale Dreyfus spins, after an initial run of apparent successes, artificial intelligence had bogged down because it had no way of coming to grips with these fundamental differences between human beings and machines. It was wedded to the notion that all human behavior —including all intelligence—can be formally described by logical rules. But human life is only as orderly as necessary; it is never completely rule-governed: life is what humans make it and nothing else. Since a computer is not involved ("engaged") in a situation, since it has no needs or wants or purposes, it must treat all facts as equally relevant at all times: it cannot make the kinds of discrimination and evaluation that are the stuff of human life and make it meaningful.

Weizenbaum's book was greeted critically, but with a modicum of respect, by his colleagues in artificial intelligence; on the other hand, hardly any computer scientist had a good word to say about Dreyfus's harsh verdict. Clashes of personality and even charges of intellectual incompetence came to dominate the debate. Regrettably, there was little serious discussion between critics and enthusiasts about the issues raised—possibly because of the different value systems involved. If one believes (with Weizenbaum) that there are certain areas where computers should not be used, this is an ethical, or perhaps a religious, judgment; and if one believes (with Dreyfus) in a phenomenological approach to understanding, where the feelings of the experiencing human body are central, one is committed to an epistemological tradition foreign to virtually everyone in the world of computer science and artificial intelligence.

(I ought to point out that Dreyfus's book went into a second edition in 1979, and that he feels that certain trends in artificial intelligence—for example, the adoption of organizing schemas or frames—go some distance toward incorporating the human approach to experience. As for the computer science community, at least a minority now feels that Dreyfus has raised issues that deserve to be addressed seriously. Nonetheless, Dreyfus's next book is tentatively entitled *Putting Computers in Their Place.*)

Perhaps most disturbing to A.I. workers was the negative review given to their field by a supposedly disinterested English observer, Sir James Lighthill, who had been requested by his government's Science Research Council to evaluate the state of the art in British artificial intelligence. Lighthill found relatively little to admire and wrote disparagingly about the distance between initial expectations and actual achievements in the first twenty years:

> Most workers in AI research and in related fields confess to a pronounced feeling of disappointment in what has been achieved in the last 25 years. Workers entered the field around 1950, and even around 1960, with high hopes that are very far from being realized in 1972. In no part of the field have the discoveries made so far produced the major impact that was then promised. . . . In the meantime, claims and predictions regarding the potential results of AI research had been publicized which went even farther than the expectations of the majority of work- ers in the field, whose embarrassments have been added to by the lamentable failure of such inflated predictions. (1972, p. 17; see also Lighthill et al. 1973)

Lighthill went on to comment:

> When able and respected scientists write in letters to the present author that AI, the major goal of computing science, represents "another step in the general process of evolution"; that possibilities in the 1980s include an all-purpose intelli- gence on a human-scale knowledge base; that awe-inspiring possibilities suggest themselves based on machine intelligence exceeding human intelligence by the year 2000 [one has the right to be skeptical]. (1972, p. 17)

There was one bright note in Lighthill's deflationary document. He singled out for special approval Winograd's thesis: in his view, SHRDLU succeeded by using principles that suggest genuine knowledge and sensi- tivity to the demands of natural language within a limited universe of discourse. That Lighthill was able to make this distinction indicates that he was not bent on dismissing all of artificial intelligence equally, and also points once again to the special contribution made by this one dissertation which appeared in the early 1970s.

Indeed, it seems fair to say that artificial intelligence has bounced back from these knocks of the early 1970s and has had some singular successes during the late 1970s and early 1980s. As Margaret Boden, a philosopher sympathetic to A.I., has declared:

> Suffice it to say that programs already exist that can do things—or, at the very least, appear to be beginning to do things—which ill-informed critics have asserted

a priori to be impossible. Examples include: perceiving in a holistic as opposed to an atomistic way; using language creatively; translating sensibly from one language to another by way of a language-neutral semantic representation; planning acts in a broad and sketchy fashion, the details being decided only in execution; distinguishing between different species of emotional reaction according to the psychological context of the subject. (Boden 1981, p. 33)

Even as the sights have been lowered from the "absurd overoptimism" of the 1950s, the actual achievements by certain workers are notable and have convinced most observers outside of the field itself that the experiments are at least interesting and should be taken seriously.

Innovations in the 1970s

While the critics of A.I. were not easily silenced, there were, by general consensus, a new burst of energy and several significant achievements in the field in the early 1970s. This second wave is epitomized by Winograd's SHRDLU, the shift from generalist to expert knowledge systems, and the fusion of features of declarative and procedural approaches. At this time, there was another vital, though rather controversial trend: the increasing use of a top-down approach to the understanding of language and other cognitive domains.

As exemplified in the work of Roger Schank and his colleagues at Yale University (Schank 1972; Schank and Abelson 1977), an "understanding" mechanism has several expectations of what a text is like in general; it also incorporates a core set of knowledge structures about details of the subject matter under discussion. These structures are built in as part of a prior knowledge base; they can then be brought to bear upon a particular text in an effort to comprehend how that text resembles, but also how it differs from, other instances of its genre. In the best-known formulation, Schank has introduced the notion of a *script*—the canonical set of events one can expect in an often encountered setting, such as a meal at a restaurant or a visit to a doctor's office. The script then allows one to make sense of different meals, ranging from a snack at McDonald's to a banquet at Maxim's; or of a series of visits to different medical specialists. Such a structured framework allows the "understander" to deal expeditiously with a variety of otherwise difficult-to-assimilate texts (much as Frederic Bartlett's story schemas allowed his subjects to make sense of an otherwise mysterious ghost story).

Another influential top-down approach is Marvin Minsky's (1975) notion of a frame: an expected structure of knowledge about a domain that consists of a core and a set of slots. Each slot corresponds to some aspect of the domain being modeled by the frame. In a frame, a description is created and then maintained by substituting observed for predicted values. Thus, for example, when a robot enters a room through a doorway, it activates a "room frame" which leads into working memory and arouses a number of expectations about what might be seen next in a typical room. If the robot then perceives a rectangular form, this form, in the context of a room frame, might suggest a window. The slots include those at a top level—fixed parameters representing things that are *always* true about a proposed situation (like a room having four walls). Lower levels have many terminals—slots that must be filled with specific instances of data: for example, objects, like a window, that one is more or less likely to encounter in a room. It is assumed that individuals possess many hundreds of organizing and interpreting frames, and that combinations of these frames will be invoked in any reasonably complex situation.

Pluralisms

Minsky has also put forth an intriguing conception about how the mind works, leading to novel proposals about how computer programs should be crafted. Rather than believing in a simple general processor or central processor, through which all information must be passed, or in an organized or unified mind that oversees all activity, Minsky now views mental activity as consisting of many agents, each of which is a specialist of some sort. According to this "society of minds" view, the mind consists of several dozen processing centers, or "agents," which can handle different types of knowledge simultaneously. Each of the local agents has a function, which is called upon in certain circumstances, and each has access to other agents. The agents communicate by emitting excitation and inhibition rather than by transmitting symbolic expressions. They can also censor information, much like a Freudian superego. Under this scheme, some parts of the mind know certain things, while other parts know things about the former. In fact, knowledge about *which* agents can know or accomplish which things becomes a crucial component of this new way of thinking about the mind (Minsky 1979, 1982).

Minsky's idea of a frame and his "society of minds" metaphor are not in themselves theories which can be subjected to clear-cut scientific tests, but are better thought of as organizing frameworks (frames, if you will) which lead to the devising of programs that perform more effectively and model human behavioral activity more faithfully. In that sense, his ideas can be seen as reactions: reactions against those approaches that fail to build in prior knowledge or expectations, and as well against those approaches that feature detailed knowledge of a specific area but have absolutely no generality or connection to any other domain. The ultimate impact of Minsky's new ideas on artificial intelligence is not yet known.

With these widespread shifts in how the knowledge base is conceptualized, there has also been increasing dissatisfaction with the kind of computer that usually serves the A.I. researcher: the serial digital "von Neumann" computer. Scholars like Minsky himself, and younger ones like Geoffrey Hinton and James Anderson (1981), raise an intriguing possibility: since the brain is itself a parallel rather than a serial mechanism, with millions of neural events occurring simultaneously, the simulation of human activities ought to be carried out by computers that also operate in parallel fashion. The brain is an apparatus that learns, that executes many special-purpose activities, and that has information dispersed throughout large reverberating circuits. Hinton, Anderson, and their colleagues call for a computer that more closely parallels the operation of the human brain, and for programs that feature many cooperating individual agents. Most of these efforts thus far involve the simulation of visual processing—an area well enough understood in neurophysiological terms to permit a plausible anatomical simulation. A growing number of experts speculate that the next innovative wave of artificial intelligence will utilize "parallel kinds" of architecture for information processing (Feigenbaum and McCorduck 1983). I shall take a look at some of these ideas about "non–von Neumann" style computing in the discussion of visual perception in chapter 10.

Understanding of Language

In addition to this influx of new ways of thinking, there have also been impressive achievements in some of the specific subject areas of artificial intelligence—achievements that reflect new concepts and can be said to atone for the contrived performances of the earlier generation of programs. In the area of language, for example, Roger Schank and his colleagues at Yale University, as well as his students who have now moved to other research centers, have produced programs that give précis of stories, skim newspaper articles, and answer questions and draw inferences about plot, character, and motivation in stories (Schank and Abelson 1977; Wilensky 1983).

Schank's claims about his programs, as well as his more general theories of language, have generated much controversy. He traces the failure of early language programs to their narrow focus on grammar and calls for programs that truly "understand the language," or at least parts of it. But many critics feel that *understanding* is being used in an illegitimate sense. I shall review this line of criticism when I come to John Searle's general skepticism about machines engaging in any kind of "intentional" behavior. There has also been debate about Schank's characterization of language. He maintains that everything we can talk or think about boils down to a small group of basic conceptual elements, and goes so far as to declare just what those elements are and how they work, thus doing apparent violence to subtleties of meaning. For instance, he claims that all the verbs of everyday speech can be analyzed in terms of twelve primitive actions (for example, move, ingest, grasp), which concern the handling, movement or transference of things, abstract relationships, and ideas. Schank provides no theoretical justification for his list but puts forth many examples of how one can analyze verbs in light of these primitive cores. Upon these verbs one should be able to construct a general understanding of language, one focusing almost entirely on semantics, to the exclusion of syntactic factors.

Schank's linguistic formulations have not convinced those who work in the Chomskian tradition of linguistic processing. From their perspective, Schank has created a set of *ad hoc* mechanisms which, however successful in certain limited circumstances, are completely unprincipled. There is no systematic criterion for determining when a particular script should be activated, or a theoretically motivated reason to choose one particular conceptualization of a verb over another. For example, why analyze eating in terms of ingesting, rather than including the muscular movements, thoughts, and reactions of an agent who is eating food? Or why invoke a script of a doctor's office rather than an office in general, or an oral surgeon's in particular, when going to a dentist? To such critics, there is no point in proceeding with the task of language understanding until one has a viable theory of the structure of language—a theory that includes the various aspects of language, including syntax, and can be applied to any kind of linguistic input (Dresher and Hornstein 1976).

Though many observers would agree on the theoretical limitations of Schank's pursuit, the fact that his programs work reasonably well at their appointed task cannot be readily dismissed. Moreover, many scholars believe that Schank has hit upon the level of generalization that may be appropriate for the creation of an "understanding system." He focuses on units of meanings, not individual words; uses words to retrieve expectations rather than to craft sentences; and focuses on semantics rather than on syntax. Just as the top-down approach has helped to rejuvenate cognitive psychology, Schank's strategic "bets" have proved surprisingly successful, at least up to now.

While the prospect of a program that understands natural language as human beings do still seems far off, there have been significant advances in other aspects of natural-language competence. Some approaches, such as those of William Woods (1975) and Ross Quillian (1968), follow the road of semantics; while others, such as those of Mitchell Marcus (1979), prefer the trail of syntax. Raj Reddy's HEARSAY (Reddy et al. 1973) program addresses the problem of understanding speech by drawing on several kinds of knowledge—semantic, pragmatic, syntactic, lexical, phonemic, and phonetic—and analyzing the signal at a variety of levels from the single-sound segment to the complete phrase. Each knowledge source takes a look at the hypothesis generated by all the others (and "displayed" on a central blackboard) and then makes a "best" guess about what has been said. While this system certainly lacks elegance, or the tightness of a theoretically motivated approach, it exploits that quality of piecing together bits of evidence that may be involved in understanding speech under less than optimal circumstances.

Perception

There has been analogous, and perhaps more unambiguous, progress in the area of visual perception. Around 1960 a brief flurry of excitement surrounded PERCEPTRON, a mechanism designed by Cornell's Frank Rosenblatt for the purpose of recognizing letters (and other patterns) placed in front of its "eyes." PERCEPTRON consisted of a grid of four-hundred photocells, corresponding to neurons in the retina; these cells were connected to associator elements, whose function was to collect electrical impulses produced by the photocells; connections were made randomly, because it seemed the best way to mimic the brain (Bernstein 1981; Dreyfus 1972). (When random wiring did not work, PERCEPTRON was rewired in a more deliberate way, which improved its performance in pattern recognition.) Another set of components entailed response units: an associator would produce a signal only if the stimulus was above a certain threshold.

Marvin Minsky and Seymour Papert at M.I.T. believed that the machine was built upon erroneous concepts, and that it was more profitable to find the principles that will make a machine learn than to build one in the hope that it just might work. As they saw it, it was necessary to build some prior structure in the machine and to provide the system with informative feedback about successes or failures. Minsky and Papert eventually published a book in which they demonstrated conclusively the limitations of PERCEPTRON theory (1968). For a while their critique put a damper on the field, because A.I. workers drew the conclusion that nothing further could be accomplished in the area of form recognition using systems based on the model of neural networks.

However, at M.I.T. by the early 1970s, more impressive efforts had been launched in the area of visual perception. Patrick Winston's program (which seems to have escaped an acronymic fate) was able to learn how to distinguish those block configurations that were arches from those that were not. The program learned to recognize tables, arches, pedestals, and arcades by being shown examples and counterexamples of each. The program searched for those differences between positive and negative instances which affected proper identification. A tentatively posited concept was then enriched by analyses of subsequent instances. While (like SHRDLU) the Winston program worked only in a very narrow domain, it made use of deep insights about how shapes can be juxtaposed.

Building on several other lines of work (Clowes 1971; Roberts 1965), David Waltz (1975) at M.I.T. devised a program capable of analyzing an entire graphic scene. Not only could it contrive a three-dimensional description of objects in a drawn scene, but it was also able to recognize two different pictures as being representations of the same scene. Waltz exploited an empirical discovery: if you can label the elements of which an image is constituted, you can so constrain the physically possible scenes that, in most cases, there is but a single interpretation of the scene. In fact, it was even possible to resolve ambiguity in the figure. As Patrick Winston declared:

Waltz' work on understanding scenes surprised everyone. Previously it was believed that only a program with a complicated control structure and lots of explicit reasoning power could hope to analyze complicated scenes. Now we know that understanding the constraints the real world imposes at junctions is enough to make things much simpler. A table which contains a list of the few thousand physically possible ways that edges come together and a simple matching program are all that is required. . . . It is just a matter of executing a very simple constraint-dependent iterative process that successively throws away incompatible line arrangement combinations. (1977, p. 227)

Even more impressive accomplishments in the area of visual perception came from another M.I.T. researcher, David Marr, who took upon himself the task of modeling the early phases of the perception of objects and scenes. Marr was impressed by Chomsky's theoretical approach to what a language is and how any organism can learn a language; accordingly, Marr pondered what is involved in *any* artificial-intelligence program and in *any* visual system as well as the actual details involved in recognizing a complex scene in the real world. And while he did not himself work directly with the visual nervous system, he designed his programs to be consistent with the processes known to characterize the visual system. Marr's sophistication in formulating the problem as well as certain striking results won him widespread admiration before his untimely death at the age of thirty-five in 1980. I shall take a closer look at Marr's accomplishments (Marr 1982) when I focus in chapter 10 on the issue of how one recognizes an object.

Of course, many other researchers and programmers could be mentioned: both those involved in "mainline" work in language, visual perception, and problem solving; and those tilling peripheral soils, such as Christopher Longuet-Higgins's (1979) work in the recognition of musical keys or Richard Young's (1974) work simulating children's cognitive processes on Piaget-type tasks. There are also under way promising new efforts, whose overall impact cannot yet be judged. For example, Douglas Lenat (1976; 1984) has developed an approach to heuristic reasoning as a supplementary means for solving problems and even for finding new heuristics. In any event, the general point should be clear: there has been a second burst of energy in the field of artificial intelligence since the crisis of the early 1970s. If the accomplishments are not yet up to human snuff, they can no longer be readily dismissed as resting on superficial procedures or depending on cheap tricks, but are clearly addressing central issues in human intelligent behavior.

The Chinese Room

Nonetheless, not all observers are convinced of the ultimate worth of artificial intelligence. In what may well be the most searching critique of it yet, the Berkeley philosopher of language John Searle has written an article entitled "Minds, Brains, and Programs" (1980). Because Searle's article was published in a journal of open peer commentary, where it generated several dozen responses from sympathetic as well as angered critics, the issues involved in the debate have become well known and, in a sense, serve as a capsule summary of the principal themes in contemporary artificial intelligence.

Searle begins by excluding from his critique the claim of weak or cautious A.I.: that is, that artificial intelligence can illuminate the processes of human behavior. He has no problem (at least as far as his article is concerned) with this variant of A.I., where the computer serves as a tool for the study of mind, allowing hypotheses to be rigorously tested. Searle's quarrel lies with the claim of strong A.I., that the appropriately programmed computer really is a mind and can be said literally to understand and to experience other cognitive states. While few scholars hold the "strong" view as baldly as does Searle's hypothetical target, the vehemence of certain responses to Searle's critique confirm that he struck a raw nerve.

Searle's Conundrum

To combat the strong view of A.I., Searle introduces his provocative Chinese room example. Suppose, he says, that an individual (in this case, Searle) is locked in a room and given a large batch of Chinese writing. Suppose that he knows no Chinese writing and may not even be able to discriminate Chinese from other kinds of squiggles. Suppose next that he is given a second set of Chinese characters together with a set of rules for collating the second batch with the first. The rules are in English and are therefore understood by Searle. The rules teach him to correlate one set of formal symbols with another set. This process is repeated with other materials so that the speaker becomes accomplished at correlating the characters with one another and, hence, can always provide the "right" set of characters when given an initiating set. Then, to complicate the situation further, suppose that the speaker is also given questions and answers in English, which he is also able to handle. The speaker is then faced with the following situation:

> Suppose also that after a while I get so good at following the instructions for manipulating the Chinese symbols and the programmers get so good at writing the programs that from the external point of view—that is, from the point of view of somebody outside the room in which I am locked—my answers to the questions are absolutely indistinguishable from those of native Chinese speakers. Nobody just looking at my answers can tell that I don't speak a word of Chinese. Let us also suppose that my answers to the English questions are, as they no doubt would be, indistinguishable from those of other native English speakers, for the simple reason that I am a native English speaker. From the external point of view—from the point of view of someone reading my "answers"—the answers to the Chinese questions and the English questions are equally good. But in the Chinese case, unlike the English case, I produce the answers by manipulating uninterpreted formal symbols. As far as the Chinese is concerned, I simply behave like a computer: I perform computational operations on formally specific elements. For the purposes of the Chinese, I am simply an instantiation of the computer program. (Quoted in Hofstadter and Dennett 1981, p. 33)

Searle's argument is more complex and subtle than this single quotation reveals, but its general tenor can be grasped. He believes that the Turing test is no test whatsoever of whether a computer program has a mind or is anything like a human being, because humanlike performance can be faked by any individual or machine that has been supplied with a set of formal rules to follow under specific circumstances. So long as one is simply following rules—so long as one is engaged in syntactic operations —one cannot be said to truly understand. And the computer is a machine *par excellence* for formal operations, unencumbered by any semantic knowledge, by any knowledge of the real world, or by any intention to achieve certain effects by its specific response. Therefore, it is a fundamentally different kind of entity from a human being who understands the semantic content of an utterance, and has his own purposes for communicating. Conclusion: the program of strong A.I. is bankrupt.

Counterattacks

Knowing that his argument will not go unchallenged, Searle himself anticipates the major counterarguments. He reviews the Berkeley or "systems reply": the claim that while the individual in the room may not understand the story, he is part of a whole system—ledger, paper, data banks, and so on; and the system itself understands. Searle's response is that the individual could memorize or internalize all the materials in the system (for example, memorize the rules in the ledger and the data lists of Chinese symbols and do all calculations in his head) and still would not understand.

A second response is the robot response of the Yale Contingent. According to this line of argument, a computer could be put inside a robot, and the robot could walk around and do all the sorts of things that real people do; being thus in touch with the real world, such a robot would really understand. But Searle says that, while this reply tacitly agrees that understanding is more than formal symbol manipulation, it still fails to make its case—because Searle could, unbeknownst to himself, actually become the robot. For example, the Chinese symbols might actually come to him from a television camera attached to the robot: thus, the Searle-robot would appear to be perceiving. Analogously, the symbols that he is issuing forth could make motors move the robots, arms, and legs: thus, the Searle-robot would act. In either case, however, Searle would actually be making all of the formal manipulations of symbols by himself and still would know nothing of what is going on. In one sense, he would be the homunculus of the robot but would remain in total ignorance of the Chinese meanings.

A third line of argument, traced this time to Berkeley and M.I.T., is the brain-simulator reply. This response suggests another scenario: a program now simulates the actual sequence of neuron firings at the synapses of the brain in a native Chinese speaker when he is engaged in, for example, story understanding or question answering. The machine now taking in stories simulates the formal structure of actual Chinese brains in processing the stories, and gives out Chinese answers as output. Searle says that even creeping up this close to the operation of the brain still does not suffice to produce understanding. Instead, he says, imagine that rather than a monolingual man being in a room shuffling symbols, the man is equipped with an elaborate set of water pipes with valves connected to them. When the man receives the symbols, he looks them up in the program and then determines which valves to turn on and off. Each water connection corresponds to a synapse in the Chinese brain, and the whole system is so rigged that eventually Chinese answers pop out. Now, points out Searle, the man does not understand Chinese, nor do the water pipes. The problem with the brain simulator is that it is simulating the wrong things about the brain. Searle indicates that

> as long as it simulates only the formal structure of the sequence of neuron firings at the synapses, it won't have simulated what matters about the brain, namely its causal properties, its ability to produce intentional states. . . . That the formal properties are not sufficient for all the causal properties is shown by the water pipe example: we can have all the formal properties carved off *from* the relevant neurobiological causal properties. (Quoted in Hofstadter and Dennett 1981, p. 340)

Searle goes on to list other replies, and combinations of replies, and responds to them in similar fashion, but it is in his response to the brain simulator reply that he tips his hand. He believes understanding is a property that comes from a certain kind of machine only—a machine like the human brain which is capable of certain processes, such as having and realizing intentions. As he says, it is not because I am an instantiation of a computer program that I am able to understand English; but, as far as we know, "it is because I am a certain sort of organism with a certain biological (i.e., chemical and physical) structure, and this structure, under certain conditions, is causally capable of producing perception, action, understanding, learning, and other intentional phenomena" (quoted in Hofstadter and Dennett 1981, p. 344).

In the journal, respondents attacked Searle's argument at every point. Some, steadfastly embracing positions Searle has already attacked, said that he had misunderstood them, or that when properly pursued, particular responses could indeed accomplish what Searle denied. Other critics accused him of being a mystic, antiscientific, antitechnological, or just another philosopher gone bad. Much was made about the caricature embodied in his single fake Chinese speaker. Respondents claimed that Searle's example is just not plausible: in order to be able to carry off the behavior successfully, the man or the system would need to achieve genuine understanding, or what we would unhesitatingly call genuine understanding were it to be found in a human being. There are orders of magnitude Searle ignored (for example, the effort it would take to anticipate and translate all possible messages) and only this sleight-of-hand allows him to make his case. Searle has also been accused of confusing levels: it is the person who understands, and not the brain; and similarly, it is the computer as a whole that understands, and not the program.

To my mind, when Searle remains on his own ground—in putting forth the example of the man equipped with a set of formal rules for responding in Chinese—he is convincing. While I would not join Searle in ruling out the possibility of any machine's understanding a natural language, I certainly feel that the word *understand* has been unduly stretched in the case of the Chinese room problem in its various manifestations.

It is Searle's positive explanation of why the rest of us understand, when he speaks about the intentionality of the brain, that can be legitimately attacked. The whole notion of the brain as a causal system that displays intentionality is obscure and difficult to understand, let alone to lay out coolly like a computer program. Zenon Pylyshyn, a computer scientist from the University of Western Ontario, scores telling points: "What Searle wants to claim is that only systems that are equivalent to humans . . . can have intentionality. His thesis thus hangs on the assumption that intentionality is tied very closely to specific material properties —indeed, that it is literally *caused* by them." Pylyshyn wonders whether Searle is proposing that intentionality is a substance secreted by the brain (1980*a*), and then poses this puzzle:

[Suppose] if more and more of the cells in your brain were to be replaced by integrated circuit chips, programmed in such a way as to keep the input-out *function* of each unit identical to that of the unit being replaced, you would in all likelihood just keep right on speaking exactly as you are doing now except that you would eventually stop *meaning* anything by it. What we outside observers might take to be words would become for you just certain noises that circuits caused you to make. (P. 442)

Searle's argument, it seems to me, loses its force if, by definition, only human brain or brainlike mechanisms can exhibit properties of intentionality, understanding, and the like. If this is true by definition, then there is no point to the controversy. If, on the other hand, Searle allows (as he must) that nonprotoplasmic entities can also possess the "milk of human intentionality," he must explain what it takes to be intentional, to possess understanding, and the like. Such explanation is going to be difficult to provide, because we have no idea how the causal properties of protoplasm allow individuals to think; and, for all we know, the process is as odd as one of those Searle so effectively ridicules.

In an effort to address these concerns, Searle has written a book on *Intentionality* which he defines as the property of mental states and events by which they are directed at objects and states of affairs in the world. Intentional states include beliefs, fears, desires, and intentions (1983*a*, p. 1). In the book, he declares:

> My own speculation, and at the present state of our knowledge of neuro-physiology it can only be a speculation, is that if we come to understand the operation of the brain in producing Intentionality, it is likely to be on principles that are quite different from those we now employ, as different as the principles of quantum mechanics are from the principles of Newtonian mechanics; but any principles, to give us an adequate account of the brain, will have to recognize the reality of, and explain the causal capacities of, the Intentionality of the brain. (P. 272)

Indeed, Searle seems to believe that, to do cognitive studies, one needs only two levels of explanation—the level of intentionality (a plain English discussion of the organism's wishes, beliefs, and so on)—and a neuro-physiological explanation of what the brain does in realizing these intentional states. He finds no need for a level of symbolic representation, which dominates work throughout the cognitive sciences (1983*b*). To the extent that these lines of argument sound like mere handwaving, Searle's positive assertions about intentionality have little force. To the extent that he can specify just what he means, and show that intentionality is not in principle restricted to organic brains, a genuine scientific issue will have been joined. Thereafter, researchers in artificial intelligence can try to simulate the very behavior that Searle believes lies beyond their explanatory scope.

It is possible, however, that the issues between Searle and his critics —and perhaps even between those in sympathy and those out of sympathy with A.I.—transcend questions of a scientific nature. In an angry critique of the Searle paper, computer scientist Douglas Hofstadter makes the following conjecture:

> This religious diatribe against AI, masquerading as a serious scientific argument, is one of the wrongest, most infuriating articles I have ever read in my life. . . . I know that this journal is not the place for philosophical and religious commentary, yet it seems to me that what Searle and I have is, at the deepest level, a religious disagreement and I doubt that anything I say could ever change his mind. He insists on things he calls "causal intentional properties" which seem to vanish as soon as you analyze them, find rules for them, or simulate them. But what those things are, other than epiphenomena, or innocently emergent qualities I don't know. (Quoted in Searle 1980, p. 434)

If Hofstadter is right about the underlying reasons for the disagreement, then there is no way in which either side can convince the other. At stake is a matter of faith, in which reason will not even be considered relevant by either side.

Critics and Defenders: The Debate Continues

Whatever the merit of Searle's arguments, they do not question the legitimacy of most current work in artificial intelligence; in fact, as he indicates, he has no qualms about accepting the utility of A.I. as an aid in conceptualizing and testing theories of human intelligence. But, as we have seen, some critics challenge A.I. at an even more fundamental level. As one example, Joseph Weizenbaum (1976), raises ethical questions about whether A.I. should be allowed to impinge on territory that has hitherto been restricted to human beings, such as issues of justice or love.

Another line of criticism suggests that efforts to simulate human intelligence are perfectly valid, but that most of the A.I. community has heretofore used superficial models which do not approach the core of human thought processes. Initially, this line of criticism came from those in the camp of transformational linguistics, like Elan Dresher, Norbert Hornstein (Dresher and Hornstein 1976), and Kenneth Wexler (1978). From their perspective, rather than trying to build upon deep principles of language (or whatever area happens to be modeled), artificial intelligence is simply a practical, trial-and-error pursuit and is unlikely ever to come up with anything that has generality and explanatory power. For instance, as they see it, Schank's program is too vague and unspecified, and there are no algorithms for determining the "primitive verb" or the script that is relevant to a given linguistic string. In contrast, Winograd's program is criticized for being too specifically tied to a given "micro-world" and thus being inapplicable to any new specimen of language. According to this "purist" philosophy, scientists ought to be spending their time analyzing systems in themselves, studying competent human beings, or fashioning theoretical explanations of what intelligence or competence amounts to: theories that can stand up to the standards of the "hard" sciences. Perhaps, once the *real* operative principles are understood—as they are beginning to be understood in the area of syntactic processing—it should be relatively trivial to program the computer to carry out these operations. In the next chapter, I shall examine this transformationalist vision of acceptable explanatory models in cognitive science.

These critics are arguing that artificial intelligence has not yet attained the standing of a genuine scientific endeavor. Instead, it is just a convenient tool whose operating principles are of scant theoretical interest—views that have been recently echoed by some of the most active workers in artificial intelligence. Terry Winograd, once the darling of the A.I. community, has been pondering the limitations of computer-based understanding and has moved away from simulation experiments. He and Daniel Bobrow declare:

> Current systems, even the best ones, often resemble a house of cards. . . . The result is an extremely fragile structure which may reach impressive heights, but collapses immediately if swayed in the slightest from the specific domain (often even the specific examples) for which it was built. (Bobrow and Winograd 1977, p. 4)

Schank has conceded the difficulties involved in devising systems without having good models, and has newly acknowledged the philosophical nature of many problems:

> AI is very hard. What is the nature of knowledge? How do you abstract from existing knowledge to more general knowledge? How do you modify knowledge when you fail? Are there principles of problem solving that are independent of domain? How do goals and plans relate to understanding? The computer is a way of testing out ideas. But first, we need to understand what we're supposed to be building models of. (Quoted in Waldrop 1984a, p. 805)

Workers like John McCarthy (1984) have been pondering what Daniel Dennett (1983) terms the "smoking gun" problem of artificial intelligence: how a program can decide which of the unexpected features in a situation can be ignored. (For example, if it is to resemble human intelligence, a frame of a boat trip should ignore the fact that the oars on a rowboat are blue rather than green but dare not ignore the fact that one of the oarlocks is broken.) John Seely Brown and Kurt van Lehn, researchers at Xerox PARC in Palo Alto, admit that most current A.I. work fails to meet traditional criteria of scientific theories, and decry the absence of "competitive argumentation" whereby the power of one simulation can be rigorously compared with the power of another. By such comparison, it is possible to indicate *why* one accepts some computational principles, while rejecting others. In lieu of such argumentation, these authors wryly suggest, artificial intelligence theories have stood on the toes rather than on the shoulders of their predecessors (van Lehn, Seely Brown, and Greeno 1982).

The realization that one's chosen discipline may not have been operating in a scientifically impeccable manner is not in itself an instant panacea, but it is an important first step—maybe the most important step in the maturing of a discipline. A second valuable trend, in my view, has been the growing number of workers in A.I. who seek systems reflecting the deep principles at work in a particular domain of knowledge. Spurning both the search for the most general properties of problem solving (which proved elusive with the General Problem Solver) and the interest in those expert systems that perform well simply by drawing with brute force on massive amounts of stored knowledge, these researchers take seriously the principles that appear to be at work in the only other intelligent system we know—the human being. I shall examine some of their promising efforts in the latter chapters of this book.

It is possible, of course, as a result of a careful study of different areas, we will discover that the deepest principles do indeed operate across areas, and that we will ultimately require a general knowledge base or problem solver rather than a host of separate experts. As I suggested with respect to the work of John Anderson (1983) in cognitive psychology, such a dream may still materialize, but the likelihood seems small.

My own analysis suggests that, after a period of excessive claims and sometimes superficial demonstrations, artificial intelligence has advanced to a more measured view of itself and has, in the process, attained a set of reasonably solid accomplishments. This maturing process has involved a recognition that the practice of A.I. entails deep philosophical issues which cannot be ignored or minimized. Involved as well has been a recognition that there are limits to what can be explained by current A.I. methods and that even whole areas of study may lie outside of artificial intelligence, at least now and perhaps permanently. It is important to have genuine demonstrations and not just verbal descriptions of possible programs: this insistence has been among the greatest contributions of Newell and Simon. But it is equally important that these demonstrations reflect robust principles and are not just fragile constructions with limited application.

Given my own view that the future of cognitive science lies in the study and elucidation of particular domains of knowledge, I believe that the field will achieve scientific status when it freshly illuminates the domains and knowledge systems with which it is concerned. As the psychologist John Marshall declares:

> I just don't care what members of the AI community think about the ontological status of their creations. What I do care about is whether anyone can produce principled, revealing accounts of, say, the perception of tonal music . . . , the properties of stereo vision . . . , and the parsing of natural language sentences. Everyone that I know who tinkers around with computers does so because he has an attractive theory of some psychological capacity and wishes to explore certain consequences of the theory algorithmically. (1980, p. 436)

Christopher Longuet-Higgins makes the same general point in a somewhat different way:

It is perhaps time that the title "artificial intelligence" were replaced by something more modest and less provisional. . . . Might one suggest, with due deference to the psychological community, that "theoretical psychology" is really the right heading under which to classify artificial intelligence studies of perception and cognition. . . . The task of the theoretician is to formulate hypotheses and to elicit their logical implications as carefully as he can, with due attention to matters of internal consistency and predictive power; the duty of the experimenter is to confront the predictions of a theory with firm and relevant observations, and to suggest points at which the theory needs modifying in order to bring it into line with experiment—if that is indeed possible. The time has now come, it seems, when the task of theory construction is altogether too intricate to be consigned to spare moments away from the laboratory; it is at least as much of a discipline as good experimentation. (1981, p. 200)

Marshall and Longuet-Higgins are pointing to the increasingly close ties being forged between experimental cognitive psychology and artificial intelligence. Psychologists can benefit from the careful simulations made by A.I. researchers, and can put their own typically informal models to rigorous tests; A.I. scientists can determine whether their hypothesized models of human behavior are actually realized by the subjects about whom they have been speculating. It seems plausible to me that parts of psychology and parts of computer science will simply merge into a single discipline or, as I suggested in the previous chapter, that they will form the central core of a newly forged cognitive science.

Of course, there may well be areas of computer science, as well as of psychology, that do not take part in this merger. This would be quite proper. The idea that artificial intelligence must be able to handle all psychological (or all philosophical) issues, or it will be unable to handle any of them, must be exorcised. Similarly, there is no more reason for us to think of humans as being completely identical to computers than for us to cling to the notion that there are no useful resemblances or parallels between these two kinds of (potentially) thoughtful entity.

Nonetheless, the issue of the actual degree of similarity between humans and computers cannot be permanently ignored. One of the principal findings of recent artificial intelligence is that the digital serial von Neumann computer seems in many ways an inadequate model of human cognition. To the extent that this finding is reinforced—and much of the research in the latter part of this book can be cited as supporting evidence —then we will have confirmation of the computational paradox. Artificial intelligence has demonstrated that the computer can be a useful tool for studying cognition and that it serves as a reasonable model for some human thought processes. But whether it is the best model for the most important processes is still very much an open question.

Artificial intelligence and cognitive psychology may well merge as the central components of a new cognitive science, but they cannot in themselves constitute the field. Philosophy will remain a source of important questions, a repository of invaluable reflections on those questions, and a valuable critic of cognitive scientific practices. But an equally important partner in this newly fashioned line of inquiry will be those disciplines that take as their appointed task the analysis of particular domains of cognition. Of the various disciplines that must assume this burden, linguistics is, by all accounts, the discipline that has accomplished the most and is thus most centrally involved in cognitive science. Moreover, and perhaps for this reason, other disciplines look to linguistics as a possible model of how to study a particular domain and to apply the powerful (and perhaps too powerful) tools of the psychologist and the computer scientist. Because of the intrinsic importance of language among the human cognitive faculties, because of linguistics' role as a possible model for domain-specific studies, and because of the tremendous strides made in linguistics over the past few decades, it is appropriate to turn now to the scientific study of language.

7

Linguistics: The Search for Autonomy

At First, There Were Colorless Green Ideas . . .

Enigmatic Sentences

At first reading, one of the most famous sentences of twentieth-century science makes little everyday sense. This is Noam Chomsky's oxymoronic proposition "Colorless green ideas sleep furiously." After all, ideas don't have colors, ideas don't sleep, something can't be simultaneously colorless and green—and for that matter, what does it mean for any entity to sleep furiously?

And yet a certain sense can be squeezed out of this sentence. It is certainly clearer than "ideas furiously green colorless sleep" or some other random concatenation of these five substantives. In Chomsky's sentence, one knows that a proposition is being asserted about *ideas*; one senses a contrast being drawn between an apparent state of blandness, as against a more active state of energy and color. The sentence is even susceptible to a figurative reading. One thinks of the revolutionary impact of apparently innocuous ideas—the kinds of idea Noam Chomsky himself put forth in his 1957 monograph *Syntactic Structures*.

The fact that we have clear intuitions about apparent nonsense like "Colorless green ideas sleep furiously" (or "Twas brillig and the slithy toves did gyre and gimble") underlies Chomsky's central contributions to linguistics and, for that matter, to cognitive science in a broader sense.

What Chomsky accomplished in his monograph, and in the numerous writings that followed, was to call attention to certain properties of sentences which all normal speakers and hearers intuitively know, but which derive from a deeper understanding of the language whose properties may be explicitly known only to the linguist. Chomsky called attention to and offered a convincing explanation of differences between apparently similar sentences: "John is easy to please" (where John is the recipient of the pleasing) versus "John is eager to please" (where John does the pleasing). "Ted persuaded John to learn" (where John is to do the learning) versus "Ted promised John to learn" (where Ted does the learning). Chomsky provided an account of sentences where meaning can be preserved despite shifting of the principal terms ("The cat chased the mouse" versus "The mouse was chased by the cat") as against those sentence pairs where one cannot simply reverse clauses ("Many men read few books" versus "Few books are read by many men"). He singled out and suggested mechanisms underlying the human ability to detect and unravel the ambiguities contained in such sentences as "Flying planes can be dangerous," "The shooting of the hunters disturbed me," and "I didn't shoot John because I like him." And he marked for study sentences that seem acceptable: "John seemed to each of the men to like the other" as against those superficially similar sentences that violate some putative rule of the language: "John seems to the men to like each other." We can say "We like each other" meaning each of us likes the other, but we can't say "We expect John to like each other"—indeed we're not even sure what this could mean (Marshall 1981).

That human beings have intuitions for sentences like these was not an insight unique to Chomsky. After all, Lewis Carroll exploited similar knowledge in *Jabberwocky*. The influential linguist of the early part of this century, Edward Sapir (1921), had called attention to many of the very relationships among sentences that were later to occupy Chomsky. But Chomsky went beyond his predecessors, including insightful linguists like Sapir, in his goal of setting out the rules that allow individuals to make, or to generate, all of the correct sentences listed above; to know that they are correct and what they mean; and to be able to pick out those sentences that violate these rules and are hence ungrammatical, though not necessarily devoid of meaning. To do this, the speaker must possess *at some level* a detailed set of rules or procedures indicating when different parts of speech can occur in given places in an utterance: that is, the rules must capture the intuitions of native speakers about the relations obtaining within and among sentences. Chomsky's statement of this explicit goal for the study of language—or, more precisely, for the study of syntax—and his success in developing methods directed toward the achievement of this goal instantly made his work stand out from that of other students of language. And his more general conviction that the several domains of mind (such as language) operate in terms of rules or principles that can be ferreted out and stated formally constitutes his main challenge to contemporary cognitive science.

In *Syntactic Structures,* Chomsky first announced a set of goals and then described the kind of grammar that appeared necessary if the proper regularities in English—or, indeed, in any language—were to be discerned. Rather than simply looking at the data of language, and trying to discern regularities from empirically observed utterances, as his predecessors had typically done, Chomsky insisted that the principles would never emerge from a study of the utterances themselves. Instead, it was necessary to work deductively. One must figure out what kind of a system language is, much in the way that one figures out what a particular branch of mathematics is like; and one must state one's conclusions in terms of a formal system. Such an analysis should lead to positing of the rules that can account for the production of any conceivable grammatical sentence (and there is, of course, an infinite number of such sentences), but at the same time the rules should not "generate" any incorrect or ungrammatical sentences. Once the system has been set up, one should then examine particular utterances to determine whether they can, in fact, be appropriately generated through adherence to the rules of the linguistic system.

In embarking on this program, Chomsky made two important, simplifying assumptions. One assumption was that the syntax of language could be examined independently of other aspects of language. If syntax were inextricably bound up with other aspects of language—for example, with meaning or with communicative utility—then it might not be possible to figure out its governing laws. The second but closely related tacit assumption was that the discipline of linguistics could proceed independently of other areas of the cognitive sciences. Once again, if the study of language were integrally tied to the study of other areas of human cognition—to other mental organs, as Chomsky would later phrase it—then progress might be impossible or agonizingly slow.

For the most part, these working assumptions about linguistic autonomy—the autonomy both of syntax from other aspects of language, and of linguistics from other aspects of cognitive science—worked out propitiously and made linguistics a rapidly developing area of science. But whether these assumptions can ultimately be sustained—whether the assumptions of autonomy are truly justified—constitutes a problem that has yet to be resolved. I shall return to these issues in the concluding section, after reviewing Chomsky's principal discoveries, the history of the field prior to his own entry, and certain current issues in the science of language.

Before entering into the heart of Chomsky's contributions, it may be well to say a word about the focus of this chapter. While the work of other scholars has been central in other chapters, in no other chapter of this book has so much attention been focused on a single individual. In part, this is an expositional device—a way of presenting the principal (and often complicated) ideas of modern linguistics in as accessible a fashion as possible. But, also, in no other contemporary cognitive science is the work of a single individual so key and so irreplaceable. In a nontrivial sense, the history of modern linguistics *is* the history of Chomsky's ideas and of the diverse reactions to them on the part of the community.

Chomsky's Approach

To achieve his ambitious goal, Chomsky first had to show that current methods for analyzing syntax and accounting for acceptable sentences would not work. By pushing a precise but inadequate formulation to its unacceptable conclusion, one could show *why* that formulation was inadequate—and, in the process, obtain a deeper understanding of the linguistic data it had vainly sought to explain. Chomsky proceeded by proving that the theoretically most plausible method for generating sentences could not in principle work. To begin with, he considered a finite-state grammar: a machine with a finite number of internal states which generates sentences in the following manner. Starting in a unique initial state, the machine passes into a second state by producing the first word of a sentence; then, while emitting a word at each transition, the machine proceeds from state to state until it has reached the final state, at which time a complete sentence has been generated. Chomsky showed that such finite-state grammars are inherently incapable of representing the recursive properties of English constructions: that is, by its nature, a finite-state grammar cannot generate sentences in which one clause is embedded in or dependent upon another, while simultaneously excluding strings that contradict these dependencies.

As an example, consider the sentence "The man who said he would help us is arriving today." Finite-state grammars cannot capture the structural link between *man* and *is arriving* which spans the intervening relative clause. Moreover, as its name suggests, a finite-state grammar cannot handle linguistic structures that can recur indefinitely, such as the embedding of a clause within another clause ("the boy that the girl that the dog . . . ," and so on). Even though such sentences soon become unwieldy for the perceiver, they are strictly speaking grammatical: any grammar must be able to account for (or generate) them. At the most general level, English (and, for that matter, other languages) does not work by slotting a word and then indicating what words can follow "to the right" of it; it works at a higher level of abstraction, where certain elements, under certain circumstances, can be placed wholly within other elements. Thus, Chomsky was making (with respect to language) precisely the point that Karl Lashley had urged about serial behavior in all of its manifestations.

Chomsky also demonstrated the unwieldiness—though not the utter impossibility—of a second kind of grammar, a *phrase-structure grammar* (or an immediate constituent analysis). Here the linguist works with an initial set of strings, together with a finite set of phrase-structure or "rewrite rules," where one phrase can be rewritten in another permissible form. Chomsky showed that such a phrase-structure system can only generate with great unwieldiness certain sentences; moreover, it cannot capture or account for many of the regularities any English speaker appreciates. Thus a phrase-structure grammar cannot explain the different structures of "What are you looking for" and "What are you running for" (Lees 1957, p. 386), or the ambiguity of "The teacher's marks are very low." Nor is there any way of showing that "John hit Bill" and "Bill is hit by John" bear a close relationship to one another. Nor, according to Chomsky, is it possible, using a phrase structure grammar, to generate sentences that involve the combination of two parallel clauses: to be specific, such grammars offer no mechanism for combining sentences like "The scene of the movie was in Chicago" and "The scene of the play was in Chicago" into "The scene of the movie and of the play was in Chicago." In broader terms, the phrase-structure grammar can be written only at the cost of several restatements of extensive parts of the grammar. As linguist Robert Lees points out, "if these uneconomical repetitions are permitted, then the grammar fails to state the near identity in structure between those parts which must be repeated" (1957, p. 387). More generally, while English might conceivably be described in terms of phrase-structure grammars, such a description would be so unwieldy, so hopelessly complex that these descriptions would be of scant interest.

Thus, the most plausible models for the generation of grammatical sentences were both shown to be inadequate: finite-state grammars, because countless instances of meaningful language cannot be generated on a word-by-word basis; phrase-structure grammars, because mere attention to the ways that phrases are constructed fails to capture important regularities in the language. For these reasons, Chomsky found it necessary to introduce a new level of linguistic structures which at once swept away these difficulties and made it possible to account for the full range of sentences in the language.

Inspired in part by his teacher Zellig Harris (1952), Chomsky discovered the level of transformational analysis. In a transformational grammar,

Chomsky argued, one posits a set of rules whereby sentences can be related to one another, and where one sentence (or more precisely, the abstract representation of a sentence) can be converted or transformed into another. A generative grammar, in Chomsky's sense, is a rule system formalized with mathematical precision: without drawing upon any information that is not represented explicitly within it, the system generates the grammatical sentences of the language that it describes or characterizes, and assigns to each sentence a structural description or grammatical analysis.

As described in Chomsky's 1957 monograph, the method of transformational grammar works roughly as follows. (It must be immediately added—indeed, stressed—that the system has changed several times in the intervening years.) Beginning with phrase-structure rules, one generates only the cores of sentences, or *kernel sentences,* which are short active declarative assertions. These are generated by following a set of instructions for constructing strings: for example, (1) Sentence = Noun Phrase + Verb Phrase; (2) Noun Phrase = $T + N$; (3) T = the; (4) N = man, ball; (5) Verb Phrase = Verb + Noun Phrase; (6) Verb = hit, take; and so on. Starting with the single symbol S, one can generate, by a completely specifiable set of rules, a kernel sentence like "The man hit the ball." Thereafter, all the other grammatical sentences of the language can be generated by means of transforming these kernel sentences.

Transformations are an algorithmic set of procedures that occur in a prescribed order and allow one to convert one linguistic string to another. Thus, a transformation allows one to convert an active sentence into a passive sentence, a positive statement into a negative statement or a question. On such an analysis, "What are you looking for" can be described as the "what-question" transformation of "You are looking for it"; while "What are you running for" is a "why-question" transformation of "You are running." Transformations can lay bare the links between sentences like "The boy kissed the girl" and "The girl was kissed by the boy"; the deep differences between superficially similar syntactic arrangements like "The girl is eager to please" and "The girl is easy to please"; and the fact that a phrase like "the shooting of the hunters" is ambiguous because it can be accounted for by two different transformational histories— one, in which the hunters are shot; the other, in which the hunters do the shooting.

All these transformations are structure-dependent: that is, they do not operate on single words or on strings of words of arbitrary length. Rather, the transformations are imposed on strings (abstract representations of sentences) *after* these strings have been analyzed into appropriate syntactic categories and constituents (or phrase structures), which determine when and where the transformations can be applied. Because Chomsky placed great value on formal simplicity in the selection of the appropriate syntactic description, transformational grammar won out over phrase structure. While all English sentences can, in principle, be generated by a grammar with only phrase-structure rules, one would naturally prefer a simple phrase-structure rule and a simple transformational rule over a large number of cumbersome and difficult-to-orchestrate phrase-structure rules.

(To prevent subsequent misunderstanding, I must now get a bit ahead of my story. At the time Chomsky wrote, it was not appreciated that the transformation was an extremely powerful formal device, one that could be abused to rescue an analysis which was not actually appropriate to the linguistic data. To counter these and other problems, there has since been a movement to reduce radically or even to eliminate the transformational component. Also, several prominent linguists are once again re-embracing a phrase-structure approach.)

While the transformational approach was clearly innovative, it is not easy to indicate precisely where Chomsky's work went beyond that of his contemporaries. Certainly the desire to write a complete grammar for English had motivated others of his colleagues, and the focus on syntax, to the relative exclusion of phonology and semantics, also characterized much work in that era. Chomsky did, in fact, talk about how the syntactic level interacted with phonology and semantics; but for years he has concentrated his analytic energies on the level of syntax (see, however, Chomsky and Halle 1968). Moreover, Chomsky approached this task with a seriousness of purpose, an arsenal of logical and mathematical tools, a finesse and a finality of argument that had simply not been marshaled hitherto in linguistic analysis. While other scholars had alluded to limitations of existing models, like the finite-state or the phrase-structure model, Chomsky actually proved the impossibility of the first and the essential inadequacy of the second. While others, including Chomsky's teacher Zellig Harris, had spoken about transformational rules that might link sentences, Chomsky went beyond a mere assertion that such rules might regularize relations among sentences: he asserted that there *must* be a separate level called the transformational level, and he postulated the mechanisms governing both obligatory and optional transformations.

Chomsky saw the linguist's task differently from the way his predecessors had seen it. His view of grammatical generation was based on the notion of an automaton—a machine in an abstract sense which simply generates linguistic strings on the basis of rules that have been built (programmed) into it. The resulting grammar is neutral—equally valid as a description of linguistic production or linguistic comprehension. Clearly, Chomsky was a child of the new era of Wiener, von Neumann, Turing, and Shannon, though—just as clearly—some of his specific ideas about how language works ran directly counter to information-theory notions.

Chomsky also characterized the task of the linguist in a more explicit way than had his predecessors. He devoted considerable attention to the theoretical question of how one goes about choosing one linguistic model over another. He laid out the formal criteria for an adequate theory of linguistics suggesting (and demonstrating) how these criteria might be achieved. He expounded as well an ordered set of standards of adequacy: *observational adequacy,* where the grammar gives a correct account of observed linguistic data; *descriptive adequacy,* where the account also captures the native speaker's intrinsic competence, his own internalized knowledge; and *explanatory adequacy,* where the analyst uncovers principles underlying optimal grammar for the language. An account that exhibits explanatory adequacy can explain why individuals have constructed the grammars that they have, and what kinds of abilities individuals have needed to achieve linguistic competence. Such theoretical sophistication (and presumption!) had also been hitherto absent from the writings of linguists interested in grammar.

The Spreading of Green Ideas

Left entirely on its own, Chomsky's book might have proved too remote from the rest of the field and perished on the vine. No one was interested in publishing his massive doctoral thesis, *The Logical Structure of Linguistic Theory* (1955), in which the formal proofs were laid out in detail. His initial monograph, *Syntactic Structures,* was published by the small Dutch publisher, Mouton, only after it had been strongly recommended by Roman Jakobson, the most distinguished linguist of the day. Even so issued, the monograph might well have remained obscure, at least for some years, were it not for a long, detailed, and wholly positive review in the influential journal *Language* by Chomsky's early student and associate Robert Lees (1957).

Leaving no doubt in his review that Chomsky's slim volume would revolutionize linguistics, Lees contrasted the "prescientific stage of collection and classification of interesting facts" with a scientific discipline "characterized essentially by the introduction of abstract constructs in theories and the validation of those theories by testing their predictive power" (1957, p. 376). Playing Huxley to Chomsky's Darwin, Lees asserted that "some fields of knowledge have reached such an advanced stage of development that their basic problem can be stated very succinctly, and the structure is so well understood that we can now begin to construct axiomatic theories to render explicitly and rigorously just what their content is and means" (p. 377). In Lees's view, Chomsky's book enabled linguistics to cross the line from a descriptive pre-science to an axiomatic science:

Chomsky's book on syntactic structures is one of the first serious attempts on the part of a linguist to construct within the tradition of scientific theory-construction a comprehensive theory of language which may be understood in the same sense that a chemical, biological theory is ordinarily understood by experts in those fields. It is not a mere reorganization of the data into a new kind of library catalogue, nor another speculative philosophy about the nature of Man and Language, but rather a rigorous explication of our intuitions about our language in terms of an overt axiom system, the theorems derivable from it, explicit results which may be compared with new data and other intuitions, all based plainly on an overt theory of the internal structure of languages; and it may well provide an opportunity for the application of explicit measures of simplicity to decide preference of one form over another form of grammar. (1957, pp. 377–78)

Lees said that *Syntactic Structures* was one of the first serious attempts to construct a comprehensive theory of language; but, as Frederic Newmeyer declares in his useful history of this era, "Actually the tone of the review as a whole made it clear that Lees regarded it as the ONLY serious attempt and a completely successful one at that" (1980, p. 19).

As they became aware of Chomsky's work, other linguists also discerned its power and originality. In another review, C. F. Voegelin, a leading linguist, declared that even if *Syntactic Structures* managed to achieve only part of its goals, "it will have accomplished a Copernican revolution" (quoted in Newmeyer 1980, p. 19). The distinguished British linguist C. E. Balzell remarked that "linguistics will never be the same"; and Bernard Bloch, one of the leading linguists of an earlier generation, confided to colleagues "Chomsky really seems to be on the right track. If I were younger, I'd be on his bandwagon too" (both quoted in Newmeyer 1980, p. 47).

But in heralding a revolution, Chomsky was launching a movement at someone's expense—namely, the structural linguists of an earlier generation. And, as the full dimensions of his program became clear, there was considerable and often violent opposition. For it turned out that Chomsky was not merely offering a critique of existing attempts to describe a grammar; instead, he espoused radically different views of how linguistics should work, and, indeed, of what social science (we would today substitute "cognitive science") was about. Some of these views were muted, or had not yet been well formed, at the time of the publication of *Syntactic Structures* (Chomsky was only twenty-nine at the time of the book's publication; twenty-seven at the conclusion of his doctorate); but with the publication of succeeding articles in the late 1950s and early 1960s, and the issuing of a major theoretical statement, *Aspects of a Theory of Syntax,* in 1965, the full dimensions of his program had been laid out.

To begin with, Chomsky made it clear that he was interested in language in a particular sense. Language is not a general means of communication or a blanket word encompassing all symbol systems: rather, at the core of language is the property of syntax, the capacity unique to the human species to combine and recombine verbal symbols in certain specifiable orders, in order to create a potentially infinite number of grammatically acceptable sentences. Moreover, syntax was seen as the primary, basic, or (in a technical sense) deep level of the language, with both semantics (meaning) and phonology (sound structure) being constructed upon a syntactic core. Thus, in a transformational account, the semantic and phonological components have access to the output of the core syntactic component, but not vice versa (Smith and Wilson 1979, p. 97): indeed, in such an account, the verbal symbols are manipulated without any reference to their meanings or their sounds. Recently Chomsky (1981) has nominated the shift from "language" to "grammar" in a restricted sense as one of the two most important shifts in linguistic theory over the past few decades (the other being the search for a more restricted notion of grammars, so that possibilities for explanatory adequacy are enhanced).

Chomsky was also interested in language in a more abstract sense than his predecessors had been. While the structuralists of the preceding generation examined what individuals actually said, and typically focused on uttered words, Chomsky considered language to be an abstraction—a capacity that can merely be glimpsed in impure form in an individual's actual output. Consistent with his formalistic leanings, Chomsky felt that linguists should focus on this idealized, virtually Platonic form and disregard the slight errors, pauses, lapses of memory, and the like which are associated with actual speaking in the real world. Both in his emphasis on pure syntax and in his desire to study language as an ideal form, Chomsky was dramatically at odds with the behaviorism of the time.

Verbal Misbehavior: The Controversy with Skinner

Chomsky gradually revealed his fundamental opposition to the complete set of empiricist assumptions of most scientists, and nearly all linguists, of his era. Initially, this revelation surfaced in a now notorious 1959 review of the book *Verbal Behavior,* by B. F. Skinner (1957), the archbehaviorist at mid-century. Skinner had attempted to explain linguistic behavior—and the accent was on *behavior*—in terms of the same stimulus-response chains and laws of reinforcement which he had invoked to account for the behavior of lower organisms—like the pecking of pigeons or the maze running of rats. He had, for the most part, ignored the intricate structural properties of language that fascinated Chomsky (and other linguists) and other critics of behaviorism like Karl Lashley. And Skinner had completely ignored the creative aspect of language—the fact that one is free to talk about whatever one wants, in the way that one wants to. Stressing the infinite expressive potential of language, Chomsky argued that it is senseless to think of linguistic output as restricted in any meaningful way by the stimuli that happen to be present.

With relish, Chomsky showed that Skinner's attempts to explain language along these stimulus-response lines were fundamentally flawed. They failed whether they were applied literally or metaphorically. As Chomsky put it with characteristic asperity:

> a critical account of his book must show that with a literal reading (where the terms of the descriptive system have something like the technical meanings given in Skinner's definitions) the book covers almost no aspects of linguistic behavior, and that with a metaphoric reading, it is no more scientific than the traditional approaches to this subject matter, and rarely as clear and careful. (1964a, p. 552)

But Chomsky made it clear that Skinner was also on the wrong track epistemologically. Like other empiricists of the day, Skinner had urged investigators to remain close to the data and to spurn abstract theory. Chomsky, on the contrary, felt that the data would *never* speak for themselves, that it was necessary to take a theoretical stand and to explore the consequences of that theory. Moreover, he revealed his own suspicion that the kinds of theories needed to explain language, and other aspects of human thought and behavior, would have to be abstract and, in fact, frankly mentalistic. Leaning explicitly on the work of Descartes some three hundred years earlier, and borrowing leaves as well from the writings of Plato and Immanuel Kant, Chomsky argued that our interpretation of the world is based on representational systems that derive from the structure of the mind itself and do not mirror in any direct way the form of the external world. And, indeed, once linguists accepted the impossibility of a physical definition of grammaticality—for example, one expressed in terms of actual utterances—they would realize the necessity for abstract mentalistic linguistic theory.

In this book review, Chomsky also revealed his fundamental impatience with most psychological approaches. In his view, psychological experiments were often unnecessary to prove a point: many psychologists preferred demonstrating the obvious to thinking systematically and in a theoretical vein (Rieber 1983, p. 48). One psychologist Chomsky singled out for praise was Karl Lashley. In his study of serially ordered behavior, Lashley had concluded that an utterance is not simply produced by stringing together a sequence of responses under the control of outside stimulation and interverbal association, and that the syntactic organization of an utterance is not something directly represented in the physical structure of the utterance. Rather, syntactic structure turns out to be, in Lashley's words, "a generalized pattern imposed on the specific acts as they occur" (quoted in Jeffress 1951, p. 122). Building on Lashley, Chomsky concluded that there must be "a multiplicity of integrative processes which can only be inferred from the final results of their activity" (1964a, p. 575).

A new psychological perspective appeared latent in Chomsky's formulation. At the very end of the review, he opined, "At the moment the question cannot be seriously posed, but in principle it may be possible to study the problem of determining what the built-in structure of an information-processing (hypothesis-forming) system must be to enable it to arrive at the grammar of a language from the available data in the available time" (1964a, p. 578). In the years ahead, Chomsky was to mine this intuition, suggesting that the individual is born with a strong penchant to learn language, and that the *possible forms* of the language which one can learn are sharply limited by one's species membership with its peculiar genetic inheritance. Chomsky was impressed by the extreme abstractness of the task faced by every child who must learn language, the rapidity with which the language is learned, despite the lack of explicit tutelage. Skinner's notion of learning language through imitation and reinforcement was implausible—if not impossible in the same sense as the finite-state grammar: an entirely new psychological perspective was needed to account for the rapidity and relatively error-free way in which children acquire language, despite the "poverty of stimulus," the relatively small corpus of often incomplete or error-tinged utterances they encounter in daily life.

General Messages: Chomskian Themata

Chomsky hit his public stride in this essay. No longer simply a linguist writing for a small group of colleagues about the arcane details of syntax, he revealed himself to be a full-fledged cognitivist, one interested in many dimensions of the mind and prepared to argue resolutely for his beliefs. (The fact that Skinner never responded publicly to the review signaled to many interested researchers the theoretical bankruptcy of the behaviorist position.) And, in the years following the publication of his review, Chomsky made clear others of his scientific themata. In his view, language provided the best model for how to conceptualize and study thought processes. Language should in fact be considered as part of a reformulated psychology. Both language and the rest of psychology ought to exhibit formal rigor, posit abstract models, and pursue the principles of explanatory adequacy. Informally phrased general principles (of the sort favored by Skinner and many other psychologists) were anathema. Chomsky gradually challenged the widespread belief in extremely general and broad powers of the mind—powers like learning, stimulus generalization, and the like. (In this move, he was reflecting, if not anticipating, similar shifts occurring in psychology and artificial intelligence.) He came to think of the mind as a series of relatively independent mental organs or modules, each with its own rules of operation and development, along with prescribed means of interacting with other "organs." Here was a powerful statement on behalf of the autonomy both of language as an organ—and, not coincidentally, of linguistics as a discipline. Superimposed on this *modularity* was a commitment to *mentalism*—the existence of abstract structures in the mind which make knowledge possible. And there was as well a swing to *nativism,* the belief that much of our knowledge is universal and inborn, and that, without the need for tutelage, one has access to this knowledge simply by virtue of being human. These views were as much a departure in the human sciences of the era as were Chomsky's initial claims in the area of linguistics; and they were to generate even more controversy than his initial views expressed in *Syntactic Structures.*

The full force of Chomsky's challenge to traditional linguistics became clear in 1958 at the Third Texas Conference on Problems of Linguistic Analysis of English. Here, in initially respectful but unfailingly firm terms, he told his linguistic brethren that their traditional approaches to understanding language were doomed to fail. He asserted that a complete inventory of elements in language could never give rise to a characterization of all possible sentences, and that an inductive discovery procedure could never work. He then went on to argue:

> I think that the failure to offer a precise account of the notion "grammar" is not just a superficial defect in linguistic theory that can be remedied by adding one more definition. It seems to me that until this notion is clarified, no part of linguistic theory can achieve anything like a satisfactory development. . . . I have been discussing a grammar of a particular language here as analogous to a particular scientific theory, dealing with its subject matter (the set of sentences of this language) much as embryology or physics deals with its subject matter. (1964*b*, p. 213)

Chomsky took issue with the view that the methodological burden of linguistics is the elaboration of techniques for discovering and classing linguistic elements, and that grammars are inventories of these elements and classes. Instead, he saw grammar as a *theory* of the sentences of the language; and he saw the major methodological problem as the construction of a general theory of linguistic structure in which the properties of grammars (and of the structural descriptions and linguistic levels derived from them) are studied in an abstract way (Chomsky 1964*b*).

Following his presentation Chomsky engaged in debate from the floor with leading structuralists of the past generation, whose views he was opposing. While some of them had hoped to defeat the young upstart once and for all, there was a very different outcome. As Newmeyer recounts on the basis of the transcripts, "Here we can see linguistic history documented as nowhere else—Chomsky, the *enfant terrible,* taking on some of the giants of the field and making them look like rather confused students in a beginning linguistics course" (1980, p. 35). In the years that followed, this scene was to be repeated countless times, as Chomsky's steadily growing body of admirers and followers did battle with the leaders of the once-dominant structuralist school and demonstrated with numbing regularity the inadequacy of earlier approaches and the promise of the new generative approach to grammar.

Chomsky's approach was indeed revolutionary—cataclysmic in relation to earlier linguistics; iconoclastic in relation to the prevailing empiricist, inductivist, and nominalist temperament. Just as scholars like Lévi-Strauss in anthropology, Bruner and Miller in psychology, and Quine and Putnam in philosophy had challenged the dogmas of their chosen discipline, so Chomsky confronted received opinions in the linguistics world. And because his approach was exceedingly formal, and the study of linguistics relatively advanced in the human sciences, the scope of his claims stood out with stark clarity.

Moreover, and this is part of the intellectual history of the time as well, Chomsky's talents as a polemicist and his penchant for debate were perhaps unmatched in recent scientific history. He liked to debate, was brilliant at it, and was willing to argue tirelessly with all those interested in his topic. He also inspired many students and colleagues to join him in what seemed like a crusade—a crusade against the reflexive (and unreflective) empiricism of the previous generation, a crusade in favor of his views of syntax, of language, of innate knowledge, of cognitive science, and, even in many cases, of the contemporary political scene. In the end, many of Chomsky's own supporters abandoned him, and today his *particular* linguistic views are apparently held by only a minority of workers in syntax. Yet even his most severe critics would not be studying what they are studying, in the way that they are studying it, without his indispensable and awesome example. And, indeed, both in the power of what he said and in the uncompromising way he said it, Chomsky's work made a deep impression from the first on nearly everyone who took the trouble to study it.

All the same, as the excitement of those early days of transformational grammar receded somewhat from view, it is easier to discern continuities with earlier times. At the beginning of this chapter, I noted that Edward Sapir, two generations older than Chomsky, was already dealing on an intuitive level with many of the problems to which *Syntactic Structures* was explicitly addressed. Going back much farther, the general epistemological

195

approach that influenced Chomsky was taken from the work of Descartes, and even more from those "Cartesian linguists" who were struck by the creative powers of human language and who (like Wilhelm von Humboldt) searched for ways to capture its regularities. And closer to home, Chomsky shared the belief of his structuralist teachers in the importance of studying syntax or grammar separately; the need (stressed by Roman Jakobson and Louis Hjelmslev [1953]) for an essentially mathematical or formal approach to language; the link (noted by Leonard Bloomfield) between the problem of describing a language and the problem of accounting for language acquisition; and the conviction (with Ferdinand de Saussure) that the study of *langue* (or competence) differs profoundly from the study of *parole* (or performance). What Chomsky did, however, was to put these various strands together: he showed that one could harness a formal-logical analysis to illuminate intuitive relations among sentences, in service of the goal of generating a system of rules which could account for all, but only all, the correct sentences in the language. As Freud said of his discovery of the unconscious through the "royal road" of dreams, such insight falls to one's lot but once in a lifetime.

Linguistics of an Earlier Era

As far back as the classical era, scholars were arguing about the regularities of language, and its ultimate characterization: is language part of nature or part of culture? A system of grammatical categories, based on Greek and Latin, evolved, and the study of rhetoric flourished as never since. Nor was this interest exclusive to the Western world; in India in the fourth century B.C., for example, Panini devised a grammar that was more diverse and in some respects superior to that proposed by Greco-Roman scholars. During the Renaissance, the tradition of classical philology reached great heights, when it was applied to textual and critical analysis in various fields. As scholars became aware of other languages, through travel and colonizing, empirical knowledge accrued concerning the various languages of Asia, Africa, Oceania, and the New World. There were even scientific expeditions just to collect information about exotic languages (Robins 1967).

An important event in the history of linguistics occurred in 1786 when Sir William Jones, an English orientalist, reported to the Bengal-Asiatic Society that Sanskrit bore a striking resemblance to the languages of Greek and Latin. Jones put forth the provocative hypothesis that all three languages must have come forth from a common source, which perhaps no longer exists. This statement jostled the scholarly world, which had hitherto assumed that Latin had been a sort of corrupt Greek, and that most European languages had just been derived from Latin. But a similarly offhand explanation of the relationship between ancient languages and the newly examined Sanskrit was not possible.

Jones's discovery ushered in a new conception of linguistic history, linguistic phylogeny, and the processes of linguistic change. Earlier it had been assumed that all languages had developed in the few thousand years since Creation, and that Hebrew was the original language. Now instead, linguists and philosophers became caught up with discovering the laws that governed changes in language. Working in the manner of taxonomic biologists, the linguists set up various language families (Semitic, Algonquin, Finno-Ugrian, and so on) and developed a theory of language changes. Jakob Grimm found systematic correspondences between the sounds of German and those of Greek, Latin, and Sanskrit. For example, he noted that where Gothic (the oldest surviving Germanic language) had an *f,* Latin, Greek, and Sanskrit frequently had a *p.* To account for these relationships, he postulated a cyclical "soundshift" in the prehistory of Germanic, in which the original voiceless (or unaspirated) stops became "aspirates" (thus *p* becomes *f*). But the systematization was not complete: Grimm and his associates were willing to countenance exceptions to such rules (Bolinger 1968).

The Neo-Grammarians

In the 1860s and 1870s, in a manner paralleling the Chomskian circle a century later, a group of young rebels called the *Junggrammatiker* (or neo-grammarians) attempted to put this situation in order. Not satisfied with a mere collection or taxonomy of regularities, of the sort that Grimm and his associates had noticed, the neo-grammarians claimed that the laws of phonemic change admit no exceptions. Hermann Paul asserted in 1879, "Every phonemic law operates with absolute necessity: it as little admits of an exception as a chemical or physical law" (quoted in Brew 1968, p. 177). Any apparent exceptions to these laws must be explained by reference to other laws, and there was little tolerance of theory for theory's sake. As the neo-grammarians H. Osthoff and K. Brugmann declared:

Only that comparative linguist who forsakes the hypothesis-laden atmosphere of the workshop in which Indogermanic rootforms are forged, and comes out into the clear light of tangible present-day actuality in order to obtain from this source information which vague theory cannot ever afford him, can arrive at a correct presentation of the life and the transformations of linguistic forms. (Quoted in Robins 1967, pp. 184–85)

The data-centered penchant of the neo-grammarians deeply affected thinking about language. Clues to how language worked could be sought in the physical characteristics of the utterances; and, in fact, the newly devised techniques of psychophysics seemed promising tools. However, despite efforts by the pioneering psychologist, Wilhelm Wundt, the psychologists never really got a handle on linguistic phenomena. What is interesting, in retrospect, is that at the turn of the century, the linguists were monitoring psychologists, trying to figure out which of the new psychological theories were correct; nowadays psychologists have been dogging the linguists, attempting to determine which of the linguists' perspectives is most likely to yield a psychologically valid view of language (Blumenthal 1979).

de Saussure's Signal Contributions

While comparative philologists (like Grimm) enhanced empirical knowledge about the development of language over the millennia, and the relationships among the sound structures of various languages, their writings have a fundamentally dated quality: it is as if, in their proclivity for discovering laws about the obscure past, these scholars had missed what subsequent generations would see as the major point of linguistic study. This was not true, however, of Ferdinand de Saussure, who can properly be deemed the first linguist of the modern era. A Swiss savant, active at the turn of the century, who made his first contributions to Indo-European comparative linguistics, de Saussure (often abbreviated as Saussure) led his colleagues away from their absorption with history and toward the investigation of the languages of their own time. He contrasted *diachronic linguistics* (which focused on changes of language over time) with *synchronic linguistics* (the study of language as a system at a single moment in time). And he argued that much of importance in language could be understood apart from those comparative and evolutionary concerns that had dominated the work of his predecessors and his own early training.

Comparing language to a game of chess (an analogy of which he was very fond), Saussure (1959) noted that, in the course of a game, the state of the board is constantly changing: still, at any one time the state of the game can be fully described in terms of the positions occupied by the various pieces. On this view, it does not matter by which route the players have arrived at their current positions. By a similar argument, though languages are constantly changing, the successive or delimited states of language can be described independently of one another and without respect to their prior history.

Language, to Saussure, resembled a game of chess in still other ways. First of all, the actual size and shape of the linguistic tokens is irrelevant:

just as any piece can stand for a bishop, any sound can stand for the concept *apple:* all that is required is conventional agreement. Second, no entity by itself has meaning: an entity accrues meaning only in terms of its relationship to the other entities in an ensemble. Thus, the meaning of a rook is only achieved in relation to what the other pieces can do in principle and to what position they occupy at the present time; by the same token, the meaning of a word (or a part of speech) is significant only in terms of the other words in the language, and of the particular words with which that given word happens to be concatenated at a specific moment in time. Just as any move in a game of chess influences the complexion of the game, and alters all the relations, so, too, any introduction of a new word has reverberations across all other words in the utterance, text, or entire language. And so language must be seen as an organized totality, whose various parts are interdependent and derive their significance from the system as a whole.

Saussure's focus on language as a system, and his interest in describing that system in synchronic terms, were probably his most lasting contributions to the emerging science of language. (The Gestalt psychologists were, at the same time, making similar points about the interrelationships among visual perceptual elements.) However, other expeditions which he made into the region of language were also telling. Saussure introduced a distinction between language (or *langue*) as a total system of regularities (like the rules governing every game of chess) and speech (or *parole*) which are the actual utterances themselves (like the moves of a particular game). While *parole* constitutes the immediately accessible data, the linguist's proper object is the *langue* of each community: the regularities in the lexicon, grammar, and phonology which each person imbibes by being reared in a particular speech community. Saussure shrewdly pointed out that a parrot may speak the words but does not know the system of language; whereas a person who knows the language of English may choose not to speak it. (Shades of Searle's Chinese room conundrum!)

In some ways Saussure anticipated linguistic theory of today, and several of his distinctions and conceptualizations are now part of the working assumptions of every practicing linguist. For instance, he viewed language as a cognitive system contained within the head of the individual speaker—a mentalistic perspective that came perhaps readily to a French-speaking scholar. But it is important to note differences between his outlook and that of current workers. For one thing, Saussure was wedded to a description or inventory of the elements in language and to building up from the simplest to the most complex elements. This atomistic orientation stands in sharp contrast to the Chomskian goal of a system of generative rules which will yield only acceptable utterances. Moreover, Saussure paid little attention to the properties of a sentence; in contrast, in Chomsky's top-down approach, the rule-governed properties of the words in a sentence and the relations that obtain among sentence types are of paramount importance. Yet Saussure's concentration on the systematic and language-specific properties of linguistics, and on the feasibility of explaining language in its own terms, makes him a partner of contemporary writers. As he insisted at the conclusion of his course, "From the incursions we have made into the borderlands of our science, one lesson stands out. It is wholly negative, but is all the more interesting because it agrees with the fundamental idea of this course: *the true and unique object of linguistics is language studied in and for itself"* (1959, p. 232). An important blow struck for the autonomy view.

The Prague School

Having launched a science of linguistics, the Saussure school saw centers rise around the world. Linguists in America, in France, and in Scandinavia all acknowledged a debt to the master of Geneva. But the Saussurean program was most successfully pursued by linguists working in Prague in the 1920s and 1930s. Under its leaders Roman Jakobson and Nikolay Troubetskoy, the Prague school exhibited wide interests but was probably best known for its work on phonology. Rather than taking the phoneme as the minimal unit of analysis, however, members of the Prague school viewed phonemes as sets of distinctive features. Each phoneme was composed of a number of articulatory features and was distinguished from every other phoneme in the language by the presence or the absence of at least one feature (Vachek 1966).

Jakobson explained the idea through a pithy example. Suppose one meets someone at a party but does not get his name. It could be Mr. Ditter, Mr. Bitter, Mr. Pitter, Mr. Titter, or the like. One's ability to figure out the person's name depends upon hearing certain minimal contrasts. For example, *ditter* and *pitter* differ on two concurrent minimal distinctions—which happen to be called *grave* versus *acute,* and *tense* versus *lax.* Moreover, any nonidentical set can be similarly described in terms of the features on which they differ.

Each of these distinctive features involves a choice between the two terms of an opposition, a contrast that can be perceived by a listener. Consider, for example, the sounds /p/ and /t/. These sounds feature a contrast between grave and acute. In /p/ there is a concentration of energy at the lower end of the sound spectrum, whereas in /t/ there is a concentration of energy in the upper end of the spectrum. Thus the two sounds have relatively different pitches, represent different distributions of energy in production, and reflect resonating cavities with different sizes and shapes. By the same token, all other distinctive features can also be defined in terms of such perceptual, physical, and motor properties. These distinctive features become aligned into simultaneous bundles of sounds which are the phonemes of language. While one might think that there is a huge multiplicity of features, Jakobson and his colleague Morris Halle reported —again, in the significant year 1956—a mere twelve basic oppositions out of which each language makes its own selections.

In its treatment of phonology along these lines, the Prague school made its most characteristic and enduring contribution. Note that this approach, while superficially similar to that of the descriptive structuralists, was actually motivated by different concerns. The Prague scholars were interested in explanation, not just description, and had no hesitation in imputing psychological reality to their linguistic accounts. Rather than viewing the features as simply "convenient" ways of describing sounds, members of the Prague school believed that they possessed physical and psychological reality: the nervous system had evolved so as to ensure the proper production and discrimination of these features. Features can be defined independently of their appearance in any particular language; and when found, they are accounted for by their place in a general theory of phonology. Theory guides the discovery of phenomena rather than the other way around.

The phoneme marked an important advance. First, it turned out that the phonemic system of every language could be characterized in terms of a small number of binary feature oppositions. Second, the features allowed the formulation of generalizations that could not be stated in other structuralist models. Also, the positing of features made possible the development of an evaluation procedure: the optimal analysis should need the least number of feature specifications *per* phoneme. These factors were soon to exert influence on linguists who sought to bring comparable rigor to the still fledgling study of syntax.

By no means did the Prague school restrict itself to phonology. Indeed, Roman Jakobson and his colleagues were driven by a lust to write about nearly every aspect of language, from phonology to poetry, and about a large band of languages as well. Invading the field of psychology, Jakobson (1941) sought to apply his interest in sound laws to a wide variety of populations. He discerned a sequence of sound development in normal children, one that follows what he called the *law of maximal contrast;* and he went on to demonstrate that this developmental progression is reversed in an orderly way as a result of damage to the human brain. Jakobson showed, furthermore, that the same kinds of contrast that had worked for the description of phonology could also be applied to choices made at other linguistic levels, ranging from syntax to pragmatics. And in a fertile methodological contribution, Jakobson pointed out that most linguistic contrasts are not equivalent or reversible: one pole of the contrast is more basic (or unmarked), while the other is essentially defined in relation to the basic pole, and is therefore marked. For example, at the level of sound structure, a voiceless sound is unmarked in contrast to a marked one; at the level of lexical semantics, the word *long* is unmarked, in contrast to the word *short* which is marked. The concept of *markedness* found its way into descriptions at each level of language and, as we shall see, exerted a major influence on adjacent fields.

By virtue of his knowledge of languages, his wide scope of interests, and his boldness in theorizing, Jakobson inspired a whole generation of linguists. And like other seminal scholars, he also exerted a pivotal effect on other fields of knowledge. Probably his greatest impact occurred in anthropology. Jakobson had met Claude Lévi-Strauss in the early 1940s in New York City, and the two of them had spent much time in consultation and comradeship. At that time Lévi-Strauss was searching for methods that would aid in making sense of the masses of data about kinship and social organization he had gathered during his field work in Brazil (Lévi-Strauss 1963). Introduced by Jakobson to the structural methods of linguistic analysis, he seized upon them as a way of conceptualizing *all* cultural data, not just those of language. For Lévi-Strauss, as we shall see in chapter 8, the example of linguistics was *the* one to be followed by other, more backward social sciences. But a vast problem inhered in deciding just how to apply the phonological model in a region where it had not been explicitly formulated. In a more modest sense, this was the problem facing the Prague school as well. One could readily use principles of analysis developed with reference to phonology, but just how to apply these principles in more complex aspects of language, such as those involved in syntax or poetry, was not always transparent.

Such reservations did not greatly trouble Jakobson. He was by temperament a conquistador, not a doubter. Though chauvinistic about his chosen discipline, he was not concerned to erect boundaries, to protect the sanctity of phonology or linguistics from territorial snipers; in fact, he strained to find connections to other fields. "I am a linguist," he would often declare "and nothing human is alien to me." Such forays and speculative leaps were spurned by the strict conscience of the Chomskyites, and for a time Jakobson's intellectual ambitions were seen as somewhat overarching and anachronistic. But now as the autonomy of linguistic study is once more being challenged, his more synthetic viewpoint may regain credibility.

Bloomfield Fashions a Field

Linguistics in America was also constructed in the shadow of Saussure's program but, by virtue of the overwhelming influence of a single linguist, Leonard Bloomfield, took a somewhat different historical tack (Hockett 1968*a*). From a contemporary cognitive perspective, Bloomfield made two contributions—one wholly beneficent, the other far less so. His positive work involved the development of methods and notations for the study of unfamiliar languages. As a young instructor, Bloomfield began to study various exotic languages—for example, Tagalog, the principal Indonesian language of the Philippines. Bloomfield worked from dictation, taking down an extended discourse, which he then subjected to detailed analysis. Rejecting the model of Latin grammar, which had guided many of his predecessors, Bloomfield recorded the sound patterns of each particular language, noting both its similarities and its departures from other classical languages. From the study of Tagalog, Bloomfield moved to Malayo-Polynesian and Algonquin. In each case he developed appropriate methods for recording the language and struggled to find the best way of describing its sound patterns and grammatical regularities. The identification of constituent structures, as a means of syntactic analysis, is an outgrowth of Bloomfield's work.

In mastering the properties of these various languages, Bloomfield was not content simply to pursue his own research. He came to see the need for a cadre of trained linguists. Soon he founded a linguistics society and launched a series of publications. He saw linguistics as a natural science —one patterned after physics:

> As the physicist need not follow the path of each particle, but observes their resultant action in the mass, and their individual actions only when these in turn group themselves into a deflection of the mass condition (as in radio-active substances) and rarely has occasion to watch the impingement of a single particle, so in linguistics we rarely attend to the single utterance or speaker, but attend to the deviations of utterances and speakers only when they mass themselves into a deflection of the total activity. (Bloomfield 1925, p. 2)

In campaigning for the discipline of linguistics, and in modeling how to record new languages, Bloomfield set an enviable standard. Like Wundt, he deserves credit for founding the principal institutions in his field. Yet, again like his German counterpart, Bloomfield's substantive vision had its narrow aspects and, in the latter's case, ended as counterproductive for the further development of his science.

In the early 1920s, Bloomfield fell under the influence of A. P. Weiss, a behaviorist at Ohio State, and gradually embraced a completely behaviorist view of language. The view evolved by Bloomfield became physicalist (and hence anti-mentalist): he thought of all language as a purely physical phenomenon and rejected any special psychological or mentalistic features in the explanation of linguistic behavior. Thus, for instance, while he would have liked to be able to account for *meaning,* Bloomfield came to the conclusion that it was dangerous to deal with this concept. He declared that, in order to give an accurate definition of meaning, one would need a scientifically complete knowledge of everything in the speaker's world. This being impossible, Bloomfield preferred to speak in simple behavioral terms of the recurrent features of a situation in which a certain form is used (Newmeyer 1980, p. 9).

Ultimately he reached a most conservative conclusion: "The only useful generalizations about language are inductive generalizations. Features which we think ought to be universal may be absent from the very next language that becomes accessible" (quoted in Newmeyer 1980, p. 4). He declared his stand in favor of strict behaviorism, mechanism, and operationalism. One only studies elements that are overtly visible or tangible, lend themselves to mechanistic explanations, and will ultimately yield stable predictions. He inveighed against mentalism, declaring that it would be as thoroughly discredited as Ptolemaic astronomy had been. Indeed, in the effort to avoid mentalistic explanations, he restricted his gaze to "private . . . events of physiology," on the one hand, and to the external stimuli of objects or people, on the other.

By dint of his clear precepts and his forceful personality, Bloomfield dominated the American linguistic scene for most of the first half of the present century. His *Language* (second edition, 1933) was for many years the standard text: all students of linguistics were familiar with, even if they did not wholly endorse, the behaviorist and antisemantic tone of the volume. It was against the ghost of Bloomfield, and such lively and loyal followers as Charles Fries (1963) and Charles Hockett (1958), that Chomsky and his colleagues launched their transformational revolution.

But if Bloomfield dominated the linguistics scene, he did not wholly control it. Indeed, Edward Sapir, who had been trained by the pioneering anthropologist Franz Boas, put forth a set of views that were to intrigue anthropologists as much as Bloomfield's views captivated the main line of linguists. Sapir did not avert meaning: indeed, he devoted some of his most probing writings to this troublesome but essential component of language. And he put forth the provocative hypothesis that a person's very processes of thinking are structured, if not controlled, by the particular properties of the language one speaks. As he expressed it in his textbook *Language:*

Human beings do not live in the object world alone, nor alone in the world of social activity as ordinarily understood, but are very much at the mercy of the particular language which has become the medium of expression for their society. It is quite an illusion to imagine that one adjusts to reality essentially without the use of language and that language is merely an incidental means of solving specific problems of communication or reflection. The fact of the matter is that the "real world" is to a large extent unconsciously built up on the language habits of the group. . . . We see and hear and otherwise experience very largely as we do because the language habits of our community predispose certain choices of interpretation. (1921, p. 75)

In the hands of his student Benjamin Lee Whorf, Sapir's ideas were further developed. Whorf did not shrink from the conclusion that even our most basic notions might be derived from language. While Newtonians might think that space, time, and matter reflect the same intuitions everywhere, Whorf demurred. He claimed that the Hopi Indians have totally different conceptions of these Kantian categories, and that these distinctions have grown out of the different ways in which their language parses the universe. As he put it:

We dissect nature along lines laid down by our native languages. . . . The world is presented in a kaleidoscopic flux of impressions which has to be organized by our minds—and this means largely by the linguistic systems in our minds. . . . No individual is free to describe nature with absolute impartiality but is constrained to certain modes of interpretation even while he thinks himself most free. (1956, pp. 153, 213–14)

Many linguists were intrigued by the work of Whorf and Sapir, even as many psychologists and anthropologists found it an excellent source of fertile hypotheses. (In chapter 12, I shall examine some of the cognitive scientific work it inspired.) And yet, like much of the work in semantics of the period, it was considered peripheral to the mainstream of linguists —too difficult to lay one's hand on, too much contaminated by the "real world" and by the dangerous notion of "meaning," not susceptible to sufficient documentation or proof. Indeed, Sapir and Bloomfield stood in marked contrast to one another. Bloomfield assumed the pose of a rigorously scientific worker, concentrating on methodology and formal analysis. His insistence on a strictly mechanistic approach to meanings and his pessimistic attitude toward semantics contributed to the relative neglect of that subject matter. Far more reminiscent of Jakobson, Sapir ranged widely and was not afraid to touch on culture, conceptualization, and the world of meaning. Paradoxically, he shared many of Chomsky's intuitions about linguistic structure but little of the formalistic inclinations of either Bloomfield or Chomsky. A union of Bloomfield-Sapir approaches and insights has yet to take place in linguistics.

The Crisis of the Early 1950s

When Bloomfield died in 1949, from most perspectives the discipline of linguistics appeared in fine shape in the United States. Commentators spoke of "great progress," "far-reaching advances," "a flourishing state," and "definitive results." The first half of the century had seen the confluence of historical, comparative, and structural descriptions of language; the discovery and development of the phonemic principle; and the attempts to put grammar and other aspects of a descriptive analysis on a firm footing. Phonology served as a model for grammar, semantics was seen as separate from grammar, and language was viewed as inherently systematic. Inductive discovery procedures were endorsed, and the assumption prevailed that one could gradually build up from the simplest level—that of sound—to word level (morphology), to syntax, and thence to semantics. While not all the decisive steps had yet been taken, it was widely assumed to be only a matter of time before the various forms and levels of language were completely understood (Newmeyer 1980).

Adding to this sense of progress and accomplishment were the rapid advances in allied fields. Theories of information (dealing with channels of communication) and techniques like stochastic modeling (dealing with probability) seemed like natural allies for the analysis of language. The invention of the sound spectrograph for the analysis of speech samples promised to lay bare the physical properties of the linguistic signal. As historian Newmeyer puts it, "many linguists felt that the procedures had been so well worked out that computers could take over the drudgery of linguistic analysis. All one would have to do (in principle) would be to punch the data into the computer and out would come the grammar!" (1980, p. 2).

Yet, on closer analysis, the scene was not as auspicious as most commentators of the time thought. First of all, as I have noted in earlier chapters, the hegemony expressed by empiricist philosophy and behaviorist psychology was breaking down rapidly. As these views began to fall into disrepute, the basis on which Bloomfield's linguistic platform had been built was undercut. Even scholars not influenced by this philosophical revolution had begun to raise doubts about the methods used by linguists. It was not as easy as it seemed simply to collect the data and to describe them objectively: one's own expectations, one's own knowledge of meaning, inevitably colored the data and lent an unsettling circularity to apparently objective descriptions. Even Hockett, a defender of the contemporary approach, declared in 1955 that it was not possible to analyze a language objectively—one had to "empathize" with the information (quoted in Newmeyer 1980, p. 17).

Efforts to repair the house of structuralist linguistics occurred from within. Probably the most successful attempts were those of Zellig S. Harris (1952) who met difficulties in a purely descriptive approach to syntax by positing transformations—rules that make explicit the intuitive relations among certain sentences. But while the techniques Harris invented were subtle and genuinely useful for organizing the data, he resisted strenuously an attempt to tie all the transformations into a single theoretical framework, or to posit an abstract level of analysis. Chomsky learned about these methods from his teacher Harris; and, as has been suggested by several commentators, it was inevitable that someone of a more theoretical bent than Harris would try to draw out the implications of such a transformational approach for the contemporary efforts to write grammars. The result, as we have seen, was Chomsky's *Syntactic Structures,* a work in which he posited a level of analysis more abstract than the surface sentence, on which the transformation(s) would be imposed. More generally, rather than simply noting possible transformations between sentences, Chomsky posited a system of rules that map from abstract underlying structures onto the articulated sentences of language.

The Evolution of Chomsky's Thought

Period Pieces

It is not possible in a survey to detail the particular models, with their numerous alterations, put forth by Chomsky and his followers in the years following the publication of *Syntactic Structures.* Nonetheless, it is important to stress that Chomsky's contribution did not occur at a single moment in time and does not consist of a single body of theory. Indeed, few of the specific notions put forth in *Syntactic Structures* have remained in their original form (even though the overall program has been maintained with considerable fidelity). Kernel sentences were soon dropped; the number of transformations was reduced and simplified enormously; the relation among the levels of syntax, semantics, and phonology has come to be understood along somewhat different lines. Certain topics introduced in that initial volume have been abandoned; while others, merely hinted at in 1957, have spawned entire research programs.

The first major new statement came in Chomsky's monograph *Aspects of the Theory of Syntax* (1965). This book presented what is now termed the "Standard Theory," the theory that for many years was the staple of introductory textbooks in linguistics. In the Standard Theory, there are no longer initial kernel sentences. Instead, one now starts with the base grammar, which generates an initial phrase marker, the *deep structure.* Major operations are performed upon this deep structure. There is a transformational component which converts the initial deep structure into other structures, the final of which is the *surface structure;* in this theory, most of the transformations are obligatory.

Two interpretive components operate on these core syntactic components. Deep-structure relations are interpreted by a semantic component: thus, the information necessary for semantic analysis must be represented in the deep structure. Phonological interpretation occurs on the surface-structure string: thus, the initial deep syntactic structure is "read" for meaning, while the ultimate surface structure is "read" for sound. In the 1965 version, both the base and the transformation rules were unconstrained, permitting a large variety of possible base and transformational systems.

The Standard Theory was a more ambitious theory, attempting in part to accomplish for semantics what had been modeled for syntax alone in *Syntactic Structures.* It also proved far more controversial and, because of various insufficiencies, eventually had to be abandoned. Particularly controversial was the notion of deep structure. *Deep structure* is a technical term, having nothing to do with profundity. Nonetheless, it was frequently misinterpreted in this fashion. Moreover, even among those who understood its technical scope, deep structure was seen as "too deep" by some critics and as "not deep enough" by others. The move of making semantics an interpretation of core syntactic arrangements was also widely debated.

We can distinguish two broad lines of attack on Chomsky. One line of attack came from the conservative branch of linguistics—from scholars still attached to the structuralist perspective of the Bloomfield days. Charles F. Hockett selected himself to answer Chomsky on behalf of the traditional interest groups in structural linguistics. In *The State of the Art* (1968*b*), Hockett argued that the fundamental program of transformational linguistics was flawed. Chomsky had bet on the wrong scientific model. He had compared language to a formal discipline like logic or mathematics; whereas it is an empirical science like chemistry. Only humanly invented systems like logic have the regularity Chomsky sought in language; in contrast, natural language is ill defined, and the theories of computability and algebraic grammar he sought to apply are irrelevant. "This knocks the props out from under current mathematical linguistics, at least in the form of algebraic grammar, whose basic assumption is that language can be viewed as a well-defined subset of the set of all finite strings over a well-defined finite alphabet" (1968*b*, p. 61). Hockett also rejected the separability of grammar and semantics (which he had earlier espoused) and the separation of both from the rest of culture. Autonomy within linguistics, and from other disciplines, was abandoned. In his view, the "grammar of language" in Chomsky's sense simply does not exist.

What is striking was the absence of response to this monograph. Except for a dismissive review by Chomsky's one-time associate George Lakoff (1969), this work of criticism was ignored. Apparently by the late 1960s, ripostes from the earlier generation had simply become irrelevant. In accordance with Thomas Kuhn's (1970) description of paradigm changes in the sciences, the Chomsky point of view took over, not by convincing the previous generation that it had been in error, but by winning the allegiance of the most gifted students of the succeeding generation.

Some members of the younger generation felt, however, that Chomsky was not sufficiently radical. In the late 1960s a major attack on his work was launched by certain linguists who had been sympathetic to his general position. Led by Chomsky's former students, George Lakoff and J. R. Ross (1976), these critics questioned the simple positing of two levels of analysis—a deep structure, to be interpreted semantically, and a surface structure to be interpreted phonetically—and also called into doubt the autonomy of syntax from semantics. Ultimately, these critics abandoned simple deep structure in favor of grammars whose underlying structures were much deeper and closer to semantic representation themselves. (Another group of critics, which eventually included Chomsky himself, embraced grammars in which the underlying structures were shallower and closer to surface structure than had previously been envisaged, and were equipped with much richer lexical components than had earlier been the case.) The generative semanticists contended that there was no clear-cut distinction between syntactic and semantic rules, and that a level of syntactic deep structure defined as the initial generating component could not be sustained. Instead, they set up rules that take semantic representations as their input and yield surface structures as their output, with no intervening level of deep structure. In contrast, the interpretive semanticists, including Chomsky, transferred more of the work of syntax into the semantic component, so that deep structure has gradually moved closer to the surface structure of a sentence (Smith and Wilson 1979).

The debates between the generative semanticists and the traditional Chomskians, and, eventually, between the generative semanticists and the interpretive semanticists, were ardent and often vicious. At stake were particular claims about how best to represent word meanings, as well as competing views about how to construct linguistic theories. Names were called and epithets were hurled in a manner that shocked even seasoned polemicists. When all the hue and cry had died down, however, the generative semanticist school lost its steam, and most of its principal adherents abandoned the field of syntax altogether. Meanwhile, in his persistent way, Chomsky has continued to investigate syntax. It is true, however, that the problems pointed out by the generative semanticists have stimulated the Chomsky contingent to develop certain notational forms (using symbolic logic) as well as a plethora of new and highly abstract mechanisms, all designed to deal with inadequacies in the traditional transformational approach. Perhaps most decisively, generative semantics helped to sound the death knell for the transformational component; this once central component has been entirely eliminated on some accounts or radically simplified on others.

Since the late 1960s, Chomsky's brand of *generative grammar* (as it came to be called) has undergone a series of changes. It is not possible to introduce and follow the intricacies of the extended standard theory or of its current replacement government and binding theory, let alone the specifics of trace theory or X-bar theory—the major landmarks in the development of his approach up to the present. I can, however, indicate some of the broad trends in the theory. Over the years, Chomsky has steadily narrowed the definition of his object of study. Never interested in language as an overall communication system, he now questions whether language *per se* is a system worth trying to study at all. Viewing language as a more abstract notion than grammar, more remote from actual mechanisms, Chomsky is more firmly convinced than ever that linguists should concentrate on solving the issues of syntax (1982, p. 14). There are no more attempts to systematize semantics.

Responding to many criticisms, Chomsky has attempted to reduce the expressive power of transformational structures. It turns out that the original grammars had been so powerful that they could not illuminate the crucial issue of what is permissible in a *human* language (see Peters and Ritchie 1973). If one wanted to know which grammars might characterize human performance, it was necessary to restrict what a candidate grammar could do. This attempt to weaken transformational power has been part of what Chomsky has called the second major shift in linguistics—the search for principles that would constrain the set of syntactic rules of natural language.

Chomsky has tried to reduce the class of transformations by discovering general conditions that rules must meet: he has sought to eliminate the possibility of compounding elementary operations to form more complex transformational rules. As he now puts it:

[M]uch effort has been devoted to showing that the class of possible transformations can be substantially reduced without loss of descriptive power through the discovery of quite general conditions that all such rules and the representations they operate on and form must meet. . . . [The] transformational rules, at least for a substantial core grammar, can be reduced to the single rule, *"Move alpha"* (that is, "move any category anywhere"). (Mehler, Walker, and Garrett 1982, p. 21)

It may even be possible to eliminate the phrase-structure rules wholly or in large part. As transformational rules and phrase-structure rules become less prominent, more attention is being paid to the lexicon—to the particular rules governing specific words. The lexicon now contains much of the information that used to be part of the transformational apparatus. And the notion of surface structure (now sometimes reconceptualized as *S-structure*) becomes much richer. In fact Chomsky has even commented that his new theory could be considered as a "one level theory," consisting merely of base generation of S-structures (see comment in Longuet-Higgins et al. 1981, p. 279).

How then, to characterize Chomsky's current approach to language or, more strictly speaking, to grammar? He describes his pursuit in theoretical terms as a search for *universal grammar* (or U.G.). U.G. is genetically determined at its initial state (in the organism) and is specified, sharpened, articulated, and refined under conditions set by experience, to yield the *particular grammars* found in specific groups of individuals (1980, p. 234). A theory of universal grammar is said to be an *explanatory theory*. To know a language is to be in a certain state of mind/brain: this state is described by a core grammar which consists of certain principles of universal grammar, which are to be discovered by linguists. Thus, Chomsky takes a purely realistic stance: language knowledge *is* a series of states in the brain.

What are these principles to which Chomsky refers? Here we come to what he considers to be another major shift in his theory. Until fairly recently, his goal had been to describe the various *rules* that individuals must somehow know if they are to know a language. But now he has come to the conclusion that it is more productive to speak of various *principles* that govern language use. These principles begin in human biology. They determine the kinds of grammar that are available in principle (Chomsky 1979). The principles of U.G. are various subsystems, which go by names like *binding theory, control theory, government theory, theta theory,* and the like—each of which features a limited degree of parametric variation.

If U.G. is sufficiently rich, then even limited linguistic data in the environment should suffice for developing rich and complex linguistic systems in the mind. There is no need to talk of the acquisition of rules. Rather, each of the systems of U.G. has certain parameters associated with it, and these are set or fixed in light of the data encountered by a person (ordinarily a young child) in the course of acquiring his native language. Slight changes in the values of the parameters proliferate throughout the system to yield what on the surface may be rather different language structures (Chomsky 1982). The grammar of a particular language that ultimately emerges can be regarded as a set of values for each of these parameters: the overall set of rules, principles, and the like constitute U.G., part of the human language faculty.

We see here the union of two visions in the science of the mind. One vision, stemming from philosophy and dating back to Plato, features language as a kind of idealized object, governed by a small set of universal principles, having relatively few parameters (Chomsky 1981). The other vision, coming from biology, puts forth language as an organic system, or module, which has the potential to develop in a small and delimited range of ways; the particular path of development yielding a "core grammar" is determined by the kinds of information encountered by the organism. Embracing these two visions, one can account at once both for the similarities across all languages (thanks to universal grammar) and the distinct differences among particular languages (thanks to the variations in parameter setting).

What is one to make of such a complex theory which has undergone critical changes in the course of a few years and will doubtless change further? One approach, sometimes adopted by Chomsky's former students, is to stress the differences in the theory from one period to another and to attribute these differences to efforts to shore it up in the light of competing accounts. Such a critical point of view has been put forth by George Lakoff (1980). In the view of this former Chomsky student, Chomsky had to eliminate deep structure and transformations because it had proved impossible to maintain the principal assumption of modularity —the independence of syntax. Once Lakoff and his associates had shown that meaning and use affect virtually every rule of syntax, Chomsky had to narrow progressively the domain of syntax: rules once regarded as clearly within the domain of syntax were redefined as part of semantics. On this account, Chomsky has conceded the validity of criticisms in practice while, in his explicit remarks, denying that he has done so. The historian of American linguistics, Frederic Newmeyer, offers another interpretation of this phenomenon. In his view each generation of Chomsky students continues to work on the major ideas proposed by their teacher during their own intellectually formative years:

> Chomsky in the early 1960's was an "abstract syntactician"—and many of his students from that period still are! Chomsky in the late 1960's proposed the lexicalist alternative to abstract syntax—and those who were then his students are still developing this model. And we can predict that Chomsky's 1970's students will be refining trace theory long after Chomsky has developed his ideas along other lines. (1980, p. 207)

In my own view, Chomsky has certainly been influenced by the criticisms leveled at him, both by former students and from others who have some general sympathy with generative grammar. However, he does not like to concede this influence explicitly. He is not easy to dispute with, and does not suffer criticism gladly, and so tends to be dismissive in writing even (or perhaps especially) of those scholars whose work has had some influence on him. This rhetorical style tends to polarize discussion.

Despite undeniable shifts in emphasis and strategy, however, it is remarkable how Chomsky has adhered to the program he initially presented to the scholarly community in *Syntactic Structures* and had been pursuing from his early twenties. The centrality of syntax, the belief in a transformational component, the view of semantics as an interpretation of basic syntactic relations—all these have endured.

Chomsky is correct in saying:

> My major interest has been to make precise the basic principles which enter into the knowledge of language that has been attained by the speaker-hearer; and beyond that, to try to discover the general theoretical principles which account for the fact that this system of knowledge, rather than something else, develops in the mind when a person is placed in a certain linguistic environment. In a general way, I might say that I am still working very much within the framework of . . . early unpublished work. (1979, p. 113)

Any growing science will be constantly changing. Chomsky has been one of the principal revisers of his own theory, sometimes in radical directions, even though the same vision has guided him from the start and he has been relentless in pursuing it.

As he moves to increasingly abstract characterizations, involving technical argumentation, he has indeed lost adherents. This does not seem to bother Chomsky, who (like many another revolutionary figure) has always seen himself as somewhat of a loner. As he declared in a recent interview:

> The particular domain into which I put most of my energies, the structure of language, seems to me to have been a very exciting one just in the last seven or eight years. I don't pretend to speak for any consensus in the field here, in fact, I'm in a very small minority in the field in this respect, but I believe it's been possible in the past few years to develop a theory of languages with a degree of deductive structure that provides a kind of unification and explanatory power going well beyond anything that would have been imagined even a decade ago. Again, I don't think many linguists would agree with me about this. . . . I suppose I'm in a very small minority in the field today. But then, that has always been the case. With regard to me, it doesn't seem very different now from what it was ten or twenty years ago. But my own views are not what they were then, and I hope they will not be the same ten years from now. Any person who hopes to be part of an active growing field will take that for granted. (Quoted in Rieber 1983, pp. 62–63)

213

Reactions in Other Cognitive Sciences

By the early 1960s, when Chomsky was gaining widespread support in linguistics, his work was also coming to the attention of workers in other fields. Since cognitive science has placed its trust in such cross-disciplinary exchanges, it is important to consider the course of interaction between contemporary linguistics and other cognitive fields.

One of the very first scholars outside linguistics proper to become aware of Chomsky's work was the psychologist George Miller. By the early 1960s, Miller (1962) had become a convert to Chomskian linguistics and soon helped to turn the psychology of language into a testing ground for Chomsky's transformational claims. Miller and his students tried to figure out ways in which to demonstrate the "psychological reality" of transformations: they hypothesized that the steps by which a sentence is theoretically generated and transformed are also realized by the "live" individual in the process of comprehending or producing sentences. This effort was not particularly successful, but important methods of psycholinguistic research were worked out in the process (Fodor, Bever, and Garrett 1974).

Miller and his colleagues succeeded in bringing Chomsky's work to the attention of the psychological community. Chomsky got a fair hearing, and a minority of students fully bought his program for language and cognitive science. Still, at this writing, the majority of workers in psychology have remained skeptical about the overall relevance of his theory for their pursuits. Although Chomsky himself describes linguistics as part of psychology, his ideas and definitions clash with established truth in psychology. He has had to contend not only with the strong residue of behaviorist and empiricist sentiment but also with suspicion about his formal methods, opposition to his ideas about language as a separate realm, and outright skepticism with respect to his belief in innate ideas. While Chomsky has rarely been defeated in argument on his own ground (for a recent dramatic example, see his debate with Piaget), his particular notions and biases have thus far had only modest impact in mainstream psychology (Piattelli-Palmarini 1980).

There is one area of psychology where Chomsky's ideas and example have had enormous influence: the psychology of language, or *psycholinguistics,* as it is often called. In the past few decades, psycholinguistics has become a major area of inquiry, encompassing studies of normal language in the adult, the development of linguistic capacities in children, the breakdown of language after conditions of brain damage, and the use of language in exceptional populations such as the deaf. A great deal of work in each of these areas has focused on syntactic capacities, with models for analysis generally supplied by Chomsky. At times these models have been used as a means of characterizing the data collected; at other times, the data have been used to test the "psychological reality" of models—the extent to which linguistic behavior unfolds according to the principles put forth by Chomsky.

After two decades of psycholinguistic work, most psychologists have despaired of applying Chomsky's work in any direct way to their own research. Not only are Chomsky's formulations highly abstract and subject to frequent change (typically in a more abstract direction); but when they have been applied, the results have not been consistent with his models, at least in any straightforward way. For example, any number of developmental psycholinguists have sought to account for language acquisition in terms of Chomsky's categories and derivations, but these efforts have generally been judged failures. Recently there have been interesting attempts to develop *learnability theory*—a formal account of the constraints that must be built into a child's cognitive apparatus if one is to learn language from the data to which one is exposed (Wexler 1982; Wexler and Culicover 1980). Steven Pinker (1984) has attempted to interpret the data of language acquisition in terms of principles of learnability. It is too early to say whether this approach will signal a new use for a Chomsky-inspired (or "generative") approach within psycholinguistics or whether a Chomskian perspective will continue to be a minority taste.

For the most part, then, Chomsky has been more influential in psycholinguistics because of the kinds of question to which he has drawn attention than because of any direct utility of his theory for experimentation. Sometimes he and his followers have discounted empirical research in psycholinguistics, with the disclaimer that their theories have to do with idealized competence, and not with the facts of individual performance. To my mind, this is an unjustified maneuver. Chomsky and his followers are only too happy to cite empirical data when it appears to accord with their theory. However, it is often far from clear just how directly Chomskian ideas are meant to be translated into empirical work; and, in that sense at least, the Chomskian reservation is justified.

Chomsky's new ideas were introduced to the philosophical world primarily through the work of two young Princeton graduates, Jerrold Katz and Jerry Fodor, who were teaching at Massachusetts Institute of Technology in the early 1960s. Collaborators for several years, Katz and Fodor (1963) also developed a model of semantics which became incorporated into the "standard version" of transformational grammar. As has been the case in psychology, Chomsky's ideas about language have persuaded a minority of younger philosophers, but many others are decidedly ambivalent about his specific claims. The formalism itself presents less of a problem, but a number of the core ideas have had a checkered history in philosophy. Philosophers have reacted coolly to Chomsky's promotion of seemingly discredited rationalist notions and to his enthusiasm for innate ideas. His ready use of terms like *rules, structures, systems,* with (apparent) disregard for the nontrivial technical problems involved in such concepts, and his facile reinterpretation of leading philosophical figures of the past (Descartes as a hero, the empiricists as villains) have proven difficult for most philosophers to swallow. Also Chomsky's lack of interest in semantics has troubled many philosophers, who find in the work of semanticist Richard Montague some of the same formal elegance others have admired in Chomsky's syntactic discussions (Thomason 1974).

Yet it is fair to say that, as in psychology, topics of discussion have been materially affected by the fact that Chomsky has spoken and written. Whether the impact of Chomsky's notions will be greater in a half-century than they are now, or whether they will be seen as a curious aberration within the general triumph of empirically oriented and anti-mentalistic sciences is too early to say. Except in the field of linguistics itself, it remains uncertain whether Chomsky's ideas will emerge as germinal and essential.

And what of other cognitive sciences? While his approach arose from many of the same roots as artificial intelligence, several of Chomsky's main ideas are not readily implemented in computational formats. For example, there is no guarantee in principle that one can parse sentences using transformational grammatical approaches. Moreover, A.I. is very much oriented toward practical problems of designing programs that understand sentences or stories, and Chomsky's syntax-centered framework is not suited for the main issues of understanding discourse. Accordingly, computer scientists like Roger Schank have been publicly hostile to the theory, taking the position that semantics and pragmatics are central in language and that syntax is relatively unimportant. Schank has also attacked the modular notion: "It is impossible to produce a model of language alone . . . apart from beliefs, goals, points of view and world knowledge" (1980, p. 36). Other scholars, like Terry Winograd, have borrowed some ideas from transformational grammar but have not made Chomskian theory pivotal to their systems. Efforts to parse sentences using transformational ideas have been few thus far (though see Berwick and Weinberg 1983; Marcus 1980). Even through Chomsky's formal elegance has appealed to A.I. researchers, his Platonic view is even more remote from most computer scientists than from the average psychologist and philosopher. For his part, Chomsky has been rather critical of research in artificial intelligence, finding it mostly unmotivated and *ad hoc:* he does, however, admire David Marr's work on vision (1982).

Rival Positions within Linguistics

Those linguists who continue to work in the generative grammar tradition, but who have broken from Chomsky's particular perspective, have sometimes been attracted to the artificial-intelligence perspective. One such researcher is Joan Bresnan, formerly a colleague of Chomsky's at M.I.T., who has concentrated on developing a theory of language which is psychologically real (1978, 1981). In opposition to Chomsky, who (as I noted) pays little attention to how his derivations might be realized by an individual speaker operating under "real-world" constraints, Bresnan and her colleagues have fashioned a perspective designed to illuminate how an individual will perceive or produce language. In her *lexical-functional theory*, there is no transformational component. The information traditionally embedded in the syntactic components is now placed in the individual's lexicon—one's knowledge of specific words. Lexical-functional grammar provides each sentence with two structures: a *constituent structure*, which is similar to a surface structure (or phrase-marker tree) in the standard theory of Chomsky; and a *functional structure*, which includes all the grammatical relations relevant to the semantic interpretation of the sentence. The functional structure is generated by annotated phrase-structure rules working in conjunction with lexical entries for the various morphemes in a sentence.

In recent years, Bresnan has begun to work closely with colleagues in the area of artificial intelligence and in psycholinguistics. The purpose of this collaboration is to determine whether the modifications she has introduced into standard syntactic theory make her position "psychologically viable" in a way Chomsky's has never been. The results thus far suggest that the kinds of parsing mechanisms devised in the light of her theory do comport better with experimental data on language processing and with the models of understanding being developed by workers in computational linguistics. For similar reasons, in his work on learnability theory, Steven Pinker (1984) has embraced lexical-functional grammar, which he views as a "central tendency" (or modal position) among contemporary linguistic theories. The work of Bresnan and her colleagues has also become central in the new, Stanford-based Center for the Study of Language and Information, in which the avowed goal is to achieve an integrated theory of human linguistic competence. The Center has just been launched, and it is too early to say whether its dream of uniting the philosophical, psychological, and computational aspects of language will be met; but all of us involved in the cognitive science movement will be monitoring progress there with abiding interest.

Much of the appeal of Bresnan's theory also accrues to another point of view which has recently gained adherents—the theory of Gerald Gazdar of the University of Sussex. Reverting to the generalized phrase-structure grammars that Chomsky strongly attacked in his early publications, Gazdar (1981) argues that one does not need transformations, and that even unusual surface structures can be stated in a straightforward way; moreover, it is important to do this because sentences thought to be the same by transformational grammarians are often actually different from one another. In Gazdar's theory, semantic interpretation is applied directly to the surface structure generated by a grammar. There are explicit semantic rules for each syntactical rule. Gazdar believes that his theories are more straightforward than Chomsky's; comport better with analyses done in formal language theory (which, in turn, are relevant to the devising of language systems on computers); and provide a more appropriate entry to problems of language acquisition. Carving out territory in opposition to Chomsky, he asserts:

> When one realizes that the syntactic theory that Chomsky has been developing over the last ten years has embraced phrase structure rules, complex symbols, a level of S-structure, a level of D-structure, a level of "Logical Form," filters, transformations, interpretive rules, stylistic rules, coindexing conventions, and abstract cases, among other things, it is a little surprising to hear him castigating as "needlessly complex" an alternative syntactic theory that employs only phrase structure rules, complex symbols, and a level of surface structure. (Quoted in Longuet-Higgins, Lyons, and Broadbent 1981, p. 281)

To readers not intimately involved in linguistics, the differences between Gazdar and Bresnan are not easy to comprehend, and even their divergences from Chomsky may seem relatively modest. (Chomsky himself tends to minimize these differences, often terming the different theories "notational variants" of the same core ideas.) Yet inasmuch as these theories are rivals in the search for programs or mechanisms that can "truly comprehend," it is important to determine which model is most appropriate. Current supporters of both Bresnan and Gazdar are working at the new Center for the Study of Language and Information, and they expect to determine whether the Bresnan or the Gazdar model is more appropriate for handling linguistic data or whether (as Chomsky might predict) the differences between the positions prove minor. What might constitute a crucial test of the theories, however, is not apparent. Linguistics is not (yet) mathematics or physics.

A Tentative Evaluation

While it is far from clear whether Chomsky's particular positions will ultimately prevail—either in linguistics proper or in neighboring disciplines—he has framed the issues for debate. His notions of which issues are important in linguistics continue to dominate discussions in much of the profession: and his ways of formulating issues have influenced all cognitive scientists, even scholars overtly inimical to his work and young students only dimly aware of the source of their views.

If the index of importance of a scholar is the extent to which one could be replaced within a discipline, Chomsky clearly emerges as the most important figure in the linguistics of recent times—equal in importance to de Saussure and to Jakobson in earlier eras and one who may ultimately exert an even greater influence on the direction of his field. Within the broader cognitive sciences, his contribution is more controversial and less secure. But on the bases of his demonstrations of the mathematical precision implicit in language, his modeling of the importance of theory-driven research, and his potent arguments for mentalism, nativism, and modularity, I would offer my opinion that he is one of the two or three most important and least replaceable thinkers of the whole movement. Piaget may have turned up a greater number of important phenomena; Herbert Simon and Allen Newell may have put forth a paradigm more widely emulated by other investigators; but no one has framed the issues of a cognitive science with as much precision and conviction as has Chomsky. Moreover, while not even he has fully lived up to the rigorous criteria he has demanded of a linguistic theory, the criteria he devised in his early works continue to be those by which subsequent linguistic theories (and theorists) are judged. Whether his impact will be as broad in other cognitive sciences may depend upon whether the model, which has proved fertile in the area of language, proves equally useful in other areas, such as visual perception, logical classification, or the study of consciousness.

Chomsky himself might feel of two minds about this. On the one hand, he is possessed of a rigorous scientific conscience and would like to see his degree of formal precision and his criteria for explanatory adequacy invoked everywhere. On the other hand, he has long insisted that the rules governing language may be unique to that domain, and he is loath to endorse notions of general cognitive structures that cut across diverse contents. And so, while the study of linguistics in which he has pioneered may serve as a model of how one goes about investigating other fields, it remains an open question whether any parallels of substance will emerge.

This paradoxical situation is epitomized by Chomsky's view of linguistics as a part of psychology. In repeatedly giving voice to this sentiment, Chomsky may appear to be suggesting that the study of language ought simply to be incorporated into a more general study of psychology (a catholic view). Yet it seems clear to me that Chomsky would not approve of incorporating linguistics into psychology as currently practiced. Psychology would need to be reconfigured in Chomskian terms (a far narrower point of view which might find little sympathy in psychology circles).

What, then, about the claims for autonomy in the area of language? Chomsky has for almost thirty years insisted that syntax can be approached as a module, one operating in independence of (though, of course, interacting with) other facets of language. While many researchers have sought to follow Chomsky in this belief, it now appears that the links of syntax to other aspects of language—to lexical semantics (*à la* Bresnan) and to pragmatics (*à la* Gazdar) in particular—may be sufficiently integral that the thesis of the autonomy of syntax is in jeopardy.

The point is not whether syntax can be looked at separately—of course, any component can be examined in isolation. The question is, rather, what is to be gained or lost by adhering rigorously to such a research program. In calling the autonomy of syntax to account, critics argue that the most important operations of language are better conceived along different lines. They call for consideration of models where the interactions among various factors are brought to the foreground (as, say, in lexical-functional accounts) in place of a model where efforts are directed chiefly at determining the operations of syntax in isolation, and where the relation between syntactic and other components is relegated to a later phase of research.

In short, then, Chomsky's demonstration of autonomous syntax is still important on methodological grounds, but it is less evident that it can be considered a viable characterization of the central aspects of language. Instead, collaborative approaches in computational linguistics—where the pragmatic and communicative aspects of language are frankly conceded and the interactions between semantic and syntactic factors are presupposed—may carry the day.

And what of the relation of language study to other cognitive sciences? One tack is to bring other disciplines to bear on language, while continuing to treat language as a domain apart, worthy of investigating on its merits. Here language—the province of linguistics—is illuminated by other disciplines—as happens in neurolinguistic studies of speech production or in psycholinguistic investigations of phoneme recognition. Many scholars (including the original advisers to the Sloan Foundation) have felt that language is the best testing ground for an integrated cognitive science. There could then be parallel studies of an interdisciplinary type directed at other domains of knowledge, such as vision, motion, and motor action. This is clearly a model for cognitive science—one designed along "vertical" lines, and one for which I have much sympathy.

The degree to which the study of language ought to remain separate from other scholarly disciplines depends to some extent on the issues one is most interested in illuminating. If one is interested in language as an abstract system—be it the creation of some divine force or simply a pattern emerging from the brain—then language is appropriately studied in terms of the kinds of taxonomic and structural category favored by linguists. (Language here becomes a "distanced" object of study, analogous to the solar system probed by astronomers.) If, however, one is interested in language as it participates in human intercourse, then a view of linguistics as divorced from other disciplinary pursuits becomes less tenable.

Consistent with this latter point of view, some scholars have come to adopt (or to readopt) a more horizontal model of cognitive science. On this view, it is wrong to think of the subject matter of any discipline (for example, language as the subject matter of linguistics) as privileged: indeed, it is more important to connect any human activity to the range of related fields that can be investigated. Furthermore, language does not belong to any discipline but is instead a part of every cognitive scientific discipline, efforts to cordon it off being artificial or wrong-headed. This was the faith that influenced scholars like Jakobson in the area of poetics, Sapir in his studies of language and thought, and de Saussure in his historical studies of language. Calling for a closer integration of fields, Roy Harris, a harsh critic of Chomsky's, declares:

> Language cannot be studied in isolation from the investigation of "rationality." It cannot afford to neglect our everyday assumptions concerning the total behavior of a reasonable person. . . . An integrational linguistics must recognize that human beings inhabit a communicational space which is not neatly compartmentalized into language and non-language. . . . It renounces in advance the possibility of setting up systems of forms and meanings which will "account for" a central core of linguistic behavior irrespective of the situation and communicational purposes involved. (1981, p. 165)

Chomsky (1980) has sometimes conceded that language may be less of a "cordoned off" territory than he would like, and that the demands of communication or the intrusion of belief structure may suffuse all linguistic activity. Should this be the case, however, language would not be worthy of study because it would prove to be hopelessly intermeshed with everything else. In Chomsky's words:

> If non-linguistic factors must be included in grammar: beliefs, attitudes, etc. [this would] amount to a rejection of the initial idealization to language as an object of study. *A priori* such a move cannot be ruled out, but it must be empirically motivated. If it proves to be correct, I would conclude that language is a chaos that is not worth studying . . . Note that the question is not whether beliefs or attitudes, and so on, play a role in linguistic behavior and linguistic judgements . . . [but rather] whether distinct cognitive structures can be identified, which interact in the

real use of language and linguistic judgements, the grammatical system being one of these. (1979, pp. 140, 152–3)

We confront here the most basic issues of scientific strategy. It may be that, in the last analysis, Chomsky is wrong. Perhaps the connections between syntax and semantics, between the "language system" and other mental organs, or between linguistics and other disciplines, is stronger or differently configured than he had imagined. It may, nonetheless, be the case that Chomsky has selected the optimal research strategy. For even if, ultimately, everything turns out to be connected to everything else, a research program rooted in that realization might well collapse of its own weight.

One of the most attractive features of cognitive science is its positing of methods and models that are sufficiently rigorous to allow the analyst to determine where those models are insufficient or unsatisfactory. The computational paradox in fact arises because computational methods have helped us to recognize some of the ways in which humans deviate from a simple-minded logic machine. Chomsky's work is exemplary in this regard because he has fashioned rigorous methods for syntactic analysis. Whatever role syntax ultimately turns out to play in human cognition, its mechanisms *are* beginning to be understood, and its relations to other components of language *are* beginning to be clarified. This remark can be made about few other areas in the cognitive sciences. For providing a paradigmatic example of clear-cut scientific progress in this new field, Chomsky has earned the respect of cognitive scientists everywhere.

As exchanges continue to be conducted with other cognitive scientists, it will become easier to assess the overall impact—and the ultimate limitations—of Chomsky's single-minded vision. How language fits into the wider culture—a topic ruled off limits (for methodological reasons) by Chomsky—will certainly be an issue addressed in a broad field. Of particular import in determining the limits of a Chomskian approach will be intense collaboration between linguistics and anthropology, two fields whose histories have commingled from the very beginning. In just what ways these connections were originally forged, and how they are manifest today, will become clear as I consider anthropology as a cognitive science.

8

Anthropology: Beyond the Individual Case

Lucien Lévy-Bruhl Examines the Mind of the Primitive

Initially, Lucien Lévy-Bruhl had seemed a progressive voice in the long-standing debate about the rationality of the savage mind. Yet, during his career, the sentiments among his anthropological colleagues changed to such an extent that ultimately he was perceived as being conservative, almost reactionary, in his views. Finally, by the end of his life, the French thinker had undergone an almost complete change of mind: he renounced the very position that had initially drawn attention to his work. In examining closely the reasons for these shifts, we not only gain a better understanding of a paradigmatic figure in the history of anthropology, but also confront the central enigma of cognitively oriented anthropology.

When Lévy-Bruhl began his study of the thinking processes of primitive peoples almost a century ago, the general orientation in the anthropological community was evolutionary. It was assumed that members of "advanced" Western civilization represented the height of reasoning, and that "lesser individuals" around the world were simply inferior copies of the Western mind. Lévy-Bruhl challenged this received opinion: "Let us then no longer . . . want to reduce their mental activity to an inferior form of our own." Primitives do not reason badly; rather, they reason differently. Lévy-Bruhl proposed that the primitive mind follows a kind of logic, a "pre-logic," which is fundamentally different from our own: these pre-logical thoughts had best be understood on their own terms (quoted in Cazeneuve 1972, p. 41).

Lévy-Bruhl proposed two major characteristics of primitive thought. First of all, such thought partakes of the *law of participation*. Primitive individuals see objects, beings, and other external phenomena as at once identical with themselves and also as something other than themselves. Thus, the Trumai (a tribe in north Brazil) say that they are aquatic animals, meaning not that they are only fish, but rather that they are *both* human beings and fish at the same time. Second, and in a fashion no less incomprehensible to the Western mind, primitive individuals can emit and receive mystical forces, properties, and qualities, which are felt as outside themselves, without their ceasing to be what they are. Thus, a newborn child can suffer the consequences of everything his father does, eats, says, and the like (Cazeneuve 1972). Given these properties, the primitive mind does not abstain from contradiction. There is no need to give up an idea because it collides with another one: both notions can be entertained simultaneously.

In positing different ways of thinking, Lévy-Bruhl pointed up the problems involved in extrapolating from one human population to another. There is no substitute for a careful study of the "mental" representations of each group. As a result of such study, he concluded, the mind of the primitive emerges as quite different from that of contemporary Europeans: dominated by emotion and affect, little concerned with logic, tolerant of contradictions and mystical forces that would be taboo in a civilized Cartesian context.

Scholars typically defend their views when attacked by the succeeding generation. But, at least privately, Lévy-Bruhl violated this pattern. Indeed, in the papers of his posthumously published notebooks, Lévy-Bruhl engaged in a debate that was as severe and tortured as any in professional publications. He became dubious that primitives really do exhibit a different, pre-logical form of thought:

> The step which I have just taken, and hope is decisive, consists, in a word, in abandoning a badly posed problem . . . even allowing for the numerous and characteristic cases of *participation* of which my six volumes are full, there still exist doubts about the explanation. . . . I started by positing a primitive mentality different from ours . . . a position which I have never been able to defend well, and in the long run an untenable one. . . . The thesis thus extenuated and weakened is no more defensible. . . . Let us entirely give up explaining participation by something peculiar to the human mind. . . . There is not a primitive mentality distinguishable from the other. (Quoted in Cazeneuve 1972, pp. 86–87)

In these later musings, Lévy-Bruhl virtually adopted the position he had originally opposed. He concurred with those who see differences between primitive and civilized as a question of degree, and was no longer remote from those who doubted there was any fundamental difference whatsoever. Lévy-Bruhl took refuge in the argument that, perhaps, it was scientific thought that is unusual: in the paraphrase of Jean Cazeneuve, "What has been described to us under the name of primitive mentality is undoubtedly a permanent structure of the human mind but in our society this structure is blurred by the supremacy of scientific thought whereas it remains in the foreground among preliterate peoples" (1972, p. 22). He concluded with a sentiment that would gain widespread endorsement today: "The fundamental structure of the human mind is the same everywhere" (p. 12).

The debate that raged in Lévy-Bruhl's mind echoed a discussion that has been widespread in the West ever since humans first became aware of the existence of exotic populations and began to ponder their relation to more familiar pockets of humanity. Though the debate extended to the morals and values of these alien populations, keen interest always centered on the quality of their thought processes. Did they have the same logics as "we" do, or were there logics peculiar to each group of individuals? How could we get inside the mind of the primitives, and discern the world in the way they see it? Those scholars who acquired a professional interest in these questions were "at risk" to become anthropologists.

In the time of Lévy-Bruhl, early in this century, the sources of evidence were principally textual: one read the myths or, less frequently, transcripts of conversations with preliterate individuals, and then drew conclusions about the kinds of thought reflected in them. But such hermeneutic methods could not attain scientific status. And so, increasingly in the twentieth century, anthropologically oriented scholars repaired to the field to examine firsthand the thought processes of "their people." This move to "case studies" was certainly an important step in an empirical direction. The problem with individual fieldwork, however, was that it left a great deal of discretion—perhaps too much—in the hands of a single investigator or a small cadre of fieldworkers.

A significant chapter of the history of anthropology in this century has been a search for methods of inquiry that were less idiosyncratic, more reliable (Herskovits 1953; Kardiner and Preble 1961). Since it was generally not practical for large teams of investigators to visit the same site—and if investigators visited at widely disparate times, they might not be witnessing the "same" peoples (Freeman 1983)—a premium was placed on more objective methods which could be employed by a single investigative team. This need gave rise in the 1960s to the field of *ethnoscience,* a seemingly objective set of empirical measures by which one could assess the thinking processes of peoples everywhere.

Ethnoscientists had no problem in invoking a representational level.

What for other more experimentally oriented disciplines constituted a major leap came naturally to anthropologists. Problems lay in another direction. While it seemed for a while that the new empirical procedures might place anthropology on a firmer scientific footing, there has recently been a disaffection with these methods: however elegant, they seem to bypass too much of what is central in the thinking and the experience of a culture. There has been at least a partial return to the view that anthropology ought to re-embrace the holistic methods of the in-depth case study, and perhaps align itself more with the humanities and less with the sciences. Continuing uncertainty about whether anthropological investigation ought to adopt the methods of experimental cognitive science constitutes a second major theme of the discipline.

Speculations about different populations date back to classical times. At least as far back as Herodotus, it was known that human behavioral patterns differed from one society to another, and attempts were made to document and explain (or explain away) such differences. Students of the Bible often traced the existence of exotic peoples back to some episode— for example, the dispersion of the three sons of Noah, or the offspring of the banished Cain, whose face had been covered with darkness. Quite often, it was assumed that certain exotic populations, like American Indians or Arabian nomads, represented a corruption or degeneration of a "pure" human: they stood in contrast to a strain that had descended directly from Adam or Abraham, and was, of course, related to contemporary Europeans.

With the revived interest in scholarship, and the far-flung travel that characterized the Renaissance, such age-old speculations gained new force. Some commentators continued to hold to the view of degeneracy; others stressed resemblances between the contemporary savage and the predecessors of civilized man. When comparisons were made between the early Europeans and contemporary savages, the implication followed that contemporary savages were simply at an earlier stage of development than contemporary Europeans. As one commentator has put it, "Europe and America . . . settled the matter by placing its [sic] own nations on one end of the social series, and the savage tribes at the other, arranging the rest of mankind between these limits according as they correspond more closely to savage or cultural life" (Hodgen 1964, p. 483).

Some scholars simply sought to understand the differences. Exemplary in this regard was the French savant Charles Louis Montesquieu, who concentrated on the study of laws, customs, and morals from different parts of the world. In an effort to explain why societies differ from one another, Montesquieu postulated factors like population density, geographical barriers, degree of isolation, stages of technological development, subsistence patterns, state of commerce, climate, and soil. In his view, natural surrounds and conditions of climate played a more decisive role in savage societies than in more developed societies. As an early functionalist, he sought within each society a motivated basis for such seemingly brutal practices as cannibalism, slavery, or idol worship (De Waal Malefijt 1974).

The advent of the Enlightenment, with its ardent belief in rationality and equality, sharpened the debate about the mentality of the primitive. On the one hand, to the extent that rationality was the standard, the Western mind *seemed* qualitatively more advanced than that of the apparently confused savage. On the other hand, to the extent that equality was stressed, another set of conclusions seemed warranted. Such practices as slavery, and such beliefs as the superiority of one group over another, were seen as regressive or anachronistic. These emerging egalitarian points of view posed difficulties for those of a religious persuasion, who needed to explain why some groups believed in a single God, while others clung to polytheistic notions. The notorious Bishop Whately claimed that savages could not be helped and were best thought of as members of a different species. Darwin posed a different threat to members of established churches who now had to contend with his demonstrations that all humans were descended from a line of forerunners, dating back millions of years, and that human beings could not be thought of apart from the rest of the Natural Order (De Waal Malefijt 1974).

Edward Tylor Launches the Discipline of Anthropology

The stage was set for more systematic thinking about different human groups. Various scholars helped to initiate the scientific study of society and culture, but the person most often granted this honor (or responsibility) is an Englishman of the late nineteenth century, Edward Tylor. Working at the same time as Wilhelm Wundt, the founder of modern psychology, Gottlob Frege, the inventor of modern logic, the neo-grammarians in linguistics, and the first generation of experimental neuroscientists, Tylor published his magnum opus, *Primitive Culture,* in 1871. Having toured America and Mexico in the 1860s and obtained thereby a vivid notion of cultural differences, Tylor undertook in his book a rationalist assault on the divine inspiration of religious beliefs. According to his revisionist perspective, human culture and religions were products of a natural, law-governed evolution of human mental capacities.

A new field requires definitions, and Tylor produced the most-often quoted description of culture: "That complex whole which includes knowledge, belief, art, morals, law, custom, and any other capabilities and habits acquired by man as a member of society" (1871, p. 1). The term *acquired* was critical: Tylor was declaring that human capacities are not simply part of one's birthright: they are rather derived from one's membership in a group and presumably could be changed, if the individuals were reared in a different group or if the group itself altered its practices or its values. This emphasis on learning also undercut any notion that individuals behave as they do because of particular inherited characteristics or their niche along an evolutionary scale. If behavior can be learned or acquired, it can also be altered.

Tylor was clearly under the sway of Darwinian evolutionary ideas. According to his own scheme, humanity could be arrayed along a linear track, ranging (in his terminology) from savagery, to barbarism, to civilization. He believed in psychic unity, however, and held that all peoples were capable of making this progression. Further, even those individuals at the height of civilization were not bereft of earlier traces. According to Tylor's scheme of *survivals,* every individual possesses many habits, beliefs, and customs that date back to earlier times and have endured despite their current lack of utility. As a timely example of a survival, the phrase "God bless you" long since has lost its original meaning and yet is ritualistically invoked when someone sneezes. Conversely, Tylor also held that even the most irrational customs are products of a reasoning capacity like our own; like Montesquieu, he believed that if one only understood the origins and circumstances of a custom, it would make sense.

In addition to contributing new ways of thinking about culture and about the relationships among different groups, Tylor also made important methodological contributions to the science he was helping to found. Noteworthy was his method of *adhesion,* whereby he attempted to determine which customs or practices hang together. This he accomplished by preparing massive lists of the practices carried out in various cultures, and noting which tended to occur at the same time. By such correlation, he could show, for instance, a predictable relation between teknonymy (naming one's parents after children) and living in the house of the mother's relatives; moreover, this practice of naming parents after children proved even more closely related to practices of avoidance, where individuals with a potentially tense relation assume a protective distance from one another. This method of correlation was a signal contribution to the new field. According to Robert Lowie, an anthropologist active in the first half of the twentieth century, "Nothing that Tylor ever did serves so decisively to lift him above the throng of his fellow-workers" (quoted in Kardiner and Preble 1961, p. 75). Instead of metaphysical speculations about why a certain practice came about, Tylor could now ferret out statistical relations between different institutions or practices.

From our contemporary perspective, Tylor's views may seem to blend with those predecessors who saw the primitive as just a pale version of civilized modern man. In fact, however, Tylor helped to undermine this view. To argue that culture actually exists among all men, in however crude or primitive a form, was a major step toward a more relativistic point of view. Moreover, Tylor's belief that all groups harbor vestiges of the past, and that behavior can be understood and justified if seen in context, served to bring the primitive person closer to the circle of civilized modern man (Stocking 1982). As Abram Kardiner and Edward Preble have commented, to overcome the ecclesiastics "who would create an impassable gulf between civilized man and his primitive ancestors, Tylor had to show that the 'rude savage' was potentially an English gentleman" (1961, p. 77). Could Shaw's *Pygmalion* be far behind?

The British Scene

Tylor's work on primitive societies links the armchair characterizations of earlier centuries with the empirically oriented work of the present era: the course from speculation to correlation. Following his pathbreaking work in England, one could witness both of these forces struggling for the ascendancy. Representing the old guard was the student of ancient societies, Sir James Frazer, whose multivolumed *The Golden Bough* (originally published in 1890) may well be the most famous anthropological book ever written. In this beautifully wrought work, which influenced many humanists even as it mesmerized the general reading public, Frazer traced a connecting thread from the pagan ceremonies of the past to the practices of Christianity and other modern religions. He described early forms of magic where one could control another individual simply by gaining possession of some vestige of that individual. These totemic practices anticipated the rise of religion where individuals gave up the belief that they themselves could control events, and instead posited nonhuman higher powers which govern the world. And finally, Frazer described the highest stage of development, that of science, where man once again began to manipulate nature, but this time sought to uncover and test the relevant physical laws. On this view, early men and contemporary primitives were seen as relatively irrational, though perhaps possessing the same potentials as modern man (Frazer 1955).

Though Frazer's work was much admired by nonscientists, and read by most anthropologists, the tradition he represented eventually yielded to a less grandiose, more empirical approach. An event that symbolized this trend was the launching, just before the turn of the century, of a large-scale expedition to the Torres Straits in the South Pacific. Never before had so many men of a scientific stripe embarked on a mission simply to document what life was like among a very different group of people. Proceeding (paradoxically) at Frazer's suggestion, A. C. Haddon, once a zoologist, organized the Cambridge Anthropological Expedition. Haddon was interested in primitive mentality but, unlike his predecessors, proposed to take systematic measurements of psychological characteristics in the field. Accompanying Haddon were experts in psychology, medicine, linguistics, and music, including W. H. Rivers, C. S. Myers, and William McDougall —all psychologists with medical training who would later become major social scientists (Rivers 1900).

The scientists on the expedition carried out many investigations. Especially when viewed from our current perspective, they did not focus on "higher" cognitive functions; instead, following the practices of psychiatrists of that era, they probed abilities to make discriminations in various sensory modalities, to appreciate illusions, and to name colors. Nor were the results particularly decisive with respect to the controversy about primitive mentality. There were some provocative findings: for example, a hint that the language available to individuals might influence the way in which they see or group colors; documentation of the Papuan's keen powers of observation (in the face of unremarkable visual acuity); a suggestion that the perception of spatial relations may also be culturally conditioned; and the documentation of capacious memories for family genealogies. McDougall also claimed that the sense of touch of natives was twice as delicate as that of Englishmen, while sensitivity to pain was only half as great. In general, however, the scientists reached no consensus on the scope of differences between the groups nor, in the case of the differences, on which reasons would best account for them (R. Brown 1956; Stocking 1982).

But the Torres expedition was a landmark in the history of anthropology, not because of its results, but for having taken place at all. That six major scientists could spend several years in the field, carrying out careful observational and experimental studies, was a dramatic demonstration that cultural differences need no longer be simply speculated about: they could be examined critically. It took some years before the full significance of this model had been absorbed by the rest of the scientific community. But, in the end, the kind of speculative statements offered by Frazer simply could not compete with empirical findings "in the field."

The American Version

Boas's Scholarly Hegemony

Thanks to the unstinting efforts of a recently transplanted German physicist, Franz Boas, the same lessons were being driven home in the United States (Herskovits 1953; T. Kroeber 1970; Stocking 1982). Boas had originally come to the New World to execute his doctoral research—an improbable study of the color of sea water. He had become dissatisfied with the laboratory study and wanted to study the color of sea water firsthand—or so goes the legend. Boas found himself in the Arctic area, near Baffinland, carrying out geographical studies, when he first encountered Eskimos and became intrigued by their languages and their behavior. Thus arose a lifelong fascination with natives in this part of the world and a long-term commitment, by a gifted and energetic man, to the founding of a scientific anthropology (as he declared) "before it was too late."

Faced with the conflicting claims of the physicist—who sought objective explanations of color—and the explorer—who sought to capture the atmosphere of exotic cultures—Boas strove to reconcile these perspectives. He concluded that validity must be granted both to the scientific view of the outsider and to the subjective view of the particular individual or culture. Here, then, was Boas's resolution of the "universal" versus "particular" dilemma which confronts all anthropological workers. He brought this lesson to the larger arena of anthropology, where he undertook a long-term study of Indian societies in the Pacific Northwest. In addition, he began to train nearly all of the next generation of anthropologists, including not only those who remained faithful to his credo, but even those who went on to found rival schools.

Apart from Boas's total commitment to the calling of anthropology, it is not simple to summarize his contribution: He steadfastly avoided strong theoretical statements, preferring to adopt a more inductive approach. Still, one can readily point out the directions in which he led anthropology, directions that remain discernible even in today's complex disciplinary terrain.

First of all, Boas opposed the notion of the linear evolution of culture. Taking issue with Tylor and those who had gone before him, Boas felt that each culture was best studied in terms of its own practices, needs, and pressures, rather than in relation to some other culture which represented a more or less advanced mode of organization. In his view, one should carefully document what is done and try to understand why, rather than evaluate how advanced or simple it might be (as the evolutionists insisted in doing), or where it came from (as the diffusionists were wont to do). This focus on the well-documented individual case, along with an abjuring of evolutionist or diffusionist temptations, has characterized anthropology in the post-Boas era.

Boas emphasized the importance of language and of linguistics for all of anthropological study. Gifted at learning languages, he developed methods for the careful notating of languages and stimulated many of his students to document the Indian languages while they were still in use. The pioneering American linguist Leonard Bloomfield paid tribute to Boas's remarkable achievements in this area:

> His greatest contribution to science, and, at any rate, the one we can best appreciate, was the development of descriptive language study. The native languages of our country had been studied by some very gifted men, but none had succeeded in putting this study on a scientific basis. . . . Boas amassed a tremendous body of observation, including much carefully recorded text, and forged, almost single-handed, the tools of phonetic and structural description. (1943, p. 198)

Boas saw each language as a unique creation which needed to be understood (in Saussurean fashion) as an organized totality. He emphasized that languages could converge from different sources, as well as diverge from a common source, and deplored the nineteenth-century search for a basic, or "Ur," language from which all other languages sprang. He also underlined the important role of language in all of human activity, though he expressed skepticism that a culture could be restricted by the form of its particular language. Indeed, in opposition to the Whorf-Sapir perspective, Boas saw thought as influencing language rather than vice versa. Even if some languages are less given to abstract terms than others, all are sufficiently complex to carry out the varieties of human thought. Thanks to Boas's insistent message, there has always been a tie in American scholarly circles between the fields of anthropology and linguistics— a model of the type of cooperation toward which cognitive science now strives.

Boas's thoughts about language related closely to his ideas about primitive mentality. In his view, the principal difference between the mental processes of primitive peoples and ourselves inheres in one fact: whereas the categories used by the primitive have developed in a crude and unreflective manner, contemporary literate populations have been able to systematize knowledge, in the manner of the rational scientist. This difference has emerged not because each individual in our society thinks in a more logical manner but rather because various philosophically oriented materials have become worked out more systematically over the generations and are now available to the general population. Boas's own explorations had convinced him that Indians and Eskimos could appreciate abstract language and thought if confronted with it, but that this set of concerns was simply not part of their habitual intellectual milieu. Overall, then, Boas was one of the first, and one of the strongest, advocates of the view that primitive and modern individuals possess essentially the same cognitive potential; an enduring suspicion of unwarranted or undocumented dichotomies between "primitive" and "modern" is one of his most compelling contributions to contemporary anthropological thinking.

From the start of his career, Boas had been suspicious of any attempt to evaluate one human being, or one human group, as better or worse than another; as his career thrived, he used his increasingly powerful and increasingly public platform to counteract all forms of racism. At least as formidable as his contributions to anthropology was Boas's role in challenging the still-prevalent views in the United States that members of one social or ethnic group were more intelligent or morally virtuous than another. That there was no scientific basis for labeling one group as inferior to another was the theme that Boas kept reinforcing in his writings. It is a theme that became part of the fabric of social science from the 1930s until the present.

Reactions to Boas

As Boas's contributions were primarily methodological, and as he had an instinctive distrust of overarching theories, it is not surprising that his most vocal critics in the next generation were those with a strong theoretical position to defend. Leslie White (1963) and Marvin Harris (1968), devotees of evolutionism who were sympathetic to Marxism, portrayed Boas as one who refused to take a stand on the relationship between one culture and another, and who, in his passion for data about particular individuals and groups, neglected the material and technological basis of human activities. A. R. Radcliffe-Brown (1940, 1952), one of the leading theorists on the British anthropological scene, stressed the importance in anthropology of an undergirding theory; he promoted a Durkheimian approach, in which the needs for group solidarity exert a decisive impact on kinship structures and on the actions and beliefs of individuals. Radcliffe-Brown also saw cultures as part of a social system, as "organisms" which evolve toward increasing diversity and complexity. All of this theorizing did not sit well with Boas, who distrusted generalizations about the needs of a group or about a culture as a whole.

Another line of research was the functionalist approach of Bronislaw Malinowski (1961, 1968): akin in some ways to behaviorism in psychology and to Bloomfield's structural approach in linguistics, the Malinowski approach evinced little interest in mental phenomena or in historical factors. Instead it focused almost exclusively on the painstaking description of social and sexual behavior. According to Malinowski, the anthropologist should search for the various *goals* that a particular custom, material object, idea, or belief serves within a society: the careful and imaginative field work methods developed by Malinowski were devoted to this utilitarian end. Malinowski also went further than his predecessors in presenting a comprehensive view of native life—detailing the various practices within a community and suggesting how they fit together. Malinowski's striking ethnographies ended up having considerable influence on the workaday practices of anthropologists, but his biologically and psychologically oriented explanations never captured the field: and Boas, himself a careful fieldworker, wondered what all the fuss was about.

While Boas was not without his critics, most American anthropologists adopted his general program. Moreover, Boas was quite generous to those who emerged from his shop. One student of his, Ruth Benedict (1934), went much farther than Boas would have dared in laying out the "character" of a civilization and in attempting to grasp the "meaning of culture" as a whole. Another student, Alfred Kroeber (1917, 1948) stressed the historical components of anthropology, pondered the concept of culture in its largest sense, and questioned the utility of focusing on particular groups or particular behavior. Though Boas had doubt about Benedict's ambitious program, and did not share Kroeber's various qualms about a scientifically oriented anthropology, he continued to support the work of his own protégés. In the struggle for the future of anthropology in America, personal loyalty was more potent than ideological consistency.

The Special Status of Language and Linguistics

While Kroeber had been selected by Boas to preside over anthropology in the United States, Edward Sapir had been his chosen vehicle as the leader of linguistics. Sapir shared Boas's interest in (and his gifts for) the recording of Indian languages. He also agreed with Boas that all languages are equally complex, and that (in their most fundamental respects) they develop free of environmental determinants. Moreover, unlike many of Boas's other students, Sapir had an enduring interest in the nature of mentality in different cultures. But as a consequence of his own studies, he came to conclusions at odds with Boas's sentiments. As I noted in discussing the history of linguistics, Sapir and his student Benjamin Lee Whorf came to believe that the language used by a group has been a principal determinant of the belief structures and the ways of thinking of that population. Indeed, Sapir came to see language as a guide to social reality:

> It powerfully conditions all our thinking about social problems and processes. . . . It is quite an illusion to imagine that one adjusts to reality essentially without the use of language and that language is merely an identical means of solving specific problems of communication or reflection. . . . No two languages are ever sufficiently similar to be considered as representing the same social reality. The worlds in which different societies live are distinct worlds, not merely the same worlds with different labels attached. (1929, p. 162)

The direction in which Sapir developed the relationship between language and culture was fascinating, not truly anticipated in Boas's own work but one that he came to admire as provocative. (Whether he would have endorsed the more radical directions in which Whorf eventually ventured is far less certain.) But there is another approach in anthropology, also traceable to Boas's influence, where language as a system of analysis came to be applied to cultural phenomena. This is the variety of structural anthropology pioneered by Claude Lévi-Strauss, one of the most eminent anthropologists of our time—a scholar who had become an intimate of Boas in the early 1940s, when the senior scholar's career was ending, and the younger's was just on the rise.

Lévi-Strauss has indicated his indebtedness to Boas's influence: "Boas must be given credit for defining the unconscious nature of cultural phenomena with admirable lucidity. By comparing cultural phenomena to language . . . he anticipated both the subsequent development of linguistic theory and a future for anthropology whose rich promise we are just beginning to perceive" (1963, p. 19). In his observation that neither language nor culture rise to consciousness, Boas had discerned a vast opening for anthropology. Precisely because people are unaware of these structures, they are much less likely to revise them at will or to invent *ad hoc* explanations of their nature and operation. But if Boas anticipated the general direction in which anthropology should proceed, it was a mutual friend, Roman Jakobson, who actually introduced Lévi-Strauss to those insights about language that would prove decisive in his own work (Jakobson 1941; Jakobson and Halle 1956).

As a founding member of the Prague school of linguistics, Jakobson had pointed out that certain properties of the human mind determine the ways in which language operates. These properties may not be immediately evident; but, once specified, they allow the analyst to make sense of diverse linguistic phenomena. On Jakobson's account, because human beings tend to perceive things in terms of polarities, many important distinctions in language also prove to be binary. Phonemes are constituted of distinctive features, with each distinctive feature either being present (for example, voiced) or absent (for example, voiceless). Other aspects of language, including grammar and meaning, can also be seen in terms of the presence or the absence of various binary features. These features do not exist in an unorganized fashion: they constitute a system, where the relations obtaining between the features become primary. Indeed, it is in laying out the systematic and structured relationship among the various terms that linguistics does its primary work.

The Structuralist Version

Lévi-Strauss's Canons

This much was straight linguistic theory, of the sort put forth by Jakobson and his associates in the Prague school and subscribed to, in more or less faithful fashion, by others influenced by Saussure. The decisive step taken by Lévi-Strauss, and the core of his contribution to anthropology, lay in his insistence—and his demonstration—that key aspects of culture are best thought of as linguistic in nature and are best approached by the methods of the structural linguist.

Appropriately for one who wanted to capture the attention of his anthropological colleagues, Lévi-Strauss began his inquiries by confronting an area central to the concern of all anthropologists—the area of kinship relations or kinship structures. To start with, he noted that in any kinship system one has as primary data both the system of relations between terms (father, son) and the system of relations between attitudes (intimate, distant). As a test case for his notions of structural anthropology, Lévi-Strauss selected the classic problem of the avunculate: the relationship where the maternal uncle represents family authority and exerts certain rights over his nephew, and yet can maintain an informal, joking relationship with that nephew. Lévi-Strauss notes a correlation between this set of attitudes and the young male's attitude toward his father. In groups where familiarity characterizes the relationship between father and son, uncle and nephew have a relationship of formal respect; whereas when the father represents family authority, it is the uncle who is treated with familiarity.

Radcliffe-Brown, a keen analyst of kinship structures, had himself called attention to this phenomenon. But, said Lévi-Strauss in response to Radcliffe-Brown, it does not suffice to study the correlation of attitudes between father and son and between uncle and sister's son. Rather, playing structural linguist, one must take into account *all* the relevant terms and the relationships among them *all*. In this particular case, the four crucial relations are those between brother and sister, husband and wife, father and son, *and* mother's brother and sister's son (Lévi-Strauss 1963, p. 42).

Even as a linguist studies the phonological relations across many languages in order to determine the proper set of distinctive features, Lévi-Strauss examined the avunculate in many cultures in an effort to discover the operative factors. He then went on to propound a structural law that, in his view, ferrets out the critical factors operating in this complex set of relationships. The law reads: the relation between maternal uncle and nephew (whether it be intimate or formal) is to the relation between brother and sister as the relation between father and son is to that between husband and wife. According to Lévi-Strauss, if one knows one pair of relations, it is possible, as in any analogy, to figure out the other (1963, p. 42); he then illustrates his "law" by reviewing supporting examples. Lévi-Strauss goes on to maintain that, even in quite different forms of descent, one always encounters the same fundamental relationship between the four pairs of oppositions required to construct the kinship system. One has thus unlocked the key to such relationships by having figured out the appropriate unit of analysis. As he says, "This structure is the most elementary form of kinship that can exist. It is, properly speaking, *the unit of kinship*" (p. 46).

Lévi-Strauss's early writings on kinship, while certainly controversial, established his mark as a major anthropological thinker and also promoted the injection of linguistic techniques (and, to a lesser extent, formal logical analysis) into the research carried out by anthropologists. Acclaim also greeted a second wave of work in social organization, another staple interest of anthropologists. Here Lévi-Strauss clarified the obscure nature of dual organizations—where two parallel kinds of clans, often exogamous, exist within the same village. Lévi-Strauss adduced evidence that these dual organizations actually mask the underlying dynamic force, which arises from the exchange of women and other commodities. It is this exchange, rather than the external residence patterns, that reflects the actual social relations found in the village.

In the early 1950s, Lévi-Strauss attended a conference of linguists and anthropologists where he presented some of the material I have just outlined. During his remarks, Lévi-Strauss alluded to an "uninvited guest which has been seated during this conference beside us and which is *the human mind"* (1963, p. 7). Lévi-Strauss felt that in their focus on the material and social organizational aspects of culture, anthropologists had given short shrift to the key factor involved in understanding any culture—the ways in which the human mind takes in, classifies, and interprets information. Not coincidentally, Lévi-Strauss was pointing out the need for anthropologists to consider mental representations just as other pioneering cognitivists were beginning to redirect efforts within their own chosen disciplines—the Zeitgeist was assiduously at work.

Exploring Mind

Lévi-Strauss's remark was prophetic concerning his own work, because for the remainder of his career he has sought to discover the nature of the human mind in as pristine a form as possible. He has approached this assignment by studying the ways in which individuals classify objects and elements, and the ways in which they create and understand myths. Much of this work is put forth as being empirical—based on the classificatory systems observed around the world and on the myths related in many Indian tribes. Yet, Lévi-Strauss makes no secret of the fact that he must rely on his own intuitions (which he has dubbed "neolithic"): introducing his major study of myths he has even declared, "It is in the last resort immaterial whether in this book the thought processes of the South American Indians take shape through the medium of my thought, or whether mine takes place through the medium of theirs" (1969, p. 13). After all, he believes, it is the same mind—all human minds—in either case, and the scholar's point of entry is simply not crucial. This may be cognitive science—but it is a science built on a Cartesian confidence in one's own mind rather than on the methods of consensual validation embraced by nearly all other workers today.

While I cannot follow through all the steps of Lévi-Strauss's complex and still uncompleted project, I can say something about the methods he uses and the conclusions he reaches. In his studies of classification, he comes down decisively in favor of the proposition that the principal feature of all minds is to classify, and that primitive individuals classify pretty much along the same lines, and in the same ways, as the most civilized persons. He describes the classifying practices of primitive groups as a science of the concrete: rather than looking for the factors that *underlie* the structures or processes of the world (as the trained scientist does), the primitive mind seeks to classify everyday objects and experiences in terms of their overt perceptual and sensory properties. These methods do not always lead to the same categories and classes as those used in the Western scientific approach—they may be more or less detailed and may have differently drawn boundaries; but they reflect roughly the same kinds of analytic moves on the part of a classifier.

Nor is there an unlimited number of ways in which the human mind can work. As humans, we are constrained in the kinds of combinations we can make, in the kinds of distinctive features of opposition with which we can play. Lévi-Strauss laid his cards on the table in this proclamation:

> The ensemble of a people's customs has always its particular style; they form into systems. I am convinced that the number of these systems is not unlimited and that human societies, like individual human beings (at play, in their dreams, or in moments of delirium), never create *absolutely:* all they can do is to choose certain combinations from a repertory of ideas which it should be possible to reconstitute. (1964, p. 60)

Though the degree of analytic precision diverges from that encountered in contemporary linguistics, it is germane to compare Lévi-Strauss's Mendelian notions here with the limits on information processing proposed by George Miller in the middle 1950s or the "setting of parameters" now favored in Chomskian linguistics.

Myth Making

Lévi-Strauss's studies of myth making represent his most extensive search for the rules governing human cognition. In an early work (1963), he laid out a methodological approach for the structural study of myth. Proceeding in approved structuralist fashion, he proposed a breakdown of a myth into component parts or units (the elementary phrases of the myth) and then the assembling of all units that refer to the same theme or make the same point. For example, in the case of the Oedipal myths, Lévi-Strauss discerns a set of themes relating to the *overvaluing of blood relations* (Cadmos seeks his sister, who has been ravished by Zeus; Oedipus marries his mother, Jocasta); a set of themes relating to the *undervaluing of blood relations* (Oedipus kills his father, Laius; Eteocles kills his brother Polynices); a set of themes relating to *monsters being slain* (Cadmos kills the dragon; Oedipus kills the sphinx); and *some unusual names having to do with difficulties in walking* (Labdacos means "lame"; Laius means "left-sided"; Oedipus means "swollen-footed").

Having grouped the various myth themes into these four categories, Lévi-Strauss then lays out a formula that purports to describe the underlying message of the myth. As he describes it, the Oedipus myth in all its myriad versions has to do with either the overvaluing or the undervaluing of the importance of kinship structure, and with the question of men's origins on the earth either through autochthony (emergence from the earth, with certain creatures having to be killed so that men can be born from the earth) or through childbirth (men from the earth cannot walk initially or they walk clumsily). The myth does not resolve these issues— where men actually come from—inasmuch as myths deal with perennial mysteries; yet it does provide a point of equilibrium by laying out various competing themes and suggesting some balance among them. Ultimately Lévi-Strauss describes the Oedipal myth in this formulaic way: the over-rating of blood relations is to the underrating of blood relations as the attempt to escape autochthony is to the impossibility of succeeding in it (Lévi-Strauss 1963, p. 216).

While this elliptical example may seem forbidding to follow, and even more difficult to swallow, it actually conveys rather well the kind of enterprise in which Lévi-Strauss has been involved. To attempt to "trans-late" his account of a myth structure, or a kin structure like the avunculate, so that it is clearer and less exotic than the original is as distorting a maneuver as would be a deliberate obfuscation of his argument. As one can see, he is willing to take any kind of myth fragment or myth corpus and reduce and rearrange its elements, in order to come up with an account of the themes with which it is working and the kinds of messages that seem implicit in it.

But what is Lévi-Strauss up to? As I see it, he believes that the simple empirical categories that populate myths—percepts of smell, sound, si-lence, light, darkness, rawness or cookedness—are best conceived of as the conceptual tools for approaching the more abstract concerns with which human beings everywhere must grapple: dilemmas like the dialectic be-tween nature and culture, the status of the incest taboo, the relation be-tween sexes, the importance of particular social arrangements. These ideas are stated in terms of concrete particulars, such as emotionally laden stories of social conflicts, but they can be reformulated at a more abstract level in terms of logical propositions. In fact, if the myths are to be properly understood, the logical terms and relations must be specified, as Lévi-Strauss has attempted to do in his gloss of the Oedipal myth. Moreover, he goes on to insist that the myths themselves have a quasi-biological relationship to one another. Each myth in a sense transforms the others that go before it, and no myth can be fully understood except in relation to all the other myths in a corpus (which might ultimately include all the myths ever spun). The kinds of relationship among phonemic features that define a linguistic system are mirrored in the thematic forms that constitute a mythic system.

While myths may confuse many of us, they offer a privileged route for a Lévi-Straussian analysis. As he sees it, the myth offers a glimpse of the mind in pure form: "when the mind is left to commune with itself and no longer has to come to terms with objects, it is in a sense reduced to imitating itself as object" (1969, p. 10). And his examination has confirmed for him the essential logic inherent in all human thought:

> The kind of logic in mythical thought is as rigorous as that of modern science, and . . . the difference lies, not in the quality of the intellectual process, but in the nature of things to which it is applied. . . . Man has always been thinking equally well; the improvement lies, not in an alleged progress of man's mind, but in the discovery of new areas to which it may apply its unchanged and unchanging powers. (1963, p. 230)

And so Boas's program is vindicated by Lévi-Strauss's myth analysis.

It should come as no surprise that Lévi-Strauss's work, while it has dazzled most readers, has not convinced many of them. It is too neat somehow that all of the myths of the world, which could have arisen from such diverse sources and for such varied reasons, should converge to embody the various messages that one thoughtful but solitary Frenchman discerns in them. Lévi-Strauss himself varies in the actual claims he makes for his analyses, as in the preceding quotation. But, over all, it is his feeling that while kinship is too embedded in social action to provide a sure guide to mental processes, mythology holds the key to unlocking the laws of the mind. That systems can be found is for Lévi-Strauss the evidence that the mind has its laws of order that the anthropologist—or, he might as well say, the cognitive scientist—is challenged to discover.

Like Noam Chomsky, Lévi-Strauss has stimulated a great deal of admiration for the scope of his project and the daring way in which he has sought to reorient his field. Unlike Chomsky, his method cannot be laid out with sufficient clarity so as to be followed by anyone who exhibits good faith and hard work. Thus, rather than having a school of followers, Lévi-Strauss has chiefly imitators, who seek to carry out the kind of intuitive subjective analysis in which the master excels. Of these, the English anthropologist Edmund Leach is probably the best known as well as the most gifted (1961, 1974). But Lévi-Strauss shares with many original thinkers the desire either for complete fidelity (on the part of others) to his own system or for some formal declaration of distance. Thus, many of those initially sympathetic to him, including Leach, have eventually been left out in the cold—a situation not, apparently, displeasing to Lévi-Strauss.

Is Lévi-Strauss, then, a pivotal contributor to cognitive science or just an isolated, humanistically oriented savant? Most of my colleagues would, I suspect, consign him to the tradition of Rousseau, Montesquieu, and the French Academy (to which he was recently elected) rather than to the ranks of Simon or Chomsky, but I think that this assessment will turn out to be shortsighted. In my own view, despite his conceits and idiosyncracies, his rather cranky set of interests and obsessions, Lévi-Strauss will prove to be an enduring figure in the history of cognitive science. At mid-century he injected issues of cognition centrally into anthropological discussions. By invoking the most rigorous approaches of linguistics during his time, and applying them imaginatively in the principal domains within anthropology, he opened up new fields of inquiry. Like Piaget, he has sometimes aped system, or haphazardly borrowed terms from formal analysis, rather than being truly systematic: it is therefore up to his successors to pursue his program in a less personal and more replicable way (though how to do this is much less clear than, say, in the case of Piaget). Again, as happened with Piaget, Lévi-Strauss's strong positions on anthropological issues have served as a convenient point of departure for revisionist formulations.

When all the criticisms have been considered, few of Lévi-Strauss's *particular* conclusions may remain; but the critiques will only have been possible because of his fertile questions and provocative hypotheses. Moreover, I suspect that one hundred years from now his research program will be seen as more right-headed than that of his strongest critics—the true mark of an important thinker. Lévi-Strauss will endure because he posed questions that are central to both anthropology and cognition; outlined methods of analysis that might be applicable; and proposed the kinds of systematic relations which *may* obtain in such diverse fields as kinship, social organization, classification, and mythology.

Sperber's Variations

Of those who have some sympathy with Lévi-Strauss's enterprise, Dan Sperber, a former student of his now working in Paris (1968, 1982), endorses his teacher's once radical program of examining the products of human mentation and concurs that the model of linguistics is crucial for anthropologists. Yet, perhaps appropriately for one of a younger generation, Sperber feels that Lévi-Strauss has drawn on the *wrong* school of linguistics. The structural approach is as outmoded in anthropology as it has become in linguistics, maintains Sperber; and it is from the work of Chomsky, Fodor, and others of the transformationalist school that the anthropologist must now seek models.

Here the lessons turn out to be largely negative, for language is seen as a system that works by its own very special rules. Contrary to Lévi-Strauss's vision (and reflecting the shift toward domain-specific principles), Sperber maintains that linguistic analysis cannot properly be applied to other cultural phenomena such as myths, custom, and rituals. One should instead consider cultural phenomena as entities subject to an endless amount of mental associations or elaborations, of the sort which go on precisely *after* the usual rule-governed operations of language have been carried out. It is in the realm of the mysterious, the unanalyzable, the richly symbolic, that most cultural entities exert their powers—and not in the relatively lean aspects of language which can be apprehended and analyzed according to prescribed syntactic, phonological, and lexical regularities. Sperber points out that most human beliefs are not purely propositional but are rather semipropositional—not fully logical and far fuzzier. It is risky to apply to such amorphous belief systems the rigid classificatory grid of the syntactician or the phonologist. Instead, one needs to study the processes whereby rich penumbras of meaning are evoked.

Sperber's positive contribution inheres in his characterization of symbolic processes. Rather than being induced or constructed from experience, the symbolic mechanisms are part of the innate mental equipment which makes experience possible. These mechanisms of symbolic elaboration, working in a manner reminiscent of Lévi-Strauss's savage, start with the assumption that the "waste" of the mind ought always to be salvaged because something can be made of it. It is just because this dross harbors within it atypical or exceptional conceptual characteristics that it lends itself to unending symbolic elaboration. In such cases, the symbolic mechanism of the mind draws on one's encyclopedic knowledge, one's knowledge of more or less remote categories, and, indeed, any other modes of information or interpretation that happen to be available—all in an effort somehow to piece together these disparate elements into an overall sensible framework. Anthropology is the discipline that has access to the fullest range of beliefs, practices, and symbolic systems; hence, it is in a privileged position to lay bare the operation of those human symbolic mechanisms that supplement the (relatively) pure computational aspects involved in language, mathematics, and ordinary classification.

There is no shortage of critics of Lévi-Strauss, who fault him at every step, from the initial ethnographies he published in the 1940s to the dubious importation of methods from cybernetics, information theory, or linguistics which crowd his pages. To my mind, the most telling line of criticism questions whether polymorphous human behavioral patterns and beliefs can lend themselves to the kind of systematic, rule-bound, and "closed" analysis that has proved appropriate for certain aspects of linguistic structures. In the view of anthropologist Clifford Geertz, Lévi-Strauss has jumped prematurely to the conclusion that human thought processes can be analogized to the operations of a traditional computer (Geertz 1973, 1983). The preferred path, in Geertz's view, lies in the careful detailed study of a social group in its cultural setting: only in this way can one hope to understand the kind of symbolism it uses and the way in which it goes about making sense of the world. Geertz criticizes Lévi-Strauss's mechanistic approach, his ignorance of the particular historical conditions that spawn a given myth or social organization, the minimization of affective and emotional factors, the loss of the specific individual with his or her own needs, motivations, goals, and wishes—all in favor of an intellect that grinds out classifications and propositions. Geertz also questions the wisdom of construing symbolic products as the output of internal cognitive mechanisms: according to his more public view of mind, myths, rituals, beliefs, and the like are a socially generated form of symbolization:

> The way to look at thought is not to assume that there is a parallel thread of correlated affects or internal experiences that go with it in some regular way. It's not of course that people *don't* have internal experiences, of course they *do;* but that when you ask what is the state of mind of someone, say while he or she is performing a ritual, it's hard to believe that such experiences are the same for all people involved. . . . The thinking, and indeed the feeling in an odd sort of way, is really going on in public. They are really saying what they're saying, doing what they're doing, meaning what they're meaning.
> . . . Thought is, in great part anyway, a public activity. (Quoted in Miller 1983, pp. 202–3)

Whether the program of structural anthropology might ultimately make sense is not directly addressed; but it seems clear to critics like Geertz that the time for such an assault on the universals of thought is premature. We must first understand individual cases much better than we do; and that understanding must encompass ourselves no less than the "funny" people elsewhere whose difficult-to-pigeonhole practices have perennially stimulated the symbolic processes of anthropologists.

Ethnoscience

What Lévi-Strauss undertook pretty much by himself, armed with his own intuitions, has in the last three decades become in somewhat transmuted form a major wing of anthropology. I refer here to the field of ethnoscience, in its various lexical guises—componential analysis, ethnosemantics, cognitive anthropology—all comprising the organized study of the thought systems of individuals in other cultures and sometimes in our own.

Roots

The factors that gave rise to ethnoscience in the United States in the middle 1950s resembled those that stimulated Lévi-Strauss in France at about the same time. Both anthropological circles were affected by the example of linguistics as a social science that had achieved unparalleled rigor. Information theory, stochastic modeling, cybernetics, and computer simulation were other reminders of the advantages to be gained by formal approaches to social phenomena. Thanks to the works of the semioticians like Roman Jakobson (1963) and Charles Morris (1971), there was increasing awareness of the essentially symbolic property of all human action, and of the need to explain it in terms of its cognitive, as opposed to its practical, aspects. According to one of the first ethnoscientific practitioners:

> The model for the first experiments in the structural analysis of meaning was consciously an analogical adaptation of that which had been developed for phonemic analysis. More than one of those who were involved in the early phases of this experiment have acknowledged that the stimulus to it, as well as the eye-opener as to how it might be done, came from a combination of their training in phonemics and their reading of Charles W. Morris' *Foundation of the Theory of Signs.* (Lounsbury 1968, p. 223)

In fact, this background spawned the initial pair of publications consciously styled in the ethnoscientific mode: Ward Goodenough's (1964) revision of his analysis of the Trukese kinship terminology, which he had undertaken in the field some years earlier (1951, 1956); and Floyd Lounsbury's (1956) structural analysis of the Pawnee terminology collected for Lewis Henry Morgan by an Indian agent in 1863.

Just how have the practitioners of this new form of science conceptualized themselves? According to Stephen Tyler, the first anthologist of cognitive anthropology, the field focuses on discovering how different peoples organize and use their cultures.

> It is an attempt to understand the organizing principles underlying their behavior. It is assumed that each people has a unique system for perceiving and organizing material phenomena—things, events, behaviors, and emotions. . . . The object of the study is not these material phenomena themselves, but the way they are organized in the minds of men. Cultures then are not material phenomena: they are cognitive organizations of material phenomena. (Tyler 1969, p. 3)

Drawing on the model of a linguist's grammar, ethnoscientists search for the ways in which knowledge of a culture's rules is reflected in the behavior of natives, and especially in their speech.

Anthony Wallace, an early worker in the field, compares the ethnosemanticist to an observer with the following assignment: describe a calculus being used by a group of people who have not formulated their system in a written text. The investigator is allowed to interview and observe, and to learn the method as a novice himself. As he analyzes that data, he does not merely tabulate frequencies and give equal weight to every slip, joke, gibberish, or error:

What he does, instead, is to infer the system of rules that these people are attempting to apply. He will gain the assurance that he is on the way to an adequate understanding of these rules from the logical completeness of the system he infers and from his ability, when using it, to produce behavior that an expert will reward by saying, in effect, "That's right; that's good; now you've got it." (1968, p. 537)

Robert B. Edgerton and L. L. Langness have put it even more succinctly: "The goal of an ethnoscientific description is to write a set of rules for a culture which is so complete that any outsider could use them to behave appropriately in that culture" (1974, p. 38).

A Sample Componential Analysis

A common ethnoscientific approach is componential analysis. To illustrate how a componential analysis might actually be carried out, I have borrowed an example from an early study of English kin terms by Anthony Wallace and John Atkins (1960). These authors begin by taking a set of kinship terms: namely grandfather, grandmother, father, mother, brother, sister, son, daughter, grandson, granddaughter, uncle, aunt, cousin, nephew, and niece. Next, they define these terms with respect to genealogical relations. Thus, *grandfather* is defined as someone who is one's father's father (or, in the notation used by anthropologists, Grandfather: FaFa). The expression "Grandfather: FaFa, MoFa" is translated as "grandfather refers to 'father's father' and to 'mother's father.'" All terms are defined through the primitive forms *Fa, Mo, Br, Si, So, Da,* and some simple operators.

The rest of a kinship grid contains entries like:

Grandmother: FaMo, MoMo
Grandson: SoSo, DaSo
Uncle: FaBr, MoBr, FaFaBr, MoFaBr, and so on,

culminating in the entry after *cousin* which includes at least twelve possible relatives. In this particular kinship grid, the terms *uncle, aunt, nephew, cousin,* and *niece* have been used in an extended sense, thus including such relations as "second cousin once removed" and other distant relations within an extended family.

The third stage entails a number of observations obtained from the grid. For instance, all but one of these terms *(cousin)* specifies the sex of the relative: some (like *grandfather* but not *cousin*) specify generation; all specify whether the relative is lineally (for example, *sons*) or nonlineally (for example, nephew) related to Ego; and nonlineal terms specify whether all the ancestors of the relative are direct ancestors of Ego, whether all the ancestors of Ego are ancestors of the relative, or neither.

Now comes the crucial stage: the analyst hypothesizes that three dimensions will be sufficient to define all the terms. The *sex of the relative* (male as a_1, female as a_2); *generation* (b_1 as two generations above Ego; b_2 as one generation above Ego; b_3 as Ego's own generation; b_4 as one generation below Ego; b_5 as two generations below Ego); finally, *lineality*: c_1 is lineal; c_2 is co-lineal (brother or sister); c_3 as ablineal (cousin). Lineals are persons who are ancestors or descendants of Ego; co-lineals are nonlineals, all of whose ancestors include, or are included in, all the ancestors of Ego; ablineals are relatives who are neither lineals nor co-lineals.

In the next step the terms are now redefined as components. Thus, the grandfather is $a_1 b_1 c_1$; the grandson is $a_1 b_5 c_1$; the sister is $a_2 b_3 c_2$; an uncle is $a_1 b_1 c_2$ and $a_1 b_2 c_2$; and a cousin is a b (not marked on either sex or generation) and c_3. (Note the convention that, when a term does not discriminate on a dimension, the letter for that dimension is given *sans* subscript).

It is now possible to summarize this analysis of kin terms by means of the paradigm in the following table. Conforming to the technical definition of a paradigm, each term has been so defined that no term overlaps or includes another; every component is discriminated by at least one term; and all terms can be displayed on the same paradigm.

	c_1		c_2		c_3	
	a_1	a_2	a_1	a_2	a_1	a_2
b_1	grandfather	grandmother				
			uncle	aunt		
b_2	father	mother				
b_3	[ego]		brother	sister	cousin	
b_4	son	daughter				
			nephew	niece		
b_5	grandson	granddaughter				

Source: From A. F. C. Wallace and J. Atkins, "The Meaning of Kinship Terms." Reproduced by permission of the American Anthropological Association from *American Anthropologist* 62 (1): 58–80, 1960.

This analysis accomplishes the goal of laying out the relationships among the various kin terms in our language in a clear, exhaustive, and simplifying way. Wallace and Atkins make no claims that this is the best way, or the only way, to lay out the components of American kin structure (for an influential rival account, see Romney and D'Andrade 1964)—only that it is one possible and parsimonious way of accomplishing this task.

Wallace and Atkins's examples also convey the concerns that occupied the minds of the founders of componential analysis. These researchers felt that it made sense first to apply the method in an area that is already relatively well understood; where there is a finite number of terms that could be defined on independent grounds (like sex); and where societies differ in potentially revealing ways from one another in the kinds of terminology they use, and the ways in which these societies cut up the kinship pie. It was also important that members of those societies hold shared intuitions about their respective kinship structures. For example, among the Iroquois the primary dimensions are those of *generation* and *bifurcation* (a distinction between parallel and cross-cousin relations); whereas in Crow kin systems, the primary dimensions are *a skewed generation measure* (where females rank a social generation higher than their male siblings in certain contexts) and *bifurcation* (Lounsbury 1963, p. 572). Floyd Lounsbury declared:

> We may consider that a "formal account" of a collection of empirical data has been given when there have been specified 1) a set of primitive elements, and 2) a set of rules for operating on these, such that by the application of the latter to the former, the elements of a "model" are generated; which model in turn comes satisfactorily close to being a facsimile or exact replica of the empirical data whose interrelatedness and systemic nature we are trying to understand. A formal account is thus an apparatus for predicting back the data at hand, thereby making them "understandable," i.e. showing them to be lawful and expectable consequences of an underlying principle that may be presumed to be at work at their source. (Quoted in Durbin 1966, p. 31)

Goodenough adds a less formal note:

> One test of the adequacy of this account, I have said, is that it does not do violence to my own feel, as informant, for the structure of what is described. This is the subjective test of adequacy. An equally important test is that it provide an alien with the knowledge he needs to use my kinship terminology in a way I will accept as corresponding with the way I use it. This is the objective test of adequacy. (Quoted in Kuper 1973, p. 573)

Thus described, componential analysis may seem a relatively simple and straightforward process on whose application trained anthropologists should agree and by which they should ultimately arrive at the same conclusion. And indeed, at least compared with Lévi-Strauss's avowedly subjective measures, it is possible to train students in componential analysis. In fact, however, componential analysis turns out to be more complex and "fuzzier" than its originators had hoped.

Critiques of Ethnoscience: From Within

The area of kinship represents a positive extreme with respect to the feasibility of listing terms and the likelihood of figuring out the relevant dimensions in a reliable fashion. When one turns to other domains, ranging from color, to botany, to disease, it turns out to be more complex to elicit the relevant terms and delineate the domain, let alone to ferret out the relevant dimensions that may systematize the domain in a defensible and desirable way.

Even when the terms and dimensions have been delineated, the way in which to arrange them becomes a subject of considerable controversy. The clear-cut example of a paradigm I have just illustrated is but one of the numerous formal ways in which terms can be arrayed. There are also diagrams, mazeways, taxonomies, trees, etic grids, contrast sets, and many other ways of laying out the findings: the relationship among these ways of delineating is by no means clear, and it is possible to make combinations of them or to lay out findings in more than one way, as in box or key diagrams. Even English kinship terms can be laid out in ways other than paradigms, depending on the terms used, the methods used to elicit the definitions, and the ways in which the dimensions are aligned with reference to one another (Kay 1966).

Still thornier questions arise when one wants to determine whether a componential analysis is appropriate, or which of a number of competing analyses is most accurate. The intuitions of a native speaker or of a judicious anthropologist provide one measure, but it is also possible to use empirical methods—for example, requiring informants to answer questions, to sort items, to define terms, to group words, or even to construct their own componential analyses. The "psychological reality" of an analysis—is it in the heads of all informants, of trained and reflective informants, or only in the head of the analyst?—turns out to be one of the most complex questions in componential analysis. Indeed, one can raise, with respect to a "simulation" of a native's knowledge, the same questions posed by John Searle in his "computer-Chinese room" conundrum.

Some of these critical points were brought up early on by Wallace and Atkins (1960), who pointed out problems with homonyms and metaphors, where the same words might have different meanings, or where different words might have the same meanings. There was the problem of connotation, where words may have the same objective meaning but connote different affective values (*dad, daddy, old man, pop, father,* and so on). Other critics have argued that componential analysis is inherently circular, since one must begin by assuming the very relationship among terms whose relationship should actually be fixed only at the conclusion of the investigation. In other words, the existence and coherence of the domain is presupposed before the investigation begins (Gardin 1965). Some commentators have focused on the enormous problems of translating terms from a foreign language (particularly one of non Indo-European origins) into a familiar tongue and assuming that the same kinds of analysis can be applied to the translations (Crick 1976; Keesing 1976). For example, in a culture where men and women do few things together, it is risky to transfer the same meanings to the foreign terms as we would apply to male and female; and the terms *male* and *female* themselves have very different frequency and usage than do *man* and *woman* (Lyons 1968).

Critiques of Ethnoscience: Outside the Ranks

Criticisms from those who are not aligned with formal analytical approaches are more severe still. Clifford Geertz points out that knowing how to talk about something is not the same as doing something. One has to pay attention to the logic exhibited in actual life, not to some kind of abstracted set of symbolic elements whose validity for the inhabitants— let alone the formal logical relations that may obtain among them—is questionable at best. "Nothing has done more, I think, to discredit cultural analysis than the construction of impeccable descriptions of formal order in whose actual existence nobody can quite believe" (Geertz 1973, p. 18). Gary Witherspoon argues that many aspects of importance are simply not marked in the language and concludes:

How a Navajo thinks and what categories he can employ in his thinking are not the same. . . . The assumptions that kin terms have primary . . . referents in all cultures, that kinship and kinsmen are basically the same in all cultures, and only partitioned differently by various sets of kin terms, and that kin terms correspond to and express the kin categories of a given culture seem extremely naïve. (1971, p. 116)

Michael Silverstein (1978) views cognitive anthropology as a natural outgrowth of the importation of Bloomfieldian views into anthropology. Words are seen as standing directly for things. Reflected is an utterly atomistic conception of language, functionally ordered into data arrays, without any sense of how words function in a social context, the kinds of actions in which they are embedded, and the ways in which they interact with and influence one another. Language as a structured system, not language as a set of isolated tokens referring to isolated objects, should be the model of choice for anthropologists.

Perhaps most telling in any discussion about the fate of ethnoscience is the hegira of Stephen Tyler himself. Initially a staunch proponent of componential analysis and its first anthologist, he became completely disillusioned in the intervening decade. In 1978 he published *The Said and the Unsaid*, in which he spurned the earlier view of language as offering a reliable window on the cognitive systems of individuals. In his formulation:

> Common to both logical positivism and transformational linguistics is their view of language-as-mathematics. Both focus on language as a system of primitive or elementary units which can be combined according to fixed rules. However useful this analogy may be in certain limited ways, it creates problems in understanding how the purely formal system of elements and rules relates to something other than itself. Both create dualistic systems which oppose formal linguistic competence to empirical components. (1978, pp. 13–14)

Tyler now stresses the functionalist facets of language. On this account, language is not merely a means of representing ideas but equally a means for expressing wishes, feelings, and emotions—and, above all, a way of getting things done in the world. As he phrases it, language is a means of establishing relations rather than an object consisting of relations. What we take to be someone's intentions, purposes, plans, and attitudes are clues to what that person means.

Tyler ends up endorsing a hermeneutic approach. In this perspective, one looks at what is said and unsaid—the background of unspoken presuppositions and implications—created conventionally by the said and created intentionally by the speaker and hearer. He rejects the assumed independence of semantics from pragmatics:

> No less than the death of meaning should we have forecast from a manner of thought that emptied thought of all content, and what else could we expect from a method of analysis that presumed to show that meaning might mysteriously emerge from the mechanical concatenation of meaningless elements? . . . Whether in art or science nothing is clearer than the intellectual poverty of formalism. (1978, p. 465)

Tyler's benediction over componential analysis has not by any means spelled the death of this movement. However, there is now abroad considerable awareness that the original methods of componential analysis, while suitable in some domains, may not be widely extendable. Such techniques may be useful in studies of kinship and color; they may be plausible with other possibly finite categories like plants, animals, or everyday objects; but they rapidly become dysfunctional when applied to slippery areas, like emotions or diseases, where the line around the domain is not announced in advance and where an individual's (or a group's) idiosyncratic interpretive system comes more readily to the fore.

In the case of illness, for example, one's responses are so intertwined with the values of one's culture, the nature of pain, the prevailing theories of causation and cure of disease, the distinction between observable and experienced symptoms that the analyst rapidly loses confidence that diverse informants are talking about the same thing or even the same domain. Sensing these difficulties, Roger Keesing, another early supporter of the new ethnography, declared as early as 1976:

> For almost fifteen years, cognitive anthropologists have pursued "the new ethnography" as far as it would lead them. For the last five, at least, it has been obvious that this would not be very far—that the messianic promises of the early polemic were not to be realized. "The new ethnographers" have been unable to move beyond the analysis of artificially simplified and delineated (and usually trivial) semantic domains and this has discouraged many of the originally faithful. (1976, p. 307)

It is not by any means the first occasion in cognitive science where formal methods turn out to work most effectively with those aspects of behavior that seem least central to mankind's concerns. Clearly, the computational paradox resonates in anthropological circles.

Stephen Murray (1982), a historian who has reviewed the rise and subsequent decline of "classical ethnoscience," discerns two different reasons for the evanescence of this form of study. The first stems from a much-touted promise that was not fulfilled. In the middle 1960s, a major study of drinking in Chiapas, Mexico, was designed to test the powers of ethnoscientific research. According to the plan, investigators were supposed to apply the same procedures for analyzing patterns of drinking to data secured from five villages. However, problems of analyzing the data were never solved and the investigators themselves eventually moved on to other problems. As Paul Kay, one member of the team, reports,

> It turned out that after collecting a huge amount of material and spending two or three years looking for a set of objective procedures—or even semi-objective procedures—that could be applied to this material to reduce it to some kind of logical statement, we gave up, because we could not find such a set of procedures. Drinking is an institution in Chiapas that permeates the entire lives of a people: religion, politics, family life, even agriculture is inextricably tied up with drinking, so to do the ethnography of drinking there is to do the total ethnography. (Quoted in S. O. Murray 1982, p. 169)

Kay's colleague Brent Berlin suggests, "We were not convinced that what could be said from the elicited data was that much more revealing than what could be said on the basis of old-fashioned participant observation" (p. 169).

The experience in Chiapas may have signaled an important lesson for anthropologists. While certain domains may permit themselves to be bracketed from the rest of the culture, most domains of interest may be inextricably bound up with the surrounding context. To study drinking without studying everything else may (from the anthropological point of view) be a scientifically untenable posture: in this case, to isolate is to destroy. Berlin and Kay, who began as enthusiasts of the enthnosemantic method, are here underlining its limitations. Contextual, historical, and cultural effects may be of the essence in most of the anthropological terrain.

Murray cites another reason for the decline of ethnoscience: that is, this anthropological subspecialty never cohered into a single integrated perspective but was, at best, a loose confederation. Murray believes that self-styled revolutionary groups, which demand total commitment and are organized under a single visionary leader, are more likely to prevail in academic competition. (The example of Chomsky in linguistics springs to mind.) A loose confederation offers less resistance to competitors and ultimately ceases to exist as a recognizable approach. Instead, "having achieved a measure of recognition and success, ethnoscience grouping encountered the seeming price of success: splintering. . . . By the late 1960s new students were not being attracted and classical ethnoscience was no more" (1982, p. 172).

There is scarcely any consensus within anthropology about which steps ought to be taken in lieu of a strict ethnoscience. Some authorities have continued to carry out studies in the tradition but have substituted more modest goals. Others have adopted the perspective of Clifford Geertz (1973, 1983), who feels that anthropologists have erred in attempting to mimic the natural sciences, and that the anthropologist has greater affinity with an interpreting literary critic. (I shall consider a Geertzian critique again in later discussions of cognitive science.) Still others feel that notions and concepts developed in other areas of cognitive science can be usefully imported into anthropological study.

Psychological Forays

While componential analysis made the biggest splash on the anthropological scene, the importation of methods from other disciplines has also flourished in past decades. In the tradition of the Torres Strait expedition, some investigators have analyzed the perceptual capacities of diverse populations. In an ambitious study, Marshall Segall, Donald Campbell, and Melville Herskovits (1966) attempted to resolve a dispute about environmental contributions to visual perception by studying the susceptibility of several groups to various optical illusions. They subjected individuals from fourteen non-European cultures to a variety of illusions. Supporting the position that one's experiences influence the way one sees, these investigators found that on certain items, such as the Müller-Lyer illusion,* European and American samples proved more susceptible to illusions. These seemed to reflect life in a "carpentered" environment, replete with many square and rectangular objects. In contrast, on certain other perceptual arrays, non-Western samples proved more susceptible to the illusion. For example, among individuals who live in an equatorial terrain, where one must look at flat and wide spaces, there is a greater tendency to fall prey to the horizontal-vertical illusion. Thus, in an issue long of interest to culturally sensitive students of psychology, these investigators were able to discern intriguing regularities.

A second line of psychologically inspired studies addresses the capacities of individuals from non-Western societies to reason in the manner of a Westerner. In this regard the measures used by intelligence testers, and also those developed by Jean Piaget in his work with children, have proved most transportable. An early wave of studies was sympathetic to the notion that people outside the West, and particularly those who had not attended school, performed far more poorly on tests of abstraction, conceptualization, and classification (Dasen 1972; Dasen and Heron 1981). (Results were much more comparable on tests of perceptual and motor skill.) But before it was possible to conclude that the non-Westerners were less intelligent or could not think as well, some important methodological adjustments were made by Michael Cole and his colleagues (Cole and Scribner 1974). It emerged that, when familiar materials were used, or when requested behavior was explained to or modeled for the subjects, many of the documented differences between individuals from the two cultures now evaporated.

As a result of these instructive demonstrations, much greater stress is now placed on using materials that are "culture-fair" and on testing those capacities that are basic, rather than those likely to be transmitted only in schooled settings. Most evidence now suggests that, as Boas long believed, the fundamental operations of thought are the same everywhere, and it is the *uses* to which these processes are put that differ dramatically across cultures. Superimposed upon this basic continuity is the advent of certain

*In the Müller-Lyer illusion, one of the two lines appears longer than the other, even though both are exactly the same length.

abilities to reason without the usual contextual supports, or to carry through certain complex chains of reasoning, which seem to develop chiefly among individuals exposed to years of Western-style secular schooling.

Investigators have been revisiting some of the issues about language and thought that had been raised many years ago. While strong experimental support for the Whorf-Sapir hypothesis had never been obtained, there was a widespread suspicion among anthropologists that the differences between conceptual systems in remote cultures were vast and that these might well reflect variations in the structure or the contents of language. However, in a line of study which continues to exert wide influence in several cognitive sciences, Eleanor Rosch (1973a, 1973b—then Eleanor Heider) strongly challenged the Whorfian line: she demonstrated that, even in cultures with few color terms, individuals still sort, classify, and otherwise deal with the color spectrum in roughly similar ways. The language does not affect basic psychological processes. Paralleling this line of work, Rosch's colleagues at the University of California at Berkeley, anthropologists Brent Berlin and Paul Kay (1969), showed that the color terms used by diverse societies all follow a systematic pattern. That is, if a society has only two color terms, those terms will divide the spectrum between white and black; if a language contains three terms, then it contains a term for red; if it contains four terms, then it contains a term for green or yellow (but not both) and so on to the most complete languages which contain eleven basic color terms (white, black, red, green, yellow, blue, brown, pink, purple, orange, and gray). While these lines of work have engendered controversy (as we shall see in chapter 12), they have helped swing the pendulum of anthropological analysis back to the pole of universalism: most researchers now believe that individuals the world over perceive and classify in relatively similar ways, and that the ways in which they classify reflect the operation of deep principles of mind which cannot easily be dislocated.

Committed anthropologists thus face a dilemma. On the one hand, as enemies of racism and cultural chauvinism, they are delighted by the evidence that individuals the world over appear to think and process information in similar ways. One of the fundamental puzzles of anthropology appears to have been resolved. On the other hand, as scholars who value the peculiar profiles of different cultures, they do not want these reassuring signs of universalism to invalidate or render superfluous their careful study of individual cultures. Thus, they take care to stress that the identity of mental processes should not in any way lessen the importance of chronicling and then explaining the vast differences around the globe in behavior, in patterns of thought, and in the uses to which both are put.

One productive way in which the anthropological community can have its cake and eat it too is to continue the careful case studies that have been the lifeblood of the field, but to inform these studies with promising concepts or methods from cognitive science. In this vein a number of careful studies have been carried out by Michael Cole and his associates. For example, Jean Lave (1977) has contrasted the mathematical skills exemplified by Liberian tailors within their ordinary working context with their performances on standard kinds of mathematical tasks. Sylvia Scribner (1984) has documented that dairymen at work in the New York area can carry out complex forms of numerical estimation while at work in their customary environments. Edwin Hutchins (1980) has shown that individuals engaged in debates about land rights in the Trobriand Islands exhibit logical reasoning of considerable complexity. And Cole, working with Sylvia Scribner (Scribner and Cole 1981), has studied the effects of different varieties of literacy on the general reasoning and mnemonic capacities of the Vai group in Liberia. All these efforts cherish the individual details of particular groups in their home context: they pointedly spurn premature generalizations or excessive reliance on arbitrary sorting tasks. Still, when proper caution is taken, forms of thinking in remote settings do lend themselves to comparison with the kinds of thought process exhibited and the kinds of measure used in traditional Western-schooled settings. Anthropology can, indeed, be infiltrated by cognitive scientific concepts, without any need for a wholesale abandonment of traditional methods or classical problems.

One final point of contact between anthropology and the rest of cognitive science should be noted. While most energy in recent years has been devoted to the increasingly fine-grained analysis of particular domains—ranging from kin terms to folk theories of emotions—some investigators remain interested in the general conundrums dating back to Tylor, of how culture is possible, how it is constituted, and how it is acquired. Part of the interest unfolds in an evolutionary framework. Investigators working with other primates, with the skulls of earlier humans, or with other relics of the paleontological or archaeological record seek clues about how human beings became cultural animals—about the sources of language, of social behavior, of rituals and art. Moving to a briefer time frame, other investigators have raised the question of how children in a society "learn" culture. In Roy D'Andrade's formulation (1981), culture consists of a large pool of information passed from one generation to another, including learned programs for action and understanding. Yet unlike the classical computer programs, these programs tend to be unspecified and inexplicit, absorbed through a slow process of guided discovery, and involving the manipulation of content-centered rather than formal-based symbolic systems. Every individual must acquire hundreds of thousands of chunks of cultural information to be competent in the business of society, and yet the mechanisms whereby these bits are acquired remain obscure. D'Andrade does venture his opinion that culture is unlikely to be picked up without considerable modeling and guidance, but that the way this instruction takes place has not been illuminated thus far by standard psychological accounts. Here, again, the model of how individuals learn language presents itself as a tempting, if possibly perilous analogy.

Lévy-Bruhl Revisited

In the century since the term *culture* became formally introduced, and the discipline of anthropology was first formulated, massive amounts of empirical information have been obtained about individuals in different cultures. We know much more than earlier observers about kin terminology, social organization, modes of behavior, ways of classification, use of language and myth, powers of reasoning. As in many other areas of cognitive science, the basic scientific dilemma—Do primitives think the way we do? —has not lost its urgency. But the ways in which scholars think about this question have become much more sophisticated. Nowadays most investigators take for granted that the basic modes of perception and classification are the same everywhere, but that particular elements in the environment can affect how—and the extent to which—these processes develop. Thanks to research in this tradition, many instructive differences among individuals in diverse societies have been uncovered, even as the fundamental continuities in mental processes everywhere seem increasingly to be confirmed. Here is where future work is likely to proceed.

As anthropologists have tackled the issues vividly raised in Lévy-Bruhl's own writings, they have found themselves engaged in an odd assortment of activities. There have been flirtations with aggressively cognitive measures—the formal musings of Lévi-Strauss and the more publicly verifiable componential analysis of the American school. While neither has proved a panacea for explicating the thought processes of any group or individual, let alone an exotic one, clear insights have been gained about at least some domains in some societies. Thus, Lévi-Strauss has tackled the broadest questions, but has failed to provide sufficiently rigorous descriptions of his analytic methods; in contrast, the componential analysts have developed relatively precise analytic tools but have not successfully applied them beyond certain relatively restricted domains.

The success of the cognitive scientific approach to anthropology will hinge on whether the rigor of componential analysis (or some other computationally inspired approach) can be wedded to the broad issues that have traditionally attracted scholars to the study of exotic cultures. We have seen that the componential approach achieved reasonable (though not unmixed) success in dealing with constrained categories like kinship or color but has not so far been particularly revealing with broader categories such as emotions or diseases.

In a sense, it is useful to think of anthropology as representing a kind of "upper bound" for cognitive science. Anthropology clearly deals with issues representing very large bodies (such as entire cultures) and spanning a quite wide scope (such as the relationship between a culture's linguistic practices and its thought patterns). If cognitive-scientific methods can deal successfully with such global issues, they will clearly have established their utility in illuminating human thought.

It may turn out, however, that cognitive scientific methods are only partially successful in dealing with such a broad assignment or can only be usefully brought to bear upon the most constrained (and possibly the least interesting) domains. While issues of context, culture, and history can be bracketed in other cognitive sciences, they may be of the essence in anthropology. If, in the last analysis, anthropology proves to lie largely outside of the mainstream of cognitive science, this will be an important (if somewhat disappointing) finding. And it may signal the even less happy outcome that large areas of psychology, philosophy, and linguistics may also fall outside of cognitive science, at least as currently practiced.

In the years since Lévy-Bruhl debated with himself about the status of the primitive mind, the pendulum has swung decisively to a belief in the essential unity of the human mind everywhere. But the question of how to study that mind remains hotly debated. For every believer in empirical cognitive methodology, for every supporter of the structuralist or ethnosemantic approach, there is now a Geertzian, who believes that cognitive-science approaches are essentially inadequate in the anthropological realm, and who calls instead for a sympathetic reading of the cultural data, much in the manner of a literary critic. It is worth noting, however, that in the last several years a moderate middle ground seems to be emerging. According to this tack, anthropology remains the field where careful case studies are indispensable and where keen attention to particularities remains of enduring importance. At the same time, there is no reason why these studies cannot be informed by the most salient and useful cognitive concepts and analytic frameworks. And thus a new cadre of workers has learned to speak the language and to carry out the approaches of cognitive science, even though such researchers practice it in an area where the specifics remain all important. Cognitive science can contribute to anthropology, without enveloping it.

While the historical and particularistic aspects of each society continue to be valued, there is fresh recognition that, in the last analysis, all that can be attained by any individual in any culture is restricted by the particular species to which one belongs, and, more specifically, by the nervous system that one possesses by virtue of one's humanity. For this reason, anthropologists of every stripe—from Lévi-Strauss to Geertz—have savored discoveries about the human as an organism: the evolution of the brain, the development of the skeletal musculature system, the nature of sexual ties at different ages. Such insights from the areas of biology and neuroscience will not in themselves answer questions about culture—the levels of analysis are simply too disparate. (Indeed, neuroscience serves as a kind of "lower bound" to cognitive science and thus is maximally distant from anthropology.) But, in due course, findings from the study of the human nervous system may well illuminate how an individual becomes able in such short order to assimilate and to transmit to others the practices of the culture in which he or she happens to live.

9

Neuroscience: The Flirtation with Reductionism

Karl Lashley Poses a Research Agenda

Karl Lashley, the pre-eminent American neuropsychologist of the first half of the twentieth century, liked to recall his initiation into the intricacies of the nervous system. As a seventeen-year-old laboratory aide in zoology in 1907, "I found in a box of trash . . . a series of Golgi stained sections of a frog's brain. I proposed . . . that I work out all the connections among the cells, so that we might know how the frog works. . . . I have never escaped from the problem" (quoted in Beach et al. 1960, p. *xvii*).

True to this testimony, Karl Lashley devoted his research career to an investigation of the nervous system. Some of his early work was conducted with J. B. Watson, who was shortly to found behaviorist psychology; but the main influence on his scientific development was Shepherd Ivory Franz, a neuroanatomist who was skeptical about the possibility of localizing behavior in specific regions of the nervous system. Among his principal discoveries, Franz had found that a lesion in the frontal lobes of mammals does not abolish learned behavior unless the destruction of the tissue is massive; that long-established habits tend to persist in any case; and that habits lost by extensive destruction can be relearned. Under Franz's tutelage, Lashley began a lifetime's effort to discover the neural substrate of particular behaviors (Boring 1950).

The Lesion Technique

In carrying out his research, Lashley made extensive use of the technique of *ablation,* where specific areas of the nervous system (often regions of the cerebral cortex) are destroyed by means of a surgical lesion. The basic goal of the ablation technique is to determine which behavior is impaired or destroyed following a punctate lesion, and thereby to infer which functions are typically served by that region of the brain. Lashley was inclined to be skeptical about the possibility of attributing specific behavior to specific regions of the brain; but in no way did the apprenticeship with Franz foreshadow the extent to which Lashley would go to pursue this problem or the bold conclusions he was to reach some decades later. The experiences of the student cannot foretell the achievements of the mature scientist.

In the decade following his initial training by Franz, Lashley conducted dozens of experiments on the nervous system of the rat. His typical study involved ablation of an area of the visual cortex of the rat brain and a determination of the effects wrought on the rat's perceptual powers. By 1929 Lashley was ready to summarize his findings in a major work entitled *Brain Mechanisms and Intelligence.* He strongly questioned the significance of specific neural zones and connections: "It is very doubtful that the same neurons or synapses are involved even in two similar reactions for the same stimulus" (1929, p. 3). Describing experiments on maze running after cortical ablation was examined, Lashley concluded:

The capacity to learn the maze is dependent upon the amount of functional cortical tissue and not upon its anatomical specialization. . . . The results are incompatible with theories of learning by changes in synaptic structure, or with any theories which assume that particular neural integrations are dependent upon definite anatomical paths specialized for them. . . . The mechanisms of integration are to be sought in the dynamic relations among the parts of the nervous system rather than in details of structural differentiation. (P. 3)

With these words, Lashley hurled a set of sharp challenges to the neuroscientific community. After all, a principal lure of neuroscience is the hope that the specific neural bases of particular behavior can be found— and what better prize than discovery of the neural focus of a particular act, thought, or sequence of behavior? Yet here was a major neuroscientific researcher declaring, on the basis of decades of research, that such a search was forlorn. Lashley was calling into question *localization*—the belief that specific behavior resides in specific neural locations. At the same time, if less explicitly, he was also posing difficulties for *reductionism,* the scientific program that seeks to explain behavior entirely in terms of neural (or other lower-order) principles.

Equipotentiality and Engrams

Having established to his satisfaction that particular behavioral patterns cannot be consigned to specific cortical regions, Lashley spent the rest of his scholarly life searching for a viable alternative to the classic localizationist position (Beach et al. 1960). He was attracted to the principal ideas of Gestalt psychology, according to which the organism perceives overall patterns initially and only subsequently becomes sensitive to their component parts. From Lashley's perspective, this approach to psychology made neurological sense as well: perhaps, rather than responding to specific forms of information, the brain works as an integrated unit, responding as an organized totality to complex patterns of stimulation.

Lashley developed several related concepts. He spoke of *equipotentiality*—the capacity of any part of a functional area to carry out a particular behavior. Equipotentiality is mediated by the *law of mass action,* according to which the efficiency of performance of a function may be reduced in proportion to the extent of the brain injury within an area. In other words, impairment in performance is due not to the site of the injury, but rather to the amount of tissue destroyed. As Lashley put it:

> The alternative to the theory of the preservation of memories by some local synaptic change is the postulate that the neurons are somehow sensitized to react to patterns or combinations of excitation. It is only by such permutations that the limited number of neurons can produce the variety of functions that they carry out. . . . All of the cells of the brain are constantly active and are participating, by a sort of algebraic summation, in every activity. There are no special cells reserved for special memories. (1950, p. *xi*)

Finally, he pondered the property of *plasticity*—the potential for remaining areas of the nervous system to take over when a specific region has been damaged.

Given this belief in generalized patterns of representation and behavior, what was one to make of the search for the *engram,* the discrete representation in the nervous system of specific ideas, concepts, or behaviors? Lashley came to the conclusion that one would never find such an engram. As he put it in a provocatively negative formulation, "This series of experiments has yielded a good bit of information about what and where the memory trace is not. It has discovered nothing directly of the real nature of the engram. I sometimes feel, in reviewing the evidence on the localization of the memory trace, that the necessary conclusion is that learning just is not possible" (1950, p. 501). In Lashley's view, during learning, information comes to be represented widely within large regions of the brain, if not throughout the brain as a whole. Within these areas, all the cells acquire the capacity to react in certain definite patterns. Whether the cells can be mobilized to carry out an impaired function depends upon the percentage of them still remaining after brain injury, the degree to which the pattern of behavior has been mastered beforehand, and the strength of motivation of the animal. Particularly in the case of brain-injured animals, motivation might have to be quite potent if the organism were to display its still-preserved abilities.

Lashley's experiments strike a severe blow against any unmodulated account of the nervous system as a set of discrete centers, each having its own unique functions, so that destruction of a set of cells would result in complete loss of a particular function and in total sparing of all remaining ones. At the same time, he helped to cast doubt on the *reflex arc*—the bond whereby each response is triggered by a specific stimulus—which had been the principal neural model of behavior in higher (as well as lower) organisms. Things were simply not that simple. In study after study, Lashley deduced the implications of the localizationist position, designed a supposedly critical experiment, and showed that abilities persist despite the predictions of the localizers, thus giving the lie to those scientists who claimed that impulses have to be transmitted over certain established paths in order for specific behavior to be performed.

Lashley's Iconoclasm

In addition to providing a devastating critique of a simple-minded localizing position, Lashley also impressed on the next generation of workers the difficulty of coming up with a viable model of the nervous system. In possibly his best-known paper, the Hixon contribution "The Problem of Serial Order in Behavior" (Jeffress 1951), which I discussed in chapter 2, he evocatively laid out a whole set of problems that neurobiology had ignored. Drawing on examples from language, walking, playing the piano, and the like, Lashley demonstrated that many sequences of behavior exhibited long planning units which unfold too quickly for them to be altered or corrected "live." In his view, it was necessary to reconceptualize current associationist models of the nervous system to allow for effects that can be manifest for a significant period after initial stimulation. And so, to choose a single example, in order to understand a *double entendre,* one would have to retain in mind (and in the brain) a meaning latent in the body of the joke, which only becomes "activated" by the punch line. No simple stimulus-response bonds can explain this behavior: one needs a model of the nervous system which is hierarchically arranged and features feedback and feed-forward mechanisms.

Lashley's unorthodoxy manifested itself in the new talk about computers. At the time of the Hixon Symposium, many noted scholars were eager to analogize the brain to the digital computer. Lashley voiced a note of caution:

> The brain has been compared to a digital computer because the neuron, like a switch or valve, either does or does not complete a circuit. But at that point the similarity ends. The switch in the digital computer is constant in its effect, and its effect is large in proportion to the total output of the machine. The effect produced by the neuron varies with its recovery from [the] refractory phase and with its metabolic state. The number of neurons involved in any action runs into millions so that the influence of any one is negligible. . . . Any cell in the system can be dispensed with. . . . The brain is an analogical machine, not digital. Analysis of its integrative activities will probably have to be in statistical terms. (Quoted in Beach et al. 1960, p. 539)

By his careful experimental example and his polemical style of expression, Lashley called into question central dogmas of the time. He was saying to his colleagues that their vaunted stimulus-response model, their reflex arc, cannot explain behavior. As his student Karl Pribram recalls, "Lashley had a genius for skepticism, for poking holes in all the myths that had grown up about how the brain works" (Hooper 1982, p. 170).

Less directly, but with equal decisiveness, Lashley's descriptions undermined unreflective assumptions about reductionism. So long as accounts were based upon specific cells or particular reflex arcs, neuroscientists could rest easy in their belief that behavior could be explained at the neurological level. A particular lobe controls vision or subserved volition, and that was that. On this assumption, the need for explanation on the psychological or mentalistic level might fade away. But ever the scholarly troublemaker, Lashley spent the last years of his professional life describing behavior—for example, long sequences carried out without feedback—that eluded current mechanistic models and strongly implied more abstract and hierarchically organized forms of representation. While Lashley himself did not call for explanations on the mentalistic level—he was still too much of a Watsonian—his work (and his talk of "plans" and "structures") cleared the way for Simon's belief in a symbol system, Piaget's call for mental operations, Miller's TOTE system, and Chomsky's resorting to rules and representations. In our terms, Lashley helped to set the stage for a cognitive-scientific approach to behavior and thought.

While Lashley's substantive contributions to cognitive science should not be minimized, his actual claims within neuroscience met a less positive fate. As has happened with other workers who put forth strong and falsifiable programs, succeeding researchers have put many of his claims to the test. Today few of his specific propositions would still command wide assent. For instance, the nervous system turns out to be far more specific, far less equipotential than Lashley had contended. His belief that the brain works in a Gestalt-like fashion would find few adherents today. But in framing the questions sharply, and in introducing the key terms of scientific debate, Lashley for a long time dominated, and still exerts appreciable influence on, that work in neuroscience that impinges upon cognitive and behavioral concerns.

The work of Lashley, and of other experimental researchers working at the intersection of the brain and behavior, raises another issue—and one crucial for my inquiry here. It has been held by many scientists, especially neuroscientists, that the optimal way to account for human behavior and thoughts is in terms of the structure and functioning of the human nervous system. To some investigators, this neuroanatomical account can complement accounts proffered in psychological or behavioral language; but for others, neuroanatomical accounts may eventually render unnecessary accounts in terms of representations, or symbols, or other psychological argot. In the view of this latter reductionist group, cognitive science emerges as, at best, a holding operation: a temporary account of mental activity destined to vanish once an account in terms of synapses can be attained. And such reductionists find themselves in sharpest opposition to functionalists—true-blue cognitivists who believe that behavior and thought must be accounted for completely on the level of representations, without any regard whatever to the "hardware" in which it happens to be embodied. The debate about the possibility—and the desirability—of reductionism lurks in the background in any account of neuroscientific work (see Mehler, Morton, and Jusczyk 1984).

How Specific Is Neural Functioning?

Debates about the specificity of function go back a long time in scientific history. Descartes, among the first to concern himself with the relationship between the body and mind, put forth his own notions of localization. He recognized that different parts of the brain control different bodily functions, and located the interaction between the soul and the body at the pineal gland at the base of the brain. Juan Huarte, a contemporary of Descartes, rejected the doctrine of the localization of faculties in separate ventricles, and suggested instead that the brain works as a unit (Diamond 1974). Even at the dawn of the scientific era, it seems, dispute was already raging about the plausibility of the reductionist position and the viability of a holistic (as against a localizationist) account of neural representation.

It is not surprising that scientists have long been interested in the issue of how processes and information are represented in the brain. Unless one subscribes to a wholly mystical account of human behavior—in which case one is not a scientist—it becomes important to try to understand the bases of human behavior and thought. Even the Greeks put forth theories about this issue, though the particular accounts they wove strike us today as more poetic than plausible. Once the brain had been selected as the region of the human body most likely to be involved in matters of mind, discussion about the neural basis of thoughts and actions necessarily came to center on this circumscribed region.

Understanding of the nervous system developed rapidly in the eighteenth century (see Gardner 1975; Herrnstein and Boring 1965). Luigi Galvani showed that electrical charges can cause muscles to contract. Charles Bell and François Magendie independently discovered the anatomical separation of sensory and motor functions in the spinal cord. Animals could continue to move even after being anesthetized, just as animals could still undergo sensation after being paralyzed. Johannes Müller put forth the *law of specific energies,* which held that the quality of experience is determined not by the features of the objective stimulus but rather by the particular neurons that respond to it.

Building on such discoveries, Francis Joseph Gall was able to propound the most far-reaching (and most notorious) theory of localization. The title of one of his works summarizes his major claim: "On the functions of the brain and each of its parts: with observations on the possibility of determining the instincts, propensities, and talents, or the moral and intellectual dispositions of men and animals, by the configurations of the brain and the head." In his writings, Gall defended the proposition that the brain is so divided as to be able to carry out many discrete functions. These dispositions are innate, and "the brain is composed of as many particular and independent organs as there are fundamental powers of the mind" (quoted in Robinson 1976, p. 339). In the hands of some of his more extreme followers, Gall's doctrine of phrenology led to the claim that one could even discern an individual's unique intellectual profile by examining the specific configurations of his skull.

While appealing widely to the public of the early nineteenth century, Gall's claims did not go over well in the scientific community. His chief critic, Pierre Jean Marie Flourens, carried out experiments that demonstrated common actions of different parts of the brain. Flourens insisted that the cerebral regions function as a whole and that the magnitude of a deficit cannot simply be reduced to the area or even the amount of brain involved. While conceding some specificity in the nervous system, Flourens added that "there should, moreover, properly be brought to light another order of phenomena that includes both this efficacious *Unity* of the nervous system that joins all the parts of the system together, in spite of their diversity of action, and also the degree of influence that each of these parts contributes to the common activity" (quoted in Herrnstein and Boring 1965, p. 222).

Evidence for Localization

Toward the end of the nineteenth century, the pendulum began to swing from Flourens toward Gall. Gustav Theodor Fritsch and Eduard Hitzig (1870), two German neurophysiologists, were able to demonstrate unequivocally that stimulation of different areas on the cortex of a dog was followed by the contraction of specific muscles. David Ferrier, working in England a few years later, directed his attention to the prefrontal areas of the cortex. Though neither motor nor sensory functions were demonstrable in this region, Ferrier maintained that

[it] is important for intellectual work. . . . [Following ablation] I could perceive a very decided alteration in the animal's character and behavior. . . . Instead of as before being actively interested in their surroundings and curiously prying into all that came within the field of their observation, they remained apathetic. . . . They had lost, to all appearance, the faculty of attentive and intelligent observation. (Quoted in Diamond 1974, p. 244)

Soon such localizations of higher cortical functions were also being discovered in human beings. In the 1860s, Paul Broca (1861), a French surgeon, reported the cases of two aphasic patients, individuals who had lost language as a result of injury to the brain. In a finding whose importance for subsequent scientific inquiry is difficult to overestimate, Broca claimed that this damage to language had not simply resulted from random injury to the nervous system but was restricted to insults to the left cerebral hemisphere. Narrowing his focus even further, he claimed a special priority for expressive language, in the lower portion of the third convolution of the frontal lobe. Subsequent case reports confirmed the gist of Broca's claim and also suggested an association of other kinds of linguistic breakdown with injuries to related sites in the left hemisphere. Just a few years later, Carl Wernicke (1874) traced difficulties in understanding language to an injury in the left temporal lobe; while Jules Déjerine (1892) attributed difficulties in reading and writing to lesions in the left parietal lobe and the parietal-occipital cortex (see Gardner 1975).

It was a heyday for scholars of a localizationist persuasion. With increasingly sophisticated methods for testing animals, claims were made for specificity in each region of the cortex. In a parallel fashion, as additional case studies of brain-injured patients accumulated, claims about the astonishing specificity of certain cognitive deficits were forthcoming. Perhaps—the dream went—if studies of sufficient particularity were made, the functional significance of all areas of the brain might be laid bare. Localizationism would triumph; reductionism would gain in plausibility.

The followers of Flourens, skeptical about localization claims, were not about to give up the game. A few decades after Broca's epoch-making publication, Pierre Marie, a French neurologist, declared to the Paris Neurological Society that "the third frontal convolution plays no special role in the function of language" (1906, p. 241). Marie had re-examined the brains originally studied by Broca and come to the conclusion that the master's original claims were simply not justified. Each of Broca's patients had far more extensive lesions than Broca had reported, and the range of accompanying deficits had not been documented with sufficient precision. Marie countered that there was but one form of aphasia, which could arise from lesions in various cortical areas; reports of localization had been greatly exaggerated.

The Resurgence of Holism

Marie's protest might have been enunciated in a void; but, in fact, it generated many echoes. Within a few years, a variety of neurologists had endorsed his claims that cognitive functions are not highly localized in the nervous system. They adduced evidence that the same kinds of deficits could be obtained from individuals with lesions in a wide variety of areas; and conversely, patients with similar anatomical lesions often exhibited contrasting sets of deficits or even at times no deficits at all. These neurologists, who came to be known as the "holists" (in contrast to the "localizers" or "diagram makers") regarded the brain as a single highly integrated organ, one involved as a whole in all intellectual activities and not susceptible to specific impairment from discrete lesions. They spoke of the plasticity of the nervous system, the capacity of uninjured areas to take over from injured areas, and the loss of abstract thinking and other functions as a consequence of the *size,* rather than the *site,* of lesion (Gardner 1975).

The holist position assumed by neurologists like Pierre Marie, Kurt Goldstein, and Henry Head was reinforced by certain events within the field of psychology. Like Karl Lashley, their counterpart in the world of animal neuropsychology, these investigators were much impressed by the findings from Gestalt psychology. It was clear that the organism reacted not just to single stimuli but rather to the relationship among stimuli, to overall patterns, and to stimuli perceived as part of a given context. Moreover, the Gestalt assumption that the nervous system is organized in terms of neural fields, operating across wide regions of the cortex, struck a responsive chord with these neurologists. The opponents of localization in neurology, like the opponents of atomism in psychology, served as a bulwark against the elementarist bias of the behaviorists during the early part of the century. At the same time, holists were far more sympathetic to the notion that behavior could not be explained satisfactorily in terms of neural circuitry. As they saw it, there was a continued need for explanation on the psychological level—particularly the global or holistic kinds of explanation offered by the Gestalt psychologists.

Once again, then, there was a correlation between skepticism about localization and skepticism about reductionism—not a logically necessary association, to be sure, but rather a meeting of two ideas in the minds of many scientists. In the view of these investigators, even if it could be shown that certain functions regularly break down as a result of damage to specific areas of the brain, the significance of such a finding was not clear. Hughlings Jackson, a forerunner of the holist school during the nineteenth century, had declared that localization of symptoms did not signify localization of function (Jackson 1932). To give a specific example, just because naming breaks down following lesion in the angular gyrus, it is an unwarranted assumption that naming actually takes place in this specific site of the brain. Richard L. Gregory has stated this point crisply:

> The removal of any of several resistances in a radio set may cause the emission of strange sounds, but it cannot therefore be concluded that the function of the resistances is to inhibit howling. . . . The southern region of British railways is a complex system of railway lines, signal boxes, stations and control systems. A breakdown of a section of the line, a power failure or a slip in the central control room at Waterloo, may disrupt traffic over a wide area. But we cannot therefore say that the function of the system is localised in the . . . power station, the central control room . . . all are essential. (Quoted in Rose 1973, p. 94)

We have here what looks like a scientifically untenable situation. One school of investigators, represented by the localizers, was claiming increasingly fine kinds of informational specificity in the nervous system. From their perspective, it was only a matter of time before every behavioral function could be adequately mapped in the brain of the organism. The rival school of investigators, equally respectable and equally vocal, considered the localizationist approach to be bankrupt: not only was evidence mounting in favor of the trio of mass action, equipotentiality, and plasticity; but even to the extent that the localizers could demonstrate links between lesions and deficits, the significance of this association remained unclear.

Evaluating the Evidence

When respectable groups of scientists have such opposite points of view, it is necessary to step back and attempt to gain some perspective. It is possible, of course, that one school is entirely correct and the other entirely wrong; but neither school dismissed the experimental claims of the other, so this dénouement was not likely. It is also possible that each school was talking about different phenomena and was therefore correct in its own bailiwick. Thus, perhaps the localizers were correct for certain organisms, for certain behavior, for certain portions of the life cycle; while the holists were correct for other organisms, other behavior, or other periods of life. And, indeed, each school of investigators did look to somewhat different clusters of evidence in order to bolster its conclusions. A holist typically turned to maze-running rats, while a localizer was likely to gravitate toward the varieties of aphasia in adults.

At any rate, by the end of the 1940s, many investigators were seeking some rapprochement between the rabid holists and the extreme localizers. It was becoming clear that claims about highly specific syndromes following highly specific lesions could not be maintained; the variation across patterns, and across clinics, was simply too great. On the other hand, any number of lines of investigation undercut the extreme holist position. Even Lashley himself conceded that there was a fair degree of localization within the visual system—the system he happened to know the best. Studies by neuroembryologists like Paul Weiss (1952) and Roger Sperry (1951) revealed that the developing neurons contain highly specific information: when budding limbs were surgically transplanted to a new position, the nerves would still reconnect with the place of origin, even if it meant that the organism was unable to move toward its usual targets. Such findings challenged extreme versions of the plasticity hypothesis and demonstrated considerable specificity and committedness even in the immature nervous system. Most dramatically, the Gestaltist claims about "fields of brain representation" were undercut by experiments in which various encumbrances were placed in the brain itself. Lashley placed gold foil to disrupt neuroelectric fields (Lashley, Chow, and Semmes 1951); Sperry inserted insulated mica strips into the brain (Sperry and Miner 1955); and Karl Pribram (1971) put aluminum hydroxide cream in minute amounts over the cortical surface. Pattern discrimination remained intact despite marked disruption of direct currents and electroencephalographic activities. These results were difficult to explain on a localizing account; yet, at the same time, they discredited the major theoretical account put forth by the Gestalt holists. Faced with the results of these experiments, Gestaltist Wolfgang Köhler, the chief proponent of field theory, is said to have declared in desperation "that ruins not only my Direct Current field [theory] but every other current neurological theory of perception" (quoted in Pribram 1971, pp. 110–11).

Donald Hebb's Bold Synthesis

A theoretical synthesis is at a premium when the competition between theories becomes too strident. Probably the person who most successfully mediated between the Gestalt and the atomist-localizing points of view was the Canadian neuropsychologist Donald O. Hebb. In his now classic monograph *The Organization of Behavior* (1949), Hebb argued that behavioral patterns, such as visual perceptions, are built up gradually over long periods of time through the connection of particular sets of cells, which he called *cell assemblies.* To this extent, behaviors or percepts can indeed be localized in specific regions, perhaps even in specific cells of the brain. However, with time, more complex behaviors come to be formed out of sets of cell assemblies, which he called *phase sequences.* These phase sequences are less localized, and involve much larger sets of cells drawn from disparate sections of the nervous system. A phase sequence inevitably involves some equipotentiality: it includes alternative pathways so that if some are destroyed, a behavioral function can still be carried out with greater or lesser effectiveness by those that are spared. Finally, by the time the organism has reached maturity and is capable of performing the most complex forms of behavior, it is difficult to attribute any behavior to a discrete set of neurons in a delineated region of the brain.

One can see how Hebb's position could comfortably accommodate portions of both the holist and the localization points of view. On the one hand, early in life, the localizer can be seen to have the edge, since simple perceptions depend on specific sets of cells: no holism here. Yet, with development, more complex cell assemblies and phase sequences are formed, and these are able to participate in numerous kinds of behavior: plenty of holism here. Still, it would be an oversimplification to see the developmental course as proceeding from localizing to holism; for, in other respects, the sequence is exactly the reverse. As Hebb pointed out, learning early in life is flexible, so that it can take place despite the destruction of large parts of the nervous system; in contrast, later learning depends specifically on certain developed structures, and there is relatively little plasticity in the system. In this respect, then, it is more plausible to view the developmental sequence as running from holism to localization. A beneficial effect of Hebb's work was to point up these various complexities and competing tendencies, making it less plausible for anyone to adopt a rigid localizing or an inflexible holist position. This intermediary position came to carry considerable weight and has recently been embraced by computer scientists who are attempting to simulate vision (see chapter 10).

The Hixon Symposium Revisited

The need to reconcile these extreme positions was also manifest at the various pivotal conferences during the late 1940s and early 1950s. During the Hixon Symposium (Jeffress 1951), the major neurologists, neurophysiologists, and neuropsychologists debated with one another the tenability of the localization position. Psychologist Heinrich Klüver reported astonishingly specific behavior consequent upon lesions in the temporal lobes of monkeys: these organisms exhibited psychic blindness, strong oral fixations, an excessive tendency to react to each and every visual stimulus, profound changes in emotional behavior, a remarkable alteration in dietary habits, and an increase in the amount and diversity of sexual behavior. Neurologist J. M. Nielsen described specific forms of agnosia (failure to recognize objects) which accompany lesions in the occipital lobes. Neuropsychologist Ward Halstead discerned predictable mental difficulties in planning and in abstraction following damage to the frontal lobes.

In response to these strands of evidence in favor of localization, Karl Lashley reviewed his own long series of experiments on pattern recognition and maze running in rats. Pointing out that he had found a remarkable *lack of evidence* for localization, he taunted Halstead:

> In fantasy, I have thought perhaps that my most important contribution when I reach retirement age would be to have my frontal lobes removed and see what I could do without them. I have less confidence than Dr. Halstead that it would preclude the production of something of interest. We have little experimental evidence of intellectual defect from uncomplicated removal of the prefrontal lobes. (Quoted in Jeffress 1951, p. 145)

Wolfgang Köhler voiced his own skepticism about localizationalist accounts: "The atomistic character of Dr. McCulloch's neurophysiology prevents any direct approach to relationally determined facts such as visual shapes. . . . If we think of cortical function in terms of continuous field physics rather than of impulses in neurons, the difficulty never arises" (quoted in Jeffress 1951, p. 65). Such, then, was the situation in the early 1950s: Köhler and Lashley defending a top-down perspective, against proponents of a view based on specific neural structures. Lines were still drawn between these two factions, along with a growing feeling that each of them must hold part of the truth, and a widely discerned need for a more integrative point of view (like Hebb's) which could give each position its due.

Hubel and Wiesel's Decisive Demonstrations

In the late 1950s, David Hubel and Torsten Wiesel, two young neuro-physiologists, began to record with microelectrodes from single cells in the cortex of the cat. Over the next two decades, they were to record impulses from the nervous systems of numerous cats and other animals as well, and to do so throughout the visual system at various depths and in other regions of the brain. For this work, widely recognized as pathbreaking, Hubel and Wiesel were awarded the Nobel Prize for Medicine or Physiology in 1981. Much of our current knowledge of localizing has been obtained from this line of study (Hubel and Wiesel 1959, 1962, 1979; Hubel 1979; see also Lettvin et al. 1959).

Hubel, Wiesel, and their associates documented two important phenomena. First of all, they demonstrated beyond any doubt that specific cells in the visual cortex respond to specific forms of information in the environment. The exquisitely organized cerebral cortex contains cortical columns, and *simple cells* within the columns respond to such punctate properties of stimuli as orientation, or presence or absence of light. So-called *complex cells* react to lines kept in optimal orientation as they sweep across a receptive field; perhaps this mode of reaction corresponds to some early stage in the brain's analysis of visual forms. Some cells respond to input only from one or the other eye, while others can be influenced independently by both eyes. For some *hypercomplex* cells, the most effective boundary shape is a corner; for others, a tongue shape. Following such demonstrations, no one could any longer doubt that the nervous system was highly specific in its mode of functioning.

The second and equally important line of work emanating from the Hubel-Wiesel laboratory concerns the critical role played by certain early experiences in the development of the nervous system. While some perceptual and motor abilities are clearly "wired in" at birth (or else how could the organism function well enough to survive?), this is by no means true for all functions (or else, how could the organism change and learn?). The visual system of the cat will not develop—in fact, parts of it will atrophy —if the animal is not exposed to patterned light after birth. Moreover, the cat must be exposed to a visually varied environment, permitted to use both eyes, and allowed to move about its environment. If exposed to horizontal patterns only, the cells normally destined to carry out vertical processing will either atrophy or will be "taken over" to execute other functions. It should be noted, too, that the timing of these early experiences can be specific. For example, if, between the third and fifth postnatal weeks, one of the eyes is prevented from seeing forms, it will become functionally blind thereafter, even if normal registration and imaging are restored.

While Hubel and Wiesel's work stands at the center of this line of research, their efforts have been complemented and strengthened by those of many other workers. Jerome Lettvin and his colleagues at Massachusetts Institute of Technology showed early on that receptors in the eye of the frog are also extremely specific and respond to small round bloblike shapes which are rather reminiscent of bugs—hence, the term *bug detector* (Lettvin et al. 1959). Vernon Mountcastle (1978) documented columns in the somesthetic sensory cortex that have specific response patterns analogous to those of the visual cortex. Recording from the inferior temporal lobes of monkeys, Mortimer Mishkin (1967) finds cells that participate in coding the physical attributes of visual objects; these cells appear to be involved in activities much closer to the recognition of objects (and some distance away from that sensitivity to punctate forms of stimulation which excite the neurons in the primary visual cortex). There are even cells in the monkey's cortex that respond maximally to the shape of a monkey's hand (Gross, Rocha-Miranda, and Bender 1972). For those in sympathy with specificity and localization of function, the last few decades have yielded much confirming evidence.

The Molar Perspective

Though sets of cells responding to objects, or major portions of objects, represent a more molar form of pattern recognition than do cells responding to spots of light or individual edges, they are still some distance removed from the "higher" forms of thought which occupy most cognitive scientists. Another set of studies carried out at a molar level also bears upon the claims of the localizers and the holists.

Sperry on Split Brains

Because they were suffering from intractable epilepsy, a small group of patients were subjected, in the late 1950s and early 1960s, to a radical operative procedure: a surgical intervention where the two halves of the brain were disconnected from one another. Roger Sperry grasped the pivotal scientific implications of this unusual form of surgery and, with his colleagues at the California Institute of Technology, devised methods for testing separately the two halves of the brain. These studies were also of epoch-making importance and resulted in Sperry's sharing the Nobel Prize in 1981 with Hubel and Wiesel (Gazzaniga 1981; Sperry 1974; see also Geschwind 1965).

The major thrust of Sperry's work was to document important differences in the functioning of two hemispheres. From a plethora of tests carried out on the dozen patients available for scrutiny, Sperry reinforced the impression of clinicians (Geschwind 1965) and experimentalists (Kimura 1973; Milner 1967) that the left hemisphere is dominant for language and other conceptual and classificatory functions, while the right hemisphere assumes a dominant role for spatial functions and for other fine-grained forms of discrimination. So far, then, support for the localizing point of view—and remarkable support, too: for each hemisphere of the same person can be tested separately, in such a way that the other hemisphere is not even "aware" of the testing going on with its neural neighbor.

Yet, once again, a line of study also offered some support for the holistic point of view. Through the use of ingenious techniques, the Sperry team was able to show that the right hemisphere of right-handed persons was capable of far more linguistic functioning than had hitherto been thought: for example, there was considerable ability to understand written language (Zaidel 1977, 1978). Perhaps in the normal individual, the very dominance of the left hemisphere may prevent documentation of the latent linguistic capacities of the right (or nondominant) hemisphere. Second and of equal importance, there were wide individual differences among the commisurotomized patients (Gazzaniga 1983). In particular, the younger they had been at the time of their operation, the more likely it was that patients would reveal well-developed capacities in both hemispheres. By contrast, those patients who sustained epilepsy and underwent surgery relatively late in life exhibited the usual pattern of considerable lateralization of function found in most brain-damaged patients. Finally, the two hemispheres themselves differed, with the right hemisphere relatively dominant for more holistic or Gestalt-forms of perception.

Gradients of Plasticity and Hierarchy of Functions

Sperry's results suggest that there is indeed considerable plasticity in the immature human nervous system: the human being has the opportunity—if not the necessity—of exploiting those portions of the nervous system that under ordinary circumstances would not be mobilized for these specific purposes. The earlier the time of trauma, the more likely that one will prove able to carry out the desired function, irrespective of the site of injury. Indeed, even if one loses an entire left hemisphere during the first year or two of life, one will nonetheless be able to learn language; at this time, the relevant zones of the right hemisphere are sufficiently plastic or equipotential to assume this function. If the same operation were to take place later in life, however—say, after adolescence—there would be far less language recovery; in all likelihood, one would remain discernibly aphasic or even mute thereafter (Dennis 1980).

Other factors also influence the degree of plasticity. In general, younger individuals, those who are left-handed or who have sustained some brain injury early in life also exhibit more plasticity than those who exhibit contrasting traits. Thus, support for the localizing position is provided by data obtained with older right-handed persons; while that for the holistic position is more likely to arise from studies of younger, left-handed persons.

Studies conducted with brain-damaged patients in other laboratories have also increased our understanding of the neural representation of cognitive capacities (Geschwind 1974). From the work of Alexander Luria (1966) and his colleagues in the Soviet Union, it is now clear that, with development, different nervous centers gain dominance, and the hierarchy among behavioral functions alters. For instance, in young children, sensory regions are dominant; but in older individuals, the association cortexes and the "planning regions" of the frontal lobes become ascendant. Thus, lesions of the sensory regions are more lethal in younger subjects, while lesions of the frontal lobe are more pernicious in mature subjects.

According to Luria's studies, no function is carried out fully by a specific region, but nor is it the case, as Lashley implied, that all regions figure equally in a specific function. Rather, several anatomical regions may figure in the performance of a particular behavior, but *each of them makes a characteristic and irreplaceable contribution.* Thus, in the case of drawing, the left hemisphere is responsible for the mastery of details, while the right hemisphere contributes the overall sense of form. Hence, the kind of disruption seen in an individual's drawings generally reveals the site of that person's brain damage. We thus move from a simple assertion that one hemisphere carries out one function and the other hemisphere a rival function, to the more sophisticated claim that each hemisphere, or each region within a given hemisphere, contributes to a given activity in characteristic ways.

Many sentences have been written about the optimal way in which to describe the dominance patterns of the two hemispheres. Characterizations range from the mundane (language in the left, spatial function in the right) to the grandiose (science or rationality in the left, art or intuition in the right) to a distinction that captures current debates in neuroscience (localized function in the left hemisphere, synthetic or holistic functioning in the right). The precise characterization of the functions of the two hemispheres—or, more probably, determination that such a neat dichotomization is simply not possible—awaits the results of further studies (Beaumont, Young, and McManus 1984). Yet whatever the mission of each isolated hemisphere, there is a clearly dynamic interaction between the two hemispheres. When the left hemisphere is aroused (for instance, by the sounds of language), it promotes certain kinds of analytic and linguistic functions. In contrast, arousal or stimulation of the right hemisphere brings spatial and holistic functions to the fore (see Kinsbourne 1978).

While, in general, it is preferable to sustain an injury to the brain early rather than late in life, and to exploit the plasticity of that developmental stage, early is not always better. There are at least three caveats. First of all, sometimes an early injury manifests no apparent deficits at the time but produces severe deficits later in life. Thus, injuries to the frontal lobe in a young monkey may produce no immediate impairment of functioning, but long-term sequalae become evident at the time when the planning or mnemonic functions of the frontal lobes would normally mature (Goldman-Rakic et al. 1982; Goldman and Galkin 1978). Second of all, when another area of the brain takes over, the "rescuer" may well sacrifice the potential for carrying out *its* own preordained functions. Thus, the right hemisphere may assume language functions in the left-hemisphere–injured child, but the child will eventually display spatial deficits, because of the resulting unavailability of the relevant right-hemisphere zones (B. T. Woods 1980). Finally, even when another area of the brain assumes a function, it may not do so in an optimal way. Individuals with only a right hemisphere do learn to speak, but they end up using different linguistic strategies, which render them relatively insensitive to crucial syntactic features of language (Dennis and Whitaker 1976). At least for right-handers, there may be only one optimal way to learn language—the way that draws upon intact left-hemisphere structures that have evolved to carry out phonological and syntactic analyses. Language functions carried out with the right hemisphere depend excessively on semantic and pragmatic factors; this approach to language proves adequate for most mundane communication but unsatisfactory for the appreciation of subtle grammatical distinctions.

Even as certain regions of the brain seem preordained to carry out certain kinds of functions, other considerations militate against a purely "plastic" perspective. Work in experimental psychology documents that organisms are "prepared" to master certain behaviors and "counterprepared" to learn other ones. Thus, for example, rats can quickly learn to run or jump to escape shock but with only the greatest difficulty to press a lever in order to effect the same escape. Similarly, jumping to avoid a shock seems a natural or "prepared" response; but if a rat must jump in a box with a closed lid, learning will be slow and uncertain. It seems reasonable to contend that normal children are "prepared" to learn language very quickly, and that at least some children are "prepared" to master the tonal system of their culture's music with little exposure: it would not be surprising to find children having great difficulty in learning some kind of "nonnatural" language or musical system contrived by a diabolical experimenter or dictated by an omnipotent monarch.

The Neural Base of Cognition: Studies of Two Systems

Great scientific debates rarely die out entirely, particularly when there is a core of validity in the rival perspectives (Holton 1984). Such may be the case with the controversy between the localizers and holists, which has been evident since the time of Descartes and highly vocal since the period of Gall. Studies conducted over the last twenty-five years, in the wake of the Hixon Symposium, have, however, helped to frame the debate. It is now conceded that, at least at the level of sensory processing, the nervous system is specifically constructed to respond to certain kinds of information in certain kinds of ways. There is also evidence for "neural commitment" at much more molar levels of representation, even extending to the two cerebral hemispheres. To this extent, Lashley greatly overstated his case. On the other hand, impressive evidence continues to accumulate documenting the resilience and plasticity in the nervous system, particularly during the early phases of development. At such times, even organisms deprived of the usual neuro-anatomical structures are able to adapt and to carry out requisite functions, sometimes without incurring excessive costs. In this regard, the view of the holists and the mass-action proponents remains tenable. As a tentative conclusion, then, it seems that some localization is accepted by all, but that important islands of plasticity remain within this general framework.

But while great debates are seldom silenced altogether, they can become muted. Much less energy is devoted nowadays to debates about localization as against holism (or specificity as against plasticity), at least in terms of the operation of the nervous system. Instead, studies have reverted to a more circumscribed terrain. Neuroscientists are devoting the bulk of their time to the careful study of specific systems in specific organisms; they are guided by the hope that these systems can be well understood in their own terms, and that the knowledge obtained thereby might ultimately inform more general discussions of the neural basis of cognition, including the controversial issue of reductionism. From the many examples that could be cited, I shall mention two; these are taken deliberately from very different levels of analysis and may contribute in diverse ways to an emerging cognitive science.

Eric Kandel Bridges a Gap

Recently Eric Kandel and his associates at Columbia University have succeeded in bridging what had once seemed a vast gap—that between the functioning of the individual nerve cell and the behavior of organisms (Kandel 1979). This team of researchers has made this leap by focusing on a very simple organism—the snail *Aplysia californica*—whose nervous system can be readily described and which is also capable of simple forms of learning, such as habituation, sensitization, and classical conditioning. By studying these processes in the snail, Kandel and his associates have shown that these elementary aspects of learning are not diffusely distributed in the brain but rather can be localized in the activity of specific parts of neuronal networks. In fact, some learned behavior in the snail may involve as few as fifty neurons.

In Kandel's account, learning results from an alteration in the synaptic connections between cells; rather than necessarily entailing new synaptic connections, learning and memory customarily come about as a consequence of alteration in the relative strength of already existing contacts. In fact, Kandel and his colleagues have shown that the amount of chemical transmitter released at the terminals of neurons is crucial in altering synaptic strength. Thus, for example, when the tail of a sea slug is shocked, a neurotransmitter is released. An alteration occurs in the pores of the neuron, so that more transmitter is released in response to a later impulse. Then the next time the tail is shocked, the neuron quickly "remembers" to send out chemical commands to retract the siphon.

Kandel summarizes his position on the relationship between innate and experimental inputs to such learning:

> The potentialities for many behaviors of which an organism is capable are built into the basic scaffolding of the brain and are to that extent under genetic and developmental control. Environmental factors and learning bring out these latent capabilities by altering the effectiveness of the pre-existing pathways thereby leading to the expression of new patterns of behavior. (1982, p. 35)

Thanks to this work, we can now glimpse—perhaps for the first time— what learning entails at the chemical and neural level. The unsettling question to be addressed by cognitive science is whether, as other more complex forms of behavior are similarly described, there will remain a felt need for a separate explanation at the representational level.

The Song of Birds

A dramatically different, but equally suggestive line of study comes from work on the songs of birds by Fernando Nottebohm and his colleagues at the Rockefeller University (Nottebohm 1970, 1980; see also Konishi 1969; Marler and Peters 1977). Many species of birds sing songs, and it is well known that these species, and sometimes even subspecies, can be recognized by their peculiar song. But where does this song come from, and how does it acquire its characteristic pitches, tempo, and lilt?

It turns out that the answer differs from one species to another. In some cases, the species song is part of the bird's birthright. Thus, in the ringdove, a certain song is sung by every male member of the species. No feedback or external stimulation is needed. In fact, even if the bird is deafened at birth, it will still sing its species song.

There is less of a lockstep route toward the acquisition of song in most other species. Typically, birds begin with a period of babblelike subsong, followed by a period of plastic song, where syllables are repeated or rehearsed until they constitute short phrases. Finally, within a year, the plastic song gives rise to a stereotyped song similar to the songs produced by other normal adult males.

From the neuroscientific perspective, it is instructive that various deprivations exert predictable influences on the course of song development. Canaries, for example, require auditory feedback for normal development. They can, however, go on to produce a well-structured song even in the absence of hearing the vocalizations of other members of their species: their own songs suffice. In the chaffinch, however, both auditory feedback of one's own song *and* exposure to the songs of other birds are needed if the chaffinch is to produce a full normal song. If deafened within the first three months of life, the chaffinch will produce an extremely abnormal song, which may prove to be little more than a continuous screech. However, should it be deafened after it has learned its full song, there is no discernible deterioration in performance.

Bird song is one of the few instances of brain lateralization among infrahuman animals. Just as the left hemisphere of the brain of humans is critical for linguistic competence, so the left hypoglossal nerve in the bird proves crucial for its production of song. One can produce aphasia (or amusia) in a bird by destroying the left portion of its nervous system. But the aphasic canary can recover its prior songs because the homologous pathways of the right hemisphere have the potential of being exploited. In this recovery of function, songbirds are more fortunate (because their nervous systems are more plastic) than adult humans.

The work of investigators like Nottebohm and Kandel is based on the premise that much can be learned at this point through the careful study of a single system in a single organism. As Peter Marler, another pioneering researcher on bird song, has remarked: "The research on birdsong learning is slow and laborious. But I think in the long run this may be the only way in which we will ever gain proper understanding of the issue that confronts us . . . namely [in this case] the genesis of natural categories in the perception of animals and man" (1982, p. 93).

To be sure, the two research efforts proceed on somewhat different assumptions. Kandel hopes that by studying habituation and conditioning, he will eventually illuminate processes known to occur in a wide range of organisms, including humans: the assumption here is that certain learning processes, sometimes modified as "horizontal," cut across all manner of content (from learning music to mastering drawing), and that these can be found in relatively analogous fashion across diverse organisms (from aplysia to man). The Nottebohm line of research, on the other hand, proceeds along a different vein. Bird song is a behavior that clearly exists only in birds, though it may conceivably have some phylogenetic ties to human music or to human language. It is, in any case, a self-contained system, which allows various kinds of experimental manipulation. Interest in bird song is consonant with a belief that much cognitive activity is "vertically organized": that there exists a domain called "song" which may well follow rules different from other domains and is best understood in its own terms. Any generalizations that may be validly extended from bird song to other systems in other organisms—or even from one bird species to another—will only emerge after careful study of these systems on their own terms. In neuroscience, no less than in psychology and artificial intelligence, a tension can be discerned between a "modular" and a "general problem-solving" or "central-processing" point of view.

The remarkable success of the work of Hubel and Wiesel and their collaborators has given fresh impetus to the belief that systems may work in their own way. In 1978, David Hubel put it this way:

> We are led to expect each region of the central nervous system has its own special problems that require different solutions. In vision we are concerned with contours and direction and depth. With the auditory system, on the other hand, we can anticipate a galaxy of problems relating to temporal interactions of sounds of different frequencies and it is difficult to imagine the same neural apparatus dealing with all of these phenomena. . . . For the major aspects of the brain's operation no master solution is likely. (Hubel 1978, p. 28)

Such sentiments, articulated by one of the masters of contemporary neurophysiology, tilt in favor of attention to the specific properties of specific sensory detectors and challenge those in search of a single mode of neural explanation which pertains equally to different forms of behavior.

The work of Kandel (and to a lesser extent of Nottebohm) raises afresh the issue of reductionism. It seems to some observers that an account of the classical psychological phenomenon of habituation in terms of neurochemical reactions is an important step on the road to the absorption of cognition by the neurosciences. Once the basic mechanisms of learning have been described in this way, no additional level of explanation will be needed; in a way that would please such behaviorally oriented philosophers as Richard Rorty, these reductionists believe there is really nothing more to be said when neurophysiology has had its say. Yet most scientists of a cognitive persuasion feel that such accounts, while informative, will still prove tangential to their ultimate interests. As psychologists John Marshall and John Morton declare:

> The relationship between learning theory and natural behavior is only to be determined through functional representations of what the organism's nervous system does, not what it is. With simple organisms such as *Aplysia* this relationship can most readily be established in terms of its neurophysiology and neurochemistry. . . . With humans it can at best only be done abstractly. . . . Suppose it turned out that all human synapses were equivalent to *Aplysia's* and suppose that all the behaviors of such a synapse were expressible in terms of learning theory. Suppose further that we had all the human neurobiological information there was to have. We might then have an account of natural human behavior . . . but we would not have an explanation in terms of the questions we really wanted to ask. (Quoted in Fox 1983, p. 1222)

Pribram's Holographic Hypothesis

With this heightened interest in the operation of specific neural and behavioral systems, one might think that proponents of a more holistic view of the brain had been stilled. Not so. Neuroscientist Karl Pribram argued, in his 1971 book *Languages of the Brain,* that a belief in specific feature detectors *à la* Hubel and Wiesel can take one only a limited way: in his view, the brain is better analogized to a holographic process. Holography is a system of photography in which a three-dimensional image of an object can be reproduced (with the appearance of the third dimension preserved) by means of light-wave patterns recorded on a photographic plate or film. A hologram is the plate or film with the recorded pattern: information about any point in the original image is distributed through-out the hologram, thus making it resistant to damage. Since waves from all parts of the object are recorded on all parts of the hologram, any part of the hologram (however small) can be used to reproduce the entire image. A hologram can store a great deal of information in a small space; indeed some ten million bits of information have been usefully stored holograph-ically in a cubic centimeter.

According to Pribram's holographic view, all parts of the brain are capable of participating in all forms of representation, though admittedly certain regions play a more important role in some functions, and other regions are more dominant for other functions. In his view, just as many holograms can be superimposed upon one another, so can infinite images be stacked inside our brains. Perhaps when we recall something special, we use a specific reconstruction beam to zoom in on a particular encoded memory. Pribram also fixes upon another quality of the hologram: the fact that it records the same wave front over its surface, repeating it over and over. Even if only some of a shattered hologram is left, it will still suffice to reconstruct the entire image (Hooper 1982).

While the holographic analogy has engendered considerable skepti-cism, many neuroscientists remain sympathetic with Pribram's goal of showing that the nervous system is not simply a collection of specific modes of processing; they cling to the possibility that important forms of knowledge remain, as Lashley had so fervently believed, widely dispersed throughout the brain. Pribram notes that "the properties of holograms are so similar to the elusive properties that Lashley sought in brain tissue to explain perceptual imaging and engram encoding that the holographic process must be seriously considered as an explanatory device" (1982, p. 176). Moreover, in a manner reminiscent of the view of limited plasticity, Pribram himself has recently begun to speak of a "limited holograph," hoping thereby to avoid some of the pitfalls of a full-blown holographic account. Eric Harth comments:

What interests brain theorists about the hologram is this quality of a *distributed memory* (the phrase is Lashley's): Every piece of the hologram says a little bit about every part of the scene, but no piece is essential. The other intriguing fact is that one can superimpose any number of holograms on the same piece of film, and then reproduce the images of the original scenes one by one without interference from the others. (1982, p. 88)

The analogy with Lashley's view of the neocortex is striking and may help explain the continued appeal of a holographic theory of memory.

Three Historical Moments

We might single out three moments in the age-old debate about the degree of localization of representation in the human nervous system. The first moment involved scientific hunches. When Descartes located the soul in the pineal gland, when Gall spoke about the representation of amativeness and of criminality in different lobes of the brain, each was announcing claims without benefit of experimental evidence.

A significant step forward took place when it was possible to examine the effects of injuries to discrete areas of the nervous system. When Fritsch and Hitzig lesioned specific sites in the nervous system of dogs, when Broca and Wernicke looked at the effects of strokes in the human cerebral cortex, they were able to substantiate correlations between regions of the brain and forms of behavior.

Finally, when Hubel and Wiesel recorded from discrete cells in the visual cortex of the cat, it became possible to ascertain with great specificity the function of particular units and the circumstances under which they would function (or fail to function) normally. So powerful and precise was this technique that most researchers stopped studying the effects of damage to large and undemarcated regions of the brain, except in human beings who had the misfortune to suffer injury to portions of their brains.

It is in terms of these three historically stacked events in neuroscience that current debates about localization and plasticity can now be framed. In today's climate, it is possible to utilize highly sophisticated radiological, electrophysiological, and chemical assaying techniques to study the structure and the functions of the nervous system, the processes whereby it develops, the effects that follow upon various kinds of pathology. And the thrust of these various lines of research has had two effects: first, to render localization as a more plausible general orientation; second, to direct the attention of active scientists to the operation of specific systems, rather than to continued debate on broad conceptual issues.

And yet it is far too early to claim that the pendulum has stopped swinging, or that the pivotal questions motivating neuroscience have been answered. As Pribram's interest in the holographic aspects of the nervous system indicates, and as the recent studies of recovery of function in young animals make clear, the voices in favor of mass action and plasticity have not been stilled. Moreover, within the specific areas of higher cognitive functioning (as we shall see), there remain debates about even the most basic issues. Neuroscientists still do not agree about just how to describe the functions of the particular cells that Hubel and Wiesel have studied (for example, in terms of sensitivity to spatial frequency rather than the detection of line orientation) (Pribram 1980, p. 58); nor how to characterize the various difficulties that aphasic patients demonstrate; nor how best to label the functions of the right hemisphere in a normal individual, one who suffers from unilateral brain injury, or one whose cerebral hemispheres have been separated for therapeutic reasons. Moreover, even if localization seems (on the whole) to be more tenable than holism, it is now apparent that reductionism is a separate issue.

Will Neuroscience Devour Cognitive Science?

In some ways the neurosciences are different from the other cognitive disciplines (even as philosophy, the wholly nonexperimental discipline, is also different). Researchers in the neurosciences stand out from their cognitive-scientific peers because they most closely partake of the model of the "successful" sciences of physics and biology, because they can most readily state their questions unambiguously and monitor progress toward their solutions. While defenders can be found for the propositions that psychologists or anthropologists have made little progress, or have failed to define their central issues with sufficient progress, few, if any, informed observers would level the same charge at the neurosciences. It is for this reason, in part, that I have avoided an excessively historical approach in this chapter, and focused instead on one central issue in the field—in order to show how the question has been framed, to look at the various alterations in perspective, and to evaluate neuroscientific conclusions after a century of work on the question.

Yet it should be clear that while the neurosciences are different (and who would decry that difference?), they are not all that different. As I have observed, fundamental debate continues on many of the central questions. The uncertainty I have documented reflects the fact that, while rapidly growing, neuroscience is a young field and is still in the process of defining, rather than resolving, many principal issues. And the uncertainty points to another consideration as well.

There are those (perhaps a majority) within the neurosciences who would maintain that cognitive scientific concepts and concerns are not relevant to a biologically oriented science. On this reductionist view, the goal of any natural science should be to explain phenomena at the most elementary level possible. Just as physics moves toward explanation at the subatomic level, and biology searches for explanation at the genetic and molecular levels, so the neurosciences should become oriented increasingly toward the nerve cell and the chemical and electrical events that occur within. So long as the science remains relatively immature, it may be necessary, for the time being, to carry out psychological experiments or to engage in computer simulations of behavior. But once the appropriate neuroscientific studies have been carried out, explanations that feature behaviors, thoughts, actions, schemas, or other molar or representational concepts should become superfluous.

There is a parallel reductionist tendency within the neurosciences themselves. So long as the science remains immature, it may be necessary to speak about occurrences at molar neural levels (for example, within a column of cells, a region of the occipital lobe, or even an entire lobe or hemisphere of the brain). But ultimately such talk should disappear, as the same occurrences can be accounted for at the level of a particular cell. Thus, a strong reductionist position proceeds in two directions: it jettisons the terminology of psychology or phenomenology as rapidly as possible; and it moves from grosser regions of the nervous system to more specific sites. There are, of course, weaker reductionist positions, which permit some cognitive talk or some discussion of more molar neural systems; but they share with strong reductionism a skepticism about any concept whose relation to well-established neural facts remains obscure.

From the perspective of cognitive science—one that I happily adopt here—these lines of argument are untenable. While cognitive scientists may differ in the extent to which they are interested in, or knowledgeable about, new discoveries and favorite models of brain scientists, they are agreed about one crucial matter: that is, one cannot have an adequate theory about anything the brain does unless one also has an adequate theory about that activity itself (Mehler, Morton, and Jusczyk 1984). It is not possible to study perception—even its most fine-grained forms—without a theory of perception. It is not possible to study classification without having a theory of categorization, without substantive knowledge about domains being categorized, as well as understanding the philosophical issues involved in constructing or deploying a category. It is ill-advised to talk about mind, self, action without considerable familiarity with the pitfalls that have long resided as alligators in these particular mentalistic swamps. To paraphrase Wittgenstein, one can know every brain connection involved in concept formation, but that won't help one bit in understanding what a concept is.

From this perspective, it is not possible to enter into the nervous system as a disinterested observer who is simply chronicling the facts (as many neuroscientists assume they are doing). Both the topics studied, and the ways in which they are studied, will reflect implicit theories: theories about what perception, cognition, or language are; what is important in each; and how each of these processes occurs. Risks of generalizing from lower animals to human beings are severe; and, in any event, the less self-conscious one is about procedures, the more likely it is that one will make naïve errors.

Thus, to take an example from language, a neurologist ignorant of linguistics might rely on naïve intuitions about language: one would therefore describe an aphasic patient as unable to use "small words" or to "speak in full sentences." But a linguistically trained observer will immediately be able to pose questions and introduce distinctions at a subtler level: Which grammatical categories pose trouble? Are these troubles apparent across different linguistic contexts? Do they correlate with other phonological, syntactic, lexical, or pragmatic difficulties or distinctions? Having recourse to such linguistic insights does not guarantee an accurate analysis. (Sometimes, indeed, too strong an investment in a particular linguistic theory can blind the observer to counterparadigmatic phenomena.) Yet, to avoid any knowledge of linguistics is equivalent to blindness-by-choice: and so it is now recognized that any aphasia research team should include psychologists and linguists as well as neuroscientists.

For these reasons, I think it best to regard neuroscience as one of the border disciplines of cognitive science. Just as anthropology represents a kind of upper bound for the investigation of cognitive phenomena, so the neurosciences represent a kind of lower bound. Many of the phenomena investigated by neuroscientists are either accounted for perfectly adequately without any reference to the representational level or allow but a subsidiary role for representational aspects: thus, an account of habituation in *Aplysia* does not cry out for representational analysis. Such phenomena do not belong to the mainstream of cognitive science, any more than do discussions of the religious system of an aboriginal tribe. But once neuroscientists begin to invade domains that entail more complex forms of mentation—for example, the domains of language or perception of objects or logical problem solving—there is no longer any possibility of finessing these representational issues. It is at this point that interdisciplinary cooperation becomes an imperative. And it is at this point that the cognitive challenge arises: how best to build explanatory bridges between the level of the neuron and the level of the rule or the concept.

Thus, much as they would like to, neuroscientists cannot afford to isolate themselves from others in the cognitive sciences. While fields like psychology, philosophy, linguistics, or anthropology may not have *the* answer to questions about perception, memory, learning, or language, work in the fields over the decades is relevant to any contemporary discussion. Ignorance of them ill serves even the most gifted neuroscientist. Even those who much prefer a "wet" approach (where one "opens up" the brain and looks at, or listens to, what is there) to a "dry" approach (where one tries to develop an adequate theory of the behavior observed) are increasingly recognizing that the solution to their problems is more likely to come about through extended interdisciplinary collaboration. I shall examine directly several such promising interdisciplinary efforts in part III.

PART III

TOWARD AN INTEGRATED COGNITIVE SCIENCE: PRESENT EFFORTS, FUTURE PROSPECTS

Introduction

In part II, I reviewed highlights from the history of six separate disciplines, which collectively constitute the cognitive sciences of today and may someday be integrated into a single cognitive science. While I have considered each discipline separately—to monitor how each discipline developed in terms of its internal standards, the principal issues it confronts, and its workaday methods—no scholarly discipline operates in a vacuum. There have been clear conversations among various disciplines—for example, between philosophy and psychology, between linguistics and anthropology, even between artificial intelligence and neuroscience. To put it in the terms of psychologist E. G. Boring (1950), one can discern the *Zeitgeist* at work; or, to use the term of the structuralist historian Michel Foucault (1970), a common *episteme* has been imposed on disparate disciplines.

To convey the factors that seem to have been at work across disparate disciplines, I shall briefly sketch the history of cognitive science as if it were a single coherent field. Our prototypical science goes back to the Greeks—to the writings of Plato and Aristotle, the topics raised in the *Meno*. It is here that questions about the nature, the status, the sources, and the use of knowledge were first raised. The agenda of cognitive science was fleshed out during the philosophical flowering of the seventeenth and eighteenth centuries—in the debates between rationalists (like Descartes) and empiricists (like Locke and Hume) and in the attempts at synthesis put forth by Kant around 1780 and by Whitehead and Russell around 1910. Here we see the first intimations of the topics that exercise the cognitive scientist of our time.

In the nineteenth century, the province of our prototypical science became that of empirical rather than of introspective scientists. The unquestioned successes of physics and chemistry, and the inspiring example of Darwin in the biological sciences, fanned hopes for a comparable science of human behavior and thought. Aided by the advent of graduate studies, the rapid growth of technology, and the emergence of a society at once affluent and yet beset by new social and economic problems, the disciplines of psychology, linguistics, anthropology, and neuroscience all began to emerge within a few decades of one another. While the focus of these disciplines differed, the forerunner of our prototypical cognitive science was based on the premise that human behavior and thought have evolved over the millennia, have adapted to the various environments in which cultures arose, and could be subjected to study by empirical and perhaps experimental methods. It should be possible at last to secure reliable answers to age-old questions about human perception, language, classification, and reason.

The leaders of these new disciplines at the end of the nineteenth century were ideally suited to the task: they were not only deeply rooted in the natural science and philosophy of the era but were also imaginative empiricists and inveterate organizers, capable of launching societies, editing journals, and arguing tirelessly with sympathizers and skeptics. Helmholtz, James, Wundt, de Saussure, Frege, Tylor, and Boas are just some of these pioneers.

These researchers succeeded in establishing new sciences, but their specific initial agenda—grandiose and optimistic—did not always take hold. There arose in the early part of the twentieth century a series of reactions to the visionary first generation. For the most part, this reaction was atomistic and functionally oriented: behavior was to be analyzed in terms of its constituent elements and viewed in light of its role within an organism's life and with respect to the goals of a society. The behaviorist vogue swept over psychology (Watson) and linguistics (Bloomfield); functionalism dominated anthropology (Malinowski); logical empiricism held sway in philosophy (courtesy of the Vienna circle). The only exception to this ideal pattern was neuroscience, where (perhaps appropriate for a "border discipline") the reaction was in the opposite direction: the localization views of an earlier generation were swept aside for a while by a holistic perspective.

The several disciplines were not completely enveloped by the behaviorist mentality. Within each, some scholars adapted a holistic or a structuralist position. The Gestalt psychologists and Piaget, the Prague linguists, the structural anthropologists like Radcliffe-Brown, kept alive the broader visions of a science of mind. And during the very time that mentalism was in disrepute, mathematicians and engineers were laying the groundwork for the breakthroughs that would eventually undermine the hegemony of behaviorism.

Behaviorism prevailed in the United States and, to a lesser extent, abroad in the period from 1920 to 1950. But as the Hixon Symposium, and the Macy conferences were being held, as Craik and Turing and Wiener wrote, and as Bruner, Chomsky, Lévi-Strauss, Miller, Newell, and Simon were pursuing their studies, a cognitivist revolution was brewing. Scholars were discovering (or rediscovering) the centrality of high-level linguistic and conceptual activities and the utility of the new tools of computing for investigating these phenomena. What were once iconoclastic statements by such scholars became (with surprising rapidity) the new orthodoxy. Behaviorism was not so much defeated as rendered irrelevant by frontal approaches to human cognitive processes.

In the late 1950s and early 1960s, there was excitement in the already established disciplines and euphoria in the new, quintessentially cognitive discipline of artificial intelligence. But the promise of the cognitive sciences would not be so readily realized. There ensued serious debates about how best to approach the discipline: whether by top-down or bottom-up techniques; by general problem solving or expert systems; by programmatic long-term experimental work, highly selected demonstrations, or detailed case studies. And when it became clear that early predictions would not be confirmed, a reaction set in, during the early 1970s: perhaps a cognitive science was not to be, at least during the lifetime of its most fervent enthusiasts.

There is another, more attractive possibility, however. Perhaps the individual cognitive sciences have gone as far as they can within each of their disciplinary constraints and paradigms. What were once merely polite and brief conversations among them need to be converted into full-scale cooperative research efforts on problems central to several of them. Stemming both from a realization that many scientific problems are simply too complex to be handled by a single discipline, and from a genuine attraction to the methods and concepts worked out in neighboring disciplines, a growing number of scientists—many of them raised in the post-1950s environment—are switching allegiance from single disciplines to the broader practice of cognitive science and are engaging primarily in inter-disciplinary pursuits.

Accordingly, in the final chapters of this book, I review several research efforts that qualify for the label *cognitive-scientific*. These represent several disciplines—either combined in one person or laboratory, or involving collaboration across individuals or laboratories—and are intended to answer the long-standing philosophical questions that originally energized thinkers in classical times. Of course, many different examples could have been chosen, and my selection is not meant in any sense to be definitive. I chose lines of research that involve the central questions in cognitive science and that are considered by the cognitive-scientific community to be of high quality. Not beyond criticism (no good scientific work is immune to critical analysis), this work has rather generated sophisticated criticism and suggested approaches that may eventually resolve such criticism. Indeed, in what follows, I have not hesitated to cite significant criticism and, where appropriate, to state my own reservations. I have chosen to focus on four sets of question that have generated cognitive science of quality.

In chapter 10, I review contemporary efforts in artificial intelligence, aided by neuroscience and psychology, to explain how humans perceive forms and objects. Central to this question is the pathbreaking work of David Marr and his associates, as well as criticisms put forth by J. J. Gibson and other believers in "direct perception."

In chapter 11, I consider the status of visual imagery: What is meant by talk of imagery, and is it proper to treat images as a means whereby knowledge is represented? My survey here focuses on the work of Stephen Kosslyn, in psychology and artificial intelligence, and on various philosophical and computational objections to this work put forth by Zenon Pylyshyn.

In chapter 12, I turn to the issue of how human beings classify objects and elements in their world. A point of departure are studies of color naming carried out by the cross-cultural psychologist Eleanor Rosch and two linguistically oriented anthropologists Brent Berlin and Paul Kay. Work here impinges on the philosophical issue of whether human classifications are arbitrary or motivated, as well as on the relationship between the languages we use and the ways in which we think.

Human rationality is the subject of chapter 13. While philosophers since Greek times have pondered the nature and the extent of human rationality, recent work by researchers like Amos Tversky and Philip Johnson-Laird severely questions the model of man as a logical thinker. This critique, drawn from psychology, linguistics, and artificial intelligence, has engendered considerable philosophical debate—reason discoursing on irrationality.

A survey of the best work, and the sharpest critiques of that work, is one way to evaluate current cognitive science. But, in the end, the way that the field presents itself—its overall charter—provides an equally important test. For the most part, I have simply presented this charter and allowed the field to speak for itself through its history and its work. In the end, however, I suspend this authorial pose and present my own conclusions about the movement whose early gropings stimulated me to write this book.

294

10

Perceiving the World

How can we recognize a circle as a circle, whether it is large
or small, near or far; whether, in fact it is in a plane perpen-
dicular to a line from the eye meeting it in the middle and
is seen as a circle, or has some other orientation, and is seen
as an ellipse? How do we see faces and animals and maps
in clouds, or in the blots of a Rorschach test?
—Norbert Wiener

Perennial Puzzles of Perception

When philosophical reflection begins—whether in a child or a society—it
typically focuses on the perception of the external world. The naïve individual is struck by the existence of a world of objects which one can see,
so long as eyes are open and there is sufficient light. The objects move, we
may also move, and yet we continue to see a stable, organized world. We
can also see forms and colors, possibly only when they are perceived as
part of an object, but perhaps also prior to, or instead of, the objects
themselves. And most of us believe that we can also perceive in the absence of objects by relying on our memories, our mental images, our
powers of imagination.

These are seemingly straightforward observations, but the history of
philosophy and psychology testifies to the difficulty of finding acceptable
accounts of how ordinary percepts come about. Problems emerge almost
immediately. Does all the information necessary for accurate perception
exist in the external world, or do we bring expectations and knowledge
to the perceptual encounter? The world is presumably possessed of a

third dimension, but how does this third dimension get recorded on the retina and then reconstructed within one's head? How different is it to perceive the world as compared with a picture of the world or with an image of the world within one's head? Why do optical illusions persist even after they have been recognized as such? And how do various visual impressions and images relate to thinking? Are they thoughts in themselves, do they provide the vehicles of thought, do they reflect the manipulation of symbolic entities, or are they but epiphenomena, vestiges that do not materially contribute to our ability to know, to learn, or to understand?

Questions like these have been pondered ever since philosophy began. Indeed, the Greeks modeled knowledge upon vision; they invested considerable effort in understanding how we come to know the visible world and how this knowledge may contribute to—or constitute—general understanding. The pre-Socratics were already engaged in debate: Metrodorus of Chios counseled his followers to disregard evidence from one's senses and to pay attention to belief; Democritus in turn acknowledged that all knowledge rests on perception (Barnes 1979). Plato believed that the soul makes perception possible, while Aristotle was more interested in discovering how the eye actually works. In more recent times, rationalists and empiricists revisited these issues. Whereas Descartes minimized the importance of sensory organs, the empiricists saw them as the point of origin for all knowledge.

Before long, practicing scientists joined these debates. In fact, probably a majority of psychologists have begun with an interest in perception, and there has been more unambiguous progress in understanding perception than in illuminating other mental processes. In my review of psychology, I have already touched upon some dominant themes: Hermann von Helmholtz's belief that there is insufficiently accurate information in the stimulus itself, and that much of perception accordingly depends upon unconscious inferences about the scenes that have been observed; J.J. Gibson's rejoinder that the senses can directly pick up from the environment information that is needed for survival; the sensationalist's contention that perception begins with the detection of elementary bits of sensation, out of which it builds up to more complex objects and forms; the Gestaltist's contrary assertion that one first perceives overall form, in a top-down fashion.

Two new lines of research entered discussions about perception. One line, already reviewed in chapter 9, sought to determine the sensitivities of particular nerve cells. If the functioning of all neurons and sets of neurons were to become known, there might be no need for more abstract or higher-level descriptions of perceptual processing.

Computer Simulations

With the advent of computers, another group of scientists became concerned with the processes of visual perception. For them, the initial challenge was less to figure out just how perception occurs in the human being than to understand how perception can be possible *in any kind of organism or mechanical device.* They approached this engineering challenge by attempting to design "seeing" machines and programs: provided with some visually presented information, these mechanisms could so parse that information as to determine the nature and form of presented objects, patterns, or scenes.

After false starts in the late 1950s and early 1960s, students of perception initiated a line of work called *scene analysis* (Boden 1977; MacArthur 1982). In a typical research program, a picture (usually a line drawing) serves as input to the computer, and the computer's task is to interpret the picture in terms of the objects depicted in it, stating the relations of objects to one another and describing the objects themselves. It seemed evident that the "real" world was too complex for current technology to parse, and the most effective programs were devised to work with artificial microworlds (of the sort that Terry Winograd had used for his language understanding program SHRDLU). As we have seen (page 170), researchers like David Waltz were able to devise programs that could unambiguously interpret most line drawings of a scene containing blocks. These approaches of the early 1970s were, however, limited in various ways. For one thing, the programs tended to use artificial line drawings, rather than real objects or photos of real objects. Moreover, the scenes usually contained a highly constrained set of forms drawn from a particular artificial microworld. Computation at the level of the image itself was minimized: there was emphasis on the manipulation of symbolic descriptions of a scene, the kinds of operations in which computers excel, as well as ample reliance on previous knowledge about forms of this sort. In contrast, the rich information available, under normal conditions, to an ordinary viewer was not taken into account. More generally, even when a scene was parsed successfully, there was a feeling that the program used clever engineering tricks, rather than psychologically plausible mechanisms.

If further advances were to take place in computer vision, it was necessary to consider not just how to perceive a particular kind of pictorial image or microworld, but rather to attack the process of perception at a fundamental level; the aim would be to come up with mechanisms that, whether or not similar to those used by animate perceivers, could at least handle the whole range of perceptible scenes and the gamut of perceptual tasks—including perception of motion, depth, surface textures, and other variables that make human perception so powerful. The combination of insights now available from perceptual psychology, neuroscience, and artificial intelligence made it possible, probably for the first time, to put forth a reasonably complete account of the early phases of visual perception—an account that explained how *any* organism is able to perceive a world of shapes and objects. The relevant input to this task came from many quarters, but the pathbreaking conceptions came largely from David Marr.

The Work of David Marr

Though tragically short, Marr's research life was amazingly productive. Trained in neurophysiology at Cambridge, England, he began his scholarly work with a study of the functioning of the human cerebellum (Marr 1969). He came to realize, however, that the most important questions about behavior could never be answered simply by looking at the brain alone—not even if one knew the function of every cell and every connection; as he said, it was like trying to understand flight simply by examining the feather of a bird. Just as a complete understanding of flight must entail an understanding of the constraints preventing any organism or machine from lifting into flight, and of the factors allowing that organism to overcome gravity, so, too, a complete understanding of perception can come about only by means of a theory that considers the actual problems involved in perceiving objects, how these constraints might be counteracted, and how they may be realized in particular mechanisms, ranging from computers to brains. This realization stimulated Marr to undertake work in the artificial intelligence laboratory at Massachusetts Institute of Technology from 1973 until his death from leukemia, a scant seven years later.

In this brief period, Marr laid out a program of how to approach visual perception in particular and of how to study knowledge systems in general. Fundamental to his perspective was the belief that vision is the construction of efficient symbolic descriptions of the images encountered in the world. As he once expressed it, the images of the world should yield a description that is useful to the viewer and not cluttered by irrelevant information. In opting for a symbolic description, Marr broke decisively from those researchers who believed in "direct perception," and entered into the camp of cognitive science.

Levels of Scene Analysis

Marr maintained that, to gain such a description, it does not suffice to have understanding at one level of analysis. One has to be able to describe the responses of neural cells, to predict the results of psychophysical experiments, and to write computer programs that analyze and interpret visual input in the desired way (Marr 1982). Accordingly, he proposed three levels of explanation—computational theory, algorithm, and implementation.

Marr's levels can be introduced through the simple example of a cash register. To understand such a device, you have to ask, at the most abstract level, what it does and why. Since its job is arithmetic, you have to master the theory of addition, which involves understanding the notion of mapping pairs of numbers to their sums, and appreciating such principles as the laws of commutativity—as in $3 + 4 = 4 + 3$—and of associativity—as in $(3 + 4) + 5 = 3 + (4 + 5)$. Such understanding of the theory of addition constitutes the computational theory of the cash register.

In the world of visual processes, the analogy is the problem of deriving properties of the world from images of it: in other words, the challenge of explaining vision in whatever mechanism happens to realize it. Such a computational theory shows what is being computed and why, for the purposes of perception, this is a useful piece of information to compute. In the case of vision, the computational theory would specify the ways in which a two-dimensional image is related to the three-dimensional world and how that image can be interpreted—the constraints that make it possible to recover the properties of the scene from the correlative image. Thus, let us suppose that vision includes such processes as recovering the shape of a rotating body from fleeting images, or the capacity for stereoscopic perception (the ability of a binocular mechanism to compute depth by combining information obtained from two slightly different points of view). Any computational theory must account for how these processes can be carried out given the information available in the image.

In order for the process actually to run, however, one has to realize it in some way and therefore choose some form of representation for each of the relevant entities. The second level of analysis of a process involves selecting, first, a representation for the input and the output of the process; and second, an algorithm (or formal symbol-manipulation procedure) by which the transformation may actually be accomplished. In other words, this second algorithmic level specifies *how* an operation is carried out. In the case of addition, one might choose Arabic numerals for the representations; and for the algorithm, one could add the smallest digits first and carry if the sum exceeds 9. Both electrical and mechanical cash registers follow this type of representation.

In the case of vision, the algorithmic level addresses itself to the question of the various ways in which a function like stereopsis might actually be represented and carried out by some mechanism. In this particular case, Marr and his colleagues had laid out an elegant set of procedures for computing stereoscopic vision; it turned out, however, that this set bore no resemblance to the processes apparently used by the brain. Marr wanted his algorithms to be consistent with what is known about animal perception: accordingly, that algorithm was replaced by one more consistent with evidence from psychophysics and from neuropsychology.

The third level concerns the device in which the process is to be realized physically. The same algorithm can be implemented in quite different technologies. Addition can be run on various electrical or mechanical machines but can also be carried out in the brain.

Any task may be achieved by various algorithms, and any algorithm is susceptible to many realizations in a given hardware. The decision about which way the algorithm will actually be realized is made by each investigator, and many students of artificial intelligence are unconcerned about the ways in which human beings happen to accomplish visual perception. Marr's interest in the level of realization clearly concerned the possibility of building computer programs to parse scenes effectively. This was the essential "existence" proof that an algorithm actually worked. As we have seen, however, he let his work be guided by the procedures that seemed to be used by the human brain—possibly because these seemed most likely to work effectively for inorganic machines as well.

Marr noted that it was easier for scientists to work on the algorithmic and the mechanical realization level—levels that lend themselves to actual experimentation. But in his view, the level of computational theory was most important to tackle at the present time. Here Marr reflects his belief that the nature of the computations that underlie perception depends more on the computational problems that have to be solved by *any system,* than on the particular hardware in which the solutions happen to be implemented in the most familiar instances.

Marr cautioned against excessive concentration on the nature of brain processes alone; as he noted, even total knowledge of anatomy and physiology would not allow one to understand why neurons have receptive fields. To understand how the neurons of the visual system actually accomplish their tasks, one must draw upon mathematical principles involved in interpreting images. Yet Marr was conscious that no discipline in itself could unravel the mysteries of perception. A true cognitive scientist, he once declared:

The moral is that ignorance in any of these three fields can be damaging. Just as the modern physicist has to know some mathematics, so must the modern psychologist, but the psychologist must also be familiar with computation and have a clear idea of its abilities, its limitations, the fruitful ways in which to think about processes and, most importantly, what it takes to understand these processes. (1982, p. 187)

Two Sketches and a Model

So much for theoretical preliminaries. Having laid out a general approach to the understanding of vision, Marr and his colleagues devoted their efforts to specifying steps governing individual processing of visual images—be it implemented by a machine or by some organism. The goal of the Marr enterprise was to explain how our brains come to compute roughly the same symbolic representations starting from initial "gray-level" variations in illumination. Briefly, Marr and his colleagues described a series of representations called "sketches" which began with the quickest and least detailed kind of parsing of visual information and culminated when the image was seen as a complete collection of objects arranged in space. (See Marr 1982 and Rosenfield 1984 for fuller accounts.)

The first representation was the *primal sketch:* this made explicit the properties of the two-dimensional image, ranging from the kinds of intensity change within a scene (areas of gray, of relative brightness as compared with areas of relative darkness) to a primitive representation of the local geometry. The next representation, the *2½-D sketch,* involves a representation from the vantage point of the viewer of the depth and orientation of the visible surfaces. The final step is the *three-D* representation. Its coordinate system is object- rather than viewer-centered; it includes a representation of volume, the space occupied by an object and not just its visualized surfaces, as well as an organized array of simple recognizable shapes of various sizes. In laying out these sketches, Marr and his colleagues were outlining the steps through which *any* mechanism necessarily passes from the time (or circumstance) in which it first attempts to make an external scene intelligible, to the time (or circumstance) when the scene has been apprehended in relatively veridical form.

A closer look at the first steps of visual processing indicates that these processes are designed to sort out factors of geometry, reflectance of a surface, illumination of a scene, and determination of viewpoint. The multiphased procedure of forming the primal sketch involves steps like detecting intensity changes, representing and analyzing local geometrical structure, and detecting illuminating effects like light sources, highlights, and transparencies. The steps reflect the fact that changes in illumination occur in a scene at the point where edges and changes in surface contour are likely to occur. This phase ends with a representation that makes explicit the size and disposition of intensity changes—allowing one to detect the boundaries in an image and what has caused them. The primal sketch consists of a set of blobs oriented in various directions; these are reminiscent of the sorts of features discerned by Hubel and Wiesel's detectors—contrasts, spatial extent, general orientation at a local level. All of these reductions and simplifications are conceived of as mental representations or symbolic depictions of the "raw information" transmitted by the light: perception consists of a series of such simplified sketches *en route* to a more veridical view of the world.

Following the achievement of the primal sketch, a number of processes operate upon it to derive a representation of the geometry of the visible surfaces. These processes include stereopsis, the use of cues of shading, texture, occluding contours, and various aspects of motion. In global stereopsis, one attains an internal representation that includes information on depth, surface orientation, and surface discontinuities. But like the primal sketch, the 2½-D sketch is constructed in a viewer-centered coordinate frame. It depends on a single vantage point and therefore cannot explain one of the most important facts about visual perception: the perceived constancy of the shape of an object despite movements on the part of a viewer.

Marr claims that the goal of early visual processing is to construct a 2½-D sketch. One avoids all the problems of traditional psychological analysis associated with intuitive distinctions like figure, ground, region, and object; the various modules of early visual processing and the 2½-D sketch itself deal only with discovering the properties of surfaces in an image. These occur in exactly the same way, whether one is viewing persons, animals, trees, or paintings. Only shapes and reflections need to be made clear to the viewer at this point. As Marr puts it, the 2½-D sketch is the final step before a surface is interpreted (as being a particular object or set of objects): in fact, it may well mark the end of purely perceptual processes.

The final step of early visual processing involves the transformation of shapes from a pure representation that is matched to the processes of perception into a representation that is suitable for recognition—a set of meaningful regions. The task now becomes object recognition: needed is a stable shape description that does not depend on a particular momentary viewpoint. Thus, the pieces of a shape must be described in terms of a frame of reference based on the shape itself. A scheme for representing shape involves the use of a coordinate system and component axes iden-

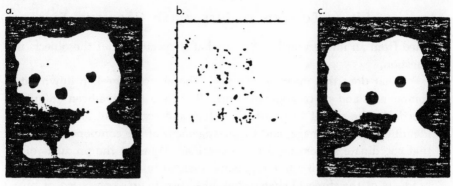

An image (a), the spatial components of its primal sketch (b), and a reconstruction of the image from the primal sketch (c).

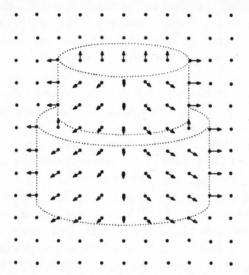

A 2½-D sketch without a representation of depth information.

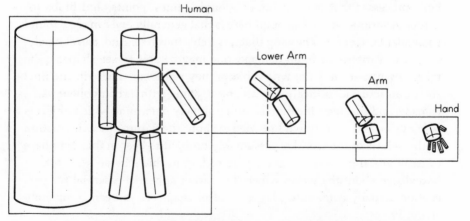

Organization of shape information in a 3-D model description. Each box corresponds to a 3-D model.

SOURCE: From P. H. Winston and R. H. Brown, *Artificial Intelligence: An MIT Perspective*, vol. 2: *Understanding Vision, Manipulation, Computer Design, Symbol Manipulation* (Cambridge, Mass.: MIT Press, 1979). Reproduced by permission.

tified from an image which capture what is specific about the objects in question.

What does this mean in practice? The object is broken down into components and subcomponents until all of its parts have been uniquely specified. The model's coordinate system and component axes must be identified from an image, and the arrangement of the component axes in that coordinate system need to be specified. Whereas the products of a primal sketch look like line segments oriented in various directions, the products of the three-D sketch look like stick figures composed of pipe cleaners. This reason is that according to Marr and his colleague Keith Nishahara (1978), the brain automatically transposes the contours it has derived from the 2½-D sketch onto axes of symmetry that resemble stick figures. By the time the three-D sketch has been constructed, the final result should be a unique description of any object one can distinguish; the same object should always yield the same unique description no matter what the angle of viewing; and different representations should reflect the similarity between different objects, while also preserving whatever differences may matter.

We have, then, a series of steps through which presumably both humans and machines must pass in making sense of a scene or an image. The first computational stage, the formation of the primal sketch, consists of description of a scene in terms of a vast collection of features like edges, lines, and blobs—the kinds of feature that may depend upon specific neural detectors à la Hubel and Wiesel. This primal sketch, an initial symbolic representation of the image, is formed by processing mechanisms that are completely independent of any "high level" knowledge about objects. The second stage involves analysis of the primal sketch by symbolic processes that are capable of grouping lines, points, and blobs together in various ways. The point here is that generally one can see a round triangular bulb before knowing that it is a chestnut tree. And, correlatively, in certain varieties of brain damage, one may be able to see shapes quite reliably without knowing what objects they represent. Then, in the final stages, an actual identification of an object, along with its component parts, is made; and this identification should uniquely determine which object is being perceived. Top-down knowledge about the nature and construction of the objects of the world is presumably brought to bear in this last phase of early visual processing. And so, according to this scheme, the sorts of knowledge about the world which had earlier appeared essential for perception actually come into play only after shapes have been completely analyzed.

I have sought to convey the boldness of Marr's approach in artificial intelligence and, without going into technical details, to suggest the way in which he conceived the steps of visual processing. It is equally important to convey the enormity of the enterprise. At the level of the primal sketch, for example, the primitives the algorithms must detect include blobs, terminations and discontinuities, edge segments, virtual lines, boundaries, groups, curvilinear organization, and other such elements. Marr himself attempted to describe the process in general terms:

> One initially selects roughly similar elements from [the image] and groups and clusters them together, forming lines, curves, larger blobs, groups, and small patches to the extent allowed by the inherent structure of the image. By doing this again and again, one builds up tokens or primitives at each scale that capture the spatial structure at that scale. Thus if the image was a close-up view of a cat, the raw primal sketch might yield descriptions mostly at the scale of the cat's hairs. At the next level the markings on its coat may appear—which may also be detected directly by intensity changes—and at a yet higher level there is the parallel-stripe structure of these markings. . . . at each step the primitives used are qualitatively similar symbols—edges, bars, blobs, and terminations or discontinuities—but they refer to increasingly abstract properties of the image. (1982, p. 91)

Implications for Cognitive Science

How does Marr's approach contribute to classical debates about visual perception? In general, he favors a bottom-up analysis of images. Rather than beginning by hypothesizing about what might be there, the perceptual system consists of many specific computational mechanisms targeted to carry out specific analyses, independent of any "real world" knowledge or any interaction among the several mechanisms. Indeed, Marr maintains that there are separate *modules* for computing such aspects of visual information as motion, stereoscopy and color, with each module operating according to its own principles and having little, if any, interaction with the others. Marr sought to hold off the importation of knowledge about possible objects and scenes until as late in the processing of visual information as possible. For once one begins to draw on such knowledge (of the sort presumably used by human beings to interpret scenes), the process of modeling would become much more complex. As Marr maintained, "Perhaps we could say that at these higher levels we are beginning to face all the problems that the linguists have" (1982, p. 313).

But if Marr was sympathetic to the bottom-up approach, so long as it proved tenable, he was equally an apostle of considerable processing and considerable symbolic representation during early visual processing. That is, he had no truck with the notion that perception can occur automatically, because of a prescribed or predetermined "fit" between the perceiver and the world. Rather, in the tradition of Helmholtz, Marr noted from the first the extensive amount of recalculation of the initial information that is necessary for effective perception to take place.

In this respect, Marr was close to his M.I.T. colleague Noam Chomsky, who had stressed the considerable computation involved in producing and comprehending language (Chomsky 1984). While Chomsky spurned the methods of artificial intelligence, and was less concerned with corroborating evidence from other disciplines, he shared with Marr a belief in the need for an account of language (or syntax) at the most abstract level—what is the nature of syntax, and how it is possible for *any* mechanism to carry out syntactic operations altogether. It is not surprising that the two men had considerable respect for one another. Just as Chomsky wished to examine syntax in its pristine form (uncontaminated by semantics or pragmatics), Marr wanted his analysis of visual processing insulated as far as possible from the intrusion of "real world" knowledge. But Marr also sought consistency with what is known about the operation of the brain. At each level of processing, he examined the relevant evidence about brain operation: he continually revised algorithms in the hope of making them consistent with the psychophysical and neurophysiological evidence—be it at the level of individual cells or of cortical lobes. Thus, with one eye fixed upon the brain, the other upon implementation of algorithms on a computer, Marr was an embodiment of interdisciplinary cognitive science.

In addition to his concerted effort to illuminate visual processing, particularly during its early stages, Marr also had strong views about how other research efforts in artificial intelligence should be carried out. He was critical of those approaches that focus only on mechanisms, that tinker with a particular problem without understanding the nature of that problem itself. By the same token, he denigrated those extremely general approaches which assumed that all kinds of problem solving should be modulated by the same mechanisms. In information processing, he maintained, the structure of each individual problem is central and must be understood first.

Marr felt it important to focus initially on those tasks humans carry out well, rather than to examine those they do poorly. Such well-executed processes were more important for human beings, in general, and more likely to entail long-standing highly organized mechanisms. In contrast, the study of tasks (like the solution of cryptographical problems) which most individuals can carry out only with difficulty would turn up only *ad hoc* and artificial-processing strategies: these were unlikely to illuminate deeply entrenched aspects of human information processing.

Marr's colleague Christopher Longuet-Higgins paid his late colleague high compliments:

If neurophysiology was a theoretical vacuum when he entered it, it is now seething with lively controversy about the validity of his ideas on the visual system. . . . Even if no single one of Marr's detailed hypotheses ultimately survives, which is unlikely, the questions he raises can no longer be ignored and the methodology he proposes seems to be the only one that has any hope of illuminating the bewildering circuitry of the central nervous system. David Marr's lifework will have been vindicated when neuroscientists cannot understand how it was ever possible to doubt the validity of his theoretical maxims. (1982, p. 992)

Their fellow countryman Stuart Sutherland offers even higher praise: *"Vision* [Marr's posthumous book] is perhaps the most important book on the subject to appear since Helmholtz' *Physiological Optics"* (1982, p. 692).

In a nontrivial sense, Marr was picking up the program glimpsed during the late 1940s when notions of cognitive science were first jelling. Workers like Wiener, von Neumann, and McCulloch, who were interested in the connections between the brain, the computer, and processes of perception, put forth various proposals about how the perceptual mechanisms actually work. When the first conception proved wrong, or impossible to verify, efforts to tie together these sources ceased for a while, and scholars withdrew into their own specialty: psychologists like Gibson, focusing on processes of visual perception; artificial intelligence experts like Frank Rosenblatt directing their energy to computer vision; neurophysiologists like Lettvin and Hubel and Wiesel stressing brain neuroanatomy. Using the computer but focusing on the theory of perception, Marr was able to move some steps toward an integration of these different perspectives. As he articulated his own vision, "The discovery of constraints that are valid and sufficiently universal leads to results about vision that have the same quality of permanence as results in other branches of science"(Marr 1979, p. 75).

Reactions to Marr

It is too soon to evaluate which portions of Marr's program are likely to survive, and which will need to be modified or altogether scuttled. Most commentators have expressed admiration of Marr's research program and awe at the amount he was able to accomplish with his colleagues in a few years, but have generally withheld public comment on which particular aspects of his effort are least robust. Conversations with scholars knowledgeable about vision have revealed areas of likely criticism.

Like many other pioneers, Marr expressed his convictions in a strong and clear-cut manner, even as he did not hesitate to criticize others. In reaction, not surprisingly, observers stress the ties between Marr's contributions and those of other workers (for example, Horn 1975) as well as the connections among the various levels of analysis that he preferred to isolate. Apparently not all of the processes described in his writings were implemented in computer programs; and until they have been, it will remain uncertain which are workable. There are reservations about how much visual processing can actually take place without top-down information: to the extent that such top-down effects may occur early on, or be more pervasive in early visual processing, or allow shortcuts to recognition, Marr's modular approach is endangered. And except at the level of the primal sketch, little neurological evidence can be related directly to the Marr model.

Questions have also been raised about the extent to which Marr's analysis successfully addresses the most central part of perception—the recognition of real objects in the real world. Most of his account focuses on the steps before object recognition takes place; the procedures he outlined for object recognition may prove applicable chiefly to the perception of figures of a certain sort—for example, the mammalian body, which lends itself to decomposition in terms of generalized cylindrical forms.

Like other pioneering researchers, Marr helped to identify the agenda for future work. A large cadre of scholars are now engaged in interdisciplinary studies of visual perception; and irrespective of their attraction to Marr's particular claims, they are working on the problems he did much to bring to the fore. A far more critical perspective on his whole enterprise can, however, readily be inferred from a group of researchers who rarely discuss his work: those inspired by the writings of James J. Gibson. The line of thinking emanating from Gibson serves as an important challenge to the general cognitive-science approach to perception and to other issues of human cognition as well.

The Gibsonian View of Perception

In Gibson's view (1950, 1966, 1979; see also Turvey et al. 1981), organisms are so constituted, and live in a world so constituted, that they will readily gain the information they need to survive and to thrive. In particular, our sense organs are designed to pick up information from the external world. Thus, when one detects the third dimension, the relevant spatial information is simply presented in the light, without one's having to infer distances or to correlate information from eye and hand; there is no need for the kinds of unconscious inference which scientists from Helmholtz on have proposed. Initially in life the information will be relatively gross, but with time and experience, it will be increasingly fine-grained; still, in any case, the information will be adequate for survival, veridical, devoid of misleading cues. The information is available in the world and needs only to be picked up. There is no need to operate upon it or process it; there is no need to draw on prior knowledge, on mental models, on interpretive schemata (Gibson 1967). If researchers understood how people attend to what is there, all the problems of perceptual psychology—indeed, perhaps all the problems of psychology proper—could be satisfactorily explicated.

On which evidence did Gibson draw in coming up with this radically simple orientation to perception? In the course of many years of experimentation, he became extremely impressed with the kinds of information available to the visual sense alone. For example, according to classical empiricist theory, the sense of touch was deemed central to an organism's ability to perceive depth. But Gibson showed that there is sufficient information in the visual sphere to allow the discrimination of depth. The gradient of texture density is an important clue. Consider a piece of paper or a linoleum floor with a recurrent checkerboard pattern: one sees the density of the texture as invariant across the entire array. So long as one peers straight ahead (or straight down) at the pattern, the density of the texture does not change. But as the stimulus slants, or as one peers at it from an angle, the density of texture changes from the near edge to the far edge, and the viewer receives precise and unambiguous information about the distance of each part of the stimulus from one's eyes (Hochberg 1978). Hence attention to texture gradient suffices to yield information about the sizes of objects on a surface or the arrangement of surfaces with respect to each other: there is no need for the use of other sensory modalities, the calculation of ratios, or other unconscious inferences.

Gibson also stressed the important contribution to perception made by a person's motions in the world. So long as one is forced to sit passively, any scene will appear ambiguous. But if you are free to walk about, changes in the optic array will be precisely tied to the voluntary movements of your body. As you continue to explore, information is routinely obtained and that information in turn yields more relevant information. Moreover, the changes in the optic array that result from motions initiated by the individual make it very easy to figure out what is occurring in the visual world. Thus, active exploring individuals exploit a perceptual system that is maximally informative about space and distance.

Based on these and many other observations and considerations, Gibson arrived at extreme skepticism about the whole computational approach. He objected to the notion of mental representations, mental operations, the *processing* (as opposed to the direct "pickup") of information, and other cognate concepts. Inferences were completely unnecessary. From his point of view, cognitive scientists have been subscribing to modes of discussion and analysis which are both unnecessary and fundamentally wrongheaded.

In the light of today's psychology, this is certainly a radical perspective. Indeed, a reader of this book might well ask why, in this cognitively oriented age, anyone would take it seriously. There are at least three reasons, I think. One is that Gibson was an extremely clever and incisive researcher, a keen student of perception, who helped to explicate many perceptual phenomena and underscored—as Marr would later stress—the extensive information already present in the environment in which the organism lives. As Marr put it, Gibson asked the critically important question: "How does one obtain constant perceptions in everyday life on the basis of continually changing sensations? This is exactly the right question, showing that Gibson correctly regarded the problem of perception as that of recovering from sensory information 'valid' properties of the external world" (Marr 1982, p. 24).

A second reason for Gibson's appeal can be found in the set of interlocking concepts he developed. He felt that psychologists ought to look to physics—most especially to optics—as a means of understanding the structure of the environment. Physics would be linked to biology as organisms make their way in the world, picking up relevant information to which they are attuned. As a central part of his fine-grained analysis of the environment, Gibson introduced the notion of *affordances*. Affordances are the potentialities for action inherent in object or scene—the activities that can take place when an organism of a certain sort encounters an entity of a certain sort. According to the notion of affordances, individuals throw things that are grabbable (that is, they afford grabbing), devour things that are edible (they afford eating), and cuddle things that are lovable (they afford loving). The concept of affordances permitted an analysis of an organism's effectiveness within its environment, without the apparent need to invoke beliefs, attitudes, or mental effort—all of which concepts made Gibson very nervous. Indeed, for him an object's meaning consists in the affordances it provides to an organism. Objects are meaningful to us because they afford things for us to do with or to them or in reaction to them.

A final reason for Gibson's persuasiveness comes from the simplicity of his point of view. Like B. F. Skinner, who toiled in a distant area, Gibson was able to provide an unambiguous theory, which apparently did away with the need for a lot of internal apparatus and representational contrivances, and substituted a straightforward realistic account, where the world simply contains whatever information is needed. "I am convinced," Gibson once declared, "that invariance comes from reality, not the other way around. Invariance in the ambient optic array over time is not constructed or deduced; it is there to be discovered" (quoted in Royce and Rozeboom 1972, p. 239).

It is here that cognitive scientists of almost every stripe have locked horns with Gibson. As Marr phrased it, the detection of invariants is exactly and precisely an information-processing problem, which must be approached by the tools of modern psychology. Gibson greatly underrated the difficulty of such detection. The only way to understand how the detection works is to treat it as an information-processing problem.

Cognitive-Science Critiques of Gibson

In order to meet the challenge put forth by Gibson and his followers, the cognitive-science community has rolled out its big guns. Shimon Ullman, a colleague of David Marr, mounted an attack "against direct perception" in *The Behavioral and Brain Sciences* (1980). Ullman points out that the direct perception of information touted by Gibson would be justified if it were not possible to break down perceptual information into more elementary constituents; but computational and psychophysical studies have amply shown that the perception of objects can be broken down into simpler units and into more elementary operations.

In Ullman's view, it thus becomes preferable to posit a continuum of perceptual mechanisms ranging from direct to indirect. Some aspects of perception, such as those involving the detection of textures or the mapping of a reliable correlation between light and layout features of gradients, seem to work in a relatively direct way. The field owes much to Gibson for having identified these perceptual capacities and clarified their mode of operation. But many other aspects of perception simply do not lend themselves to direct registration and interpretation. The raw intensity array which constitutes the first image is unmanageably vast: the only feasible first step is to replace the intensity array by a representation of the significant intensity changes in the image, as Marr and his colleagues have done in positing the primal sketch. Moreover, other aspects of perception—for example, the perception of motion—simply do not occur in a direct way but, rather, involve the devising of structural descriptions on which perceptual mechanisms can then operate. And by the time one is dealing with object recognition, one has encountered a process that is mediated by prior knowledge and by beliefs through and through and can in no way be accomplished directly by detectors. In Ullman's perspective, the richness of information in the visual array does not imply that constructs internal to the perceiver have no place in the theory of perception. On the contrary, it is only through a joint recognition of the rich information in the environment *and* of the capacity for considerable recoding and transforming that we become able to see and to recognize objects.

Ullman is challenging Gibson on two fronts. First of all, he is saying that a great deal can be gained by studying perception in terms of its component parts and phases (rather than by viewing it as an automatic kind of "resonance" between the perceiver and the world); thus a bottom-up approach has its utility. Second of all, he is insisting on the importance of an analysis in terms of an internal symbolic representation: the mechanics of perception simply cannot be modeled or accounted for except in terms of such a cognitive-scientific approach. In short, the admitted richness of the perceptual array in no way implies that the absence of constraints is internal to the perceiver.

Even more of a frontal attack against Gibson was carried out by Jerry Fodor and Zenon Pylyshyn in their article "How Direct Is Visual Perception: Some Reflections on Gibson's 'Ecological Approach'" (1981). Defending what they wryly term the "Establishment" view, these two authors single out for special attack the central notion in Gibson's scheme—that objects have properties or affordances that are resonant with the needs or goals of organisms and are therefore readily responded to or "picked up" by the organisms.

The concept of affordances allows Gibson to explain how organisms know what to do with or how to respond to what they perceive. But Fodor and Pylyshyn argue that the properties of affordances are unconstrained—that anything can be an affordance. But if any property can count as affordance—and moreover, if any such property can be picked up—then one is left with an account as empty as Skinner's alleged explanation of language learning. And so, playing Chomsky to Gibson's Skinnerian account, Fodor and Pylyshyn conclude that Gibson's explanation of why organisms handle objects in the way that they do is devoid of theoretical significance. As Fodor declares elsewhere, "The category 'affordance' seems to me to be a pure cheat; an attempt to have all the goodness out of intentionality without paying any of the price" (Fodor 1980, p. 107).

As this last quotation suggests, the key concepts missing from a Gibsonian account all have to do with meaning—with how an organism interprets, infers, or assumes an "intentional stance" to an object. Only some such notion will prevent the organism from noting everything and responding to everything. On the Establishment account, Gibson fails to appreciate that individuals are able to act appropriately in an environment because they make inferences about what they see, and because they have beliefs, goals, purposes, and other intentional states directed toward their percepts. As Fodor and Pylyshyn point out, it is not good enough that we directly perceive that a rock can be used as a weapon (because it is "grabbable" and "hurlable"); we need an account of how apprehension of such a property can occur *without* inferences. There is no "neutral" information available to a perceiver; either the information is in the world but not available in a relevant form to the perceiver; or the information is interpreted by the perceiver and hence can no longer be deemed neutral (Fodor 1984).

Thus, when Gibson talks about the light conveying information concerning a layout, he is actually talking about semantic relations—the information is *about* something; but he has no way of indicating how one recognizes such semantic relations. The question how one gets from properties of light to the properties of the layout has only one conceivable answer in the Fodor-Pylyshyn view—through inferential mediation. The pressing question for the cognitivist is to understand the sorts of empirical consideration relevant to deciding *which* properties of the light are attended to, interpreted, and then acted upon.

In Fodor and Pylyshyn's view, Gibson's longtime focus on problems of visual perception led him to underestimate the difficulty of constructing a cognitive psychology that dispenses with mental representation. The prototypical perceptual relations are extensional: they have to do with the information about features of the environment, such as those in an image. Here the need for internal representations and inferences may be less patent. But most prototypical cognitive relations—like believing, expecting, thinking, and so on—are intentional, and the constructs of mental representation are required to explain intentionality. There is a big difference between seeing x and seeing x as y, and what is central to cognitive psychology is the ability to see something as an entity—a rock as a tool or a weapon or a stool rather than just a blob.

Fodor and Pylyshyn (1981) conclude that one needs either an independent account of the meaning of a representation, as is called for by the Establishment view, or of the specification of a property, as required by Gibson. The problem of accounting for the meaning of a representation may be tractable, since the meaning of a representation can perhaps be reconstructed by reference to its function; but Gibson gives no indication at all of how to specify a property, no explanation of how a configuration of light can ever specify such interpreted properties. And so "where the Establishment line offers, anyhow, a pious hope, the Gibsonian line offers only a dead end" (Fodor and Pylyshyn 1981, p. 192). Missing the point about inference, about mental representations, about intentionality are all thus aspects of missing the same point.

An Aggressive Defense

With such a staunch attack from the M.I.T. trio of Ullman, Fodor, and Pylyshyn,* one might wonder whether the followers of Gibson would retreat (or retrench) in silence. Far from it. In their commentaries on Ullman's target article in *The Behavioral and Brain Sciences,* and in a response to Fodor and Pylyshyn even longer than the original article, Michael Turvey and Robert Shaw, two Gibsonian psychologists at the University of Connecticut, indicate that the cognitivists have missed the point of *their* own position. To start with, Turvey and Shaw remind us of the extent to which Gibson's work has illuminated fundamental questions of perception and has helped to explain the perception and the behavior of a wide range of organisms moving about in a wide range of environments. The proof is in the pudding, they say, and they reject out-of-hand the notion that the Gibson approach is as vacuous as Skinner's: they then wrap the mantle of Chomsky around themselves by claiming, "Just as Chomsky used the regularity and ease of natural language acquisition as a fact to justify treating language as a special subject matter, so Gibson and his followers have argued for the importance of doing justice to natural, effective perception" (Turvey et al. 1981, p. 239).

According to Turvey, Shaw, and their associates (abbreviated hereafter as Turvey and Shaw), Gibson's ecological approach seeks to account for an organism's apprehension of its environment and the manner in which it controls its actions with respect to that environment. The approach focuses squarely on organism-environmental relations, never on what might be in the organism's head. Indeed, many issues can simply be bypassed: for Gibson, "awareness" is *always* "awareness of some property," and so there is no need to posit inferences or symbolic calculations. Secondary become the issues of what counts as perception, of whether perception should be construed as judgment, of whether perception is direct or indirect, and of how inference figures in the scheme of things.

Once again turning Fodor and Pylyshyn's argument against them, the Turvey team concludes that the Establishment's views are insufficiently constrained and have placed a burden on inference which it simply cannot bear. Instead, Turvey, Shaw, and colleagues argue for a conception of natural law that posits meaningful relations between organisms and environment. By "natural law," they are referring to scientific principles—in this case, laws that explain why organisms perceive and behave in the ways they do by virtue of their fit with their environment. The use of the term *perception* should then be restricted to relations captured by such laws.

---

*Pylyshyn, currently at the University of Western Ontario, is a frequent visitor and sometime collaborator at M.I.T.

Ecological theorists like Gibson seek to extend the application of natural law as far as possible, because that strategy promises tight constraints and an explanation of lawful evolution of inference in principled ways. In contrast, Establishmentarians like Fodor and Pylyshyn want to extend cognition and intelligence as far as possible and thereby to limit the role of natural law. Regularities, then, must be accounted for by mental rules and representation—which are themselves constrained by very little except unsystematic intuitions (Turvey et al. 1981, p. 245). The Establishment talks a great deal about how to make the right inferences and very little about how to locate the right premises. The ecological school provides a way to get the right premises by laying out the laws of perception; it derives these laws of nature by careful observation of, and experimentation on, organisms as they pick up information from and operate effectively within their natural environments. The Establishment has to gamble that it can guess how an organism is going to know what to do in a given situation; the ecological school has the much more straightforward task of simply finding out what sorts of things this kind of organism actually *does* in this kind of a situation.

The role of natural law centers on affordances and effectivities. Gibson's "ecological science" studies the relations between *affordances*—things that are grabbable, climbable, and the like—and *effectivities*—things that can do the grabbing, climbing, and so on. The examples used by the Gibson school account for how organisms carry out these and countless other activities in their natural environments in order to survive and thrive. According to this scientific credo, psychologists are called upon to describe the lawful regularities of the environment if they wish to produce a scientific explanation of the origin, function, and causation of behavior (Turvey et al. 1981, p. 274). This tack includes laws about everyday objects and events, which have the affordances that govern behavior of importance to the organisms of the world. And so, the "ecological psychologists" fill their articles with analysis of places where wasps can lay their eggs, elements that sharks can eat, stems on which marsh periwinkles can climb, and the like—no optical illusions or ambiguous sentences for them.

Turvey and Shaw deplore the rampant tendency to ascribe to an organism neural detectors or structural descriptions that essentially represent the very property that is sensed. This practice permeates the Establishment: for Z to see, detect, register a property x of X, Z must "have" property x in some sense, neurophysiologically or conceptually. In contrast (as Turvey and Shaw have put it), the ecological school eschews rules (or computation) in favor of natural laws, representations in favor of occurrent properties, and concepts in favor of affordances. Instead of trying to stuff properties into the heads of organisms, the ecological school keeps these properties where they belong—in the natural world. All told, the ecologists make central to their science the discovery of natural laws governing the organism's relation to its environment, rather than cognitive laws, which carry out operations on mental representations.

Contrasting Perspectives

As the ecologists describe it, we are left with two sharply contrasting images. The Establishment treatment of the intentionality problem conjures up an image of an organism (such as the hermit crab), on the occasion of becoming hungry, moving about with a concept of food in mind and looking for something that will match the concept; or an organism (such as the marsh periwinkle), on the occasion of impending danger from the approaching tide, moving about with a concept of a thing that can be climbed up in mind and looking for something in the environment that will match up with that concept. The ecological approach conjures a very different image—of an organism, on a given occasion, moving in the context of one set of nested laws rather than another. Confronted with the fact that a gannet can dive accurately into the water and scoop up a fish when hungry, the ecological school asks about the various kinds of laws that can control the gannet's behavior and how the values for the gannet's dive are arrived at in accordance with some law when it dives for food. The latter image expresses belief in a natural basis to intentionality, whereas the Establishment image does not (Turvey et al. 1981, p. 299).

In the view of Turvey and Shaw, there is at stake a larger philosophy of science issue. Are the uniformities observed in nature reflections of an underlying concrete framework of laws, or are they only the insidious invention of the human mind? Turvey and Shaw criticize Kant's arrogance in saying, "The understanding does not draw its laws from nature but prescribes them to nature" (1981, p. 299), and prefer to draw constraints from biology and physics rather than from the more elusive realm of the human mind. These researchers prefer to believe that there is a natural order, which it is the scientist's role to discover—just as it is the organism's role to discover the natural properties in its environment that will give it all that it ever needs to know.

The Gibsonians attack the Establishment in terms of its conception of scientific truth. While both Gibson and his critics are involved in a scientific effort designed to figure out how perception and cognition occur, the Gibsonians are likely to find the crucial information in the environment and the organism's relationship to it; the Establishment cognitivists pay attention instead to the presuppositions and biases built into the organism and to the way information in the world becomes transformed or reconstructed upon its apprehension by the organisms.

It is possible to take the position that these are simply two views of the same basic situation: one paying far more attention to the environment; the other paying far more attention to the organism; but both attempting to explain the same set of phenomena in parallel ways. One can also divide the territory to be explained, leaving simple perception to the ecologists, complex inferencing to the Establishment. Both parties occasionally take such positions, when they are in a mediating mood; but in general, the gulf seems much deeper. The very terms that are central to the Establishment—*intentions, inferences, schemas*—are rejected by the Gibsonians as unnecessary: even as the terminology favored by the latter—*affordances, effectivities, information pickup*—is deemed by the Establishment to be vacuous or insufficient. The fundamental scientific themata are also different: Gibson reflects a belief in the real world as it is, with all the information there, and the organism simply attuned to it; the Establishment reflects a belief in the constructive powers of the mind, with the external world simply a trigger for activities and operations that are largely built into the organism. Depending upon whose view holds sway, cognitive studies will look quite different.

From one vantage point, the dispute between the Establishment and the ecological school can be depressing. Here we are, two thousand years after the first discussions about perception, several hundred years after the philosophical debates between the empiricists and the rationalists first raged, and leading scientists are still disagreeing about fundamentals. Though the current debate cannot be mapped directly onto other debates —nominalist versus realist, empiricist versus rationalist, unconscious inference versus sensory registration versus "pickup" of relevant information—the themes are familiar enough, and the arguments frequent enough, as to make one question whether there has been progress.

Yet once one transcends these statements of position—in very spare form—one finds far more agreement. Both schools certainly believe that our knowledge of the mechanisms of perception has been enhanced over the past decades. We know much more now about how perception of the world comes about than we did fifty years ago, and a good deal of credit for this knowledge accrues to Gibson himself. Disagreements about a research program lie in whether the study of organisms and environments can suffice or whether an additional layer of analysis is necessary. Marr and his colleagues have made a strong case for the proposition that perception can only be understood if the nature of the problem involved in vision is analyzed explicitly—an approach requiring logical and mathematical considerations—and if attempts are made to try to realize these considerations in terms of a well-specified model.

It seems to me that this question can be—and likely will be—resolved by future research: by ascertaining whether the Gibsonian approach is capable of handling more complex aspects of scene recognition and object recognition, or whether it requires the kinds of inferential and intentional mechanisms postulated by the Establishment. Or, to put it the other way around, the conclusion will depend equally on whether the Establishment's promissory approach actually can help us to understand the gannet in flight or the infant moving about its playpen.

Possible Reconciliations

Neisser's Ecological Approach

Recently two trends, occurring in contrasting corners of the cognitive sciences, hold promise for the reconciliation between the two perspectives outlined here. One trend embodied in the recent work of Ulric Neisser (1976, 1984) is clearly in a top-down direction. Once the prototypical cognitive psychologist, Neisser has become increasingly impatient with those artificial laboratory studies and information-processing accounts that have become the mainstay of his discipline. Following some years as Gibson's colleague, Neisser has become a moderate convert to the ecological stance. The form of this conversion consists less in a doctrinaire endorsement of Gibson's particular concepts than in a commitment to study the kinds of behavior that interested him under the "real world" conditions he favored. Thus, as noted in chapter 5, Neisser calls for studies of perception as it unfolds when an organism is making its way around the world; studies of recognition and classification of complex real world objects as they are encountered in the environment, rather than of contrived objects encountered in lab settings; and studies of memory of one's early history or of complex experiences in the natural world. Neisser hopes that, from a wedding of the concerns of cognitive science with the naturalistic approach laid out by the Gibson school, one may end up with a science fully equal to the species.

Parallel Processing in Perception

The other recent trend, which may help to moderate the Gibson-Establishment dispute, is distinctly in the bottom-up tradition. I have in mind a new wave of artificial-intelligence attempts to study the process of visual perception. Inspired by Marr's example, but diverging from it in significant respects, a sizable number of scientists are now investigating visual-processing systems modeled closely on the primate nervous system (Ballard, Hinton, and Sejnowski 1983; Brown 1984; Feldman 1981; Grossberg 1980; Hinton and Anderson 1981; Hinton, Sejnowski, and Ackley 1984; Hofstadter 1983; Rumelhart and McClelland 1982; Waldrop 1984). These approaches—variously called "parallel visual computation," "neo-associationism," "neo-connectionism," or "massive parallel processing systems" (M.P.P.S.)—begin with a critique of standard computer simulation of vision, which uses serial "von Neumann–style" symbolic processing. In their view, it makes far more sense to simulate vision by using (physical or virtual) machines involving many independent processors (perhaps as many as a million) carrying out many processes at one moment in time. Such parallel systems take the Marr scheme much further than he explicitly went. To the notion of different modules carrying out their own separate analyses, one now adds the notion of many units operating and exchanging information in ways analogous to many brain cells or columns firing simultaneously. Computation is performed by excitatory and inhibitory interactions among a network of relatively simple neuronlike units, which compete and cooperate so that certain units become active and others are suppressed. Eventually, thanks to statistical properties of the ensemble, the network settles into a state that reflects its particular "task" —for example, perceiving a given image.

In these M.P.P.S.'s, memory and perception occur in a distributed fashion: that is, instead of there being a single central control, or the complex passing of information between modules, many units operate simultaneously and achieve their effects statistically. The multiple connections allow much of the knowledge of the entire system to be applied in any instance of recognition or problem solving. There are other advantages to a distributed representation. No information inheres in a specific locus; thus, even though many units (or cells) may be destroyed, the relevant memory or concept continues to exist. Also, because of the widespread distribution of information, it is possible to arrive at a decision even if a match turns out to be noisy, or incomplete, or approximate. These properties seem closer to the kinds of search and decision organisms must carry out in a complex and often chaotic natural world.

An important feature of the M.P.P.S. approach is that it dispenses with some of the staples of artificial intelligence as the latter has been customarily conceived (and as it most annoyed Gibson). Central to the classical Newell-Simon view is the positing of symbolic structures, upon which operations are performed in a specified order, as the result of a decision procedure. In this new dispensation, it may be possible to dispose with *any* notion of symbolic processing and, instead, to model perception in a more direct fashion—just neurons connected to other neurons and dedicated to specific functions. Instead of the need for a separate knowledge store, knowledge (and even "intelligence") simply inheres in the strength and appropriateness of the connections between simple neuronlike processes. And, indeed, the machine concepts involved in this new approach bear provocative analogies to the primate brain.

In some ways, the parallel-processing approach seems a throwback to the first days (or even the gestation period) of cognitive science. The kinds of neural network being simulated resemble those that first drew McCulloch and Pitts's attention to the relations between the nervous system and the logical calculus. The desire to model the brain directly is reminiscent of early attempts to build computers that realized Hebb-type cell assemblies and phase sequences. The statistical "pandemoniumlike" aspects of these models and the clear absence of controlling "executive processes" contrast with the logical step-by-step difference-reducing programs that came to be perfected by Newell and Simon in their General Problem Solver. Yet, because of the greater rigor with which the networks are specified, and enhanced understanding of the problems involved in image processing, these approaches may be viewed as a tentative synthesis between the classical and the Marr approaches, rather than simply as a regressive force. Indeed, the facts that several of the algorithms have successfully simulated aspects of visual perception, and that the operation of these systems seems consistent with what is known about the operation of the primate visual system, give hope that such parallel systems may eventually serve as reasonably complete simulations of early visual perception.

In spite of the recent excitement about massive parallel processing systems, they leave questions unanswered. While these systems can accomplish much more in a short period of time, speed alone does not ensure understanding: the fundamental questions about the nature of perception (and of other systems) must continue to be raised and addressed. Basic computational and definitional issues do not vanish just because of speed or brute force. There remain unresolved questions about how the numerous independent processors manage to work together and whether they can simulate behavior that is truly sequential—for example, eye movements. As in Gibson's work, questions also arise concerning the extent to which mechanisms of this sort can be adapted to more complex forms of problem solving, of the sort that has classically been simulated by symbolmanipulating von Neumann machines.

In fact, some authorities have raised the intriguing notion that the brain (and hence the computer) might be most effectively thought of as entailing two *different* systems: one, massively parallel, engaged in such probablistic endeavors as object recognition: the other, sequential, dedicated to symbolic manipulation, rendering dichotomous judgments, and engaged in such deterministic activities as logical problem solving (Kosslyn 1984; Fahlman, Hinton, and Sejnowski 1983).

How does the new approach of M.P.P.S. speak to the issues being debated by the Gibsonians and the Establishmentarians? Paradoxically, the parallelists are using the mechanisms most clearly associated with the Establishment view—powerful electronic computers—in order to put forth a view of perception closer to that embraced by Gibson. He did not live long enough to pass judgment on this new approach to the simulation of vision. But several features of the new approach—its fidelity to the mechanics of the brain, its spurning of complex symbol manipulation or intricate decision procedures about what step to carry out next, its importation of vast amounts of real world knowledge, and its suggestions about how Gestalt phenomena might emerge from the competition and cooperation of various neural networks—have a Gibsonian ring to them. Moreover, to the extent that such efforts actually result in an effective simulation of vision, in a way that seems concordant with the human nervous system, the need for theoretical discussions about the "right way" to think of perception may become increasingly academic. (But see Fodor 1984 for an alternative view.)

In any case, if either of these rival schools—or one like them—turns out to be successful, then the problems of visual perception will have been largely resolved. The Marr-Ullman approach will represent more of a triumph for cognitive science: it is a self-constructed dialogue among several participant disciplines, no one of which can hold the answer to the puzzles alone; and it draws explicitly on cognitive science concepts such as representation and symbolic operations. If the Gibsonian approach were to triumph, it would call into question the need for much cognitive-science baggage; it would constitute more of an explanation in a classical psychobiological or psychophysical framework. The M.P.P.S. approach falls somewhere in between: the technology of cognitive science in the service of a view of perception which is closer to neurology than to psychology.

In my own view, Gibson's work is a logical place in which to begin the study of perception: his ecological perspective provides vital information concerning the phenomena of perception and the kinds of information in the environment to which any perceptual apparatus must be sensitive. In Marr's terms, Gibson helps us to understand the nature of the computational task involved in perception. But Gibson's work proves of limited help in understanding the actual steps involved in perceiving specific objects. In contrast, Marr has put forth a plausible account of how an organism may actually proceed from intensities of light to the parsing of the objects in a scene. He has provided a mechanistic account of perception which seems internally coherent and consistent as well with converging evidence drawn from several cognitive disciplines. And even if his particular account turns out to be wrong or incomplete, or if the approach of the parallel processors carries the day, he has defined the likely parameters for future debates about early visual perception. So, in the terms I have used in this chapter: even if Marr is wrong about the extent to which bottom-up analysis can occur before top-down factors have to be invoked, he has made a persuasive case for the importance of the symbolic or representational level of information processing. As I see it, the burden of proof is now on the Gibsonians.

Even if Marr (or the parallel-processing school) is right, and we can account for the perception of objects with relatively little recourse to knowledge about the external world, still it is patent that the recognition of objects, or even groups of objects, marks just the beginning of the cognitive enterprise. Any student of cognition must be concerned with what happens to these initial perceptions when they are invoked in planning, problem solving, or simple recollection: one must concern oneself with the way in which organisms determine the identities of objects, how to classify them, and how to reason about them. These even more challenging puzzles will occupy the following chapters.

11

Mental Imagery: A Figment of the Imagination?

Now we have already discussed imagination in the treatise *On the Soul* and we concluded there that thought is impossible without an image.

—ARISTOTLE

Introduction: Images through the Ages

Assuming a behaviorist pose vis-à-vis other organisms makes a certain sense. After all, since one cannot have access to the internal experiences and sensations of an animal or another person, it may be wise to suspend judgment about these experiences and to concentrate instead on activities that are manifest or at least readily measurable. But when contemplating one's own mental processes, exclusive perseveration on overt behavior seems unjustifiable. A psychologist may be disinclined to attribute images, hallucinations, or dreams to other individuals, but it seems self-delusion —a doubt even Descartes would have spurned—to deny these in one's own phenomenal experience. And then, once one has accepted one's own images, a new puzzle arises: Can one continue to withhold them from others?

It is not surprising, therefore, that most students of mental processes, from the time of the Greeks on, have singled out for study the capacity to conjure up in one's "mind's eye" various objects, scenes, and experiences—entities that are not present in one's surroundings (and may never have existed at all). At first philosophers, then armchair psychologists, and finally the first generation of experimental psychologists were all keen to explore mental imagery.

Why this interest in imagery? Seeing or touching the world of objects can be fascinating, once one begins to think about it, but a person could certainly pass through life without giving such experiences a further thought: they are as evident as the prose unknowingly spoken by Molière's bourgeois gentleman. But when it comes to experiences that, however vivid to oneself, are not accessible to other individuals, intriguing questions arise. It is easy to understand why one should be equipped to react to things in one's environment—how else would one survive?—but what end is served by experiences that are completely private? Is this process adaptive or can it be damaging? Why does one dream? Can one imagine anything at all and, if not, what are the limits? Does imagery occur in the same way as normal perception, merely activating perceptual structures by internal means instead of by a stimulus—or does it marshal different mental processes? To what extent can one exert control over one's imagery—and is it possible to influence the imagery of others?

The first psychologists made the study of internal imagery central in their discipline. Followers of Wundt probed their own internal imagery and painstakingly analyzed self-reports by their trained subjects. And yet hardly a quarter-century had elapsed before grave doubts were raised about the status of mental imagery as a partner fit to participate in polite psychological publications. Thanks to the skeptical accounts emerging from Würzburg, the more ephemeral and less reliable aspects of imagery were underlined. Not everyone had images, it turned out, and those who did introspected about them in different ways. There was no reliable way to define imagery in an experimental situation, no agreement about what should count as an imagistic or imaginary experience. Certainly a new science ought not to embrace such a vague and fuzzy concept as a principal mental construct, let alone as an explanation of the way in which people think. For such reasons, the ghostly image was exorcised for half a century from respectable academic psychology.

In the early 1970s, however, with behaviorism on the wane, psychologists began to report findings that were difficult to think or write about except in terms of imagery (Paivio 1971). Perhaps the most dramatic studies were carried out by Roger Shepard and his colleagues at Stanford University. In an oft-cited study, which I reviewed in chapter 5, he and

Jacqueline Metzler (1971) exposed subjects to geometric figures and asked them to indicate as rapidly as possible whether the two figures were actually representations of the same object as seen from different vantage points.

But, strikingly, the difficulty of the task (as measured by the time it took to give a response) proved readily predictable in terms of the number of degrees by which the second figure had been rotated. Thus, a figure that had been rotated eighty degrees took longer to specify as identical to the target than one rotated fifty degrees, but a model rotated one hundred degrees proved even more difficult to specify as identical to the target than had the former two. It was tempting to conclude that the subjects were mentally rotating these figures, and that the greater the distance of the rotations, the longer the road to a correct response. Moreover, there was no need just to conjecture, because the subjects themselves verified this account. It seemed reasonable—indeed, almost inescapable—to conclude that human beings generate mental images of these forms and rotate them through some as yet undefined mental space.

According to Stephen Kosslyn (1980), possibly the major contemporary student of imagery, Shepard's findings caused a sensation in the cognitive community. The data were striking and systematic, apparently reflecting a basic capacity of the cognitive system. Moreover, these elusive internal images turned out to yield a psychophysical law that was simple yet robust: time to judge identity (or non-identity) was a monotonic function of the physical distance between the forms. One of the least tangible constructs in psychology had yielded a scientific law of striking precision.

There were other reasons for the excitement. In light of Shepard's results, it made sense to think of an individual as having pictures in his head. He never employed this expression, which cannot be construed in a sensible manner anyway; but he made respectable the idea of an analogue mode of mental representation, a mode capturing certain of the relations of proximity that can also be perceived in the physical world. Shepard's results called into question current efforts to explain all of thought in terms of one kind of computational mechanism—that of the serial, digital computer which processes one kind of information. The typical approach of this era had held that information is represented in the brain in lists or networks of propositional information. But this approach—that what we know consists of lists or of propositions—seems utterly inadequate to account for the mental rotation findings and phenomena. Instead, it made more sense to think of the brain as passing through an ordered series of states, which mimic ordinary processes when physical stimuli are being observed in the world. Imagery should be thought of in its own terms, rather than as a cryptic version of verbal mediation or symbolic manipulation. Perhaps there were two separate and equally valid forms of mental representation. And perhaps a study of the less familiar imagistic mode might help to clarify some of the later stages of visual perception—and do so in a way different from either a neurological or an ecological perspective.

Stephen Kosslyn's Model

Taking off from these and other equally beguiling findings, Kosslyn and his colleagues have undertaken three major and coordinated lines of work (Kosslyn et al. 1979). First of all, they have added to the file of empirical evidence that favors the existence and flexibility of mental imagery. In a set of extremely ingenious experiments, the Kosslyn team has delineated major properties of the imagery system.

To convey the Kosslyn approach, let me introduce a representative study (Kosslyn, Ball, and Reiser 1978). Subjects are shown a map containing seven fictional locations—a rock, a tree, a beach, a patch of grass, a well, a hut, and a lake. After having had a chance to familiarize themselves with the map, one is asked to imagine the map in one's mind and then to answer various questions about it. For example, one is asked to focus on one location in the map and then to look for a second one. Assuming that the second location is on the map, a subject is directed to picture a little black speck moving as rapidly as possible from the first to the second point and then to push a button. When one cannot find the named second location, one is asked to push a second button.

Kosslyn found that the time to scan from location A to location B was a linear function of the distance between the two sites on the map. Apparently the subjects were scanning a mental image, just as one would scan the physically present map. As a check that the subjects were not simply using a propositional representation or a mental list of the locations, subjects were seen in a second condition. Now one was simply asked to indicate whether a named location was on the map. It turned out that, under this condition, there was no hint of a distance effect. Evidently subjects just consulted a list in this instance. Thus, it seems most unlikely that subjects were employing some propositional representation in the first study: for, if they had been, the results on both experiments should have been identical (Kosslyn 1983, p. 46).

What of other results demonstrated by the Kosslyn group? It takes more time to survey an image of a large object than an image of a small one; more time to survey an image that travels in a third dimension than one that only cuts across a flat plane; more time to see small details on an image than large ones; and it is more difficult to imagine objects known to be hidden or concealed by a barrier than ones known to be in a visible position. Ever sensitive to the possibility that subjects may be reasoning (rather than imagining) their ways to the correct answer, Kosslyn and his colleagues have paid particular attention to experimental conditions where subjects could not have known the correct answer. They have discovered that subjects perceive imagistic effects that even scientists could not predict from a verbal description of the task, but that individuals placed in the actual concrete situation will reliably experience. On the other hand, there are some effects—for example, certain afterimages—that individuals will perceive when confronted with actual displays but that turn out not to be experienced when one is asked to imagine the customary eliciting circumstances. These latter lines of research support the independent validity of imagery. If individuals always behaved as their knowledge dictated—using images just in those cases where they *thought that they should*—then they would not display such paradoxical effects.

Having demonstrated a massive number of results putatively due to some form of mental imagery, Kosslyn and his colleagues have gone on to devise a comprehensive theory of this capacity. While not boldly claiming that human beings have pictures in their heads, these researchers defend the notion of a "quasi-pictorial" form of mental representation called "imagery." In their view, this form of mental representation is as important for an understanding of cognition as is the more usually invoked propositional form.

Here the plot thickens. Many psychologists would be content to allow imagery back into the psychologist's lexicon and even permit it to be used as a "local explanatory construct" for certain reliable findings. But when talk shifts to imagery as a basic property of human cognition—as a primary way in which information can be symbolized or represented—then psychologists and other cognitivists grow much more cautious. After all, if as elusive a concept as an image is allowed to serve as a psychological explanation, then on what basis can other "pretenders" be excluded? For their part, philosophers also begin to get nervous: What does it mean "to have an image" or to read information off an image? What can an image in the head be anyway? (Block 1981*a*).

According to the Kosslyn account, images have two major components: the surface representation is the quasi-pictorial entity in the active memory that is accompanied by the subjective (Kosslyn's term) experience of having an image. The images are likened to displays produced on a cathode-ray tube by a computer program operating on stored data. In other words, the images are temporary spatial displays in active memory that are generated from more abstract representations housed in long-term memory.

These initial abstract representations consist of propositions and other kinds of non-imagistic information, such as that embodied in concepts. Thus, in the generation of imagery, there is an interplay between descriptive (languagelike) and depictive (picturelike) memories. But the quasi-pictorial image is not merely an epiphenomenal concomitant of more abstract nonpictorial processing. Rather, by drawing on long-term memory, one can generate images, chunk them in various ways, subject them to various transformations, and classify them in terms of semantic categories (for example, a particular imagistic configuration can be parsed as a person's nose or as the state of New Hampshire). Kosslyn speaks of a mind's-eye–like device which is necessary to interpret images or parts thereof: indeed, in his view, any representational system must include some sort of interpretive device (Kosslyn 1978). And he stresses that information is stored in images that are not languagelike but "bear a non-arbitrary correspondence to the thing being represented" (1981, p. 46). In sum, Kosslyn's model includes a cathode-ray tubelike display medium, techniques for forming an image on the display, and techniques for interpreting and transforming information in such a display.

Computer Simulation

Nowadays, in psychology, when one has a detailed description of a process, it is desirable (as well as fashionable) to attempt to develop a computer model of it—as Kosslyn and his collaborators have set out to do. They posit two kinds of data structures. The first consists of a *surface matrix* which represents the image itself. This image-data structure is represented by a configuration of points on a matrix. The matrix corresponds to a *visual buffer,* a spatial medium used to support the representations that make possible seeing during perception as well as during imaging. A quasi-pictorial image is achieved as a person selectively fills in certain cells of this matrix. The image depicts information about spatial extent, brightness, and contrast; it has limited resolution, causing contours to be obscured if an object is too small. The matrix corresponds to short-term visual memory; and, therefore, representations within it are transient and can be maintained only through effort.

The second set of data structures consists of the long-term memory files, which represent the information used in generating images. One kind of representation stores visual information about the literal appearance of an object, such as how something looks; included is information on the object as viewed in a number of different ways. The second type of long-term representation is a set of facts about the imaged objects. These facts are represented discursively, in a propositional format: included is such information as the names of the most highly associated superordinate categories and a classification of the object's size. These sets of data structures are then used in three imaging processes: routines for generating surface images, for classifying these images or parts thereof, and for transforming images.

In a highly schematic example, Kosslyn and his colleagues illustrate how these data sources and processes get mobilized in a program. For example, in generating a detailed image of a chair, the IMAGE procedure first constructs a skeletal image of the chair and then searches for factual information stored in long-term memory for the names of parts that go in the chair. It may find, for example, that chairs have cushions, and that these are the foundation part of the chair. PUT and FIND procedures then locate the relevant part of the image (the seat) by means of a set of procedures describing the seat. Once the seat has been found, a FIND operation passes back Cartesian coordinate information of where this part fits the image. Once the location and size are computed, an appropriate PICTURE routine is called, and the part is integrated into an overall image (Kosslyn et al. 1979, p. 542).

A chief reason for actually programming the computer, as opposed to merely producing flow charts, is that it helps one to discover the consequences of some claim and to study interactions among components (Kosslyn 1980). The fact that the simulation works also solves the homunculus problem: the program performs the integration, and there is no need for a "little man" to read the images. In some cases, Kosslyn's simulation has actually brought to light problems that were not anticipated, and has accordingly inspired a revision of the model. Thus, for example, in the original simulation there was no provision for scanning to the inactivated region of the surface matrix. Only when the program was asked to find an object in a certain image, and received an error message, did Kosslyn make needed changes in the program. In addition to calling attention to deficits in the model, the computer simulation has also suggested various new studies; these have led to further changes in the model which could be incorporated into further revision of the simulation as well.

In many ways, the Kosslyn program can be considered a prototypical cognitive-scientific enterprise. First of all, it addresses a long-standing set of philosophical issues via a systematic program of experimental research. It deals unabashedly with the level of mental representation, while avoiding many of the weaknesses of earlier attempts to posit and utilize constructs of mental imagery. Rooted in the first instance in psychology, it relies heavily on a model of computer simulation. In addition, as we shall see, there are also significant ties to work in neuroscience and in philosophy, and these are being vigorously explored at present. Many aspects of image generation—including its similarities and differences from ordinary perception or ordinary memory—have been clarified. It is not that the Kosslyn group has resolved all outstanding issues about imagery: in fact, much of the work and many of the claims remain controversial. Yet, building on the work of Shepard, Paivio, and other researchers, Kosslyn has made the study of imagery a respectable topic within cognitive science and illuminated crucial facets of this mode of mental representation. Imagery is now central in any cognitive map of the discipline.

The Debate about the Kosslyn-Shepard Perspective

Probably no research in recent cognitive studies has generated so much controversy as work on imagery. And because Kosslyn has been eager to talk of mental imagery as a form of representation, and has devoted much energy to the development, revision, and popularization of his model, discussion has focused on his own claims. Indeed, not only was there a major "target" article in *The Behavioral and Brain Sciences* (1979) on Kosslyn's work, complete with twenty-five responses by leading cognitive scientists, but several major philosophical works have reviewed imagery in considerable detail (Block 1981a; Dennett 1978; Fodor 1975).

Like any contribution that attracts widespread attention, Kosslyn's work has been criticized at almost every level, from the naïveté of the theorizing, to the mystique surrounding mental imagery, to the possibility that the experimental sample includes only those subjects who are suggestible, influenced by the instructions, or liable to confabulate their testimony about imagery. (See the response to Kosslyn et al. 1979 in *The Behavioral and Brain Sciences,* as well as Kosslyn 1980 and 1983 and Pylyshyn 1984.) Kosslyn, in turn, has written extensively on each of these lines of criticism and has, in the opinion of many observers, given satisfactory responses.

Some of Kosslyn's responses have taken the form of studies that speak to specific criticisms. For example, he was criticized because his model did not handle three-dimensional aspects of images. His student Steven Pinker proceeded to show that, having surveyed a three-dimensional scene, subjects imagined in three dimensions: that is, the time taken by subjects to scan among objects decreased in proportion to the actual three-dimensional distances between the objects and not in proportion to the two-dimensional distances captured in a photographic representation of the scene (Kosslyn 1983, p. 154). Kosslyn was also challenged because his subjects may have had previous propositional knowledge about some of the effects they reported: in this case, imagistic explanations need not be invoked. Accordingly, Ronald Finke, another associate of Kosslyn, studied a phenomenon—the perception of complementary colors as afterimages—about which nonpsychologists are ignorant (Finke and Schmidt 1978). Despite their ignorance, subjects asked to imagine the phenomenon reported precisely the same afterimages as do naïve individuals confronted with a "real life" presentation. Finally, Kosslyn's overall position has been bolstered by Martha Farah's finding (1984) that at least one of the components of his model—the image-generation component—can be destroyed in isolation by damage to the brain. Moreover, and in surprising contradiction to what the literature on brain laterality suggests, the image-generation component seems to be found in the posterior portions of the left (and not the right) hemisphere of the human brain.

There have been other criticisms as well. Some scholars have questioned the meaning of key terms in Kosslyn's model and have voiced the charge of theoretical looseness. For example, the term *quasi-pictorial,* as applied to an image, seems a clear case of wanting to exploit the connotation of *picture* without paying the price for it. There have also been general criticisms about the ecological validity of Kosslyn's research program. Ulric Neisser expresses this point of view:

> Why does the theory suggested here strike the reader as clever rather than insightful, as cute model making rather than serious psychology. I think it is because the thinking of Kosslyn and his collaborators is completely detached from everything we know about human action or perception. . . . It attempts to "account for" a sharply restricted body of experimental results (usually reaction latencies) by relating it to an equally restricted class of models (usually computer programs of something similar). (Quoted in Kosslyn et al. 1979, p. 560)

Perhaps because of the fertile experimentation emanating from Kosslyn's laboratory, the most telling lines of criticisms do not focus on the phenomena or the findings, which seem reasonably robust, but are rather directed toward his claim that there exists a separate form of representation called imagery, that it exhibits its own properties and operates independently of the canonical form of representation in propositions. Some commentators, like John Anderson and Philip Johnson-Laird, have questioned the status of these claims. Based on certain considerations of logic, Anderson has claimed that, for every line of experimentation, one can develop explanations in terms of either propositions or of imagery, and there is no principled way to ascertain which is correct. Anderson concludes that "barring decisive physiological data, it will not be possible to establish whether an internal representation is pictorial or propositional" (1978, p. 249). Johnson-Laird does not accept Anderson's proof but says that it is unlikely that imagery disputes will be settled by psychological experiment. In his view, a more productive discussion should revolve around levels of representation. Although at one level a psychological process may use only strings of symbols, at a higher level it may use various sorts of representation, including arrays, dot matrices, and the like. For various purposes, including the solving of certain kinds of problems, it may be reasonable for humans to use mental images or, as Johnson-Laird prefers to call them, "mental models" (Johnson-Laird 1983).

Pylyshyn's Penetrating Case against Imagery

Other commentators, however, argue that Kosslyn's claims are simply wrong. Probably his most tenacious and probing opponent is the Canadian computer scientist and psychologist Zenon Pylyshyn who has published approximately a dozen major articles, all designed to refute the claim that imagery merits consideration as a separate form of mental representation. Like a persistent lawyer, Pylyshyn attacks Kosslyn at every level of analysis and for every aspect of his studies (Pylyshyn 1979, 1981, 1984). But the nub of his critique has to do with the tenability of Kosslyn's claim that human beings can think—can solve problems or reason—by making use of a separate medium called imagery. If there were such a biological function as imagery, it would be a fixed human capacity: in fact, individuals would *have* to use the medium of imagery in order to solve certain kinds of problem. But, in Pylyshyn's view, imagery is simply a product of symbolically encoded rules and propositions, like beliefs and goals. In other words, an individual has available lots of knowledge encoded in propositions and simply draws on these propositions in order to construct what appears on phenomenal evidence to be an image (Pylyshyn 1981, 1984).

Pylyshyn's complex argument is worth following because it represents widespread views of how to conduct cognitive science and how to conceptualize the mind. He begins with the flat assertion that cognition *is* computation: the computer is not just a metaphor for the brain, but the mind computes in a literal fashion. He goes on to distinguish two fundamentally different explanations for the behavior of a system (1984, p. 210). The first appeals to *intrinsic properties* of the system, to processes that reflect the operation of natural laws. (This is the level J. J. Gibson was actually exploring.) The second explanatory form appeals to *external properties*—to properties of the external world which the system must be able somehow to represent. In this latter case, the explanatory principles have to take into account the goals and beliefs of the system. This second form, which touches on inferences rather than on reactions, particularly engages the cognitivist. Here we enter the land of Chomsky and Fodor.

In explicating intrinsic properties, Pylyshyn has coined the term *functional architecture* to refer to basic information-processing mechanisms of the system for which a nonrepresentational account suffices. The functional architecture includes the basic operations permitted by the biological system, as well as such built-in constraints as the size of the memory, the capacity of a buffer, the list of permissible operations, and the like. The functional architecture cannot vary in ways that demand a cognitive explanation (in terms of goals, beliefs, representations, and the like). Rather, differences in cognitive phenomena can themselves be explained by appealing to the different arrangements that can obtain among the fixed set of operations.

The notion of functional architecture allows Pylyshyn to cleave apart two fundamentally different types of processes: those whose explanations require appeal to certain kinds of representations, and those whose explanations do not. Those processes requiring appeal to the representational level are termed *cognitively penetrable:* they can be (and routinely are) affected by an individual's symbolic processes, including beliefs, wishes, and the like. Countenancing inferences, they fall outside the functional architecture. In contrast are those capacities that are *cognitively impenetrable:* part of the functional architecture, these processes are carried out in an automatic and encapsulated way, impervious to an individual's particular beliefs. Impenetrable capacities can be likened to the hardware built into a computer; penetrable capacities are programmable, hence subject to change.

It would be desirable if the human cognitive repertoire were largely impenetrable: then one could explain many processes as occurring necessarily, courtesy of neural wiring. It turns out, however, that much of human cognition is penetrable. And, in particular, in Pylyshyn's view, imagery turns out to be *cognitively penetrable:* rather than being a requirement of a certain kind of cognitive system (a part of the hardware), it can be changed in all kinds of ways simply by one's giving (propositional) instructions to oneself. If the results reported by Kosslyn were supposed to contribute to our knowledge of how the mind works, these functions must be cognitively impenetrable: they must always apply when imagery is putatively involved. But one can, in fact, claims Pylyshyn, change such functions: they are cognitively penetrable. Put concretely, you can make your attention jump from place to place in an image as easily as you can make your scanning speed change—evidence that these activities are at the behest of one's ideas and beliefs.

Pylyshyn revisits Kosslyn's map-location task but interprets it in a different vein. Where Kosslyn believes that a subject is focusing on one point after another in a mental image, Pylyshyn believes that the subject is simply imagining the "real life" situation and how one would behave in it. Thus, the experiment is probing tacit knowledge of the depicted situation rather than perception of (or within) an imaginal medium. More generally, the fact that information in an image is always labeled suggests that the representation must have been interpreted before it was generated. In Pylyshyn's view, the surface display dominating Kosslyn's theory serves little function; its elements and its interpretation are at the behest of a subject's goals, beliefs, and efforts. There are no intrinsic properties of the surface display: *all* are interpreted and subject to alteration (Pylyshyn 1979, p. 562).

Pylyshyn concludes that it is best to think in terms of one set of processes that are biologically determined—built into the hardware, so to speak—and of another set of abstract symbols or propositions that can simply be manipulated by a set of rules in a computer program. Images are not built into the hardware and thus ought to be considered as epiphenomena secondary to the manipulation of symbolic elements.

But Kosslyn will not be drawn into Pylyshyn's particular distinctions. He prefers to avoid reference to underlying abstract propositions and to refer instead to various forms of representation—such as verbal and imaginal varieties. Instead of the possibly misguided search for an irreducible form of representation, Kosslyn finds it preferable to posit the internal representations most effective in accounting for empirical findings. In fact, the issue is not whether images may be derived from more primitive propositional or symbolic representations, but rather whether a quasi-pictorial image has emergent properties permitting its treatment as a distinctive form of representation. Efforts to explain all of the imagery results reported earlier in terms of a propositional or symbolic code turn out to be clumsy and roundabout, whereas the kind of model developed by Kosslyn handles the current results neatly and also predicts suggestive new ones. Pylyshyn may believe that his theory is more parsimonious because he posits only one mode of mental representation, but Kosslyn's theory can readily handle a whole range of data which Pylyshyn is unable to address in a satisfying manner.

In this extended debate, Pylyshyn represents the mainstream of computer scientists who have a long-standing commitment to a digital symbol-computing model, where operations upon strings of symbols are the way in which information is processed. He places a great deal of stock in this symbol-centered approach:

The notion of a discrete atomic symbol is the basis of all formal understanding. Indeed, it is the basis of all systems of thought, expression or calculation for which a *notation* is available. . . . No one has succeeded in defining any other type of atom from which formal understanding can be derived. Small wonder, then, that many of us are reluctant to dispense with this foundation in cognitive psychology under frequent exhortations to accept symbols with such varied intrinsic properties as continuous or analogue properties. (1984, p. 51)

Pylyshyn finds a disturbing circularity in the claims for imagery. In his view, a theory of cognitive processes should explain how imagery comes to have its putative powers. One would need to show that there is an imaginal mode of processing which is indeed an inviolable property of cognition (having to do with the structure of the brain) and has to be employed in order to answer questions about locations and distances and the like. But, as Pylyshyn sees it, Kosslyn simply *assumes* a medium of imagery and then purports to explain its character by indicating the ways in which imagery works—the kinds of operation in which images are involved. Pylyshyn concludes that the question about Kosslyn's work is "whether we are entitled to take certain specific empirical regularities as revealing general constraints arising from the nature of the . . . representational *medium* or *format,* or whether such regularities are the consequences of what the subjects believe, what they take their goals to be" (1980*b*, p. 162).

For his part, Kosslyn concedes that there is a basic propositional level of coding, from which images may well be generated, at least in part. He takes his "anti-reductionist" or "anti-monist" stand on the legitimacy and importance of a separate mode of representation which can be productive in its own right. Not only do mental images play a causal role in thinking but, once formed, they remain encoded in a form that can then be put to various uses. Pylyshyn's notions are simply not productive: for example, despite his criteria of cognitive impenetrability, he is not able to give examples of any process (beyond the most elementary perceptual ones) that is insensitive to beliefs, wishes, and other intentional phenomena. Kosslyn has the weight of experimental evidence on his side, for when he makes claims about imagery, or offers a simulation, he can invoke a great deal of supportive data. In fact, as I have noted, neural evidence can now be cited in support of Kosslyn's model. Of course, since Pylyshyn is trying to make a basic conceptual point, he is not likely to be persuaded by yet another study or empirical demonstration.

To my own way of thinking, Kosslyn has the stronger line of argument within the empirical cognitive sciences. If one is trying to model the way the mind works, and a certain line of modeling consistently produces rich and revealing results, then it is folly to dismiss that line just because of some theoretical objections—which would be very hard to disprove. (Indeed, in my own view, further research might well reveal several imagery systems, analogous to the one described for the visual system, but capturing and transforming other kinds of information, such as linguistic, musical, or tactile.) Moreover, as Ned Block (1983) has pointed out, the various questions anti-imagists have raised about the difficulty of finding images (or "quasi-pictures") in the mind can actually be leveled against the propositionalists as well. After all, it is hardly obvious what it would mean for there to be propositions in the mind; it is just that the idea is somewhat less vivid (somewhat less imagistic!) and may therefore be somewhat easier to swallow.

But if Kosslyn's approach seems reasonable enough within the mainstream of cognitive science, it has raised considerable hackles within the wider philosophical community. Philosophers have raised the problem of what it means when one begins to use the term *imagery* and falls readily (and nonreflectively) into the use of various associated expressions: scanning the image, focusing on particulars thereof, transforming the image, and the like. Since it is clear that there are no pictures (or even any "quasi-pictures") in the mind (who or what is there to see them? what is the medium of the picture? and so on), the question must be raised just what is gained, and what is risked, by elaborating on this metaphor (Schwartz 1981). Georges Rey (1981) poses some unsettling questions. He asks of images, which appear to exist in two dimensions, in what kind of space do they live? Is the mental image really as brilliantly colored as the "live" physical configuration? He also challenges Kosslyn's seductive model. Cathode-ray tubes are perceived by human eyes, but surely there is no further eye located in the recesses of the brain. People often report that they see things that do not really exist—perhaps on this score, what one should try to do is to explain what people report, including their recital of images, rather than try to study images that may not exist in any meaningful sense.

A Wittgensteinian Critique

Pushing this line of criticism yet further is William Shebar (1979), a philosophy student who worked with Kosslyn and then subjected some of his ideas to a Wittgensteinian critique. As I noted in chapter 4, Wittgenstein had little regard for psychological theorizing: in his view, concepts were often adopted unwittingly from certain seductive features of our language. Thus, a Wittgensteinian approach calls for careful attention to the language involved in such expressions as "imagining" or "having an image," and is skeptical about images as an explanatory construct within psychology.

As Shebar puts it, a careful look at the language involved in talking about images reveals the many traps concealed therein. One should not think of an image as a thing, for what kind of a thing is it? It is preferable instead to talk about the action of imagining, which is something that individuals legitimately do. You can tell someone to imagine a house—because that is something that people can do—but you cannot tell someone to "see a house," for seeing is a different kind of action from imagining, and not one subject to voluntary control. By the same token, it is equally misleading to analogize an image to a picture. One needs materials to make a picture but not to make an image; yet this form of locution leads us to think of imagery as a private slide show which we can see on the private screens of our minds. Thus, you obviously cannot draw someone else's picture, but you do have the capacity to imagine it.

Shebar objects to Kosslyn's characterizations of his results. The same results can be explained without the need for an analogy with imagery. Anyone knows that it takes longer to scan further distances on real pictures and thus, when asked to imagine this process, conceives of it along the same lines. The fact that it takes a longer time to press the button does not imply the existence of a particular process called imagery—or a particular element called an image—which is longer; it is simply an affirmation that whatever happens when one scans a longer distance takes more time.

In Shebar's view, the term *internal representation* is loaded from the start with connotations of external representations on which it is modeled. But it is not proper to talk about a hidden picture as a representation—for to whom would it represent anything if one could see it? Shebar senses a pernicious circle. Subjects are understanding the instructions given by Kosslyn by grasping the very analogy that has been used to make the predictions and is later used as an explanation for the result. As Shebar puts it, a subject's understanding of the "inner process" talk in the instructions depends upon one's grasping of the "outer" process talk on which it is modeled; and thus, one is bound to produce just those regularities that *look* like evidence for the theory.

Shebar's critique is potentially devastating for imagery studies and possibly as well for other areas of psychology which dabble in internal representation. From his perspective, psychologists think they are studying processes but are actually examining the effects of adapting a certain way of talking about things. The researchers are using a form of locution that actually reflects pretheoretical ways of discussing experience, rather than mechanisms that can actually be investigated and understood. According to this account, the problems of psychology will be solved not by newer data or more precise terminology but, rather, by the realization that they are not genuine problems.

In my view Shebar's critique is tonic, perhaps slightly toxic, but not as fatal as he might wish. There are, in fact, considerable risks in adapting a certain vocabulary, for it carries associations that may be unconscious—and, therefore, even more destructive to the users. But the cure for this problem is more careful attention to one's way of talking, more scrupulousness of one's theory, rather than necessarily abandoning a line of study. Certainly, studying how individuals perceive is worthwhile—as not even Wittgenstein would have denied; and if the appearance of internal images seems to be part of perception, or seems to have properties akin to "live" visual perception, such phenomena are worth studying also. But since those capacities are less overt, less readily subjected to intersubjective reliability, one needs to be all the more alert.

A Wittgensteinian perspective raises profound questions for cognitive science. This aspiring discipline rests on the assumption that it is valid to speak about internal representation: that is, about a separate level between the nerve cells of physiology and the behavioral norms of a community. Wittgenstein was unwilling to embrace this assumption, though he avoided simple-minded behaviorist critiques of "internal constructs" and introduced a sophisticated view of how the community provides ways of conceptualizing the world.

It might seem that studies of imagery are made to order for a Wittgensteinian critique. It is relatively straightforward to talk about an individual's perceptions of objects or about one's actions in the world; and even talk about language or music is directed toward a symbolic system that can be readily analyzed. But discussion of those inherently mysterious phenomena called mental images is bound to stimulate metaphors (like the "mind's eye") and exotic models (like a cathode-ray tube) that will differ in certain telltale respects from the phenomena being modeled. Food for philosophical lions!

Cautious cognitive scientists, such as Pylyshyn, might seem well advised to jettison talk of imagery and to retreat to firmer grounds. There is, however, another, bolder scientific ploy to which Kosslyn, Shepard, and their colleagues can lay claim. If the case for cognitive science can be made with respect to the relatively tenuous (and tendentious) phenomenon of imagery, if the Wittgensteinian critique can be met there, then the case can be readily transported to firmer ground. Viewed in this perspective, the obstacles involved in studying imagery may actually confer considerable power upon efforts undertaken successfully in this area.

Still, there is at least one sense in which Wittgensteinian skepticism could prevail. Should a persuasive case be made for a tight cognitive-scientific account of veridical perception and also for that second-order form of perception involved in mental imagery, these forms of mental activity can still be carried out wholly—or at least in large part—without reference to language and to organizing conceptual systems. (After all, it may well be that nonlinguistic animals have images; and there is little doubt that they perceive in ways similar to human beings.) But any cognitive science worth its name will eventually have to offer accounts as well of those cognitive capacities that are heavily infiltrated or penetrated by linguistic and conceptual processes. In entering this area, cognitive scientists confront the most vexing issues within their science—and also those issues about which human beings care most deeply.

12

A World Categorized

In defining the human being as a featherless biped, the Greeks were not simply providing a succinct definition of their own species. They were exemplifying their belief that common objects of the world can be classified into groups, and that these groups can be defined by certain criterial attributes. Thus, all human beings belong to a single class called humans, and that class can be defined reliably by the whimsical phrase to which I have alluded.

Consider the set of accomplishments inhering in this terse formulation. While all living creatures respond in similar ways to entities they deem similar, these responses are typically unreflective. Noting that humans everywhere group entities together constitutes an important achievement. Realization that these categorizations can form a nested hierarchy is a further insight. For instance, a person treats different views of a terrier as instances of the same terrier; groups together all terriers; then groups terriers with poodles into the categories of dogs, dogs and cats into the category of domestic animals, and on up the hierarchy to mammals, vertebrates, animals, living things, and, simply, entities (Keil 1979). Moreover, in addition to forming and organizing categories, human beings also ferret out the traits defining each category. If one can supply a satisfactory definition of a terrier, a dog, a domestic animal, and the like, one will then have a rationale for placing every entity into one or more appropriate categories.

From the days of Aristotle, such practices of naming, defining, and categorizing have undergone philosophical scrutiny. By the middle of this century, a certain position had become entrenched as the "right way" to think about categories, concepts, and classifications (a trio of terms I shall use here interchangeably). And yet in the past thirty-five years, during the very period when cognitive science has been in the ascendancy, this view of how we categorize the world has undergone the most severe attack, until today virtually no one holds it in its pure form.

In this chapter, I shall first review the major points of the classical view of concepts and then consider the major attack on this position in the fields of psychology, anthropology, and philosophy. Today it is no exaggeration to say that the *classical* view of concepts has been replaced by a *natural* view of concepts. The new view is not without its critics, including a fair number of commentators who yearn for the less ambiguous days of the classical view, as well as radical scholars who doubt altogether the utility of inventing categorization. After surveying a range of responses to the natural view, I shall take stock of what has now been established about human classificatory practices, and how this knowledge can inform an emerging cognitive science.

The Classical View of Classification

I provided an initial glimpse of the classical view in introducing Jerome Bruner's study of how individuals learn to form or attain concepts (Bruner, Goodnow, and Austin 1956). Recall (p. 93) that subjects were asked to recognize instances of geometric concepts like *large red triangle* or *tall blue cylinder*. In such cases, a category was arbitrarily defined (any set of attributes could have been targeted), and each item unambiguously fitted (or failed to fit) into that category. The traditional recipe: a category and a set of defining features, just like the featherless biped. Nor was this point of view restricted to experimental cognitive psychology. Philosophers' favorite definitions of concepts adhered to the same procedure: a bachelor is an unmarried adult male. Anthropologists looked for similar structures in their studies of kinship (an uncle is male, of an older generation, and not a direct lineal antecedent). Even in the area of neuroscience, a search was on for detectors that registered unambiguously to all lines that were oriented in a certain direction but to none otherwise oriented.

Playing a classicist to the classical theory, I shall lay out its defining features (see Smith and Medin 1981):

1. Categories are arbitrary. Nothing in the world or in our nervous system determines how we must slice up our observations. Cultures and languages do this work. Items can be grouped together in any number of ways to form categories, and people can learn to identify or construct those categories defined by their culture.

2. Categories have defining or critical attributes. All members of a

category share these defining attributes, no nonmembers share them, and there is no overlap between members and nonmembers.

3. The *intension* (or set of attributes) determines the *extension* of a category (which items are members). Hence, it makes no sense to talk about a category as having an internal structure, with some items standing out as better members than other items. Either the triangle is tall and red, or it is not. Boundaries are sharp and not fuzzy.

These assumptions have been stated in bold form: one can find objections to such a sober vision of categories in writings dating back to the British empiricists. Nonetheless, some variant of this classical position was widely held until the middle of this century, when Ludwig Wittgenstein and his followers hurled a challenge which has in recent decades been reinforced by considerable behavioral-scientific work. Eleanor Rosch, possibly the cognitivist whose critique did most to undermine the classical view, described the pervasive wisdom around 1950:

> The processor was assumed to be rational, and attention was directed to the logical nature of problem-solving strategies. The "mature western mind" was presumed to be one that, in abstracting knowledge from the idiosyncracies of particular everyday experience, employed Aristologian laws of logic. When applied to categories, this meant that to know a category was to have an abstracted clear-cut, necessary, and sufficient criteria for category membership. If other thought processes, such as imagery, ostensive definition, reasoning by analogy to particular instances, or the use of metaphors were considered at all, they were usually relegated to lesser beings such as women, children, primitive people, or even to nonhumans. (Rosch and Lloyd 1978, p. 2)

In one sense, this classical view of categorization was consonant with the aura of cognitive science—a science built upon the unambiguity of the computer. But just as the general view of the computer as a single all-purpose logical machine eventually gave way to a plurality of computational stances, so, too, this general view of classification was not able to withstand the force of arguments and empirical data from several quarters. A strong blow against it came from work in a domain the classical view had initially adopted as its own—the area of color naming.

The Universe of Color Terms

From a purely physical point of view, there are no indices to designate where one color ends and another begins: the color spectrum (or sphere) is a continuum throughout. Yet every human group has some means of naming and labeling colors, and these means of subdividing the spectrum seem quite diverse. Some cultures have just two or three names for describing all colors; while other societies, including our own, feature a family of terms—unmodified (blue) as well as highly modified (light sky blue). Since each culture apparently carves up the color sphere as it sees fit, there are apparently no natural laws at work here. Rather, one culture decides to cut the color spectrum at a certain point (for example, at wavelength x); while another culture divides it at wavelength y, or divides it a different number of times. The task of a person within a culture is to learn the color name that that culture has arbitrarily hit upon, just as one learns the name of family members, flora and fauna, and various human artifacts, ranging from tools to forms of government.

One scholar who had been thinking along these lines was Roger Brown, psycholinguist at Harvard University. Working in the early 1950s with his graduate student Eric Lenneberg, Brown had become interested in the way in which a culture's particular parsing of the color spectrum may affect how individuals from that culture classify and later recall specific hues. In a review written in 1975, Brown has caught the *Zeitgeist* of that period: he has also suggested the ways in which it came to be undermined by Eleanor Rosch, who happens to have been his student nearly twenty years later.

As Brown recalls in his review, he and Eric Lenneberg (1954) wanted to test the Whorf-Sapir hypothesis: that is, one's conceptualization of the world reflects the particular terms and concepts of one's culture (see also chapter 8, p. 235). These researchers selected color for two principal reasons: first, because colors can be described in an objective "culture-free" way, drawing upon an extensive psychophysical apparatus; second, because the cross-cultural records documented many cultures with disparate color lexicons.

For various reasons, the original study by Brown and Lenneberg actually involved only native speakers of English. Subjects were shown some twenty-four colors and asked to name them: those colors that were readily named were called "codable." Another group of subjects was then briefly exposed to a small set of colors and thereafter shown a large set of hues and asked to indicate which they had seen before and which they had not. The colors in the new set included ones that had been rated as codable and ones that had not been so labeled. The results provided support for a weak version of the Whorf-Sapir hypothesis: specifically, subjects were somewhat better able to recognize those chips that had been rated as highly codable than those that had not. The authors judged that the existence of names within the American lexicon had exerted an influence on the subjects' behavior, by making those colors that were readily named easier to recognize.

Rosch's Critique of Classical Views

In the decade or so following the original Brown and Lenneberg investigation, several follow-up studies were conducted. This research proceeded in various meandering directions but was no more conclusive than the original Brown-Lenneberg study. There was modest support for the Whorf-Sapir hypothesis, little conclusive evidence against it. But around 1970, Eleanor Rosch (then Eleanor Rosch Heider) had the opportunity to visit the Dani in New Guinea. The Dani, a Stone Age people, have but two color terms—*mola* for bright, warm hues, and *mili* for dark, cold ones. Curious about the effects of such an unusually limited color vocabulary on the Danis' behavior with various color tasks, Rosch exposed the Dani to forty color chips, representing four brightnesses and ten hues. Each subject was asked to name each of the chips; then subsequently in a recognition condition, a subject was shown a test chip, asked to wait in the dark for thirty seconds and then asked to pick, from the array of forty, the one he had seen. On the naming task, the Dani clearly confirmed that they are from a culture different from ours. At the far end of the color curves, the Dani agreed among themselves about which colors were *mili* and which were *mola*. But intermediate chips were not consensually validated because individual subjects located the boundary between the two color terms at diverse points.

On the recognition condition, however, the results were completely unexpected. The Dani turned out to recognize colors in a manner very similar to the Americans—making the same confusions, for example— though their overall scores were not as high. Thus, differences in naming structure were not paralleled by differences in the way in which colors were stored in memory or accessed for recall (Heider 1972; Rosch 1973*a*; Rosch 1973*b*).

As a further check, Rosch and her colleague Donald Olivier (1972) selected hues immediately adjacent to one another in the color sphere and matched on saturation and brightness. Sometimes the members of a hue pair lay on the same side of a color name (whether English or Dani); at other times, they lay on opposite sides of the line, hence reflecting different color categories (for example, green and blue). Even with this simplified task, recognition proved equally keen for perceptually adjacent hues whether or not they lay on different sides of a language line—decisive evidence against a classical Whorfian position. As Brown puts it: "The fascinating irony of this research is that it began in a spirit of strong relativism and linguistic determinism and has now come to a position of cultural universalism and linguistic insignificance" (1975, p. 152). Or, in Rosch's own words, "In short, far from being a domain well suited to the study of the effects of language on thought, the color space would seem to be a prime example of the influence of underlying perceptual cognitive factors on the formation and reference of linguistic categories" (Heider 1972, p. 20).

Why, then, was this set of findings damaging to the classical view of concept formation? For many years, it had been assumed that the lines between colors were arbitrary, drawn as seen fit by a culture; individuals would simply mirror these boundaries in their own classificatory and mnemonic behavior. Now Rosch was calling into question these various lines of argument. The naming practices turned out to be incidental. The ways in which individuals from different cultures remember colors seemed to reflect the organization of the nervous system, not the structure of particular lexicons. Certain colors are "good" instances of a color because of the physiology of the human visual system and not because of specific naming practices. Indeed, a lexicon codes aspects of color that are *already* salient rather than making these aspects salient.

Rosch was by no means content simply to conduct studies of color naming among an exotic population (Mervis and Rosch 1981; Rosch 1977, 1978). Following her return to America, she probed a wide gamut of domains and concluded that the story on color is highly pertinent elsewhere as well. According to the classical view of classification, based primarily on the use of artificial stimuli, each category is defined by a finite list of criterial features: members display these features; nonmembers do not. But this classical picture does not apply to the world of natural objects —like birds—nor does it prove particularly illuminating in the realm of numerous man-made objects, like furniture or tools. In the world of everyday reality, highly correlated (non-independent) features prove the rule. For example, given the capacity to perceive feathers, furs, and wings, a perceiver soon comes to realize that in the empirical world, wings occur with feathers more than they do with furs. There is, in other words, considerable redundancy in the appearance of members of the same category—not the independence of features posited in the classical view. Recognition mechanisms exploit these redundancies.

There are other intrusions from the world as it actually is. For example, with respect to man-made entities, objects with one sort of appearance are more likely to be grouped together as chairs (because they possess the potential for being sat upon) while another group of objects is more likely to be grouped as drinking vessels (because they possess the potential for being held and poured from). While some characteristics may appear to demark chairs and others to demark drinking vessels, one looks in vain for a set of defining criteria; instead, the kinds of action these objects seem to elicit (or afford) constitute a more useful aid to classification.

Rosch has discerned a basic structure which seems observable across a wide range of categories. Categories are built around a central member or *prototype*—a representative example of that class which shares the most features with other members of the category while sharing few, if any, features with elements drawn from outside the class. A robin is a more prototypical bird than a chicken or a penguin: accordingly, it is more readily recognized as a bird and less likely to be misclassified as a member of another category (such as a mammal or a fish). Similarly, a sedan emerges as a more prototypical car than does a convertible or a limousine. Indeed, even with respect to artificially designed categories—for example, a series of dot patterns or a set of nonsense figures whose members have been fashioned according to certain prescribed criteria—the same findings apply. That is, the data on recognition or memory of these forms seem more adequately accounted for by assuming that subjects are erecting prototypes, than by assuming that they are looking for (or devising) a fixed list of features. The classical view founders even on its own home turf.

Rosch has called attention to other aspects of category structure as well. In many common categories of experience, she discerns a certain level at which subjects most readily can learn names, have ready access to them, remember them, and the like. She dubs this the *basic level.* Objects at the basic level within a category share many perceptual similarities and functional characteristics. For example, in the realm of furniture, a chair is a *basic-level* object; with respect to the animal world, a dog or a bird would be a basic-level object. The basic-level object contrasts with a higher level called the *"superordinate"* (furniture, in the case of a chair; animal, in the case of a bird), and can also be contrasted with the *"subordinate"* level (rocking chair in the case of chairs; robins or wrens in the case of birds). Young children strongly favor naming all objects at the basic level—all four-legged beasts thus being "dogs" for a time, and the categories of animal and collie emerging only later. Ultimately individuals become able to name and classify at these various levels but tend, whenever possible, to embrace the basic level of organization.

As a final point, Rosch questions the existence of strong or fixed boundaries between categories. While one can, of course, construct categories that have defining features and fixed boundaries, categories in the real world tend to have fuzzy boundaries and to blend into one another. These views echo those introduced some years earlier by Ludwig Wittgenstein.

In propounding such ideas, Rosch challenged each of the major tenets of the classical view. Rather than being arbitrary, categories are seen as motivated. Conceived of in a Gibsonian vein, categories reflect the perceptual structure of the perceiver, the kinds of actions one can carry out, the physical structure of the world. Categories do not have criterial features but harbor prototypes, with less prototypical members being apprehended with reference to the extent that they resemble (or fail to resemble) the prototype. Categories exhibit internal structure and that structure yields psychological consequences: basic-level objects turn out to be the most readily named and recalled; less psychologically accessible, but still useful and necessary for various purposes, are the finer-grained level of the subordinate and the overarching level of the superordinate. Finally, the categories do not have firm boundaries: many members sit astride the border of two or more categories.

Several factors may have contributed to this state of affairs in the world of categorization. Having evolved over many years to be able to deal efficiently with their environment, human beings tend to group together into categories entities that appear similar to their perceptual apparatus or call upon similar actions, or both. Moreover, what looks similar is not in the least arbitrary. For example, our visual system is so designed as to treat certain reds as being better than others, and to draw the line between red and orange, or between orange and yellow at specific points on what looks (to the instruments of the physical scientist) like a continuous spectrum. This view makes clear contact with what is known about the physiology of color vision, and links are forged as well with recent work in logic: the new variety of *fuzzy set logic,* which deals with degree of membership in a class, turns out to fit well with the claims being made by Rosch and her colleagues. And so one telltale finding about color naming in a remote Stone Age tribe has fostered a revolution in the way we conceptualize concepts.

While nearly everyone agrees that the Rosch findings undermine a strong view of the classical theory of concepts, critics question whether the natural view, taken alone, can replace it. In one study, Sharon Armstrong, Lila Gleitman, and Henry Gleitman (1983) examined the structure of a category that was clearly defined in the classical criterial way: the category of odd number. To their delight, these authors determined that individuals are as likely to organize such a concept around a prototype as they will a natural category like bird or vegetable (seven turns out to be the prototypical odd number). The researchers concluded that Rosch has no way of distinguishing between a classically defined and a natural concept. However, it seems to me that this line of evidence could as readily be cited as showing that even "true" classical concepts have the kind of categorical structure Rosch has ferreted out elsewhere. According to the latter analysis, the tendency to discern naturalistic features in all categories is viewed as a confirmation, rather than a refutation, of the natural view.

Another critical view, put forth by Daniel Osherson and Edward Smith (1981), asserts that the prototype theory cannot account for the ways in which more complex concepts (for example, the concept *pet fish*) are apparently composed of elementary concepts. These authors propose a hybrid theory: that is, while categorization continues to need a core concept, along the line of classical concept theory, this core aspect must be combined with an identification process (the way in which one determines category membership). Rosch's approach is seen as an explanation of how one identifies instances of the natural and artificial sort. In the view of Osherson and Smith, such a hybrid theory is important because "the ability to construct thoughts and complex concepts out of some basic stock of concepts seems to lie near the heart of human mentation" (1981, p. 55).

To my mind, neither the findings of Armstrong and colleagues nor the Osherson-Smith argument undermines the broad thrust of the Rosch position. The classical theory remains feeble; the natural view emerges as a more veridical description of how individuals form and utilize categories. And yet the two lines of criticisms that I have reviewed do make an important point: certain aspects of human cognition—such as the capacity to apply the definition of *odd number* in a reliable manner or the ability to form more elaborate concepts out of simpler ones—seem inexplicable in terms of the natural view. At least some aspects of categorization may employ the kind of computational operations classicists cherish.

Berlin and Kay on Basic Color Terminology

Remaining within the field of choice, Brent Berlin and Paul Kay of the University of California at Berkeley provided intriguing evidence about the "naturalness" of color names (1969). As I have noted earlier, these anthropologists studied the color-naming practices of individuals drawn from twenty genetically diverse languages, ranging from Arabic to Ibo (Nigeria) to Thai, and found that cultures differ dramatically from one another in the number of basic color terms they possess, from two (like the Dani) to eleven (like the English).

Dwarfing these differences are two important phenomena, both documented by Berlin and Kay. First of all, when confronted with chips spanning the full spectrum of hues, their informants selected the same focal areas for colors, irrespective of whether they had names for them: that is, informants from these diverse cultures agreed about what was a "good blue" or a "poor green," even if their culture lacked names for these colors. Indeed, the differences among individual speakers of one language were comparable to those among speakers of different languages. Berlin and Kay attribute this universal agreement to the structure of the nervous system of the primate, which renders certain hues more salient than others (de Valois and Jacobs 1968).

The second and remarkable finding was a fixed order in the construction of color lexicons. Studying color lexicons from ninety-eight different cultures, Berlin and Kay uncovered the following sequences. If (like the Dani) a culture has only two color terms, terms will code for black and white. If a third term is added, it will be red; fourth and fifth will be yellow or green (followed by whichever one of the two has not been used); blue and brown will be the next pair, competing for sixth and seventh places; and purple, pink, orange, and gray will be the last four names to be coined. These results are virtually impossible to account for through a series of historical accidents or diffusions. Instead, the kinds of distinction cultures make among colors, and elect to capture in their lexicons, apparently reflect distinctions most salient in their perception of the world, presumably (again) for neurophysiological reasons.

The Berlin and Kay findings were as epoch-making in the area of anthropology as Rosch's were in psychology. Just as psychologists had to reconsider their beliefs in classical definitions of concepts and in the arbitrariness of categories, anthropologists had to re-examine their beliefs in the flexibility of naming and categorization schemes and in the influence of language on thought structures. But some anthropologists feel that the conclusions drawn by Berlin and Kay are too broad. John Bousfield, for example, suggests that it is one thing to know that the color spectrum is divided into two segments, but quite another to translate the terms as "black" and "white." In his view, such a pair of terms would acquire far more meaning (since they are the only ways to talk about colors) than they do in a multicolor-term culture:

> It is absolutely crucial to remember that we would be changing the meaning of these two English terms if we now had to assign more or less every hue and shade in the room to one category or the other. We could do so, just as the taste of wines can be located on the dry-sweet dimension. . . . But we have lost something if we do not realize that this change has occurred in the meaning of our terms, and if we think instead that their terms "mean the same" as ours. (1979, p. 208)

In his critique, Marshall Sahlins, an anthropologist at the University of Chicago, goes even further (1976). Initially, he accepts the Berlin and Kay finding without modification, saying that "relativism will simply have to come to grips with the cross cultural regularities of color categorization" (1976, p. 2). But he proceeds to interpret the findings in virtually the opposite way. Rather than agreeing that the perception of colors directs a culture's naming practices, Sahlins maintains that the human perceptual apparatus itself is exploited by more pervasive cultural concerns: "The true ethnographical existence of color terms and percepts [inheres in] their actual cultural significance as codes of social, economic and ritual value" (p. 8). In Sahlins's "semantic" view, colors have nothing to do with a score of sample chips—an arbitrary invention of Western technology—but, rather, signify crucial cultural differences between life and death, noble and common, pure and impure. Even in our culture, terms like *red* or *yellow*, or *blue* or *green* are appropriated to emphasize significant distinctions in "charged" domains like politics, bodily states, religion. It is owing to their deep concerns about phenomena like anger or patriotism or mourning— phenomena that become associated with characteristic hues—that humans attend to colors at all. To adopt this semantic point of departure, Sahlins insists, is not to ignore biology but simply to assign it a proper place.

To my mind, it would be a mistake to get involved in a "chicken-egg" question of which came first—the cultural distinctions motivating all humans or the ability to discriminate colors *per se* along certain lines. I read Sahlins as making a different point. As he sees it, one does not confront perception *per se*, except perhaps in an artificial situation where one asks subjects to examine color chips. Perception is always marshaled in the service of some cultural end. And so, à la Lévi-Strauss, one ought to think of the perceptual system—and globally, of the mind—as an implement of culture, as an organizational structure to be exploited by the human cultural enterprise. As Sahlins concludes, "It seems to me that *Basic Color Terms* opens up very exciting prospects for an ethnography of color whose general aim, quite beyond the determination of the empirical correlates of semantic categories, might consist especially in the correlation of the semiotic and perceptual structures of color. For colors, too, are good to think (with)" (1976, p. 16).

In such reactions to the Berlin and Kay findings, we see the same impulse for territorial preservation which greeted the Rosch work. Just as some psychologists felt the need to defend the classical view of concepts, so, too, some anthropologists seek to ensure that the terrain of culture does not disappear now that some potent universals have been demonstrated. Perhaps scholars will eventually find some way of blending the strengths of the two points of view, as Osherson and Smith attempt in psychology and Sahlins attempts in anthropology. But to my mind, neither of these lines of criticism undermines the main point of the natural view of categories. They are commentaries or cautionary notes, rather than convincing revivals of the classical view in psychology or anthropology.

A New Philosophical Cast on Concepts

Just about the time that Eleanor Rosch had repaired to the wilds of New Guinea, a shift in many ways parallel to the trends in psychology and anthropology was coming to a head within the philosophical community.

As has happened more than once, this philosophical shift was previewed in the thinking of Ludwig Wittgenstein (1968). In the early part of the century, as a principal contributor to, if not the inspirer of, the Vienna circle (see pp. 62–65), Wittgenstein had stressed the importance of logic and the need for precision in language (as well as the desirability of keeping silent when such linguistic accuracy was not possible). But in the second phase of his scholarly career, Wittgenstein came to focus on the way in which ordinary language is used, and arrived at the controversial conclusion that philosophical problems typically inhere in one's use of language. He saw language as a loose and fragmentary set of elements and as the necessary means of communication among individuals, but as prone to obscure as well as to enlighten because it is the web through which all other experience necessarily passes. Concepts are neither mental constructs in the head nor abstract ideas in the world, but ought to be seen as *abilities* which individuals can employ in ways acceptable to the rest of the community—roughly speaking, as ways of accomplishing things.

In Wittgenstein's skeptical view, the most an analyst can hope to achieve is greater insight into how language as a system works, and into how our own ideas have come to be formed by the linguistic practices of our community. Efforts to figure out what "really" happened, to sweep aside the veil of language, are doomed to fail. And the glorification of logic, or of abstract concepts bereft of utility within a community, is an irrelevant move, lacking philosophical force.

While Wittgenstein was calling for a radically different view of language and conceptualization, the attack on logical empiricism was also being pursued by once-sympathetic philosophers in the Anglo-American tradition like W. V. O. Quine (1953) and Nelson Goodman (1955). As I noted in chapter 4, the distinction between the analytic and the synthetic, the contrast between the immediate and the mediate, the possibility of verifying observational sentences—these were all being spurned. More modest goals for philosophy, or even the merging of philosophy with psychology, as a kind of "naturalized epistemology," were being advanced.

Ultimately, a still more radical attack on the classical view of concepts was put forth virtually in tandem by the American philosophers Saul Kripke (1972) and Hilary Putnam (1975*b*). This pair of scholars came to question the belief that the world is a welter of sensation which can be parsed with equal plausibility in an indefinite number of ways. Rather, in a move analogous to the Roschian maneuver within psychology, these philosophers embraced a view of naming and classifying that smacked of the rankest realism. Kripke, Putnam, and their associates argued that there is a *real* structure to the world, and that much of our conceptual armament is designed to capture this genuine and attainable structure. Putnam (in his talk of "natural kinds") and Kripke (in his talk of "rigid designators") assumed that there are many objects, ranging from gold to goldfish, and also many entities, like the persons "Richard Nixon" or "Greta Garbo," that ought not be defined in terms of a list of criterial attributes. For practical purposes, these concepts have no definition, no intension; they have only an extension, or a relation extending from the term to its concrete referent in the world. Richard Nixon is the person whom his mother named as such; he cannot be anyone else; and the only way to make sure that he is Richard Nixon is to have a confirmed history that he is the same individual that his parents so dubbed in the year 1913. By the same token, gold is what it is; scientists may define it today as the atomic weight 79, but it will remain gold even if the scientist's understanding of gold changes.

According to this view, all instances of the same natural kind possess a definite underlying structural property in common. Thus, all lemons ultimately possess the same structure even though any two randomly selected lemons may lack a specific perceptible property in common. A category is organized around stereotypes that enable a layperson to recognize exemplars: such an organization proves essential inasmuch as one will not necessarily be privy to the underlying genetic properties all lemons really share.

As Stephen Schwartz (1979) has explained, we rely on experts to help us to determine the appropriate use of such *natural-kind* terms. We assume there is someone (or some procedure) that can confirm the identity of Richard Nixon; we assume there is someone who can confirm that this sphere is a lemon or that this metal is gold. Such natural-kind terms prove susceptible to the formation of stable generalizations, such as, "If you do X to gold, it will turn. . . ." To use the natural-kind term appropriately, you do not need to know the trait governing the extension—indeed, at present no one may know it; you just have to believe that it can be discovered eventually. In other words, a nature is there (in principle) to be discovered.

The question arises why we have natural-kind terms. Schwartz voices the opinion that such terms turn up whenever the same stuff or thing characteristically assumes a lot of different forms. Water can take different forms, as can diseases, animals, plants, and so on. Seeing these changes occurring on the "same" object, one assumes that there is some underlying trait making the stuff continue to be of the same kind. In contrast, "artificial kinds" do not necessarily exhibit dramatic changes: cars do not necessarily rust, rings need not bend: these are simply vicissitudes to which any man-made object *may* be subject. Schwartz goes on to discern a unity in the changes exhibited by natural-kind terms, as all members of a particular kind must go through the changes. Something of a law-governed nature must remain the same in the transition from ice to water or from larva to butterfly.

"Likewise the reason why I believe that tigers share an essence, the reason why I am compelled to postulate an underlying trait for tigers that makes tigers tigers, is that big tigers, by a perfectly natural, unconscious, and ineluctable process, produce little tigers" (1979, p. 315). Or to put it in Kripke's terms, we come to think of objects in terms of what could happen to them, in terms of the modal possibilities, the regularities and the exceptions.

To those somewhat removed from philosophical frays, the move to natural-kind objects, the willingness to accept an ostensive definition, ("This is gold") or a history of occurrences ("This has always been Nixon"), rather than a list of necessary and sufficient conditions ("Gold is *A,B,C*, or Nixon is *X,Y,Z*) may seem innocuous enough. But within the philosophical world, the moves first launched by Wittgenstein and then extended in new and unanticipated directions by Kripke and Putnam are considered very radical. Some sacred cows dating back to Aristotle are directly challenged; some strong and biologically oriented contentions ("A lemon has an essence . . .") are being introduced to a world that has been comfortable in its empiricism and its nominalism. Rather than meanings being located inside someone's head, the Putnam-Kripke tradition suggests that meanings are located in the world—an imperative imposed by the real structure of objects and the ways in which individuals come to learn about them.

Discussion of the new theory of reference has been widespread within the philosophical community. The talk of essences, of a "real" structure in the world, of a connection between proper names (like Richard Nixon) and natural-kind terms (like lemon or gold) is sometimes seen as a reactionary move, one that recalls errors to which philosophers from a bygone day were prey, but that had ostensibly been exorcised by several centuries of empiricist philosophical analysis. The practice of collapsing diverse elements into the same category because of ostensible underlying structural identities is seen as risky. Indeed, the reversion to realism has such strong philosophical implications that even Putnam himself (though not apparently Kripke) has had second thoughts about the dangerous lair into which such an analytic line may lead.

Yet whatever misgivings an individual philosopher may feel, an observer of the cognitive sciences is struck by the extent to which parallels were occurring across several fields. The findings emerging empirically from the laboratories of psychologists and from field trips to New Guinea were closely reflecting the discussions engaged in by scholars who might never think to conduct an experiment or join an anthropological team but were deeply steeped in over two thousand years of argumentation on related topics. From these widely different avenues came a common rejection of the classical view of concepts, a sharp impatience with criterial lists of attributes, and a correlative belief that there are natural categories in the world, best defined by examples (called variously "stereotypes" or "prototypes"), and possibly reflecting underlying structures, which we as humans have the potential to recognize and to understand. In each case, the extent to which the revisionist claims could take over the field remained in doubt, and some critics yearned for the good old classical days: yet the challenge posed to the classical formulation was widely recognized and frequently endorsed.

We have, then, a prototypical example of how several disciplines in the cognitive sciences have combined to suggest a solution to a long-standing philosophical puzzle. In this particular case, the puzzle surrounds the human capacity to group together elements as members of a category, and then to distinguish that category or class from others in the same general domain of experience. A consensus had developed over the years that such categorization was relatively arbitrary, with the culture determining which entities ought to be grouped together. Most any set of criteria could be proposed; and once proposed, these criteria could be applied reliably to instances, as means of determining which belonged to the category and which did not. Classes were relatively clear; boundaries, relatively fixed. Thus, it was appropriate for researchers like Jerome Bruner to conduct experiments using artificially contrived classes: after all, they were thought to represent well the kinds of classes we must utilize every day.

From the fields of psychology, anthropology, and philosophy, working initially in relative independence of one another, but possibly reflecting the same factors or spirit, came an increasing realization that this classical view is wrong. Categorization is anything but artificial and unambiguous; rather, it relies on information in the natural world to which we as a species are geared to respond. Categories have an internal structure, centered around prototypes or stereotypes, with other instances being defined as more or less peripheral depending upon the extent to which they share pivotal features with the central prototype. Perceptual information is crucial in defining the dimensions of a category; language, for the most part, follows upon the discriminations made by the individuals, rather than playing a controlling role in how one classifies in the world.

There is an irony in the decline of the classical theory—an irony we have encountered in other contexts. The classical theory of concepts was tailor-made to a computational model of mind—a set of precisely defined dimensions which could, taken conjunctively, yield a category. Computers were the perfect devices for simulating (or epitomizing) this mode of mind. It is therefore striking that, at the very time that science had available a device fully equal to simulating a certain view of concepts, that view was found to be radically flawed. Not surprising, therefore, that there was resistance across several disciplines to the relatively radical implications of the natural view of categorization. Many analysts hold out for a range of categories, some of which are relatively natural, others of which are more arbitrary and lend themselves readily to the kinds of analyses put forth in the classical theory. And it is certainly true that the natural theory deals better with colors or plants than with legal terms, religions, or self-concepts; moreover the extent to which the natural theory handles man-made artifacts satisfactorily is far from settled.

Indeed, to my mind, the principal challenge to the natural view of categorization inheres in the extent to which it can move beyond an explanation of those basic-level entities that we are "biologically prepared" to perceive and classify. Color is most likely to lend itself to a natural-kind account, because our perceptual system is primed to consider certain colors as focal; and there is every reason to think that primates the world over see colors in similar ways (unless they happen to be color-blind). The evidence concerning other "natural" entities—such as plants, fruits, or animals—is not as well worked out, but there is reason to expect that an account in the natural-kind tradition may suffice (Berlin, Breedlove, and Raven 1973).

But much of our classification in everyday experience extends beyond the objects evolution has prepared us to classify in certain ways. There are the multitude of man-made objects, ranging from tools to machines to works of literature or art. There are more abstract concepts such as political principles, religious precepts, belief systems, and economic laws. And there are concepts that impinge much more upon an individual's own personal concerns: concepts having to do with personality, motivation, sexuality, emotions, and the self. Anthropologists in the ethnoscientific tradition have attempted to apply to these concepts the approaches that worked in simpler areas like kinship systems, plants, and colors. As I noted in chapter 8, these attempts have not been notably successful; and, in fact, the discipline of ethnoscience, in *both* its classical and its natural form, is quiescent at the present time. One might say that the critique of the classical view has been relatively successful but that the natural approach has not yet proved genuinely illuminating with more complex, less "built-in" concepts.

Can Categorization Be Studied from a Cognitivist Perspective?

Which leads to a more radical critique, of the sort associated with Clifford Geertz of the Institute for Advanced Study, and other members of the school of symbolic anthropology. Geertz (1973, 1983) opposes his position to the central cognitive-scientific "dogmas," where thought is viewed as unified, bound to the individual psyche, and governed by statable laws; in place of this Newell-Simon vision, Geertz urges a view of thought as a collective product, which is coded differently across cultures thanks to historical forces that have exerted their effects over the millennia.

The existence of numerous cultures with diverse and idiosyncratic histories makes comparison across cultures difficult, if not suspect. Rather than comparing the psychological processes of one population with another, one must ponder the commensurability of the conceptual structures of one community with those of another community. Geertz sees little reason to expect that a mimicry of the natural or the physical sciences will be helpful here. Rather, he calls for the utilization of approaches associated hitherto with the humanities. The anthropologist bent upon understanding the conceptual structures or categorizing practices of an alien community may share more with a literary critic trying to understand a text, with a historian trying to make sense of documents, or with an art critic analyzing a painting than with a chemist mixing elements or a biologist carrying out experiments. In this approach, the analysis of culture is not an experimental science in search of laws but is rather an interpretive or "hermeneutic" scrutiny in search of meaning. The method needed here is an imaginative leap where one tries to place oneself inside the head, or the experience, of the "native." The preferred route is through careful idiographic case studies: one studies the categories of religion or animal life by observing the practices of daily living and not by requesting definitions or administering tasks of classification.

Symbolic anthropology alerts us to another risk. Critical issues in the study of perception, recognition, classification, logical reasoning, and other cognitive operations may not be given to us by nature in the way, say, that the movement of the heavenly bodies or the laws of the atom might reasonably be taken as given, even by the proverbial observer from Mars. Rather, *our* ways of conceptualizing precepts, concepts, and the like are the products of a particular intellectual and cultural history, traceable in significant measure to a mode of analysis that arose at the time of the Greeks. We are involved in the pursuit of an understanding of concepts that come out of our own philosophical and historical tradition; and we make a grave error in assuming that this agenda has to be *the* agenda, the only feasible one to pursue. Perhaps the Hindu or Dani tradition would parse cognition in a radically different way or reject the concept of cognition altogether. Such a line of argument makes contact with the critique of work on color vision put forth by Sahlins (1976): on this account, the issues that individuals or cultures choose to make central dominate whatever cognitive operations are provided by nature.

Of course, resolution of so fundamental a controversy cannot be provided in advance: it is, as they say, an empirical issue or perhaps a question of which line of explanation will prove most satisfactory and revealing in light of the canons judged to be relevant—be they canons of the natural sciences, the social sciences, the humanities, or the arts. It is not, however, simply a matter of taste.

In my own view, even if the processes by which individuals reason or classify may be similar the world over, the actual products and the ways they are thought about may be so different as to make illuminating generalizations elusive. And to the extent that particular concepts are the result of biases lurking within the linguistic system of a given culture, one risks entering a Wittgensteinian-Whorfian morass from which few investigators have yet returned. It seems to me that the important lines to be drawn are between those concepts and those principles of reasoning that have evolved since the early hominid era, as against those that have developed only comparatively recently and reflect the particular history, customs, and values of one or another social or cultural group. Clearly, there are ways in which humans form concepts of colors or of animals, and these may well be the same the world over. In formulaic terms, concepts may not be formed classically, but a naturalistic approach to certain aspects of conceptualization and reasoning appears possible.

But when one enters the world that is entirely man-made, in arts, rituals, or sciences, the possibility for effective generalization seems less evident. Here, forces of history and culture may prove so dominant that the differences may outweigh the similarities. While certain generalizations can be formed, the ones that seem most revealing about a particular circumstance may not extend beyond that circumstance. What tells us the most about the Balinese may tell us the least about the Belgians, and vice versa.

Scientists cherish their own reflections and use them to guide their studies. They devise artificial, criterially defined categories (else their work could not begin), and they follow strict canons of logic (otherwise their work would not be accepted). In their efforts to model thought processes, they have sought such categories and such operations in normal individuals. But in their search for marks of the scientist in nonscientific man (or even in the scientist, when not "playing" scientist), these investigators have been disappointed. Faced with an artificial concept, the subject attempts (if inappropriately) to treat it as if it were a natural concept. Asked to reason logically, subjects have embraced images and stereotypes. So we confront the paradoxical situation where scientists have attempted—for experimental purposes—to make the natural world artificial; but their subjects, faced with the difficulty of dealing with these artificial concepts, have simply (if sometimes inappropriately) invoked their naturalistic modes of reasoning and classification.

Returning to the issues raised in the earliest philosophical debates, we find that progress has indeed been made. At the very least, classical views have been strongly challenged. Among natural-kind concepts, there are some factors reminiscent of "ideal forms" and "universals"—Plato might take some comfort in this vindication. Similarly, there is modest support for the view that, under certain circumstances, the language one uses does influence the way in which one conceptualizes the world; indeed, as one moves toward complex, abstract, and less immediately perceptible realms, the role of one's symbolic systems may become predominant. Yet in those areas investigated thus far—like the classification of common objects or common sensory experiences—the position of the naked nominalist or the rabid Whorfian is not supported.

And how does cognitive science fare in this cooperative enterprise? Once again, progress has depended upon convergences among disparate fields. The particular disciplines most intensively involved in issues of classification have been philosophy, where the problems have been defined and discussed; psychology, where certain critical experiments have been devised; and anthropology, where pertinent cross-cultural studies have been carried out. Scholars such as Eleanor Rosch, Brent Berlin, Paul Kay, and Hilary Putnam epitomize this ecumenical spirit. Until now, the constraints on classifying imposed by neurophysiology have been modest; still, when results like those with color naming prove consistent with what is known about physiology, everyone feels on firmer ground. It is, in part, the immense distance between our understanding of abstract concepts and our understanding of the nervous system that renders remote, at the present time, the hope for a conclusive account.

No less than was the case with perception and imagery, probing critiques have been leveled at the whole enterprise. Just as Gibson has questioned the representational views of perception, and as Wittgenstein has questioned the explanatory power of imagery, so Geertz and other anthropologists wonder whether comparative ethnoscientific studies of categories valued in the West can illuminate the most vaunted forms of thought. The anthropologists may well be correct in their view that complex concepts elude current investigative techniques; and, at least for a while, more of interest and importance may be learned through approaches informed by literary sensibility. At the same time, the processes whereby categorization takes place are recognizable across diverse populations and diverse domains of experience; in that sense, we know more (and we know differently) about categorization than we did before the advent of cognitive science.

In confronting questions of categorization, we have moved into a distinctly human terrain, involving both language and reasoning capacities. Few would quarrel with the claim that this area is less advanced than the study of perception; indeed, as Geertz suggests, the possibility remains that the most crucial questions about categorization may continue to elude cognitive-scientific methods. Perhaps cognitive science as a field will prove unequal to the task of explicating the genesis, nature, and use of our more complex and evocative concepts and categories.

Yet, even if issues of categorization turn out to be susceptible to a cognitive-scientific analysis; even if (say) the naturalistic view turns out to be fully vindicated, there will remain crucial unresolved questions. For classification or categorization is ultimately a tool—a means whereby individuals organize their world so as to solve certain problems and to achieve certain ends. The ultimate achievements of this field will depend on whether the principles evolved to deal with relatively simple concepts and modest classification will prove applicable to complex concepts and systems of concepts.

Just what sort of an organism will utilize these capacities, and toward what ends will they be used? Here cognitive scientists have found themselves confronting value-laden aspects of human cognition—and, in particular, have directed considerable attention to the question whether individuals can be thought of as proceeding in a logical or rational fashion. This question is of importance for scientific reasons, since much of cognitive science is based on the model of the logical computer; it also has important political and social implications. The answers to questions of human rationality, with which I shall deal in the following chapter, turn out to be surprising, and not particularly reassuring to those who place their faith in reason.

13

How Rational a Being?

Whenever there is a simple error that most laymen fall for,
there is always a slightly more sophisticated version of the
same problem that experts fall for.

—AMOS TVERSKY

While the Greeks sometimes defined man as a featherless biped, they had
far more invested in another definition: man as rational being. Only humans can invoke a form of thought that adheres explicitly to rules and
leads to conclusions that can be judged by the community as valid or
invalid. Unpacking this Greek notion a bit, it proves possible to distinguish
between the individual who reaches valid conclusions—and can therefore
be deemed *rational*—and the procedure by which these conclusions are
reached—a procedure termed *logic.* And so, one might conceive of a crea-
ture who is rational but reaches conclusions by means other than logic—
for example, by shrewd intuition, lucky guessing, or being programmed to
issue only valid responses.

Though surrounded (in a sense) by evidence of the irrationality of
human beings, philosophers have clung to the notion that human beings
are logical and rational—or at least to the ideal that human beings should
strive for rationality and that they have the potential to achieve it. This
preoccupation with an ideal of rationality is hardly surprising, since philosophy itself has sought to proceed by rational means. Indeed, Bertrand
Russell once speculated that Aristotle was the first to define man in terms
of rationality (quoted in Pylyshyn 1984, p. 257). Over the years, the
development of the field of logic has been closely intertwined with the
history of philosophy: just as the logic of Aristotle's time informed Greek
philosophy so the logics of Frege, Whitehead and Russell, and Kripke have
informed the philosophy of today.

Cognitive science was conceived in the shadow of contemporary logic. As I noted in discussing the Hixon Symposium in chapter 2, both early work on computers and the model of the neuron as a logical circuit encouraged a view of thought as logical (Jeffress 1951). Furthermore, the first generation of cognitive scientists embraced a model of human beings that was decidedly rationalistic. Jerome Bruner, Herbert Simon, Allen Newell, and Jean Piaget all elected to investigate issues involving the abilities of human beings to reason validly. In fact, the problems solved by the first computer programs were problems in logic; the classification tasks investigated by psychologists required logical deductive processes; Piaget went one step further, not only studying problems of logic, but assuming that "developed" humans reason by invoking principles of logic. As he once put it, "reasoning is nothing more than the propositional calculus itself" (Inhelder and Piaget 1958, p. 305).

But the faith of the initial generation in a study of logical problems and its determined search for rational thought processes may have been misguided. Empirical work on reasoning over the past thirty years has severely challenged the notion that human beings—even sophisticated ones—proceed in a rational manner, let alone that they invoke some logical calculus in their reasoning. Once again, a computational age has documented departures from computerlike precision. This realization has seeped through many lines of research, but few would quarrel with my selection of Philip Johnson-Laird (from Great Britain) and the team of Daniel Kahneman and Amos Tversky (originally from Israel) as the spokesmen for this particular chapter of cognitive science. Not only have these scholars developed stunning demonstrations of human departures from rationality; they have also offered explanations of the reasons we humans often go wrong in the ways we do.

The Illogic of Human Reasoning

Cards with Numbers

Consider the following problem developed by Peter Wason and Philip Johnson-Laird (Johnson-Laird and Wason 1970; Wason 1966; Wason and Johnson-Laird 1972). Four cards are laid out with their faces displaying, respectively, an E, a K, a 4, and a 7. You are told that each card has a letter on one side and a number on the other. You are then given a rule, whose truth you are expected to evaluate, "If a card has a vowel on one side, then it has an even number on the other." You are then allowed to turn over two, but only two, cards in order to determine whether the rule is correct as stated.

If you have already met this problem, or one of its close relatives, you should have little trouble getting it correct. (In this case, your memory is being tested, not your powers of reasoning.) But if this is your maiden encounter, you will almost certainly miss it, as have over 90 percent of subjects (including many logicians) to whom it has been presented in many settings. Most subjects realize that there is no need to select the card bearing the consonant, since it is clearly irrelevant to the rule; they also appreciate that it is essential to turn over the card with the vowel, for an odd number opposite would infirm the rule. The difficulty inheres in deciding which of the two numbered cards to pick up. There is a strong temptation to pick up the card with the even number, because the even number is mentioned in the rule; and this temptation proves fatal to a majority of subjects. But, in fact, it is irrelevant whether there is a vowel or a consonant on the other side, since the rule does not actually take a stand on what must be opposite to even numbers. On the other hand, it is essential to pick up the card with the odd number on it. If that card has a consonant on it, the result is irrelevant. If, however, the card has a vowel on it, the rule in question has been infirmed, for the card must (according to the rule) have an even (and not an odd number) on it.

The fact that this problem proves hard (even though, once explained, it seems evident enough) gives one pause: ready explanations for this result elude those who place great faith in the logical capabilities of their fellow humans and themselves. But to my mind there is an even more interesting twist to the Wason and Johnson-Laird demonstration. Consider the following problem, again using four cards, each representing a journey. Each card has a destination on one side and a mode of transportation on the other. This time the cards have printed on them the legends, respectively, "Manchester," "Sheffield," "Train," and "Car"; and the rule is: "Every time I go to Manchester, I travel by train." While this rule is formally identical to the number-letter version, it poses relatively little difficulty for individuals. In fact 80 percent of subjects realize the need to turn over the card with the word "car" on it. Apparently, one realizes that if the card with "car" on it has the name "Manchester" on the back, the rule is infirmed; whereas it is immaterial what it says on the back of the card with "train" on it since, as far as the rule is concerned, one can go to Sheffield any way one wants.

Why is it that 80 percent of subjects get this problem correct, whereas only one tenth know which cards to turn over in the logically identical vowel-number version? Possibly a person is much better at solving a problem entailing familiar material—material that enables one to place oneself inside the situation, to figure out what one would do, what it would be reasonable to do. Indeed, you are more likely to succeed on the aforementioned problem if you are British (and hence know of Sheffield and Manchester) and if you are of an older generation (and so have grown up with trains as a likely mode of travel).

The results clearly challenge any notion that individuals are "logic machines," capable of applying the same modes of reasoning, independent of the specific information in a problem. Thus, humans are notably different from an ideal computer: the actual contents of a problem (vowels versus vehicles) cannot make any difference for such a syntactically governed apparatus. Yet just as the particular structure of each category colors a subject's classifying strategies in a Roschian experiment, so, too, the content of specific problems determines how all of us (except, perhaps, highly trained logicians) will proceed on an apparently simple reasoning task.

Results on these and many other puzzles have convinced Philip Johnson-Laird, a leading cognitive scientist, that people do not employ a mental logic in solving problems (1983). The kinds of logic described by logicians simply seem irrelevant to normal individuals. We do not construct truth tables and look up the result: we do not use formal rules of inference. But Johnson-Laird maintains that there can be reasoning without logic. The dilemma facing the cognitivist is to allow both for rationality *and* for human error.

Puzzles about traveling or games with vowels and numbers may seem a shade artificial, but there is nothing contrived about the syllogism. This form of reasoning goes back at least to Greek times and was considered by Aristotle (often our judge in these matters) as the core of logic. It is used unreflectively by ordinary individuals as part of daily experience; and as Johnson-Laird neatly shows, it is even drawn upon by critics who wish to belittle the importance of syllogisms. One might say, "Syllogisms are artificial." Furthermore, "Psychologists shouldn't study things that are artificial." Therefore, "Psychologists should study the kinds of inferences that are used regularly in daily life." In the very act of dismissal, this critic has invoked syllogistic reasoning.

Artists and Beekeepers

According to Johnson-Laird's analysis, there are sixty-four kinds of syllogism—all variations of the following example:

All the artists are beekeepers.   (All A's are B.)

All the beekeepers are chemists.   (All B's are C.)

The subject (and anyone can play) is asked to figure out which conclusions, if any, follow from these two premises. Johnson-Laird and his colleagues have found that such syllogisms pose considerable difficulties; and that, often as not, people will draw invalid conclusions from them. Moreover, explaining the patterns of success and failure on such problems has proved difficult for the logicians and psychologists who have sought a comprehensive account. These misadventures have resulted because experts on syllogistic reasoning assume that individuals untrained in formal logic nonetheless use some variant of it (for example, visual aids like Euler circles or Venn diagrams) to solve the problems.

These experts have evolved elaborate accounts purporting to show how the average person approaches syllogisms. These methods can perhaps work in principle—if, for example, one has unlimited memory capacity and has mastered sophisticated mathematical notations; but Johnson-Laird illustrates convincingly that even the talented college student cannot proceed by embracing these methods: "The present theories are too fragile to bear the weight of human reason" (1983, p. 93). Either the theorists succeed in accounting for deductive errors but fail to account for the rationality that is exhibited by subjects, or they explain the ability of subjects to reason adequately under ideal conditions but fail to illuminate the kinds of error made by human subjects. The trick is to offer an explanation that can account for both human rationality and human error. Johnson-Laird therefore introduces his major contribution to cognitive science: the notion of a mental model.

He asks us to pretend that we have the power to conjure up individuals who fulfill one or more of the roles stated in the premises. Clearly, we can create individuals who are at one time artists, beekeepers, *and* chemists —who exhibit the trio of roles discussed in the premises. These individuals can be represented in mental model form as

    artist–beekeeper–chemist
    artist–beekeeper–chemist
    artist–beekeeper–chemist

We also know that there are individuals who are beekeepers and chemists but not artists:

    beekeeper–chemist
    beekeeper–chemist
    beekeeper–chemist

And we know from common sense (as well as from careful consideration of the problem) that there can be chemists who are not beekeepers:

    chemists
    chemists
    chemists

We now have created a mental model that arrays all of the information that can be taken directly from the premises given. We see that there are three categories of individual: those who represent all three occupations; those who are beekeepers and chemists; and those who are just chemists. (The fact that I have listed three instances in each category is accidental; one may conjure up as many exemplars as one wishes.) Reading off of these arrays, we can now proceed to answer questions or draw conclusions. For example, if we want to determine whether all the artists are also chemists, we can simply look at the tableaus and confirm that all the artists are indeed chemists.

Johnson-Laird's approach is important in that it proceeds differently from other tacks, which in some way follow the laws of formal logic, either explicitly or implicitly. There is no need to translate the premises, implicitly or explicitly, into the *p*'s and *q*'s of formal logic, to say that all *p*'s are *q*'s, and all *q*'s are *r* and to deduce, according to an algorithm, what follows from that array. Nor is there any need to draw overlapping circles (the visual embodiment of formal logic in a system like Euler circles) and to read off which aspects overlap one another under each circumstance. Rather, the individual engaged in constructing a mental model is simply employing whatever medium is comfortable to him (words, images, some hybrid) in order to represent the information for himself in a convenient and readily accessible manner.

According to Johnson-Laird, one first represents the individual tokens (artists, beekeepers) in some manner and thereby forms a *mental model* of the first premise. Next, one adds the information in the second premise (that beekeepers are chemists) to the mental model of the first premise, taking into account the different ways in which this can be done. An advisable strategy here is to establish the possible arrangements (whether an individual can be a beekeeper without being an artist) using as few "imaginary actors" as possible, though, as I have noted, the precise number of actors depicted proves irrelevant to the syllogistic inferences that are eventually drawn. Finally, after all of the mental pictures have been constructed, an integrated set of pictures is submitted to a test: a search is undertaken for an interpretation of the premises that is *inconsistent* with the model. An inference is valid if, and only if, there is no way of interpreting the premises that is consistent with a denial of the conclusion.

In the example just given, it is possible to arrive at a valid conclusion simply by constructing one mental model. Thus the solution of this problem is relatively simple: one avoids the explosion of combinatorial possibilities that plague conventional formal approaches to syllogistic reasoning. Of course, some other problems prove far more complex to model. For example, Johnson-Laird introduced the following syllogistic premises:

All the bankers are athletes.
None of the councillors are bankers.

If you believe that this syllogism is easy, you are almost certain to be wrong. (Even if you know it is hard, you will probably fail.) In fact, as Johnson-Laird shows, there is only one fool-proof conclusion:

Some of the athletes are not councillors.

This conclusion is difficult to draw correctly because it requires a subject to devise three separate mental models and then to integrate them so as to reach a single conclusion. Of the sixty-four possible syllogisms investigated by Johnson-Laird, four are as fiendishly difficult as this one: they require individuals to construct and evaluate three separate models and, to make matters worse, fail to exhibit certain surface or "figural" cues that ordinarily help one to solve syllogisms.

So far what Johnson-Laird says seems reasonable, but why accept it as the best account of the thinking involved in syllogistic reasoning? He sets out several criteria for a theory of reasoning and proceeds to show how his approach meets these criteria. First of all, it is necessary to have a way of characterizing all sixty-four kinds of syllogism and to predict which will pose the most problems for subjects. Empirical work with subjects has confirmed the basic outlines of this claim. Second of all, it is necessary to lay out the requisite processes by which individuals solve these problems and then differentiate among the most and the least successful subjects in terms of whether they can exhibit each of the hypothesized component skills. Johnson-Laird's model predicts that the decline in performance reflects the number of separate models that have to be constructed. A third desideratum is the capacity of the theory to explain how children handle syllogisms and to pinpoint the factors that will improve their performance. It turns out that young children cannot handle syllogisms that require more than one model; indeed, children succeeded best in that form of syllogism which Aristotle considered perfect:

All the A are B.
All the B are C.
Therefore all the A are C.

All of these research maneuvers are carried out from the perspective of psychology, though admittedly a psychology informed by a sophisticated grasp of the ways and traps of logic. But Johnson-Laird penetrates into the heartland of cognitive science because (like Stephen Kosslyn working in the area of imagery) he has implemented his theory via a computer program. The computer program consists of three basic steps:

1. Construct a mental model of the first premise.
2. Add the information in the second premise to the mental model of the first premise, taking into account the different ways in which this can be done. (This turns out to be the trickiest aspect of the process, the one that determines whether one, two, or three different models need be constructed.)
3. Frame a conclusion to express the relation, if any, between the "end" terms that hold in all the models of the premises.

These steps constitute what Johnson-Laird terms an *effective procedure*—a procedure that, if carried out rigorously, guarantees that one will reach the appropriate conclusion. In his view, cognitive science rests upon discovery of such effective procedures which can be carried out not only by those imperfect mechanisms called human beings but also by those impeccable mechanisms called digital computers. Johnson-Laird's procedure worked perfectly on his computer and thus is effective.

Johnson-Laird attributes the power of his theory to the fact that it is compatible both with the sorts of errors that subjects make and with a completely valid set of deductions. He concludes:

> There appears to be no branch of deductive inference that requires us to assume the existence of a mental logic in order to do justice to the psychological phenomena. To be logical, an individual requires, not formal rules of inference, but a tacit knowledge of the fundamental semantic principle governing any inference: a deduction is valid provided that there is no way of interpreting the premises correctly that is inconsistent with the conclusion. Logic provides a systematic method for searching for such counter-examples. The empirical evidence suggests that ordinary individuals possess no such methods. (Quoted in Mehler, Walker, and Garrett 1982, p. 130)

Mental Models as a Panacea?

Syllogisms are but one of several areas examined by Johnson-Laird in his effort to demonstrate the power of his mental-models approach. In his recent book *Mental Models* (1983), he applies his approach with impressive success to such topics as inference, word meaning, grammar, and the comprehension of discourse. In each case, he describes the nature of the problem to be solved, the competing explanatory models (including models based on propositions, schemas, images, and other staples of a cognitive-scientific diet), and attempts to show why the mental-models approach illuminates the processes exhibited by human beings and can be effectively realized on a computer. This is more than a series of effective demonstrations: it is a persuasive argument for a certain approach to cognitive science. *Mental Models* may well serve as a mental model for the next generation of cognitive scientists.

When it comes to describing what a mental model is and how it differs from other competing accounts, Johnson-Laird is less than completely successful. It may be that he is simply placing too great a demand on a single concept—stating, for example, that "all our knowledge of the world depends on mental models" (1983, p. 419). As one sympathetic critic has declared, "Johnson-Laird succumbs to the temptation to see his nascent theory of mental models as the solution to everyone else's problem" (Stich 1984, p. 189).

Johnson-Laird seems to sense this difficulty, though he may view it as less of an obstacle than an opportunity. He embraces the versatility of such models:

> Since mental models can take many forms and serve many purposes, their contents are very varied. They can contain nothing but tokens that represent individuals and identities between them, as in the sorts of models that are required for syllogistic reasoning. They can represent spatial relations between entities, and the temporal or causal relations between events. A rich imaginary model of the world can be used to compute the projective relations required for an image. Models have a content and form that fits them to their purpose, whether it be to explain, to predict, or to control. (1983, p. 410)

Despite these probably excessive and perhaps unsustainable claims, mental models turn out to be useful devices for accounting for a subject's behavior in delimited domains, like syllogistic reasoning. First of all, Johnson-Laird's approach explains how individuals can succeed on some questions—and also can fail on others—without the need for invoking formal logical methods. Thus, it can account for a wide range of performances. Second of all, the various predictions built into the model have been tested not only with human subjects but also with a computer program. Again, while a computer program is no guarantor of success, the fact that simulations have proved workable indicates that at least there are no hidden errors or contradictions in the theory. In its own terms, the model works.

In his discussion of rival explanatory modes in the cognitive sciences, Johnson-Laird makes a telling point. In his opinion, it is too simple to say that images are (or are not) modes of representation, to argue (as have scholars like Pylyshyn [1984]) that all representation is best thought of in propositional forms, or to maintain (as has John Anderson [1978]) that it is impossible in principle to decide whether a process entails propositions or images.* Johnson-Laird prefers to posit at least three types of mental representation: propositional representations that resemble natural lan-

---

*Anderson has constructed a proof showing that it is always possible to construct an alternative account using a different sort of representation that behaves in an equivalent way (1978).

guages; mental models which are structural analogues of the world; and images that are the perceptual correlates of models from a particular point of view (1983, p. 165). We ought to think of individuals as representing information at several different levels of abstraction: moreover, the form of representation at one level need not be the same as the form of representation at another level. Just as a computer may have several different languages, ranging from machine code to a high-level programming language, so, too, a psychological process might use only strings of symbols at one level but involve images or mental models at a higher level of representation. This ecumenical approach seems to do more justice to the wide range of human psychological processes brought to bear on such problems as text understanding or inference than does a stubborn adherence to a single mode of mental representation.

Returning to the puzzle of logical reasoning, we find that Johnson-Laird has enriched our understanding in two ways. To begin with, he has shown that the ways in which human beings were once thought to approach problems of reasoning simply do not hold: one does not reason as classical logic would suggest. Yet humans are not irrational either. Through a careful analysis of syllogistic reasoning, the conduct of experiments with subjects of different ages and degrees of expertise, and the simulation of his model on a computer, Johnson-Laird has arrived at a picture of reasoning that seems robust and viable. A combination of several of the cognitive sciences has yielded a genuine clarification of a long-standing philosophical issue—the degree of rationality of human beings.

Why does logic fail? As anthropologist Roy D'Andrade has noted, the vocabulary of the logician is a second-order vocabulary (1982). It is a statement not about things or events but, rather, about the consistency or the inconsistency of statements. Ordinary language statements do not usually refer to truth conditions but refer rather to states of affairs in the world: people appear to be so designed (or so educated) that their major interest focuses on what can happen in the world under such-and-such conditions. The soundness, the speed, and the complexity of the reasoning that individuals exhibit seem primarily a function of the degree of familiarity and organization of the materials being processed, rather than a function of any special or general ability of the person doing the reasoning. And so there are appreciable differences in how a given person can reason about different topics, topics that, from a formal point of view, call upon the same degree (and even principles) of logical expertise.

This line of reasoning drawn from the analyses of Johnson-Laird, Wason, and D'Andrade suggests that we can better understand the logical reasoning of humans not by imputing to them any formal logical calculus but by attending instead to two factors. The first has to do with content:

the greater the familiarity and the richer the relevant schemata which are available, the more readily can one solve a problem. The second attribute has to do with form: one succeeds on problems to the extent that one can construct mental models that represent the relevant information in an appropriate fashion and use these mental models flexibly. Just how one learns to construct such mental models, to integrate them with "real world" knowledge, and to deploy them appropriately in the proper circumstances are fertile questions for developmental and educational psychology.

If Johnson-Laird and company are correct, the kinds of principles devised by logicians—and invoked by researchers like Piaget—will turn out to have only limited applicability to how we reason in the real world. Apparently we have evolved as creatures who are most likely to succeed on tasks that contain familiar elements and allow the ready construction and manipulation of mental models. Considerations of pure logic, a field that developed long after our survival mechanisms had fallen into place, may be useful for certain kinds of information under certain circumstances by certain individuals. But logic cannot serve as a valid model of how most individuals solve most problems most of the time.

Biases in Human Cognition:
The Tversky-Kahneman Position

As if the onslaught from Johnson-Laird and colleagues were not enough, still other attacks on the rationality of human beings have been launched in recent years by imaginative (if not insidious) researchers. A well-known set of studies was carried out in the 1970s by Amos Tversky and Daniel Kahneman, then of the Hebrew University in Jerusalem. Once again, the upshot of these studies was that individuals often performed radically differently on problems that had the same formal structure; moreover, these performances reflected strong biases in the human cognitive system which must be taken into account in any theory of human reasoning. Thus, while Johnson-Laird has illuminated the kinds of processes used by individuals in solving classical logic problems, Tversky and Kahneman have singled out the kinds of heuristics and strategies that guide—if they do not determine—the ways in which individuals reason in everyday life (Kahneman, Slovic, and Tversky 1982; Kahneman and Tversky 1982, 1984; Tversky and Kahneman 1983).

Theater Tickets and Coin Tossers

Let me consider a few of the numerous intriguing examples reported by Tversky and Kahneman: Asked to say which sequence of heads and tails is less common, HHHTTT or HTHHTT, most individuals will choose the former. Apparently individuals judge frequency of samples on the basis of their similarity to the features of the "parent" population. Since irregularity is an essential feature of randomness, irregular samples are judged more likely than regular samples, even though both series are equally likely to occur.

Imagine that you are on the way to a Broadway play with a pair of tickets which cost forty dollars (this is some years ago!) and discover you have lost the tickets. Would you pay another forty dollars? Now imagine that you are on the way to the theater to buy these tickets. Upon arrival, you realize that you have lost forty dollars in cash. Would you now buy tickets to the play? Clearly, on an objective basis, the two situations are identical because in both you are forty dollars in the hole. Nevertheless, most people report that they would be more likely to buy new tickets if they had lost the money than if they had lost the tickets. The argument is that the same loss is assigned to different "mental accounts": the loss of forty dollars in cash is entered into an account distinct from the play and so has comparatively little effect on whether one buys new tickets. On the other hand, the cost of the lost tickets is attributed to the account of "attending the theater": one is loath to accept the doubling of the cost of the play—shelling out eighty dollars for a pair of tickets.

Another example: Mr. Crane and Mr. Thomas are scheduled to leave the airport at the same time, though on different flights. They travel to the airport in the same limousine, are caught in a traffic jam, and arrive at the airport a half-hour after their scheduled departures. Mr. Crane is told that his flight left on time, while Mr. Thomas is told that his flight was delayed and left just five minutes ago. Nearly everyone agrees that Mr. Thomas will be more upset, even though in fact the two men's objective conditions are indistinguishable—after all, both missed a plane. The reason, in the view of Tversky and Kahneman, is that in the play of one's imagination, Mr. Thomas comes much closer than Mr. Crane to catching his flight, and thus the frustration experienced is greater. Similarly, an individual whose lottery ticket differs by only one cipher from that of the winning ticket is much more upset than the individual whose number is remote from the winning entry.

Imagine that you are about to buy a jacket for $125 and a calculator for $15. The calculator salesman tells you that the calculator you want to buy is on sale at the other branch of the store, twenty minutes away, for

$10. Would you make the trip? Most people say that they will. Another group is asked a similar question. This time the cost of the jacket is changed to $15, and the cost of the calculator to $125 in the original store and to $120 in the branch. Of respondents presented with this version, the majority said that they would not make the extra trip. Note that in both cases the total purchases are the same: the choice is always whether to drive twenty minutes to save $5. But apparently respondents evaluate the saving of $5 in relation to the price of the calculators. In relative terms, a reduction from $15 to $10 (or 50 percent) is less resistible than a reduction from $125 to $120 (less than 5 percent).

Finally, meet Linda. She is thirty-one years old, single, outspoken, and very bright. She majored in philosophy. As a student, she was deeply concerned with issues of discrimination and social justice and also participated in antinuclear demonstrations. You are now asked to rank, from most to least probable, a series of eight statements. Included in the list are the statements: "Linda is a psychiatric social worker," "Linda is a bank teller" and "Linda is a bank teller and is active in the feminist movement." On any rational account, it is more probable that Linda is a bank teller than that Linda is both a bank teller and active in the feminist movement. The probability of x, after all, is always greater than the probability of independent event x and independent event y. Yet more than 80 percent of subjects, including those who are sophisticated in statistics, assent more readily to the statement that Linda is a bank teller and a feminist than to the statement that Linda is a bank teller.

Why this clear flouting of rationality? Tversky and Kahneman see the laws of probability being overwhelmed by the principle of *representativeness*. People are keenly attuned to the likelihood that someone with certain characteristics will also exhibit other ones. (To the extent that someone is a social activist, she is likely to be a feminist.) Indeed, the more supporting details are consistent with this representative portrait, the more likely a subject will assent to these new details, even though (on a rational basis) the added details increasingly constrain the set and hence render it less probable in absolute terms. Thus, given the information that Linda is a certain kind of person, subjects readily fit in other events that have in the past been representative of such persons, and in the process ignore what they otherwise know about probability.

And this "otherwise" knowledge does still exist. Asked the abstract question "Which is more probable, x alone or x and y," subjects readily consent that x alone is more probable. Moreover, when confronted with the apparent contradiction between this abstract response and the Linda question, they readily admit that they have made an error. Thus, it is too simple to say that subjects were simply fooled: the response based on representativeness in the Linda problem seems to reflect a deep-seated bias in human judgment.

These are but a few of the many vivid instances studied by Tversky and Kahneman and, of the lot, among the easiest to present.* But these examples should underscore the point that individuals do not reach decisions in a way that is logically consistent or that obeys the laws of probability. I do not mean, however, that the behavior is illogical or inexplicable. Rather, Tversky and Kahneman have revealed a separate psychology of preferences which does not follow strictly from an economic calculation of gains and losses but instead focuses on how individuals "frame" selections. Among the relevant considerations are: whether a person construes the situation as one in which there is a guaranteed loss (as opposed to a likely loss); whether a result will have a substantial effect on one's customary style of life; whether one has ready access to an instance of the category in question; how one's imagination plays on what might have happened; how closely an example resembles a prototype about which one already holds strong views; the mood that one expects to be in; and the way in which a question is actually phrased (for example, does one speak of the killing of four hundred out of six hundred persons, or of the sparing of two hundred out of six hundred?).

Overall, Tversky and Kahneman conclude that statistical principles and rules of deduction are simply not imported from the kit of the measurement scientist into the reasoning of everyday life. People are not coherent in the way that it would be nice to believe they were. In even-tempered tones, these investigators conclude, "The descriptive study of preferences also presents challenges to the theory of rational choice because it is often far from clear whether the effects of decision weights, reference points, framing, and regret should be treated as errors or biases or whether they should be accepted as valid elements of human experience" (Kahneman and Tversky 1982, p. 171).

A Philosophical Critique

The results reported by Tversky and Kahneman, as well as those gathered by Johnson-Laird, Wason, and other workers, have not gone unnoticed or unremarked upon by those keepers of human rationality—the professional philosophers. One such is L. Jonathan Cohen of Oxford University, who has taken on Tversky, Kahneman, and their colleagues in a series of critiques. Cohen (1981) takes three swipes at the notion that most individuals do not behave in a logical or rational fashion. The first

*Interested readers can play subject by consulting the dozens of examples recounted in Kahneman, Slovic, and Tversky 1982.

line of argument simply holds that what is rational should be determined by the man in the street; he is the ultimate arbiter, and findings that statisticians or experimenters may choose to impose on laymen are, strictly speaking, irrelevant. On this line of argument, individuals can make errors, of course; but except for such problems of "performance," it ought to be assumed that the average person is competent. After all, no one questions judgments about grammar as rendered by the man on the street, and judgments of reason should be similarly honored. This line of argument may have a certain persuasiveness; but, in the last analysis, it strikes me as antiscientific since it essentially closes the discussion. After all, if every human (of whatever age or mental state) is considered rational, no matter how he or she happens to reason, and no matter whether he or she concurs with others, then there is no way to study rationality at all. It is ubiquitous and unchallengeable.

A second line of argument maintains that it is unreasonable to expect ordinary individuals to be aware of laws of probability and other statistical regularities: most of the claimed findings are seen as reflecting a lack of education or of special knowledge, rather than deficiencies of cognition. On this line of reasoning, we would all be superrational if we were to receive expert training. No one has yet offered to train John Q. Public on the laws of probability, but there is already plenty of anecdotal evidence and some experimental evidence to suggest that even trained experts exhibit the kinds of bias uncovered by Tversky and Kahneman (Kahneman, Slovic, and Tversky 1982).

The third—and, to my mind, the most interesting—line of argument actually challenges the relevance altogether of laws of statistics like Bayes' theorem. According to the theorem, postulated in 1763 by Thomas Bayes, one should take into account *baseline* (or *base*) *rates* when making judgments about probability in a specific situation. Thus, if one is trying to decide whether a given verbal portrait pertains to a lawyer or to a trial lawyer, it is pertinent to take into account the fact that there are far more lawyers in a society than there are trial lawyers.

Cohen directs his critical sights on the following example from the published research of Tversky and Kahneman. Subjects were told that, in a certain town, blue and green cabs operate in a ratio of 85 to 15, respectively. (In Bayesian lingo this is the so-called base rate.) A witness has identified a cab in a crash as green; and the court is told that, under the relevant light conditions, such a witness can reliably distinguish blue cabs from green cabs in 80 percent of cases. Subjects were then asked: What is the probability (expressed in percentages) that the cab involved in the accident was actually blue?

The median response in this task was 0.2. Investigators like Kahneman and Tversky claim that this response reflects a serious error because it indicates a failure to take into account the base rates—that is, the prior probabilities. The investigators reason as follows. The fact that far more cabs are blue than green must be taken into account in computing the likelihood that the cab was, in fact, green. They then make four computations: the likelihood of correct identifications of the cab as blue, given that it is blue (85% $\times$ .8 = 68%); the incorrect identification of a cab as blue, given that it is actually green (15% $\times$ .2 = 3%); the correct identification of a cab as green, given that it is actually green (15% $\times$ .8 = 12%); and the incorrect identification of the cab as green, given that it is actually blue (85% $\times$ .2 = 17%). All together, the identifications of the cab as green will be 29 percent (17% + 12%) and the fraction that is wrong will be 17/29. Consequently, according to the experimenters' mode of reasoning, the probability that the cab in the accident was actually blue is 17/29 and not 1/5.

But, argues Cohen, one need not approach this problem in this textbook way (in this case via Bayes' theorem). He claims, for instance, that jurors ought not to rely on probability if they can avoid doing so: such an invoking of probability assumes that the issue before the court concerns a long run of cab-color–identification problems, where actually the juror is only trying to decide about this particular case. Strictly speaking, jurors are here occupied with the probability that the cab actually involved in the accident was blue, on the condition that the witness said it was green. Since the jurors know that only 20 percent of the witnesses' statements about cab colors are false, they rightly estimate the probability at issue as 1/5, without violating Bayes' law. The fact that cab colors actually vary by an 85-to-15 ratio may properly be considered irrelevant to the estimate: after all, this fact neither raises nor lowers the probability of a specific cab-color identification being correct on the condition that it is an identification by this particular witness. As Cohen phrases it, "A probability that holds uniformly for each of a class of events because it is based on causal properties, such as the physiology of vision, cannot be altered by facts, such as chance distributions that have no causal efficacy in the individual events" (1981, pp. 328–29).

Cohen comes up with another example that strikes much closer to home. Suppose you are suffering from a disease which is either A or B. It is known that A is nineteen times as common as B. The two diseases are equally fatal if untreated, but it is dangerous to combine treatments. Your physician orders a test which turns out to be correct on 80 percent of the cases where a differential diagnosis must be made. The test reports that you are suffering from the much rarer disease, B. Should you nonetheless opt for the treatment appropriate to A? According to the Bayesian view, this would be the proper step. In view of the prior distribution of the disease, the probability that you are suffering from A will be 19/23. But you might choose to ignore the prior probabilities, on the supposition that the probability of *your* suffering from B is 4/5. According to Cohen, it is irrational for you as a patient to answer in terms of the overall probabilities rather than in terms of the particular diagnosis just made. Paradoxically, if you followed the point of view in the statistical textbook, it would be a waste of time even to apply the test for the disease, since whatever its results, it is still more prudent on a statistical basis to assume that you have disease A, the statistically more common one.

Cohen discerns different interests at stake here. The administrator who wants to secure a high rate of diagnostic success for a particular hospital at minimal cost would be well advised to follow the laws of general probabilities, and so should eliminate the test. But the patient is concerned with success in his own particular case, not with the probabilistic success of the system in the long run, and so needs to evaluate test results with respect to his chances. Long-run strings of success are of no relevance to him.

In suggesting that the factors affecting the promulgators of a statistical law are not identical to those influencing a solitary individual making a decision about his or her own life, Cohen makes an interesting move. But it has not won him much favor with other experts on judgment, such as those asked to comment on his article in *The Behavioral and Brain Sciences* (Cohen 1981). Cohen was castigated as an apologist for errors and for the status quo, as a person who would undo the learning of science, and who himself was incapable of putting forth an argument or reasoning coherently and thus was dependent upon unsupported assertion and illusion. These criticisms struck me as being excessively severe, as though Cohen had hit a vulnerable spot. But to my mind, rather than demonstrating that people are logical (as he has intended to do), Cohen has, in fact, provided further evidence that they depart from logic and rationality in certain systematic ways. He also has reminded us that acting in one's own adjudged self-interest is not necessarily the same as making a judgment about which outcome is more likely to happen in some hypothetical event.

Some further points can be made as well. First of all, individuals have evolved in order to survive in a certain range of biological and social environments, not to satisfy some abstract notion of logic. It may well be that the kinds of induction and deduction individuals habitually (and even reflexively) make are most likely to lead to survival. And so they are rational in this absolute sense, even if they appear irrational in the light of certain textbook principles.

Another line of argument underscores the kinds of bias that have been built into favored psychological paradigms. To the extent that experiments harbor illusions or tricks they may be seen as having limited relevance to most daily behavior. Certainly if one slips traps into questions, it is easy enough to secure wrong answers or answers that make subjects look foolish. Piaget and his colleague Bärbel Inhelder once designed a test in which one gives young children a set of five tulips and two roses and then asks, "Are there more tulips here or more flowers?" (Inhelder and Piaget 1964). Until the age of seven, children will answer that there are more tulips, seemingly oblivious to the fact that the term *flowers* subsumes all of the tulips and all of the roses. Piaget and Inhelder confidently concluded that young children are unable to compare a whole set (flowers) with one of its subsets (the tulips). But as philosopher Jonathan Adler has pointed out (1984), it may be too simple merely to assume that children are incapable of making such comparisons. Rather, the children may simply not be expecting the kind of question that violates ordinary conversational rules of being "relevant" and pertinent. Children may just assume that the comparison being asked for is the perceptually evident one—Are there more tulips or more roses?—rather than the obscure if not downright deceptive query, Are there more tulips or more tulips plus roses? On this analysis, if children are asked for comparisons where a subclass could be more legitimately compared with the entire class, they would answer correctly. And, indeed, it turns out that when such questions are posed to children—Are there more children or more people?—they emerge as sensitive to the principles of "class inclusion" (see also Donaldson 1978).

Applying this perspective to the preceding examples, we can see that individuals might well be apprehending the Tversky-Kahneman problems in light of the ways in which people usually converse and the kinds of information they usually exchange. In the "Linda-bankteller" problem, for example, one assumes that the information about Linda's previous political involvements would only have been given if the listener was supposed to draw the conclusion that she was a feminist. Thus, a listener simply makes the reasonable assumption that the speaker wants him to believe that Linda is a feminist—else why trouble to mention so much about her political and social attitudes? In the problem about the taxicab, on the other hand, it might be assumed that the information about base rates has no relation to the question at hand. For as Tversky and Kahneman have themselves pointed out, subjects respond differently when told, "Although the two companies are roughly equal in size, 85 percent of the cab accidents in the city involve green cabs and 15 percent involve blue cabs." Now the information about base rates has been tied directly to the problem at hand, and subjects *do* take it into account. It is too simple, I think, to attribute subjects' apparent irrationality simply to the ways in which these problems are phrased and the kinds of conversational postulates involved. But at the same time, it is important not to ignore the possible effects of these factors (Kahneman, Slovic, and Tversky 1982, p. 157).

Jonathan Cohen uses the Tversky and Kahneman results as a means of arguing that individuals are genuinely rational, and to suggest that experimenters are caught up in statistical fine points having little bearing upon survival in daily life. But other philosophers, far from questioning the Tversky-Kahneman findings, have reformulated their news in light of these results. Christopher Cherniak, for example, rejects the notion that any rational agent must employ a logic, such as a complete first-order deductive system (1983). Indeed, Cherniak suggests abandoning a quest for ideal rationality: to achieve this goal, one would have to marshal infinite resources. Cherniak instead suggests a standard of minimal rationality. One makes some but not necessarily all inferences that are appropriate, and even uses heuristics that are formally incorrect—sketched images and other shorthand devices—as a means to arrive at a reasonable decision within a reasonable time.

Henry Kyburg, philosopher from the University of Rochester, believes that philosophers are still entitled to describe rationality as an ideal that individuals may only approach. But he goes on to indicate that empirical data are relevant in that they show how normative principles of inference, probability, and decision making are routinely violated by human beings. Kyburg rejects Cohen's notion that the intuitions of ordinary people should be the standards of rationality, and says, "It is not clear that such an inquiry would be any more relevant to the development of normative standards of inductive or deductive logical cogency than an inquiry into people's arithmetical intuitions would be to the development of standards of arithmetical validity" (Kyburg 1983, p. 232). But, Kyburg readily acknowledges that "empirical studies may suggest certain facts relevant to the development of normative constraints" (p. 244). Such a theory should be based both upon normative factors and what people actually do. He concludes:

> Though I think it is clear that the problem of characterizing rationality is a difficult one—far more difficult than many have realized—it does not seem insuperable. The very difficulties we uncover contribute to our understanding. And the fact that we progress at all—the fact that we listen to each other's arguments and recognize an obligation to deal with them—suggests that our goal can be approached. (P. 245)

Cherniak's and Kyburg's messages from the philosophical flank are important for our inquiry. Rather than throwing away the issue of rationality altogether, or concluding that empirical work is strictly irrelevant, they construe the study of rationality as a joint venture—one involving the findings of empirical researchers as well as the clarifications and distinctions of philosophical analysts. They leave open the possibility that individuals may depart from strict canons of logic and yet exhibit a viable version of rationality. We see at work here a catholic model of cognitive science. Instead of particular sciences banding together—as they have done, say, in the study of psycholinguistics—there is a broader dialogue at work—a dialogue between philosophers who are continuing to ponder a classical philosophical problem, and empirical scientists who have devised ingenious methods for attacking these venerable issues. And while the examples here have been drawn largely from the realm of psychology, they are by no means restricted to that discipline. Indeed, as I have suggested, the kinds of concern explored by Wason and Johnson-Laird, by Tversky and Kahneman, also involve issues of linguistics (How are the particular questions phrased?); they can be applied to diverse anthropological settings (How is reasoning carried out by different populations exhibiting different kinds of bias?); and they may be instructively simulated by artificial intelligence (as Johnson-Laird has modeled his work on simulation). Indeed, of the cognitive sciences, only the concerns of neuroscientists stand relatively remote from work on logic, reasoning, and rationality. Whether this statement is true only at present, or whether the whole realm of rational and logical beliefs operates at a level apart from neuroscience, has not yet been adequately considered.

Conclusion

With this review of work on rationality, I complete this survey of four exemplary contemporary efforts in the cognitive sciences. Taken together, these cases confirm that interdisciplinary efforts can achieve genuine progress in clarifying long-standing epistemological issues. While strong critiques have been leveled at this work—for example, the attack fashioned by L. Jonathan Cohen—these can, in my view, be satisfactorily met without fundamental damage to the cognitive-scientific enterprise. Such a result is particularly impressive in an area like rationality, which is equally remote from the operations of the nervous system and from the kinds of elementary process involved in perceiving visual form.

The work on rationality, like that on categorization, yields an intriguing moral. Some decades ago, before the computer was invented and cognitive science had been launched, it was common to maintain that human beings typically form concepts of a classical sort and that they generally reason in a logical fashion. Now the cognitive age, with its high-powered computational techniques, has called into question the view of human beings as operating in precise fashion. I do not mean, of course, that human behavior is no longer subject to study by computational or other cognitive-scientific techniques—indeed, Johnson-Laird has shown us just how some such behavior can be accurately simulated; but the digital and deductive fashion in which humans have been alleged to think is not viable. The broader question remains whether various forms of human irrationality—those documented by clinicians like Sigmund Freud and Carl Jung or by anthropologists like Clifford Geertz and Dan Sperber—can be elucidated by the methods of cognitive science.

Even negative lessons are important, and a science cannot be responsible for the message it yields, whether cheerful or gloomy. Yet challenging the model of man-as-computer raises far-reaching questions of the extent to which cognitive science has embraced the proper view of human mentation and provided the proper methods for its study. I turn to these questions in the final chapter of the book, as there I revisit the major themes of cognitive science in light of the histories I have related and the particular lines of current research I have presented. In conclusion, I present my views about the extent to which cognitive science has lived up to its initial promise and delineate the principal paradoxes and challenges it confronts at the present time.

14

Conclusion:
The Computational
Paradox and the
Cognitive Challenge

Surveying the scientific landscape at the beginning of the century, a far-sighted observer might have felt justified in announcing the arrival of the mind's new science. After all, building on the philosophical tradition of the Greeks and the Enlightenment, and in the wake of dramatic breakthroughs in physics, chemistry, and biology, the solution to the mystery of human mental processes seemed at hand. Moreover, toward the end of the nineteenth century, a raft of new disciplines concerned particularly with human thought and behavior had been launched. Surely the opportunity to look at individuals in many cultures, in the light of the latest findings about the human nervous system and with the powerful tools of logic and mathematics, should sooner or later yield a bona fide science of the mind.

From a contemporary perspective, it seems evident that at least three conditions had to fall into place before this dream could reach fruition. First of all, it was necessary to demonstrate the inadequacies of the behaviorist approach. Second, the particular limitations of each social science had to be acknowledged. Finally, the advent of the computer was needed to provide the final impetus for a new cognitive science.

In the preceding chapters, I have shown how each of these three conditions came to be met. By 1948, when Karl Lashley gave his famous Hixon Symposium address on the problem of serial order in behavior, it had become apparent to many scientists that the behaviorist approach to human intellective activity was fatally flawed. By the same token, the limits of other schools in the behaviorist orbit—logical positivism, structural linguistics, anthropological functionalism, Pavlovian reflexology— were already becoming apparent. A fresh approach to these issues was sorely needed.

Paralleling the discovery of the limitations of the behaviorist stance was a growing realization that each of the several human and behavioral sciences, practiced alone, harbored distinct and possibly crippling limitations. Whether it was philosophy's ambivalence about the relevance of empirical data to long-standing epistemological issues, or psychology's difficulty in adjusting its experimental approaches to large-scale issues, or anthropology's problems in transcending the single case study, or neuroscience's ambitions for dealing with capacities that defy reduction to the neural level, these various sciences increasingly felt the need for fertilization with neighboring disciplines.

Finally, and perhaps most decisively, there was the coalescence of various mathematical and logical demonstrations (such as those of Shannon, Turing, and von Neumann) with important technological breakthroughs, which culminated around mid-century in the first computers. Once the power of these machines for dealing with symbolic materials had been demonstrated, many researchers became convinced that a science of cognition might be fashioned in the image of the computer. By 1956, psychologists such as George Miller and Jerome Bruner, computer scientists such as Allen Newell and Herbert Simon, and linguists such as Noam Chomsky had carried out work that (in retrospect) was cognitive-scientific in spirit. And thirty years later, building on these pioneering efforts, researchers such as David Marr and Stephen Kosslyn (working at the intersection of perceptual psychology and artificial intelligence), Eleanor Rosch (combining psychological and anthropological concerns), and Philip Johnson-Laird (synthesizing approaches drawn from philosophy, psychology, linguistics, and artificial intelligence) had demonstrated that clear progress could be made in resolving long-standing philosophical and scientific issues. Though work on the perceptual issues is further along than research on classification or on rationality, it seems reasonable to declare in 1985 that cognitive science has come of age.

It is therefore opportune, in the life of the science as well as in the course of this survey, to take stock: to revisit the principal themes of cognitive science in order to clarify what has been accomplished over the past few decades and to discern what remains to be accomplished if cognitive science is to achieve its full potential. This evaluation will entail a consideration of the central concept in cognitive science—that of the representational level—as well as a re-examination of two themes introduced in the opening chapters of this book, the computational paradox and the cognitive challenge.

The Centrality of Mental Representation

To my mind, the major accomplishment of cognitive science has been the clear demonstration of the validity of positing a level of mental representation: a set of constructs that can be invoked for the explanation of cognitive phenomena, ranging from visual perception to story comprehension. Where forty years ago, at the height of the behaviorist era, few scientists dared to speak of schemas, images, rules, transformations, and other mental structures and operations, these representational assumptions and concepts are now taken for granted and permeate the cognitive sciences.

While most researchers (and perhaps most readers) take the representational level for granted, this form of analysis must be situated with reference to competing levels of description and analysis. It has long been acceptable in empirical science to talk of the nervous system and, more generally, of biological systems. These can, after all, be seen and even dissected. While most physical scientists have been unconcerned professionally with cultural and historical matters, it has been acceptable (and uncontroversial) among scholars in the humanities and social sciences to offer explanations in terms of social forces, cultural practices, historical traditions, and the like. How else, after all, to deal with macroscopic social phenomena? The triumph of cognitivism has been to place talk of representation on essentially equal footing with these entrenched modes of discourse—with the neuronal level, on the one hand, and with the sociocultural level, on the other. Whoever wishes to banish the representational level from scientific discourse would be compelled to explain language, problem solving, classification, and the like strictly in terms of neurological and cultural analysis. The discoveries of the last thirty years make such an alternative most unpalatable.

Making the general case for representation is one thing, making it with precision and power quite another. Any number of vocabularies and conceptual frameworks have been constructed in an effort to characterize the representational level—scripts, schemas, symbols, frames, images, mental models, to name just a few. And any number of terms describe the operations carried out upon these mental entities—transformations, conjunctions, deletions, reversals, and so on. Cognitive science needs to put its conceptual house in order and to transcend slogans and "buzz" words; the field must agree upon a language for talking about a range of representational phenomena—even if that language turns out to harbor various dialects.

As a start, I would single out two varieties of representation. One form is initially or eventually built into the hardware—be it computer or brain. Such a form must be invoked in order to detail what happens to information but this variety of representation does not involve processes of which the organism is in any way conscious or aware. For example, during the early stages of visual processing described by Marr and his colleagues, the visual system must create symbolic representations of physical information and then operate on these representations. But no organism has any options about these steps, and they are accessible only to a cognitive scientist.

A second variety of representation encompasses those problem-solving and classificatory behaviors that individuals carry out with some flexibility and some degree of explicitness and awareness. In analyzing a sentence or a story, in creating an image or transforming it, one may well become aware of having created some mental representation—or mental model—and then one carries out operations upon that model. Explicit awareness is not necessary here, but it is at least a possibility. Moreover, the individual has the option of changing the mode of representation or the kind of rule that is invoked. This mental activity is appropriately described in terms of representational language but clearly warrants a separate status (or terminology) from the kinds of representations that are automatic and possibly wired in.

It may well be that there are several varieties of representation, or that there exists a continuum from implicit to explicit, or from hard-wired to flexibly programmed. But unless a taxonomy can be agreed upon, discussion of representation will seem ad hoc and unsatisfactory. If representation is indeed the linchpin of cognitive science, it must ultimately be stated as clearly and accepted as widely as quantum theory in physics or the genetic code of the biochemical sciences. Such clarity and consensus seem a long way off.

The Computational Paradox

Strictly speaking, one could have had cognitive science without the computer. After all, computational theory antedated the invention of the computer. And yet as a matter of historical fact, cognitive science was unlikely to have arisen when it did, or taken the form that it has, without the emergence of the computer in our time. Since the first generation of cognitive scientists, the computer has served as the most available and the most appropriate model for thinking about thinking. And for most, it soon became indispensable in their daily empirical and theoretical work. Though the linking of computation and cognitivism turns out to have been a contingent rather than a necessary fact, the fate of cognitive science is closely tied to the fate of the computer.

And this leads to that strange state of affairs I have dubbed the *computational paradox*. With the vigorous tradition, since the time of the Greeks, of thinking about human thought as an embodiment of mathematical principles, it is hardly surprising that the first generation of cognitivists —reared in the logical positivist tradition—should have embraced a highly rationalistic view of human thought. One of the major results of the first years of cognitive science, however, has been a challenge of that ready assumption.

To be sure, when it comes to elementary and relatively "impenetrable" processes like visual perception or syntactic analysis, an authoritative computational account may some day be given. That is, the kinds of descriptions that are legitimately offered in the terms of a digital von Neumann computer may turn out to be appropriate accounts of these human cognitive processes as well. But as one moves to more complex and belief-tainted processes such as classification of ontological domains or judgments concerning rival courses of action, the computational model becomes less adequate. Human beings apparently do not approach these tasks in a manner that can be characterized as logical or rational or that entail step-by-step symbolic processing. Rather, they employ heuristics, strategies, biases, images, and other vague and approximate approaches. The kinds of symbol-manipulation models invoked by Newell, Simon, and others in the first generation of cognitivists do not seem optimal for describing such central human capacities.

The paradox lies in the fact that these insights came about largely through attempts to use computational models and modeling; only through scrupulous adherence to computational thinking could scientists discover the ways in which humans actually *differ* from the serial digital computer—the von Neumann computer, the model that dominated the thinking of the first generation of cognitive scientists.

I must again underscore one point. By insisting on the computational paradox, I do *not* mean to assert that it is impossible to arrive at a computational account of human behavioral and thought patterns in all of their perversity, irrationality, and subjectivity. Such accounts may well be possible and—as has been known since the time of Turing—are certainly possible in principle. Rather, the paradox suggests that the portrait of human cognition emerging from cognitive science is far removed—at least at the molar level—from the orderly, precise, step-by-step image that dominated the thinking of the founders of the field (and of those who dreamed about it in the more distant past). Human thought emerges as messy, intuitive, subject to subjective representations—not as pure and immaculate calculation. These processes may ultimately be modeled by a computer, but the end result will bear little resemblance to that view of cognition canonically lurking in computationally inspired accounts.

Entailed in the reliance on the computer as a pivotal model of thought is another difficulty which has only recently begun to be recognized. Invocation of the computer leads naturally to a concentration on logical problem solving (*à la* Newell and Simon) or on orderly, highly rule-governed analysis (*à la* Chomsky). But evidence from neuropsychological and developmental studies of mental processes has indicated that our concepts of cognition need to be considerably broadened. Processes involved in musical and other artistic activities, and, quite possibly, processes involved in knowing other individuals and in knowing oneself merit the modifier *cognitive* (Gardner 1983). To the extent that this position is valid, a thoroughgoing cognitive science will need to account for these abilities as well as for more familiar logical mathematical applications of mind. Whatever their relevance for the study of human rationality or problem solving, models derived from the computer are even less likely to be adequate to account for these other uses of mind.

It could be countered that cognitive science ought to be satisfied with modeling logical thought and that these other forms of thought ought to fall by the wayside. Perhaps cognitive science should embrace a classical computational account, even if humans do not much resemble a classical kind of computer. To restrict cognitive science to one form of cognition, however, is to refashion the subject matter to fit the current tools of study. By the same token, to accept an account just because such an account can be given is a scientifically weak move. After all, the purpose of science is not to propose a possible analysis (of which there will always be an infinite number) but rather to come up with the analysis that is most appropriate, parsimonious, and convincing. All cognitive phenomena could, after all, be described in terms of atoms, or in terms of historical factors—and in either event, a representational account would not even be necessary. But now, at the very time when a representational account has been accepted, it is important to try to find the *optimal* representational account. Representation without computation is one possible outcome for certain regions of cognitive science.

The idea of representation has until this point been closely tied to our current conceptions of computers. But there is no way of determining *a priori* to what extent the ways currently embraced for describing the representations of computers will prove germane to organisms, be they paramecia or professors. The kinds of representations favored by neo-associationists like Geoffrey Hinton turn out to be radically different (and much sparer) than those countenanced by Jerry Fodor or Zenon Pylyshyn; moreover, it may turn out that neither is adequate or suited for describing an individual who is dreaming, writing a poem, or listening to music. Earlier models of thought—the reflex arc, the hydraulic engine, the telephone switchboard—are now seen to be extremely limited. It is already clear that one kind of computer does not suffice to model all thought. We must face the alternative that humans may be an amalgam of several kinds of computers, or computer models, or may deviate from any kind of computer yet described. Computers will be pivotal in helping us determine how computerlike we are, but the ultimate verdict may be "Not very much."

Even if computers emerge as viable models for certain facets of human thought, the question arises about the various aspects of human nature that have been bracketed by cognitive scientists. As I noted in chapter 3, nearly all cognitive scientists have conspired to exclude from consideration such nontrivial factors as the role of the surrounding context, the affective aspects of experience, and the effects of cultural and historical factors on human behavior and thought (see D. Norman 1980). Some take the position that this is only a temporary move, until the relatively discrete aspects of cognition have been unraveled; others take the stronger positions that cognitive science should never deal with these aspects or even that a cognitive-scientific account will ultimately render unnecessary any account of these "fuzzier" factors.

Even a brief consideration of each of these "bracketed" topics would require many pages, and since cognitive scientists have themselves steered clear of these issues, there is little work within the disciplinary tradition on which I can draw. My own belief is that, ultimately, cognitive science will have to deal with these factors in one of two ways. Either scientists will propose a cognitive account of affect in which, for example, affective states will be viewed as quantitative values along a dimension, like happiness or cruelty; or researchers will opt for a complex explanatory framework in which the interaction of traditional cognitive factors with affective or cultural factors can somehow be modeled. These will be important but enormously difficult undertakings, for which traditional computational considerations may provide scant help.

Scholars differ widely from one another in their intuitions about the extent to which these other factors may ultimately engulf cognitive factors. From the perspective of a philosopher like Hubert Dreyfus, a linguist like Roy Harris, a psychologist like Benny Shanon, or an anthropologist like Clifford Geertz, these factors are so important, so constitutive of human experience, that they, rather than cognitive factors, ought to be regarded as primary. Although I am not without sympathy for this perspective, my own view is that there is a heartland of cognition which can be accounted for on its own terms, without necessary reference to (or reliance upon) these other, undoubtedly important elements. It is this heartland that I have attempted to describe in this book, particularly in the last four chapters. The borders of this heartland may determine the limits of cognitive science.

My own doubts about the computer as the guiding model of human thought stem from two principal considerations. As Hilary Putnam (1981) has stressed, the community surrounding a cognizing individual is critical. From those around us, we come to understand which sorts of views are considered acceptable, which are false or dangerous, justified or unjustified. Such judgments cannot initially be made by an individual but must stem from a collectivity; and because we all belong to communities, it makes sense for us to invoke such judgments. In sharp contrast, it makes no sense to indicate that a computer has made a mistake or is unjustified in its beliefs. The computer is simply executing what it has been programmed to execute, and standards of right and wrong do not enter into its performance. Only those entities that exist within, interact with, and are considered part of a community can be so judged.

My other reservation about the computer as model centers on the deep difference between biological and mechanical systems. I find it distorted to conceive of human beings apart from their membership in a species that has evolved over the millennia, and as other than organisms who themselves develop according to a complex interaction between genetic proclivities and environmental processes over a lifetime. To the extent that thought processes reflect these bio-developmental factors and are suffused with regressions, anticipations, frustrations, and ambivalent feelings, they will differ in fundamental ways from those exhibited by a nonorganic system. Note that it did not *have* to be this way—biological systems might have been just like inorganic (mechanical) systems. But it is clear that they are not. I therefore believe that adequate models of human thought and behavior will have to incorporate aspects of biological systems (for example, processes of organic differentiation or fusion) as well as aspects of mechanical systems (the operation of electronic circuits). The very comparisons between organic and mechanical structures and processes may be among the most instructive aspects of the science. All told, cognitive science will have to incorporate (and connect to) neurobiology as much as to artificial intelligence.

The Cognitive Challenge

Central to my view of cognitive science is the claim that the field entails an empirical effort to answer long-standing epistemological questions. Classical philosophy has indeed supplied much of the intellectual agenda of the contemporary field: its interest in how we perceive the world, in how we classify objects, in the status of words, images, and other constructs, and in the assessment of human rationality or irrationality. And even those issues that could not have been formulated by the classical philosophers—such as the extent to which human thought is computational—have routinely been put forth in philosophical terms. Perhaps most notably, contemporary cognitive science has provided reasonable answers to selected philosophical questions, even as it has rejected certain issues and radically transformed others.

In a sense, philosophy can be seen as standing outside of mainstream empirical cognitive science. On one bank of the mainstream, philosophy supplies many of the issues to be investigated. On the other, it examines the answers that are forthcoming, helps to interpret and integrate them, and provides critiques of the overall enterprise. Thus, for example, philosophers first raised the issues of human rationality and have now participated vigorously and instructively in the interpretation of findings put forth by Freud, Piaget, Tversky, and Kahneman. Yet as members of a discipline that stands external to empirical science, philosophers concerned with cognitive science may seem in jeopardy. For, as philosophical questions are answered by empirical science, philosophers may ultimately recede from the scene—as has, in fact, happened in vast areas of physics and biology. Still, in my view, philosophers interested in cognition stand in no peril of intellectual unemployment for the foreseeable future.

But what of the relations obtaining among the other disciplines that make up the cognitive sciences? Are they likely to blend together into one seamless Cognitive Science, or can we expect them to maintain their autonomy in the years ahead? And what would be the most favorable state of affairs?

One can contrast two visions of cognitive science. The less ambitious one calls for cooperation among the six member disciplines, each still retaining its primary questions, methods, and goals as chronicled in part II. On such an account, philosophy supplies the principal issues and helps to judge the extent to which they have been successfully handled. Neuroscience and anthropology remain as border disciplines, psychology and artificial intelligence are the core disciplines, and linguistics offers an account of that ability which is most central in the human cognitive armamentarium. When collaborating, these researchers are "practicing cognitive scientists"; otherwise, they are simply doing their own thing.

This "weak" version of cognitive science is quite possibly the norm today but scarcely warrants the label of an important new science. In a stronger, more gritty version of cognitive science, there will be gradual attenuation of disciplinary boundaries and loyalties. These will be replaced by a concerted effort by scientists committed to a representational account to model and explain the most crucial human cognitive functions.

This reconfiguration of the territory of cognitive science rests on the following analysis. Today, what is most central to cognitive studies is an individual's disciplinary background: whether one works as a philosopher or an anthropologist is more salient than whether one works on issues of language or of social interaction. This organization around the traditional disciplines would be appropriate if the actual domains of cognition did not make a central difference; so long as the same processes are believed to occur irrespective of the content of a domain (musical versus spatial cognition, for example), the conventional disciplinary division of labor makes sense.

I hold a very different, and still controversial, vision. From my perspective, as elaborated in this book, the crucial divisions within cognitive science are *not* the traditional disciplinary perspectives but rather the specific cognitive contents. Therefore, scientists should be characterized by the central cognitive domain on which they work: broad domains like language, music, social knowledge, logical thought; and more focused subdomains, like syntactic processing, the early phases of visual processing, or the perception of rhythm. Scientific training and research enterprises should come increasingly to be organized around these problems. When working on these problems, scientists should fuse their necessarily different perspectives in order to arrive at a full account of the particular cognitive domain at issue. And so the ultimate cognitive-scientific picture of syntactic processing, or of language as a whole, should be a coordinated representational account which covers the full gamut of the traditional disciplines without any need even to mention them.

Yet the question of disciplines or, more broadly, of levels of explanation cannot be bypassed entirely—and here we confront the major challenge to contemporary cognitive studies. Having established the legitimacy of the representational level, cognitive workers must trace out the ways in which this level maps onto the other legitimate (and legitimized) ways in which human activities can be construed. For a time, believers in the representational level had to proceed along their own, as yet unexplored path—and adherence to this single-minded program was the genius of the pioneering generation of the 1950s. But ultimately, such splendid isolation must be shattered. We must come to understand how culture is mapped onto brains—and the royal road toward such understanding will be the representational level.

The reason for such linkage across levels is simple but crucial. Unless the significance of work in each science can be connected to that undertaken in neighboring areas, the significance (and the limitations) of that work cannot be appreciated. No one fears the demise of physics, chemistry, and biology; and yet each of these discipines has vital, articulated, necessary links to the next level, through "borderland" disciplines like physical chemistry or biochemistry.

But, paradoxically, much of the best work in cognitive science has been carried out as if only the level of mental representation existed. In the case of language (more specifically, grammar), for example, the brilliant work of Chomsky and his followers makes no reference to, and could be maintained irrespective of, the actual conditions in the brain and in the surrounding culture. If cognitive science is to mature, however, the ultimate representational account of language must relate, at one extreme, to knowledge about the neural architecture of certain regions of the left hemisphere of the brain; and, on the other, to knowledge about the structure and function of language in different cultural groups. Only such a linking of levels can indicate whether proposed representational accounts of language are in fact appropriate, in light of neural and cultural considerations. The goal of this penetration of levels is not, to repeat, so that one discipline or level can swallow the other; but rather, so that our understanding of a domain like language can touch on all the relevant scientific perspectives, from neuron to nation.

Just as many committed cognitive scientists have restricted their work to the representational level and have spurned the borderland territory, so too they have called for a narrow delineation of what counts as cognitive. Thus, Jerry Fodor (1981) has expressed skepticism about the capacity of cognitive science to explain any of the higher or more complex forms of thought, which are "permeable" to a person's beliefs; and Zenon Pylyshyn (1984) has proposed a definition of cognition which excludes areas like learning, development, and "moods."

Although perhaps a prudent research strategy in the short term, I find this a misguided overall program for the cognitive sciences. Just because our current measures or concepts are primitive, we ought not to violate a common-sense notion of what mind is about; even less should we want to bypass the most impressive achievements of the human mind.

Indeed, in my view, the ultimate goal of cognitive science should be —precisely—to provide a cogent scientific account of how human beings achieve their most remarkable symbolic products: how we come to compose symphonies, write poems, invent machines (including computers), or construct theories (including cognitive-scientific ones). Such accounts will have to incorporate the means by which humans embark on complex projects to achieve ambitious goals; how they represent their plans; how they initiate work on a project, organize their daily routines (and nonroutines!), evaluate tentative drafts in light of feedback from other people and in view of their own motives and standards, determine when such a program or product has been completed, and then initiate a new line of work.

Such an exploratory enterprise will probably entail mentalistic entities or models of a highly molar form (as well as many finer-grained entities). It will probably cut across narrow domains (like language-related processes) and also have to involve separate constructs to account for processes involved in creativity, synthesis, and/or consciousness. Ultimately, as part of the cognitive challenge, it will also be necessary to relate a representational account of these human intellectual achievements to what is known about their neural substrate and to what can be established about the role of the surrounding culture in sponsoring and then absorbing (or rejecting or refashioning) them.

Even to begin to outline the phases involved in modeling any complex human creative activity is to confront the immensity of the task and the primitiveness of our current tools. And yet it is crucial for cognitive scientists to keep this goal in mind—even to tack it over their desks or alongside the screens of their personal computers. The study of thought must not exclude its most remarkable exemplars even if their elucidation still seems remote.

Given the most optimistic scenario for the future of the cognitive sciences, we still cannot reasonably expect an explanation of mind which lays to rest all extant scientific and epistemological problems. Still, I believe that the authors of *Meno, The Discourse on Method, The Critique of Pure Reason,* and *The Origin of Species* would feel that distinct progress has been made on the age-old issues that exercised them. Thanks to the development of new logical tools, the diverse deployments of the computer, the application of the scientific method to human psychological processes and cultural practices, our deeper and more rigorous understanding of the nature of language, and the many discoveries about the organization and operation of the nervous system, we have attained a more sophisticated grasp on the issues put forth originally by Plato, Descartes, Kant, and Darwin.

How much further cognitive science can proceed, and which of the competing visions it will choose to pursue, are issues that remain open. All who style ourselves as cognitive scientists are on the spot. If we heed the lessons entailed in our scientific history and lurking in our philosophical backgrounds, if we attend to but are not stymied by the reservations aired by shrewd skeptics, if we recognize the limitations of all inquiry but do not thereby encounter a failure of nerve, there are clear grounds for optimism.

392

REFERENCES

Abel, R. 1976. *Man the Measure.* New York: Free Press.

Adler, J. E. 1984. "Abstraction Is Uncooperative," *Journal for the Theory of Social Behavior* 14: 165–181.

Allport, D. A. 1980. "Patterns and Actions: Cognitive Mechanisms Are Content-specific." In G. L. Claxton, ed., *Cognitive Psychology: New Directions.* London: Routledge & Kegan Paul.

Anderson, A. R., ed. 1964. *Minds and Machines.* Englewood Cliffs, N.J.: Prentice-Hall.

Anderson, J. R. 1978. "Arguments concerning Representations for Mental Imagery," *Psychological Review* 85: 249–77.

———. 1980. *Cognitive Psychology and Its Implications.* San Francisco: W. H. Freeman.

———. 1983. *The Architecture of Cognition.* Cambridge, Mass.: Harvard University Press.

Armstrong, S. L.; Gleitman L. R.; and Gleitman, H. 1983. "What Some Concepts Might Not Be," *Cognition* 13: 263–308.

Arnheim, R. 1969. *Visual Thinking.* Berkeley: University of California Press.

Ashby, W. Ross. 1952. *Design for a Brain.* New York: John Wiley.

Atkinson, R. L.; and Shiffrin, R. M. 1968. "Human Memory: A Proposed System and Its Control Processes." In K. W. Spence and J. T. Spence, eds., *The Psychology of Learning and Motivation: Advances in Research and Theory,* vol. 2. New York: Academic Press.

Austin, J. L. 1962. *How to Do Things with Words.* Cambridge, Mass.: Harvard University Press.

Ayer, A. J. 1936. *Language, Truth, and Logic.* New York: Dover.

———. 1973. *The Central Questions of Philosophy.* Harmondsworth, Middlesex, England: Penguin Books.

———. 1982. *Philosophy in the Twentieth Century.* New York: Random House.

Baddeley, A. 1981. "The Cognitive Psychology of Everyday Life," *British Journal of Psychology* 72: 257–69.

Bahrick, H. P.; Bahrick, P. O.; and Wittlinger, R. P. 1975. "Fifty Years of Memory for Names and Faces: A Cross-sectional Approach," *Journal of Experimental Psychology: General* 104: 54–75.

Ballard, D. H.; Hinton, G. E.; and Sejnowski, T. J. 1983. "Parallel Visual Computation," *Nature* 306: 21–26.

Barnes, J. 1979. *The Presocratic Philosophers.* London: Routledge & Kegan Paul.

Bartlett, F. C. 1932. *Remembering.* Cambridge: Cambridge University Press.

———. 1958. *Thinking: An Experimental and Social Study.* London: George Allen & Unwin.

Bateson, G.; Jackson, D. D.; Haley, J.; and Weakland, J. 1956. "Toward a Theory of Schizophrenia," *Behavioral Science* 1: 251–64.

Beach, F. A.; Hebb, D. O.; Morgan, C. T.; and Nissen, H. W., eds. 1960. *The Neuropsychology of Lashley.* New York: McGraw-Hill.

Beaumont, J. C.; Young, A. W.; and McManus, J. C. 1984. "Hemisphericity: A Critical Review," *Cognitive Neuropsychology* 1: 191–212.

Benedict, R. 1934. *Patterns of Culture.* Boston: Houghton-Mifflin.

———. 1946. *The Chrysanthemum and the Sword: Patterns of Japanese Culture.* Boston: Houghton-Mifflin.

Berkeley, G. 1929. *Essays, Principles, Dialogues with Selections from Other Writings.* M. W. Calkins, ed. New York: Charles Scribner.

Berlin, B.; Breedlove, D. E.; and Raven, D. H. 1973. "General Principles of Classification and Nomenclature in Folk Biology," *American Anthropology* 75: 214–42.

Berlin, B.; and Kay, P. 1969. *Basic Color Terms: Their Universality and Evolution.* Berkeley: University of California Press.

Bernstein, J. 1981. "Profiles: Marvin Minsky and Artificial Intelligence," *New Yorker* 57: 50–126.

———. 1982. *Science Observed: Essays Out of My Mind.* New York: Basic Books.

Berwick, R.; and Weinberg, A. 1983. "The Role of Grammars in Models of Language Use," *Cognition* 13: 1–61.

Block, N., ed. 1981*a*. *Imagery.* Cambridge, Mass.: MIT Press, Bradford Books.

———, ed. 1981*b*. *Readings in Philosophy of Psychology,* vol. II. Cambridge, Mass.: Harvard University Press.

———. 1983. "Mental Pictures and Cognitive Science," *The Philosophical Review* 92: 499–541.

Bloomfield, L. 1925. "Why a Linguistics Society?," *Language* 1: 1–5.

———. 1933. *Language.* 2nd. ed. New York: Holt, Rinehart & Winston.

———. 1936. "Language or Ideas?," *Language* 12: 89–95.

———. 1943. "Obituary of Franz Boas," *Language* 19: 198.

Blumenthal, A. L. 1979. "Psychology and Linguistics: The First Half-century." Lecture delivered at the APA centennial symposium: "Linguistics and Psychology," New York.

Bobrow, D. G. 1968. "Natural Language Input for a Computer Problem-solving System." In M. L. Minsky, ed., *Semantic Information Processing.* Cambridge, Mass.: MIT Press.

———; and Winograd, T. 1977. "An Overview of KRL, a Knowledge Representation Language," *Cognitive Science* 1: 3–46.

Boden, M. 1977. *Artificial Intelligence and Natural Man.* New York: Basic Books.

———. 1981. *Minds and Mechanisms.* Ithaca, N.Y.: Cornell University Press.

Boffey, P. M. 1983. " 'Rational' Decisions Prove Not to Be," *New York Times,* 6 December 1983, pp. Cl, C7.

Bolinger, D. 1968. *Aspects of Language.* New York: Harcourt, Brace & World.

Boring, E. G. 1950. *A History of Experimental Psychology.* New York: Appleton-Century-Crofts.

Bousfield, J. 1979. "The World Seen as a Colour Chart." In R. F. Ellen and D. Reason, eds., *Classifications in Their Social Context.* London: Academic Press.

Bower, G. 1976. "Comprehending and Recalling Stories." Address to the American Psychological Association, Washington, D.C.

Brainerd, C. J. 1978. "The Stage Question in Cognitive-Developmental Theory," *The Behavioral and Brain Sciences* 2: 173–213.

Bransford, J. D.; and Franks, J. J. 1971. "The Abstraction of Linguistic Ideas," *Cognitive Psychology* 2: 331–50.

Bransford, J. D.; Franks, J. J.; Morris, C. D.; and Stein, B. S. 1979. "Some Constraints on Learning and Memory Research." In L. S. Cermak and F. I. M. Craik, eds., *Levels of Processing and Human Memory.* Hillsdale, N.J.: Erlbaum.

Bransford, J. D.; and Johnson, M. V. 1972. "Contextual Prerequisites for Understanding: Some Investigations of Comprehension and Recall," *Journal of Verbal Learning and Verbal Behavior* 11: 717–21.

Bransford, J. D.; and McCarrell, N. S. 1975. "A Sketch of a Cognitive Approach to Comprehension: Some Thoughts about Understanding What It Means to Comprehend." In P. N. Johnson-Laird and P. C. Wason, eds., 1977. *Thinking: Readings in Cognitive Science.* Cambridge: Cambridge University Press.

Brentano, F. 1874. *Psychologie vom empirischen Standpunkte.* Leipzig.

Bresnan, J. 1978. "A Realistic Transformational Grammar." In M. Halle, et al., eds., *Linguistic Theory and Psychological Reality.* Cambridge, Mass.: MIT Press.

———. 1981. "An Approach to Universal Grammar and the Mental Representation of Language," *Cognition* 10: 39–52.

Brew, J. O., ed. 1968. *One Hundred Years of Anthropology.* Cambridge, Mass.: Harvard University Press.

Brewster, D. 1854. *North British Review.* Quoted in J. Miller, 1983. *States of Mind.* New York: Pantheon Books.

Broadbent, D. E. 1954. "The Role of Auditory Localization in Attention and Memory Span," *Journal of Experimental Psychology* 47: 191–96.

———. 1980. "The Minimization of Models." In A. J. Chapman and D. M. Jones, eds., *Models of Man,* pp. 113–27. London: British Psychological Society.

Broca, P. 1861. "Remarques sur la siège de la faculté du langage articulé," *Bulletin de la société d'anthropologie* (Paris) 6.

References

Brown, C. M. 1984. "Computer Vision and Natural Constraints," *Science* 224: 1299–1305.

Brown, R. 1956. "Language and Categories." In J. S. Bruner et al., *A Study of Thinking.* New York: John Wiley.

———. 1975. "Reference: In Memorial Tribute to Eric Lenneberg," *Cognition* 4: 125–53.

———; and Lenneberg, E. H. 1954. "A Study in Language and Cognition," *Journal of Abnormal and Social Psychology* 44: 454–62.

Bruner, J. S. 1944. *Mandate from the People.* New York: Duell, Sloan & Pearce.

———. 1973. *Beyond the Information Given; Studies in the Psychology of Knowing.* J. Anglin, ed. New York: W. W. Norton.

———. 1982. *In Search of Mind.* Preliminary version.

———. 1983. *In Search of Mind.* New York: Harper & Row.

———; Goodnow, J.; and Austin, G. 1956. *A Study of Thinking.* New York: John Wiley.

Carnap, R. 1959. "Psychology in Physical Language." In A. J. Ayer, ed., *Logical Positivism.* Glencoe, Ill.: Free Press.

———. 1967. *The Logical Structure of the World; Pseudoproblems in Philosophy.* Berkeley: University of California Press. Original work published in 1928.

Cazeneuve, J. 1968. "Lévy-Bruhl, Lucien." Entry in *International Encyclopedia of the Social Sciences,* ed. by D. Sills. New York: Macmillan.

———. 1972. *Lucien Lévy-Bruhl,* trans. by P. Rivière. Oxford: Basil Blackwell.

Cherniak, C. 1983. "The 'universal acceptance of logic.'" *Berkeley Cognitive Science Report,* no. 6.

Cherry, E. C. 1953. "Some Experiments on the Recognition of Speech, with One and with Two Ears," *Journal of the Acoustical Society of America* 25: 975–79.

Chomsky, N. 1955. "The Logical Structure of Linguistic Theory." Doctoral dissertation, University of Pennsylvania. Published as a monograph by Plenum Press, New York, in 1975.

———. 1957. *Syntactic Structures.* The Hague: Mouton.

———. 1964a. "A Review of B. F. Skinner's *Verbal Behavior.*" In J. A. Fodor and J. J. Katz, eds., *The Structure of Language: Readings in the Philosophy of Language,* pp. 547–78. Englewood Cliffs, N.J.: Prentice-Hall. Original work published in *Language* 35 (1959): 26–58.

———. 1964b. "A Transformational Approach to Syntax." In J. A. Fodor and J. J. Katz, eds., *The Structure of Language: Readings in the Philosophy of Language,* 1964, pp. 211–45. (Reprinted from A. A. Hill, ed. (1962). *Proceedings of the Third Texas Conference on Problems of Linguistic Analysis in English, 1958,* pp. 124–58. Austin, Tex.: University of Texas Press.) Englewood Cliffs, N.J.: Prentice-Hall.

———. 1965. *Aspects of the Theory of Syntax.* Cambridge, Mass.: MIT Press.

———. 1966. *Cartesian Linguistics.* New York: Harper & Row.

———. 1972. *Language and Mind.* New York: Harcourt Brace Jovanovich.

———. 1975. *Reflections on Language.* New York: Pantheon.

———. 1979. *Language and Responsibility.* New York: Pantheon. Originally published in French, 1977.

———. 1980. *Rules and Representations.* New York: Columbia University Press.

———. 1981. "Knowledge of Language: Its Elements and Origins," *Philosophical Transactions of the Royal Society of London,* Series B, 295: 223–34.

———. 1982. *Some Concepts and Consequences of the Theory of Government and Binding.* Cambridge, Mass.: MIT Press.

———. 1984. "Changing Perspectives on Knowledge and Use of Language." Paper delivered at the Society for Philosophy and Psychology, Massachusetts Institute of Technology, Cambridge.

———; and Halle, M. 1968. *The Sound Pattern of English.* New York: Harper & Row.

Clowes, M. 1971. "On Seeing Things," *Artificial Intelligence* 2: 79–116.

Cohen, G. 1977. *The Psychology of Cognition.* London, New York: Academic Press.

Cohen, L. J. 1981. "Can Human Irrationality Be Experimentally Demonstrated?," *Behavioral and Brain Sciences* 4: 317–70.

Colby, K. M. 1975. *Artificial Paranoia.* New York: Pergamon Press.

Cole, M.; and Scribner, S. 1974. *Culture and Thought.* New York: John Wiley.

Collins, A. 1977. "Why Cognitive Science," *Cognitive Science* 1: 3–4.

Copleston, F. 1964. *A History of Philosophy: Modern Philosophy: The British Philosophers.* New York: Doubleday.

Craik, F. I. M.; and Lockhart, R. S. 1972. "Levels of Processing: A Framework for Memory Research," *Journal of Verbal Learning and Verbal Behavior* 11: 671–84.

Crick, M. 1976. *Explorations in Language and Meaning: Towards a Semantic Anthropology.* New York: John Wiley.

D'Andrade, R. G. 1981. "The Cultural Part of Cognition," *Cognitive Science* 5: 179–95.

———. 1982. "Reason versus Logic." *The Ecology of Cognition: Biological, Cultural and Historical Perspectives.* Symposium, Greensboro, N.C.

Dasen, P. R. 1972. "Cross-Cultural Piagetian Research: A Summary," *Journal of Cross-Cultural Psychology* 3: 23–24.

———; and Heron, A. 1981. "Cross-Cultural Tests of Piaget's Theory." In H. C. Triandis and A. Heron, eds., *Handbook of Cross-Cultural Psychology,* vol. 4: *Developmental Psychology.* Boston: Allyn & Bacon.

Davis, M. 1958. *Computability and Unsolvability.* New York: McGraw-Hill.

Déjerine, J. 1892. "Contribution à l'étude anatomo-pathologique et clinique des différents variétés de cécité verbale." *Comp. rend. scean. soc. biol.* 9(4): 61–90.

Dennett, D. C. 1978. *Brainstorms: Philosophical Essays on Mind and Psychology.* Cambridge, Mass.: MIT/Bradford Books.

———. 1983. "Cognitive Wheels: The Frame Problem of A.I." Unpublished paper, Tufts University.

Dennis, M. 1980. "Language Acquisition in a Single Hemisphere: Semantic Organization." In D. Caplan, ed., *Biological Studies of Mental Processes.* Cambridge, Mass.: MIT Press.

———; and Whitaker, H. A. 1976. "Language Acquisition Following Hemidecortication: Linguistic Superiority of the Left over the Right Hemisphere," *Brain and Language* 3: 404–33.

Descartes, R. 1951. *Meditation on First Philosophy,* trans. by L. J. Lafleur. New York: Library on Liberal Arts: Liberal Arts Press. Original work published in 1641.

de Valois, R. L.; and Jacobs, G. H. 1968. "Primate Color Vision," *Science* 162: 533–40.

De Waal Malefijt, A. 1974. *Images of Man: A History of Anthropological Thought.* New York: Alfred A. Knopf.

Diamond, S., ed. 1974. *The Roots of Psychology.* New York: Basic Books.

Dodwell, P. 1971. "Is a Theory of Conceptual Development Necessary?" In T. Mischel, ed., *Cognitive Development and Epistemology.* New York: Academic Press.

Donaldson, M. 1978. *Children's Minds.* London: Fontana.

Donders, F. C. 1868. "On the Speed of Mental Processes." Reprinted in *Acta Psychologica* 30 (1969): 412–31.

Dorf, R. C. 1974. *Computers and Man.* San Francisco: Boyd & Frazer.

Dresher, B. E.; and Hornstein, N. 1976. "On Some Supposed Contributions of Artificial Intelligence to the Scientific Study of Language," *Cognition* 4: 321–48.

Dreyfus, H. 1972. *What Computers Can't Do: A Critique of Artificial Reason.* New York: Harper & Row.

Duncker, K. 1945. "On Problem Solving," *Psychological Monographs* 58 (whole no. 270): 5.

Durant, W. 1926. *The Story of Philosophy.* New York: Simon & Schuster.

Durbin, M. 1966. "The Goals of Ethnoscience," *Anthropological Linguistics* 8: 22–33.

Ebbinghaus, H. 1913. *Memory: A Contribution to Experimental Psychology.* New York: Columbia Teacher's College. Originally published 1885.

Edgerton, R. B.; and Langness, L. L. 1974. *Methods and Styles in the Study of Culture.* New York: Thomas Crowell.

Ehrenfels, C. von. 1890. "Über Gestaltqualitäten." *Vtljsch. Wiss. Philos.* 14: 249–92.

Evans, T. G. 1968. "A Program for the Solution of Geometric-Analogy Intelligence Test Questions." In M. L. Minsky, ed., *Semantic Information Processing.* Cambridge, Mass.: MIT Press.

Fahlman, S. C.; Hinton, G. E.; and Sejnowski, T. J. 1983. "Massively Parallel Architecture for AI; NETL, Thistle and Boltzmann Machines." Unpublished manuscript, Carnegie-Mellon University.

Fancher, R. E. 1979. *Pioneers of Psychology.* New York: W. W. Norton.

Farah, M. J. 1984. "The Neurological Basis of Mental Imagery; A Componentical Analysis," *Cognition* 18: 243–61.

Fechner, G. T. 1912. "Elemente der psychophysik." In B. Rand, ed., *Classical Psychologists,* trans. by H. S. Langfeld. Boston: Houghton-Mifflin. Original work published in 1860.

Feigenbaum, E. A. 1959. "An Information-Processing Theory of Verbal Learning." Doctoral dissertation, Pittsburgh: Carnegie Institute of Technology, 1959. *Rand Corporation Paper,* P–1817.

396

References

————; Buchanan, B. G.; and Lederberg, J. 1971. "On Generality and Problem Solving: A Case Study Using the DENDRAL Program." In B. Meltzer and D. Michie, eds., *Machine Intelligence,* vol. 6. Edinburgh: Edinburgh University Press.

Feigenbaum, E. A.; and Feldman, J., eds. 1963. *Computers and Thought.* New York: McGraw-Hill.

Feigenbaum, E. A.; and McCorduck, P. 1983. *The Fifth Generation: Artificial Intelligence and Japan's Computer Challenge to the World.* Reading, Mass.: Addison-Wesley.

Feldman, J. A. 1981. "A Connectionist Model of Visual Memory." In G. E. Hinton and J. A. Anderson, eds., *Parallel Models of Associative Memory.* Hillsdale, N.J.: Lawrence Erlbaum.

Finke, R. A.; and Schmidt, M. J. 1978. "The Quantitative Measure of Pattern Representation in Images using Orientation-specific Color After-effects," *Perception and Psychophysics* 23: 515–20.

Fodor, J. A. 1972. "Some Reflections on L. S. Vygotsky's 'Thought and Language,'" *Cognition* 7: 83–95.

————. 1975. *The Language of Thought.* New York: Thomas Y. Crowell.

————. 1980. "Methodological Solipsism Considered as a Research Strategy in Cognitive Psychology," *Behavioral and Brain Sciences* 3: 63–110.

————. 1981a. "The Mind-Body Problem," *Scientific American* 244: 114–23.

————. 1981b. *Representations: Philosophical Essays on the Foundations of Cognitive Science.* Cambridge, Mass.: MIT Press.

————. 1983. *The Modularity of Mind.* Cambridge, Mass.: MIT/Bradford Press.

————. 1984. "Information and Association." Unpublished paper, Massachusetts Institute of Technology.

————; Bever, T. G.; and Garrett, M. 1974. *The Psychology of Language.* New York: McGraw-Hill.

Fodor, J. A.; and Katz, J. J., eds. 1964. *The Structure of Language: Readings in the Philosophy of Language.* Englewood Cliffs, N.J.: Prentice-Hall.

Fodor, J. A.; and Pylyshyn, Z. W. 1981. "How Direct Is Visual Perception: Some Reflections on Gibson's 'Ecological Approach,'" *Cognition* 9: 139–96.

Foster, J. M. 1967. *List Processing.* London: Macdonald.

Foucault, M. 1970. *The Order of Things.* New York: Pantheon.

Fox, J. K. 1983. "Debate on Learning Theory is Shifting," *Science* 222: 1219–22.

Frazer, J. 1955. *The Golden Bough: A Study in Magic and Religion,* 3rd ed. New York: St. Martin's Press. Originally published in 1890.

Freeman, D. 1983. *Margaret Mead and Samoa: The Making and Unmaking of an Anthropological Myth.* Cambridge, Mass.: Harvard University Press.

Fries, C. C. 1963. "The Bloomfield School." In C. Mohrmann, A. Sommerfelt, and J. Whatmough, eds., *Trends in European and American Linguistics 1930–1960.* Utrecht: Spectrum.

Fritsch, G.; and Hitzig, E. 1870. "Uber die elektrische Erregbarkeit des Grosshirns," *Arch. Anat. Physiol. u. Wisse. Med.* 37.

Fryer, D. M.; and Marshall, J. C. 1979. "The Motives of Jacques de Vaucanson," *Technology and Culture* 20: 257–69.

Gardin, J. C. 1965. "On a Possible Interpretation of Componential Analysis in Archaeology," *American Anthropologist* 67: 9–11.

Gardner, H. 1975. *The Shattered Mind: The Person after Brain Damage.* New York: Alfred A. Knopf.

————. 1978. *Developmental Psychology.* Boston: Little, Brown.

————. 1983. *Frames of Mind: The Theory of Multiple Intelligences.* New York: Basic Books.

Gazdar, G. 1981. "On syntactic categories," *Philosophical Transactions of the Royal Society of London,* Series B. 295: 267–83.

Gazzaniga, M. S. 1981. "Nobel Prize for Physiology or Medicine," *Science* 214: 517–18.

————. 1983. "Right Hemisphere Language Following Commisorotomy: A Twenty-Year Perspective," *American Psychologist* 38: 525–37.

Geertz, C. 1973. *The Interpretation of Cultures.* New York: Basic Books.

————. 1983. *Local Knowledge.* New York: Basic Books.

Geschwind, N. 1965. "Disconnexion Syndromes in Animals and Man," *Brain* 88: 585–644.

————. 1974. *Selected Papers on Language and the Brain.* Dordrecht-Boston/Reidel.

Gibson, J. J. 1950. *The Perception of the Visual World.* Boston: Houghton-Mifflin.

————. 1966. *The Senses Considered as Perceptual Systems.* Boston: Houghton-Mifflin.

————. 1967. "New Reasons for Realism," *Synthese,* 17: 162–72.

————. 1979. *The Ecological Approach to Visual Perception.* Boston: Houghton-Mifflin.

Glass, A. L.; Holyoak, K. J.; and Santa, J. L. 1979. *Cognition.* Reading, Mass.: Addison-Wesley.

Goldman, P. S.; and Galkin, T. W. 1978. "Prenatal Removal of Frontal Association Cortex in the Fetal Rhesus Monkey: Anatomical and Functional Consequences in Postnatal Life," *Brain Research* 152: 451–85.

Goldman-Rakic, P. S.; Isseroff, A.; Schwartz, M. L.; and Bugbee, N. M. 1982. "Neurobiology of Cognitive Development in Non-human Primates." Unpublished manuscript, Yale School of Medicine, New Haven.

Goldstine, H. 1972. *The Computer from Pascal to von Neumann.* Princeton: Princeton University Press.

Goodenough, W. H. 1951. *Property, Kin, and Community on Truk.* New Haven: Yale University Press.

———. 1956. "Componential Analysis and the Study of Meaning," *Language* 32: 195–216.

———. 1964. "Language and Property in Truk: Some Methodological Considerations." In D. H. Hymes, ed., *Language in Culture and Society: A Reader in Linguistics and Anthropology.* New York: Harper & Row.

———. 1968. "Componential Analysis." In D. Sills, ed., *International Encyclopedia of the Social Sciences.* New York: Macmillan.

Goodman, N. 1955. *Fact, Fiction and Forecast.* Cambridge, Mass.: Harvard University Press.

———. 1972. "The Revision of Philosophy." In N. Goodman, *Problems and Projects.* Indianapolis: Bobbs-Merrill. Originally published in 1963.

Gross, C. G.; Rocha-Miranda, C. E.; and Bender, D. 1972. "Visual Properties of Neurons in Inferotemporal Cortex of the Macaque," *Journal of Neurophysiology* 35: 96–111.

Grossberg, S. 1980. "How Does a Brain Build a Cognitive Code?," *Psychological Review* 87: 1–51.

Gruber, H. E.; and Vonèche, J. J., eds. 1977. *The Essential Piaget.* New York: Basic Books.

Hacking, I. 1980. "Is the End in Sight for Epistemology?," *Journal of Philosophy* 77: 579–88.

———. 1982. "Wittgenstein the Psychologist" [Review of *Remarks on the Philosophy of Psychology,* G. E. M. Anscombe, ed.], *New York Review of Books,* 1 April.

Halacy, D. S., Jr. 1962. *Computers the Machines We Think With.* New York: Dell.

Hanfling, O., ed. 1972. *Fundamental Problems in Philosophy.* Blackwell: Open University Press.

Harris, M. 1968. *The Rise of Anthropological Theory: A History of Theories of Culture.* New York: Thomas Y. Crowell.

Harris, R. 1981. *The Language Myth.* London: Duckworth.

Harris, W. H.; and Levy, J. S., eds. 1975. "Holography." *The New Columbia Encyclopedia.* New York: Columbia University Press.

Harris, Z. S. 1952. "Discourse Analysis," *Language* 28: 18–30.

Harth, E. 1982. *Windows on the Mind: Reflections on the Physical Basis of Consciousness.* New York: William Morrow.

Haugeland, J. 1981. "The Nature and Plausibility of Cognitivism." In J. Haugeland, ed., *Mind Design: Philosophy, Psychology, Artificial Intelligence.* Montgomery, Vt.: Bradford Books.

Havelock, E. A. 1982. *Preface to Plato.* Cambridge, Mass.: Belknap Press/Harvard University Press.

Hayes, J. R. 1978. *Cognitive Psychology: Thinking and Creating.* Homewood, Ill.: Dorsey Press.

Hayes, P. 1982. Personal communication. March 1982.

Hebb, D. O. 1949. *Organization of Behavior.* New York: John Wiley.

Heider, E. R. 1972. "Universals in Color Naming and Memory," *Journal of Experimental Psychology* 93: 10–20.

———; and Olivier, D. C. 1972. "The Structure of the Color Space in Naming and Memory for Two Languages," *Cognitive Psychology* 3: 337–54.

Heims, S. J. 1980. *John von Neumann and Norbert Wiener.* Cambridge, Mass.: MIT Press.

Helmholtz, H. von. 1962. *Treatise on Physiological Optics. Vol. III.* J. P. C. Southall, trans. New York: Dover.

Herrnstein, R. J.; and Boring, E. G., eds. 1965. *A Source Book in the History of Psychology.* Cambridge, Mass.: Harvard University Press.

Herskovitz, M. J. 1953. *Franz Boas: The Science of Man in the Making.* London: Charles Scribner.

Hilton, A. M. 1963. *Logic, Computing Machines, and Automation.* New York: World Publishing.

Hinton, G. E. 1981. "Implementing Semantic Networks in Parallel Hardware." In G. E. Hinton and J. A. Anderson, eds., *Parallel Models of Associative Memory.* Hillsdale, N.J.: Lawrence Erlbaum.

———; and Anderson, J. A. 1981. *Parallel Models of Associative Memory.* Hillsdale, N.J.: Lawrence Erlbaum.

Hinton, G. E.; Sejnowski, T. J.; and Ackley, D. H. 1984. "Boltzmann Machines: Constraint Satisfaction Networks That Learn." *Computer Science Memo,* Carnegie-Mellon University.

References

Hjelmslev, L. 1953. "Prologomena to a Theory of Language," *Indiana Publications in Anthropology and Linguistics,* no. 7.

Hochberg, J. 1978. *Perception.* Englewood Cliffs, N.J.: Prentice-Hall.

Hockett, C. 1958. *A Course in Modern Linguistics.* New York: Macmillan.

———. 1968*a.* Article on Leonard Bloomfield. In D. L. Sills, ed., *International Encyclopedia of the Social Sciences,* pp. 95–98. New York: Macmillan.

———. 1968*b. The State of the Art.* The Hague: Mouton.

Hodgen, M. T. 1964. *Early Anthropology in the Sixteenth and Seventeenth Centuries.* Philadelphia: University of Pennsylvania Press.

Hodges, A. 1983. *Alan Turing: The Enigma.* New York: Simon & Schuster.

Hofstadter, D. R. 1983. "Artificial Intelligence: Subcognition as Computation." In F. Machlup and U. Mansfield, eds., *The Study of Information: Interdisciplinary Messages.* New York: John Wiley.

———; and Dennett, D. 1981. *The Mind's I.* New York: Basic Books.

Holton, G. 1984. "Do Scientists Need a Philosophy?," *The Times Literary Supplement,* 2 November 1984, pp. 231–34.

Holyoak, K. 1983. "Toward a Unitary Theory of Mind" [Review of J. R. Anderson, *The Architecture of Cognition*], *Science* 222: 499–500.

Hooper, J. 1982. Interview with Karl Pribram. *Omni,* October 1982, pp. 129–35, 169–76.

Horn, B. K. P. 1975. "Obtaining Shape from Shading Information." In P. Winston, ed., *The Psychology of Computer Vision.* New York: McGraw-Hill.

Hubel, D. H. 1978. "Vision and the Brain," *Bulletin of the American Academy of Arts and Sciences* 31: 17–28.

———. 1979. "The Brain," *Scientific American* 241: 44–53.

———; and Wiesel, T. N. 1959. "Receptive Fields of Single Neurones in the Cat's Striate Cortex," *Journal of Physiology* 148: 574–91.

Hubel, D. H.; and Wiesel, T. N. 1962. "Receptive Fields, Binocular Interaction and Functional Architecture in the Cat's Visual Cortex," *Journal of Physiology* 160: 106–54.

———. 1979. "Brain Mechanisms of Vision," *Scientific American* 241: 150–62.

Hume, D. 1739. *A Treatise of Human Nature.* London.

———. 1955. *An Inquiry Concerning Human Understanding.* New York: Liberal Arts Press. Original work published in 1748.

Humphrey, G. 1951. *Thinking: An Introduction to Experimental Psychology.* New York: John Wiley.

Hunt, M. 1982. *The Universe Within.* New York: Simon & Schuster.

Hutchins, E. 1980. *Culture and Inference: A Trobriand Case Study.* Cambridge, Mass.: Harvard University Press.

Hymes, D. 1974. *Studies in the History of Linguistics.* Bloomington: Indiana University Press.

Inhelder, B.; and Piaget, J. 1958. *The Growth of Logical Thinking from Childhood to Adolescence,* trans. by A. Parsons and S. Milgram. New York: Basic Books.

———. 1964. *The Early Growth of Logic in the Child: Classification and Seriation.* London: Routledge & Kegan Paul.

Jackendoff, R. 1983. *Semantics and Cognition.* Cambridge, Mass.: MIT Press.

Jackson, J. Hughlings. 1932. *Selected Writings.* London: Hodder & Stoughton.

Jakobson, R. 1941. *Kindersprache, Aphasie und allgemeine Lautgesetze.* Uppsala: Universitets Aarsskrift. English ed.: *Child Language, Aphasia and Phonological Universals.* The Hague: Mouton, 1968.

———. 1963. *Essais de linguistique générale.* Paris: Editions de minuit.

———; and Halle, M. 1956. *Fundamentals of Language.* The Hague: Mouton.

James, W. 1890. *The Principles of Psychology.* New York: Henry Holt.

Jefferson, G. 1949 "The Mind of Mechanical Man," Lister oration for 1949, *British Medical Journal* 1: 1105–21.

Jeffress, L. A., ed. 1951. *Cerebral Mechanisms in Behavior. The Hixon Symposium.* New York: John Wiley.

Johnson, M. K.; Bransford, J. D.; and Soloman, S. 1973. "Memory for Tacit Implications of Sentences," *Journal of Experimental Psychology* 98: 203–5.

Johnson-Laird, P. N. 1982. "Propositional Representations, Procedural Semantics, and Mental Models." In J. Mehler, E.C.T. Walker, and M. Garrett, eds., *Perspectives on Mental Representation: Experimental and Theoretical Studies of Cognitive Processes and Capacities.* Hillsdale, N.J.: Lawrence Erlbaum.

———. 1983. *Mental Models: Towards a Cognitive Science of Language, Inference, and Consciousness.* Cambridge, Mass.: Harvard University Press.

————; and Wason, P. C. 1970. "A Theoretical Analysis of Insight into a Reasoning Task," *Cognitive Psychology* 1: 134–48.

Johnson-Laird, P. N.; and Wason, P. C., eds. 1977. *Thinking: Readings in Cognitive Science.* Cambridge: Cambridge: University Press.

Kahneman, D.; Slovic, P.; and Tversky, A., eds. 1982. *Judgement under Uncertainty: Heuristics and Biases.* New York: Cambridge University Press.

Kahneman, D.; and Tversky, A. 1982. "The Psychology of Preferences," *Scientific American* 246: 160–74.

————. 1984. "Choices, Values, and Frames," *American Psychologist* 39: 341–50.

Kandel, E. R. 1979. "Small Systems of Neurons," *Scientific American* 241: 66–84.

————. 1982. "Steps toward a Molecular Grammar for Learning: Explorations into the Nature of Memory." Paper presented at the Bicentennial Symposium of the Harvard Medical School, October 1982.

Kant, I. 1958. *Critique of Pure Reason,* trans. by N. Kemp Smith. New York: Random House. Original work published in 1781.

Kardiner, A.; and Preble, E. 1961. *They Studied Man.* Cleveland: World Publishing.

Katz, J.; and Fodor, J. 1963. "The Structure of a Semantic Theory," *Language* 39: 170–210.

Kay, P. 1966. "Comment on B. N. Colby, *Ethnographic Semantics: A Preliminary Survey,"* Current Anthropology* 7: 3–32.

Keesing, R. M. 1976. *Cultural Anthropology: A Contemporary Perspective.* New York: Holt, Rinehart & Winston.

Keil, F. C. 1979. *Semantic and Conceptual Development: An Ontological Perspective.* Cambridge, Mass.: Harvard University Press.

Kenny, A. 1973. *Wittgenstein.* Harmondsworth, Middlesex, England: Penguin Books.

Kessen, W. 1981. "Early Settlements in New Cognition," *Cognition* 10: 167–71.

Kimura, D. 1973. "The Asymmetry of the Human Brain," *Scientific American* 228: 70–80.

Kinsbourne, M., ed. 1978. *Assymetrical Function of the Brain.* Cambridge: Cambridge University Press.

Kitto, H. D. F. 1951. *The Greeks.* Middlesex, England: Penguin Books.

Köhler, W. 1925. *The Mentality of Apes,* trans. by E. Winter. New York: Humanities Press. (Original work published in 1917.)

————. 1969. *The Task of Gestalt Psychology.* Princeton: Princeton University Press.

Konishi, M. 1969. "Experimental Studies in the Ontogeny of Avian Vocalizations." In R. A. Hinde, ed., *Bird Vocalization.* Cambridge: Cambridge University Press.

Kosslyn, S. M. 1978. "Imagery and Internal Representation." In E. Rosch and B. B. Lloyd, eds., *Cognition and Categorization.* Hillsdale, N.J.: Lawrence Erlbaum.

————. 1980. *Image and Mind.* Cambridge, Mass.: Harvard University Press.

————. 1981. "The Medium and the Message in Mental Imagery: A Theory," *Psychological Review* 88: 46–66.

————. 1983. *Ghosts in the Mind's Machine: Creating and Using Images in the Brain.* New York: W. W. Norton.

————. 1984. "Imagery and Cerebral Lateralization: A Computational Theory." Unpublished paper, Harvard University.

————; Ball, T. M.; and Reiser, B. J. 1978. "Visual Images Preserve Metric Spatial Information: Evidence from Studies of Image Scanning," *Journal of Experimental Psychology: Human Perception and Performance* 4: 47–60.

Kosslyn, S. M.; Pinker, S.; Smith, G. E.; and Schwartz, S. P. 1979. "On the Demystification of Mental Imagery," *The Behavioral and Brain Sciences* 2: 535–81.

Kripke, S. 1972. "Naming and Necessity." In D. Davidson and G. Harman, eds., *Semantics of Natural Language.* Dordrecht/Boston: Reidell.

Kroeber, A. 1917. "The Super-organic," *American Anthropologist* 17: 163–213.

————. 1948. *Anthropology.* New York: Harcourt, Brace.

Kroeber, T. 1970. *Alfred Kroeber: A Personal Configuration.* Berkeley: University of California Press.

Kuhn, T. 1970. *The Structure of Scientific Revolution,* 2nd ed. Chicago: University of Chicago Press.

Kuper, A. 1973. *Anthropologists and Anthropology: The British School 1922–1972.* New York: Pica Press.

Kyburg, H. E. 1983. "Rational Belief," *The Behavioral and Brain Sciences* 6: 231–73.

Labbe, R.; Firl, A.; Mufson, E.; and Stein, D. 1983. "Fetal Transplants: Reduction of Cognitive Deficits in Rats with Frontal Cortex Lesions," *Science* 221: 470–72.

References

Lachman, R.; Lachman, J. L.; and Butterfield, E. C. 1979. *Cognitive Psychology and Information Processing: An Introduction.* Hillsdale, N.J.: Lawrence Erlbaum.

Lakoff, G. 1969. "Empiricism without Facts," *Foundations of Language* 5: 118–27.

———. 1980. "Whatever Happened to Deep Structure?" *The Behavioral and Brain Sciences* 3: 22–23.

———. 1982. "Categories and Cognitive Models." Working paper. Berkeley Cognitive Science Report no. 2.

———; and Ross, J. R. 1976. "Is Deep Structure Necessary?" In J. McCawley, ed., *Syntax and Semantics,* vol. 7. New York: Academic Press. Originally written in 1967.

Lashley, K. S. 1929. *Brain Mechanisms and Intelligence.* Chicago: University of Chicago Press.

———. 1950. "In Search of the Engram." In *Symposia of the Society for Experimental Biology* 4: 454–82.

Lashley, K. S.; Chow, K. L.; and Semmes, J. 1951. "An Examination of the Electrical Field Theory of Cerebral Integration," *Psychological Review* 58: 123–36.

Lave, J. 1977. "Cognitive Consequences of Traditional Apprenticeship Training in West Africa," *Anthropology and Education Quarterly* 8: 177–80.

Leach, E. 1961. "Lévi-Strauss in the Garden of Eden: An Examination of Some Recent Developments in the Analysis of Myth," *Transactions of the New York Academy of Sciences II,* 23: 386–96.

———. 1974. *Lévi-Strauss,* rev. ed. London: Fontana.

Leary, D. E. 1978. "The Philosophical Development of the Conception of Psychology in Germany, 1780–1850," *Journal of the History of the Behavioral Sciences* 14: 113–21.

Lees, R. B. 1957. "Review of Noam Chomsky," *Syntactic Structures, Language* 33: 375–408.

Lenat, D. B. 1976. "AM: An Artificial Intelligence Approach to Discovery in Mathematics as Heuristic Search." Report STAN–CS–76–570. Stanford University, Computer Science Department.

———. 1984. "Computer Software for Intelligent Systems," *Scientific American* 251: 204–13.

Lettvin, J. Y. 1981. "Filling Out the Forms: An Appreciation of Hubel and Wiesel," *Science* 214: 518–20.

———; Maturana, H. R.; McCulloch, W. S.; and Pitts, W. H. 1959. "What the Frog's Eye Tells the Frog's Brain," *Proceedings of the IRE* 47: 1940–51.

Lévi-Strauss, C. 1963. *Structural Anthropology,* trans. by C. Jacobson and B. Grundfest Schoepf. New York: Basic Books. Original work published 1958.

———. 1964. *Tristes tropiques,* trans. by J. Russell. New York: Atheneum. Original work published in 1955.

———. 1969. *The Raw and the Cooked,* trans. by J. and D. Weightman. New York: Harper & Row. Original work published in 1964.

Lighthill, J. 1972. "A Report on Artificial Intelligence." Unpublished manuscript, Science Research Council.

———; Sutherland, N. S.; Needham, R. M.; Longuet-Higgins, H. C.; and Michie, D. 1973. *Artificial Intelligence: A Paper Symposium.* London: Science Research Council.

Locke, J. 1975 *An Essay Concerning Human Understanding.* P. H. Nidditch, ed. Oxford: Clarendon Press. Original work published 1690.

Longuet-Higgins, H. C. 1979. "The Perception of Music," *Proceedings of the Royal Society of London series B 205,* pp. 307–22.

———. 1981. "Artificial Intelligence—A New Theoretical Psychology?," *Cognition* 10: 197–200.

———. 1982. "A Theory of Vision" [review of David Marr's *Vision*], *Science* 218: 991–92.

———; Lyons, J.; and Broadbent, D. 1981. *The Psychological Mechanisms of Language.* A joint symposium of the Royal Society and the British Academy, London.

Lorenz, K. 1935. "Der Kumpan in der Umwelt des Vogels," *Journal of Ornithology* 87: 137–413.

Lounsbury, F. G. 1956. "A Semantic Analysis of the Pawnee Kinship Usage," *Language* 32: 158–94.

———. 1963. "Linguistics and Psychology." In S. Koch, ed., *Psychology: A Study of a Science.* New York: McGraw-Hill.

———. 1968. "One Hundred Years of Anthropological Linguistics." In J. O. Brew, ed., *One Hundred Years of Anthropology.* Cambridge, Mass.: Harvard University Press.

Lovejoy, A. O. 1964. *The Great Chain of Being.* Cambridge, Mass: Harvard University Press.

Lowry, R. 1971. *The Evolution of Psychological Theory 1650 to Present.* Chicago: Aldine-Atherton.

References

Luce, R. D.; Bush, R. R.; and Galanter, N. F., eds. 1963. *Handbook of Mathematical Psychology*. New York: John Wiley.

Luchins, A. S. 1942. "Mechanization in Problem Solving," *Psychological Monographs* 54(6), whole no. 248.

Luria, A. R. 1966. *Higher Cortical Functions in Man*. New York: Basic Books.

Lyons, J. 1968. *Introduction to Theoretical Linguistics*. Cambridge: Cambridge University Press.

———. 1970. *Noam Chomsky*. New York: Viking Press.

McArthur, D. J. 1982. "Computer Vision and Perceptual Psychology," *Psychological Bulletin* 92: 283–309.

McCarthy, J. 1984. Interview, Stanford University, February 1984.

———; Abrahams, P. W.; Edwards, D. J.; Hart, T. D.; and Levin, M. I. (1962). *Lisp I. 5 Programmer's Manual*. Cambridge, Mass.: MIT Press.

———; and Hayes, P. J. 1969. "Some Philosophical Problems from the Standpoint of Artificial Intelligence." In B. Meltzer and D. Michie, eds., *Machine Intelligence 4*. Edinburgh: Edinburgh University Press.

McCorduck, P. 1979. *Machines Who Think*. San Francisco: W. H. Freeman.

McCulloch, W.; and Pitts, W. 1943. "A Logical Calculus of the Ideas Immanent in Nervous Activity," *Bulletin of Mathematical Biophysics* 5: 115–33.

McDougall, W. 1961. *Body and Mind*. Boston: Beacon Press. Original publication in 1911.

Malinowski, B. 1961. *Argonauts of the Western-Pacific: An Account of Native Enterprise and Adventure in the Archipelagoes of Melanesian New Guinea*. New York: E. P. Dutton. Original work published in 1922.

———. 1968. Culture. In D. L. Sills, ed., *International Encyclopedia of the Social Sciences*. New York: Macmillan. Original work published in 1935.

Mandler, G. 1981. "What Is Cognitive Psychology? What Isn't?" Address to the APA Division of Philosophical Psychology, Los Angeles.

Mandler, J. M.; and Mandler, G. 1964. *Thinking: From Association to Gestalt*. New York: John Wiley.

Marcus, M. 1979. "A Theory of Syntactic Recognition for Natural Language." In P. H. Winston and R. H. Brown, eds., *Artificial Intelligence: An MIT Perspective*, vol. 1, pp. 191–229. Cambridge, Mass.: MIT Press.

———. 1980. *A Theory of Syntactic Recognition for Natural Language*. Cambridge, Mass.: MIT Press.

Marie, P. 1906. "Révision de la question de l'aphasie," *Semaine Médicale* 21: 241–47.

Marler, P. 1982. "Avian and Primate Communication: The Problem of Natural Categories," *Neuroscience and Biobehavioral Reviews* 6: 87–94.

———; and Peters, S. 1977. "Selective Vocal Learning in a Sparrow," *Science* 198: 519–21.

Marr, D. 1969. "A Theory of Cerebellar Cortex," *Journal of Physiology* 202: 437–470 (London).

———. 1979. "Representing and Computing Visual Information." In P. H. Winston and R. H. Brown, eds., *Artificial Intelligence: An MIT Perspective*, vol. II: *Understanding Vision, Manipulation, Computer Design, Symbol Manipulation*. Cambridge, Mass.: MIT Press.

———. 1982. *Vision: A Computational Investigation into the Human Representation and Processing of Visual Information*. San Francisco: W. H. Freeman.

———; and Nishihara, K. 1978. "Representation and Recognition of the Spatial Organization of Three-Dimensional Shapes," *Proceedings of the Royal Society London, B*, 200, pp. 269–94.

Marshall, J. C. 1980. "Artificial Intelligence—The Real Thing?," *The Behavioral and Brain Sciences* 3: 435–37.

———. 1981. "Cognition at the Crossroads" [review of M. Piattelli-Palmarini, ed., *Language and Learning: The Debate between Jean Piaget and Noam Chomsky*], *Nature* 289: 613–14.

Matthews, J. R. 1982. "Who's Afraid of Immanuel Kant?" [review of N. Block, ed., *Readings in Philosophy of Psychology, vols. I, II*], *Contemporary Psychology* 27: 433–34.

Mehler, J.; Morton, J.; and Jusczyk, P. 1984. "On Reducing Language to Biology," *Cognitive Neuropsychology* 1: 83–116.

Mehler, J.; Walker, E. C. T.; and Garrett, M., eds. 1982. *Perspectives on Mental Representation: Experimental and Theoretical Studies of Cognitive Processes and Capacities*. Hillsdale, N.J.: Lawrence Erlbaum.

Mervis, C. B.; and Rosch, E. 1981. "Categorization of Natural Objects," *Annual Review of Psychology* 32: 89–115.

Miller, G. A. 1956. "The Magical Number Seven, Plus or Minus Two: Some Limits on Our Capacity for Processing Information," *Psychological Review* 63: 81–97.

———. 1962. "Some Psychological Studies of Grammar," *American Psychologist* 17: 748–62.

References

———. 1979. "A Very Personal History." Talk to Cognitive Science Workshop, Massachusetts Institute of Technology, Cambridge, Mass. 1 June 1979.

———. 1982. Interview, Princeton University, January 1982.

———; Galanter, E.; and Pribram, K. 1960. *Plans and the Structure of Behavior.* New York: Holt, Rinehart & Winston.

Miller, J. 1983. *States of Mind.* New York: Pantheon Books.

Milner, B. 1967. "Brain Mechanisms Suggested by Studies of Temporal Lobes." In F. L. Darley, ed., *Brain Mechanisms Underlying Speech and Language.* New York: Grune & Stratton.

Milner, P. M. 1970. *Physiological Psychology.* New York: Holt, Rinehart & Winston.

Minsky, M. 1963. "Steps toward Artificial Intelligence." In E. A. Feigenbaum and J. Feldman, eds., *Computers and Thought.* New York: McGraw-Hill. Originally circulated in 1957.

———, ed. 1968. *Semantic Information Processing.* Cambridge, Mass: MIT Press.

———. 1975. "A Framework for Representing Knowledge." In P. H. Winston, ed., *The Psychology of Computer Vision.* New York: McGraw-Hill.

———. 1979. "The Society Theory." In P. H. Winston and R. H. Brown, eds., *Artificial Intelligence: An MIT Perspective,* vol. 1. (pp. 423–50). Cambridge, Mass.: MIT Press.

———. 1982. "Learning Meaning." Unpublished manuscript, Massachusetts Institute of Technology.

———; and Papert, S. 1968. *Perceptrons.* Cambridge, Mass.: MIT Press.

Mishkin, M. 1967. "Visual Mechanisms beyond the Striate Cortex." In R. W. Russell, ed., *Frontiers in Physiological Psychology.* New York: Academic Press.

Moates, D. R.; and Schumacher, G. M. 1980. *An Introduction to Cognitive Psychology.* Belmont, Calif.: Wadsworth.

Mohrmann, C.; et al. 1963. *Trends in Modern Linguistics.* Utrecht: Spectrum.

Moray, N. 1969. *Listening and Attention.* Baltimore, Md.: Penguin.

Morris, C. 1971. *Writings on the General Theory of Signs.* The Hague: Mouton.

Morton, J. 1981. "Will Cognition Survive?" *Cognition* 10: 227–34.

Mountcastle, V. B. 1978. "An Organizing Principle for Cerebral Function: The Unit Module and the Distributed System." In G. M. Edelman and V. B. Mountcastle, eds., *The Mindful Brain.* Cambridge, Mass.: MIT Press.

Murray, H. A. 1945. "Assessment of the Whole Person," *Proceedings Meeting Military Psychologists and Psychiatrists.* University of Maryland Press.

Murray, S. O. 1982. "The Dissolution of 'Classical Ethnoscience,' " *Journal of the History of the Behavioral Sciences* 18: 63–175.

Neisser, U. 1967. *Cognitive Psychology.* New York: Appleton-Century-Crofts.

———. 1976. *Cognition and Reality.* San Francisco: W. H. Freeman.

———. 1980. "Comments on Gestalt Psychology." Paper presented at APA Symposium, September 1980.

———. 1984. "Toward an Ecologically Oriented Cognitive Science." *Emory Cognition Project, Report 1,* Atlanta, Georgia, January 1984.

Newell, A. 1983. "Intellectual Issues in the History of Artificial Intelligence." In F. Machlup and U. Mansfield, eds., *The Study of Information: Interdisciplinary Messages.* New York: John Wiley.

———; Shaw, J. C.; and Simon, H. A. 1964. "Elements of a Theory of Human Problem-solving." In R. J. C. Harper, C. C. Anderson, C. M. Christensen, and S. M. Hunka, eds., *The Cognitive Processes: Readings.* Englewood Cliffs, N.J.: Prentice-Hall. Reprinted from *Psychological Review* 65 (1958): 151–66.

Newell, A.; and Simon, H. A. 1972. *Human Problem Solving.* Englewood Cliffs, N.J.: Prentice-Hall.

Newmeyer, F. 1980. *Linguistic Theory in America: The First Quarter Century of Transformational Generative Grammar.* New York: Academic Press.

Nilsson, N. J. 1980. *Principles of Artificial Intelligence.* Palo Alto, Calif.: Tioga.

Norman, D. 1980. "Twelve Issues for Cognitive Science," *Cognitive Science* 4: 1–32.

Nottebohm, F. 1970. "Ontogeny of Bird Song," *Science* 167: 950–56.

———. 1980. "Brain Pathways for Vocal Learning in Birds: A Review of the First 10 Years," *Progress in Psychobiological and Physiological Psychology* 9: 85–124.

Osherson, D. N.; and Smith, E. E. 1981. "On the Adequacy of Prototype Theory as a Theory of Concepts," *Cognition* 9: 35–58.

Paivio, A. 1971. *Imagery and Verbal Processes.* New York: Holt, Rinehart & Winston.

Peters, S.; and Ritchie, R. 1973. "On the Generative Power of Transformational Grammars," *Information Sciences* 6: 49–83.

Piaget, J. 1970. "Piaget's Theory." In P. Mussen, ed., *Carmichael's Manual of Child Psychology I.* New York: John Wiley.

Piattelli-Palmarini, M., ed. 1980. *Language and Learning.* Cambridge, Mass.: Harvard University Press.

———. 1983. "The Parliament of Mind" [review of J. A. Fodor, *The Modularity of Mind*], *The Times Literary Supplement,* 2 December 1983, p. 1357.

Pinker, S. 1984. *Language Learnability and Language Development.* Cambridge, Mass.: Harvard University Press.

Plato. 1956a. *Meno.* In E. H. Warmington and P. O. Rouse, eds., *Great Dialogues of Plato,* trans. by W.H.D. Rouse. New York: New American Library.

———. 1956b. *Thaetetus.* In I. Edman, ed., *The Philosophy of Plato,* trans. by B. Jowett. New York: Random House.

Popper, K. 1974. *Unended Quest: An Intellectual Autobiography.* Glasgow, Scotland: William Collins.

Posner, M. 1969. "Abstraction and the Process of Recognition." In G. H. Bower and J. T. Spencer, eds., *The Psychology of Learning and Motivation,* vol. 3. New York: Academic Press.

———; and Mitchell, R. F. 1967. "Chronometric Analysis of Classification," *Psychological Review* 74: 392–409.

Posner, M.; and Shulman, G. L. 1979. "Cognitive Science." In E. Hearst, ed., *The First Century of Experimental Psychology,* Hillsdale, N.J.: Lawrence Erlbaum.

Pribram, K. H. 1971. *Languages of the Brain: Experimental Paradoxes and Principles in Neuropsychology.* Englewood Cliffs, N.J.: Prentice-Hall.

———. 1980. "Mind, Brain, and Consciousness: The Organization of Competence and Conduct." In R. J. Davidson and M. Davidson, eds., *The Psychology of Consciousness.* New York: Plenum Press.

———. 1982. "Localization and Distribution of Function in the Brain." In J. Orbach, ed., *Neuropsychology after Lashley.* Hillsdale, N.J.: Lawrence Erlbaum.

Putnam, H. 1960. "Minds and Machines." In S. Hook, ed., *Dimensions of Mind.* New York: New York University Press.

———. 1973. "Philosophy and Our Mental Life." Paper presented at Foerster Symposium on Computers and the Mind at University of California at Berkeley. In H. Putnam, *Mind, Language and Reality: Philosophical Papers,* vol. 2. Cambridge: Cambridge University Press, 1975.

———. 1975a. *Mind, Language and Reality: Philosophical Papers,* vol. 2. Cambridge: Cambridge University Press.

———. 1975b. "The Meaning of 'Meaning.'" (Reprinted in Putnam, 1975, pp. 215–71.)

———. 1981. "Why Reason Can't Be Naturalized." Howison Lecture, University of California at Berkeley, 30 April 1981. Reprinted in Putnam, 1983.

———. 1983. *Realism and Reason: Philosophical Papers,* vol. 3. Cambridge: Cambridge University Press.

———. 1984. "After Ayer, after Empiricism," *Partisan Review* 2: 265–75.

Pylyshyn, Z. W. 1973. "What the Mind's Eye Tells the Mind's Brain: A Critique of Mental Imagery," *Psychological Bulletin* 8: 1–14.

———. 1979. "Imagery Theory: Not Mysterious—Just Wrong," *The Behavioral and Brain Sciences* 2: 561–62.

———. 1980a. "The 'Causal Power' of Machines" [commentary on J. Searle, "Minds, Brains and Programs"], *The Behavioral and Brain Sciences* 3: 442–44.

———. 1980b. "Cognitive Representation and the Process-architecture Distinction," *The Behavioral and Brain Sciences* 3: 154–69.

———. 1981. "The Imagery Debate: Analogue Media versus Tacit Knowledge," *Psychological Review* 88: 16–45.

———. 1984. *Computation and Cognition: Toward a Foundation for Cognitive Science.* Cambridge, Mass.: MIT Press.

Quillian, M. R. 1968. "Semantic Memory." In M. Minsky, ed., *Semantic Information Processing.* Cambridge, Mass.: MIT Press.

Quine, W. V. O. 1953. *From a Logical Point of View.* Cambridge, Mass.: Harvard University Press.

Radcliffe-Brown, A. R. 1940. "On Social Structure," *Journal of the Royal Anthropological Institute* 70.

References

————. 1952. *Structure and Function in Primitive Society*. Glencoe, Il.: Free Press.

Rapaport, D. 1951. *Organization and Pathology of Thought*. New York: Columbia University Press.

Reddy, D. R.; Erman, L. D.; Fennell, R. D.; and Neely, R. B. 1973. "The HEARSAY Speech Understanding System." In *Proceedings, Third International Joint Conference on Artificial Intelligence* 3: 185–93 (Stanford).

Rey, G. 1981. "What Are Mental Images?" In N. Block, ed., *Imagery*. Cambridge, Mass.: MIT Press.

Rieber, R. W. 1983. *Dialogues on the Psychology of Language and Thought: Conversations with Noam Chomsky, Charles Osgood, Jean Piaget, Ulric Neisser, and Marcel Kinsbourne*. New York: Plenum Press.

Rivers, W. H. R. 1900. "A Genealogical Method of Collecting Social and Vital Statistics," *Journal of the Anthropological Institute of Great Britain and Ireland* 30: 74–82.

Roberts, L. G. 1965. "Machine Perception of Three Dimensional Solids." In T. T. Tippett et al., *Optical and Electro-optical Information Processing*, Cambridge, Mass.: MIT Press.

Robins, R. H. 1967. *A Short History of Linguistics*. Bloomington: Indiana University Press.

Robinson, D. M. 1976. *An Intellectual History of Psychology*. New York: Macmillan.

Romney, A. K.; and D'Andrade, R. G. 1964. "Cognitive Aspects of English Kin Terms," *American Anthropologist* 66: 146–70.

Rorty, R. 1979. *Philosophy and the Mirror of Nature*. Princeton, N.J.: Princeton University Press.

————. 1982a. Personal communication. Princeton University, January 1982.

————. 1982b. "Mind as Ineffable." Unpublished manuscript, Princeton University.

Rosch, E. 1973a. "Natural Categories," *Cognitive Psychology* 4: 328–50.

————. 1973b. "On the Internal Structure of Perceptual and Semantic Categories." In T. E. Moore, ed., *Cognitive Development and the Acquisition of Language*. New York: Academic Press.

————. 1977. "Human Categorization." In N. Warren, ed., *Advances in Cross-cultural Psychology*, vol. I. London: Academic Press.

————. 1978. "Principles of Categorization." In E. Rosch and B. B. Lloyd, eds., *Cognition and Categorization*. Hillsdale, N.J.: Lawrence Erlbaum.

————; and Lloyd, B. B. 1978. *Cognition and Categorization*. Hillsdale, N.J.: Lawrence Erlbaum.

Rose, S. 1973. *The Conscious Brain*. New York: Alfred A. Knopf.

Rosenblueth, A.; Wiener, N.; and Bigelow, J. 1943. "Behavior, Teleology, and Purpose," *Philosophy of Science* 10: 18–24.

Rosenfield, I. 1984. "Seeing through the Brain," *New York Review of Books*, 11 October 1984, pp. 53–56.

Royce, J. R.; and Rozeboom, W. W., eds. 1972. *The Psychology of Knowing*. New York: Gordon & Breach.

Rumelhart, D. E. 1975. "Notes on a Schema for Stories." In D. G. Bobrow and A. M. Collins, eds., *Representation and Understanding*. New York: Academic Press.

————. 1982. "Comments on Cognitive Science." Unpublished manuscript, University of California at San Diego.

————; and McClelland, J. L. 1982. "An Interactive Activation Model of Context Effects in Letter Perception: part 2. The Contextual Enhancement Effect and Some Tests and Extensions of the Model," *Psychological Review* 89: 60–94.

Russell, B. 1961. *History of Western Philosophy*. London: George Allen & Unwin.

Ryle, G. 1949. *The Concept of Mind*. London: Hutchinson.

Sahlins, M. 1976. "Colors and Cultures," *Semiotica* 16: 1–22.

Sapir, E. 1921. *Language*. New York: Harcourt, Brace, & World.

————. 1929. "The Status of Linguistics as a Science." In *Selected Writings of Edward Sapir*. Berkeley: University of California Press.

Saussure, F. de. 1959. *Course in General Linguistics*, ed. by C. Balley and A. Sechehaye, in collaboration with A. Riedlinger; trans. by W. Baskin. New York: Philosophical Library. Originally published in 1915.

Schank, R. C. 1972. "Conceptual Dependency: A Theory of Natural Language Understanding," *Cognitive Psychology* 3: 552–631.

————. 1980. "An Artificial Intelligence Perspective on Chomsky's View of Language," *The Behavioral and Brain Sciences* 3: 35–37.

————; and Abelson, R. 1977. *Scripts, Plans, Goals, and Understanding*. Hillsdale, N.J.: Lawrence Erlbaum.

Schwartz, R. 1981. "Imagery—There's More to It Than Meets the Eye." In N. Block, ed., *Imagery*. Cambridge, Mass.: MIT Press.

Schwartz, S. P. 1979. "Natural Kind Terms," *Cognition* 7: 301–15.

Scribner, S. 1984. "Studying Working Intelligence." In B. Rogoff and J. Lave, eds., *Everyday Cognition*. Cambridge, Mass.: Harvard University Press.

———; and Cole, M. 1981. *The Psychology of Literacy*. Cambridge, Mass.: Harvard University Press.

Searle, J. 1980. "Minds, Brains and Programs," *The Behavioral and Brain Sciences* 3: 417–57.

———. 1983a. *Intentionality: An Essay in the Philosophy of Mind*. Cambridge: Cambridge University Press.

———. 1983b. "Minds and Brains without Programs." Unpublished essay.

Segall, M. H.; Campbell, D. T.; and Herskovits, M. J. 1966. *The Influence of Culture on Visual Perception*. Indianapolis: Bobbs-Merrill.

Shannon, C. E. 1938. "A Symbolic Analysis of Relay and Switching Circuits." Master's thesis, Massachusetts Institute of Technology; published in *Transactions of the American Institute of Electrical Engineers* 57: 1–11.

———; and McCarthy, J., eds. 1956. *Automata Studies; Annals of Mathematical Studies #34*. Princeton: Princeton University Press.

Shanon, B. 1985. "The Role of Representation in Cognition." In J. Bishop, J. Lockhead, D.N. Perkins, eds., *Thinking*. Hillsdale, N.J.: Lawrence Erlbaum.

Shebar, W. 1979. "Mental Imagery: A Critique of Cognitive Psychology." Paper submitted for A.B. with Honors in Philosophy, Harvard University, Cambridge, Mass.

Shepard, R. N. 1981. "Psychophysical Complementarity." In M. Kubovy and J. R. Pomerantz, eds., *Perceptual Organization*. Hillsdale, N.J.: Lawrence Erlbaum.

———. 1982. "Perceptual and Analogical Bases of Cognition." In J. Mehler, E. C. T. Walker, and M. Garrett, eds., *Perspectives on Mental Representation: Experimental and Theoretical Studies of Cognitive Processes and Capacities*. Hillsdale, N.J.: Lawrence Erlbaum.

———; and Chipman, S. 1970. "Second-order Isomorphism of Internal Representations: Shapes of States," *Cognitive Psychology* 1: 1–17.

Shepard, R. N.; and Metzler, J. 1971. "Mental Rotation of Three-dimensional Objects," *Science* 171: 701–3.

Shiffrin, R. M.; and Schneider, W. 1977. "Controlled and Automatic Human Information Processing: II. Perceptual Learning, Automatic Attending, and a General Theory," *Psychological Review* 84: 127–90.

Silverstein, M. 1978. "The Three Faces of Function: Preliminaries to a Psychology of Language." In M. Hickmann, ed., *Proceedings of a Working Conference on the Social Foundations of Language and Thought*. Chicago: Center for Psychosocial Studies.

Simon, H. A. 1969. *Sciences of the Artificial*. Cambridge, Mass.: MIT Press.

———. 1982. Interview, Carnegie-Mellon University, February 1982.

———; and Newell, A. 1958. "Simulation of Cognitive Processes: A Report on the Summer Research Training Institute, 1958." In Social Science Research Council *Items* 12: 37–40.

Skinner, B. F. 1957. *Verbal Behavior*. New York: Appleton-Century-Crofts.

Sloan Foundation. 1976. "Proposed Particular Program in Cognitive Sciences." New York.

———. 1978. "Cognitive Science, 1978." Report of the State of the Art Committee. New York.

Sloman, A. 1978. *The Computer Revolution in Philosophy: Philosophy, Science and Models of Mind*. Hassocks, Sussex: Harvester Press.

Smith, E. E.; and Medin, D. L. 1981. *Categories and Concepts*. Cambridge, Mass.: Harvard University Press.

Smith, N.; and Wilson, D. 1979. *Modern Linguistics: The Results of Chomsky's Revolution*. Middlesex: Penguin Books.

Sperber, D. 1968. *Qu'est-ce que le structuralisme? 3. Le Structuralisme en anthropologie*. Paris: Seuil.

———. 1982. *Le savoir des anthropologues*. Paris: Hermann.

Sperling, G. 1960. "The Information Available in Brief Visual Presentations," *Psychological Monographs* 24: whole no. 11.

Sperry, R. W. 1951. "Mechanisms of Neural Maturation." In S. S. Stevens, ed., *Handbook of Experimental Psychology*. New York: John Wiley.

———. 1974. "Lateral Specialization in the Surgically Separated Hemispheres." In F. Schmitt and F. G. Worden, eds., *The Neurosciences: Third Study Program*. Cambridge, Mass.: MIT Press.

———; and Miner, N. 1955. "Pattern Perception Following Insertion of Mica Plates into Visual Cortex," *Journal of Comparative and Physiological Psychology* 48: 463–69.

Sternberg, S. 1966. "High-Speed Scanning in Human Memory," *Science* 153: 652–54.

References

———. 1969. "Memory-Scanning: Mental Processes Revealed by Reaction-Time Experiments," *American Scientist* 57: 421–57.

Stich, S. P. 1982. "The compleat cognitivist" [review of J. A. Fodor, *Representations: Philosophical Essays on the Foundations of Cognitive Science*], *Contemporary Psychologist* 27: 419–21.

———. 1983. *From Folk Psychology to Cognitive Science.* Cambridge, Mass.: MIT Press (Bradford Books).

———. 1984. "Thinking as per program" [review of P. N. Johnson-Laird, *Mental Models: Towards a Cognitive Science of Language, Inference, and Consciousness*], *Times Literary Supplement,* 4 February 1984, p. 189.

Stocking, G. W. 1982. *Race, Culture, and Evolution: Essays in the History of Anthropology.* Chicago: University of Chicago Press.

Stouffer, S. A.; et al. 1949. *The American Soldier.* Princeton, N.J.: Princeton University Press.

Sussman, G. J. 1975. *A Computer Model of Skill Acquisition.* New York: American Elsevier.

Sutherland, S. 1982. "The Vision of David Marr" [review of D. Marr, *Vision*], *Nature* 298: 691–92.

Thomason, R., ed. 1974. *Formal Philosophy: Selected Papers of Richard Montague.* New Haven: Yale University Press.

Thomson, R. 1968. *The Pelican History of Psychology.* Middlesex, England: Penguin.

Tinbergen, N. 1951. *The Study of Instinct,* London: Oxford University Press.

Tolman, E. C. 1932. *Purposive Behavior in Animals and Men.* New York: Century.

Treisman, A. M. 1960. "Contextual Cues in Selective Listening," *Quarterly Journal of Experimental Psychology* 12: 242–48.

———. 1964. "Selective Attention in Man," *British Medical Bulletin* 20: 12–16.

Turing, A. M. 1936. "On Computable Numbers, with an Application to the Entscheidungs-Problem," *Proceedings of the London Mathematical Society,* Series 2, 42: 230–65.

———. 1963. "Computing Machinery and Intelligence." In E. A. Feigenbaum and J. Feldman, eds., *Computers and Thought.* New York: McGraw-Hill. Original work published 1950.

Turvey, M. T.; Shaw, R. E.; Reed, E. S.; and Mace, W. M. 1981. "Ecological Laws of Perceiving and Acting: In Reply to Fodor and Pylyshyn (1981)," *Cognition* 9: 237–304.

Tversky, A.; and Kahneman, D. 1983. "Extensional vs. Intuitive Reasoning: The Conjunction Fallacy in Probability Judgment," *Psychological Review* 90: 293–315.

Tyler, S. A., ed. 1969. *Cognitive Anthropology.* New York: Holt, Rinehart, & Winston.

———. 1978. *The Said and the Unsaid: Mind, Meaning, and Culture.* New York: Academic Press.

Tylor, E. 1871. *Primitive Culture.* London: John Murray.

Ullman, S. 1980. "Against Direct Perception," *The Behavioral and Brain Sciences* 3: 373–416.

Vachek, J. 1966. *The Linguistic School of Prague.* Bloomington: Indiana University Press.

Van Lehn, K.; Seely Brown, J.; and Greeno, J. 1982. *Competitive Argumentation in Computational Theories of Cognition* (Interim report). Cognitive and Instructional Science Series. Xerox Parc, Palo Alto.

Von Neumann, J. 1958. *The Computer and the Brain.* New Haven, Conn.: Yale University Press.

Waldrop, M. 1984a. "Artificial Intelligence (I): Into the World," *Science* 223: 802–5.

———. 1984b. "The Intelligence of Organizations," *Science* 225: 1136–37.

———. 1984c. "Artificial Intelligence in Parallel," *Science* 225: 608–10.

Wallace, A. F. C. 1968. "Cognitive Theory." In D. L. Sills, ed., *International Encyclopedia of the Social Sciences.* New York: Macmillan.

———; and Atkins, J. 1960. "The Meaning of Kinship Terms," *American Anthropologist* 62: 58–80.

Waltz, D. 1975. "Understanding Line Drawings of Scenes with Shadows." In P. H. Winston, ed., *The Psychology of Computer Vision.* New York: McGraw-Hill.

Wason, P. C. 1966. "Reasoning." In B. Foss, ed., *New Horizons in Psychology,* vol. 1. Harmondsworth, Middlesex: Penguin.

———; and Johnson-Laird, P. N. 1972. *The Psychology of Reasoning: Structure in Content.* Cambridge, Mass.: Harvard University Press.

Watson, J. B.; and Rayner, R. 1920. "Conditioned Emotional Reactions," *Journal of Experimental Psychology* 3: 1–14.

Watson, R. I., ed. 1979. *Basic Writings in the History of Psychology.* New York: Oxford University Press.

Weimer, W. B. 1973. "Psycholinguistics and Plato's Paradoxes of the Meno," *American Psychologist,* January, pp. 15–33.

Weiss, P. 1952. "Central versus Peripheral Factors in the Development of Coordination," *Research Publications of the Association for Research in Nervous and Mental Disease* 30: 3–23.

Weizenbaum, J. 1966. "ELIZA—A Computer Program for the Study of Natural Language Communication between Man and Machine," *Communications of the Association for Computing Machinery* 9: 36–45.

———. 1976. *Computer Power and Human Reason.* San Francisco: W. H. Freeman.

Wernicke, C. 1874. *Der aphasische symptomenkomplex.* Breslau: Cohn & Weigart.

Werthheimer, M. 1912. "Experimentelle Studien über das Sehen von Bewegungen," *Zeitshrift für Psychologie* 61: 161–265.

———. 1945. *Productive Thinking.* New York: Harper & Brothers.

Wexler, K. 1978. "A review of John Anderson, *Language, Memory and Thought,*" *Cognition* 6: 327–51.

———. 1982. "A Principle Theory for Language Acquisition." In L. Gleitman and H. E. Wanner, eds., *Language Acquisition: The State of the Art.* New York: Cambridge University Press.

———; and Culicover, H. 1980. *Formal Principles of Language Acquisitions.* Cambridge, Mass.: MIT Press.

White, L. A. 1963. "The Ethnography and Ethnology of Franz Boas," *Memorial Museum Bulletin, no. 6,* Austin, TX.

Whitehead, A. N. 1925. *Science and the Modern World.* New York: Macmillan.

———; and Russell, B. 1910–13. *Principia Mathematica.* Cambridge: Cambridge University Press.

Whorf, B. 1956. *Language, Thought and Reality,* ed. by J. Carroll. Cambridge, Mass.: MIT Press.

Wiener, N. 1961. *Cybernetics, or Control and Communication in the Animal and the Machine,* 2nd ed. Cambridge, Mass.: MIT Press. Original work published in 1948.

———. 1964. *Ex-prodigy.* Cambridge, Mass.: MIT Press.

Wilensky, R. 1983. *Planning and Understanding: A Computational Approach to Human Reasoning.* Reading, Mass.: Addison-Wesley.

Wilson, M. D., ed. 1969. *The Essential Descartes.* New York: Mentor.

Winograd, T. 1972. *Understanding Natural Language.* New York: Academic Press.

———. 1975. "Frame Representation and the Declarative-Procedural Controversy." In D. G. Bobrow and A. Collins, eds., *Representation and Understanding: Studies in Cognitive Science.* New York: Academic Press.

Winston, P. H. 1977. *Artificial Intelligence.* Reading, Mass.: Addison-Wesley.

———; and Brown, R. H., eds. 1979. *Artificial Intelligence: An MIT Perspective,* vol. 2: *Understanding Vision, Manipulation, Computer Design, Symbol Manipulation.* Cambridge, Mass.: MIT Press.

Witherspoon, G. J. 1971. "Navajo Categories of Objects at Rest," *American Anthropologist* 73: 110–17.

Wittgenstein, L. 1961. *Tractatus logico-philosophicus,* trans. by D. F. Pears and B. F. McGuinness. London: Routledge & Kegan Paul. Original work published in 1921.

———. 1968. *Philosophical Investigations,* trans. by G. E. M. Anscombe. New York: Macmillan. Original work published in 1953.

Wolff, R. P., ed. 1967. *Kant.* New York: Doubleday.

Woods, B. T. 1980. "Observations on the Neurological Basis for Initial Language." In D. Caplan, ed., *Biological Studies of Mental Processes.* Cambridge, Mass.: MIT Press.

Woods, W. A. 1975. "What's in a Link: Foundations for Semantic Networks." In D. G. Bobrow and A. Collins, eds., *Representation and Understanding: Studies in Cognitive Science.* New York: Academic Press.

Young, R. M. 1974. "Production Systems as Models of Cognitive Development." In *Proceedings of AISB Summer Conference.* University of Sussex.

Zaidel, E. 1977. "Lexical Organization in the Right Hemisphere." In P. Busser and A. Rougel-Buser, eds., *Cerebral Correlates of Conscious Experience.* Amsterdam: Elsevier.

———. 1978. "Auditory Language Comprehension in the Right Hemisphere Following Cerebral Commissurotomy and Hemispherectomy: A Comparison with Child Language and Aphasia." In A. Caramazza and E. B. Zurif, eds., *Language Acquisition and Language Breakdown: Parallels and Divergencies.* Baltimore: Johns Hopkins University Press.

Zangwill, O. L. 1980. "Kenneth Craik: The Man and His Work" [The Kenneth Craik Lecture, 10 March 1978], *British Journal of Psychology* 71: 1–16.

NAME INDEX

SUBJECT INDEX

bottom-up approach *(continued)*
112; and David Marr, 305; in psychology, 97

brain, 31, 264, 275, 332, 384; and forms of behavior, 284; as a holographic process, 283–84; and perception, 112, 300, 306, 307; *see also* hemispheres, mind

brain injury, 269, 277–78, 331; and the image-generation component, 331; and localization, 267; and the nervous system, 284

Brain Mechanisms and Intelligence (Lashley), 261

calculator, 142

California Institute of Technology, 10

Cambridge Anthropological Expedition, 230, 253

Carnegie Corporation, 32

case studies, 225

categories of thought, 58

categorization, 340–59; and anthropology, 341, 355–56, 358; boundaries of, 346; and the classical view, 341–42, 345, 347–48; and cognitive science, 358–59; and color lexicons, 349; and color naming, 342–50; critics of classical view, 345, 347–48; and empiricism, 342; and ethnoscience, 358; extensions of, 342; intensions of, 342; and language, 351, 354, 358; and logic, 351; natural view of, 341, 347, 348; and the nervous system, 341, 348; and perception, 349–50, 354, 358, 359; and philosophy, 340, 341–42, 350–55; prototypes, 346; and psychology, 344–48; and scientists, 357; structure of, 346–47; and symbolic anthropology, 355–56; and Whorf-Sapir hypothesis, 343

cells: complex, 273; hypercomplex, 273; simple, 273

Center for Advanced Study in the Behavioral Sciences (Stanford University), 25

Center for Cognitive Studies (Harvard University), 32

Center for the Study of Language and Information (Stanford University), 217, 218

centralists, 133

Cerebral Mechanisms in Behavior Conference, *see* Hixon Symposium

children: and learnability theory, 215; Jean Piaget's study of, 116–17, 377; and syllogisms, 366

Chinese Room problem (John Searle), 172–74, 249; critiques of, 173–74

classification, 238–39, 292; and behaviorism, 94; classical features of, 341–42; and empiricism, 56; and psychology, 93–95

Cognition and Reality (Neisser), 134

Cognition Project (Harvard University), 93

cognitive anthropology, 30, 244, 245, 250, 252; and language, 250–51

cognitively penetrable, 333

Cognitive Psychology (Neisser), 33, 133

cognitive psychology, 42, 44, 95–98, 119–20, 130; and Adaptive Control of Thought (ACT), 131; and artificial intelligence, 180–81; and bottom-up approach, 97, 126; future of, 134; and Gestalt psychology, 114–15; history of, 119; and information processing, 95–96, 119–21, 130–34; and information theory, 96; and memory, 122, 131 *(see also* memory); and mental representations, 128; methodology of, 97–98; and modular analysis, 132–33; molecular vs. molar, 97; problems in, 96; top-down approach, 97, 124–28; *see also* psychology

cognitive science: critics of, 42; definition of, 6; representations, 38; symptoms, 38

color: componential analysis, 251; lexicons, 349

color naming, 324, 343, 344–50; and classical view of categories, 342; in the Dani, 344; and nervous system, 348

color terms, 255, 258; basic, 350

compilers, 145

componential analysis, 244, 246–51, 253, 257–58; and kinship, 246–49

computation, 16–18

computational paradox, 9, 44, 133, 180, 384–88

computational theory, 299

Computer and the Brain, The (von Neumann), 29

computer languages, 369; LISP, 154–55, 161; machine, 146

computer programs, 138, 166, 256, 329, 334, 366–67; DENDRAL, 155–56, 161; ELIZA, 157; T. G. Evans, 151–52; GPS, 34, 148–51, 154; HACKER, 160; Logic Theorist (LT), 145–48; STUDENT, 152–53, 157; Turing machine, 18; on visual analysis, 152, 299

computers, 5, 12, 15, 29, 40–41, 87, 95, 118–24, 134, 145–51, 171, 172, 300, 328–29, 333, 354, 361, 366–67, 379–80, 381, 384–88; analog, 20; assemblers, 188; and behaviorism, 10–11; in Britain, 16; and cognitive science, 40–41, 381, 382, 384–88; and data structures, 328–29; difference machines, 142; digital, 44, 130, 167, 180, 264, 320, 325, 334, 385; electronic, 6, 10, 21, 321; and functionalism, 78; and intentional systems, 79–81; Johnniac, 146; list processing, 146; and logic, 361, 366–67; and memory, 30, 34, 119, 121–22, 146; and mental imagery, 328–29, 332, 334; and mental representation, 328–29; and the model of the mind, 6, 10, 40, 41, 44, 82, 148, 166, 264, 320, 331, 332, 335, 354, 380, 388; and perception, 297–98, 300, 307; and psychology, 118–24; and representations,